D0472414

Acknowledgments

To my readers—The IT Pro Solutions series is a new adventure. Thank you for being there with me through many books and many years.

To my wife—for many years, through many books, many millions of words, and many thousands of pages she's been there, providing support and encouragement and making every place we've lived a home.

To my kids—for helping me see the world in new ways, for having exceptional patience and boundless love, and for making every day an adventure.

To everyone I've worked with at Microsoft—thanks for the many years of support and for helping out in ways both large and small.

Special thanks to my son Will for his extensive contributions to this book. You've made many contributions previously, but now I can finally give you the cover credit you've earned and deserved for so long.

—William R. Stanek

Exchange Server 2016 & Exchange Online

Essentials for Administration

IT Pro Solutions

William R. Stanek
Author & Series Editor

William R. Stanek, Jr.
Contributor

Exchange Server 2016 & Exchange Online: Essentials for Administration

IT Pro Solutions

Published by Stanek & Associates, PO Box 362, East Olympia, WA, 98540-0362, www.williamrstanek.com.

Stanek & Associates publishes in a variety of formats, including print, electronic and by print-on-demand. Some materials included with standard print editions may not be included in electronic or print-on-demand editions or vice versa.

Country of First Publication: United States of America.

Cover Design: Creative Designs Ltd.
Editorial Development: Andover Publishing Solutions
Technical Review: L & L Technical Content Services

You can provide feedback related to this book by emailing the author at williamstanek @ aol.com. Please use the name of the book as the subject line.

Version: 1.0.0.5a

> **Note**   I may periodically update this text and the version number shown above will let you know which version you are working with. If there's a specific feature you'd like me to write about in an update, message me on Facebook (http://facebook.com/williamstanekauthor). Please keep in mind readership of this book determines how much time I can dedicate to it.

Table of Contents

About This Book

William Stanek has been developing expert solutions for and writing professionally about Microsoft Exchange since 1995. In this book, William shares his extensive knowledge of the product, delivering ready answers for day-to-day management and zeroing in on core commands and techniques.

As with all books in the IT Pro Solutions series, this book is written especially for architects, administrators, engineers and others working with, supporting and managing a specific version of a product or products. Here, the products written about are Exchange Server 2016, Exchange Online and Office 365.

Because Exchange Online and Office 365 are online products, the features and options for these products can be updated from time to time by Microsoft. As this book was being written Microsoft was preparing to release a new version of Office 365 and this book is written to this new version.

Print Readers

Print editions of this book include an index and some other elements not available in the digital edition. Updates to this book are available online. Visit http://www.williamrstanek.com/exchangeserver/ to get any updates. This content is available to all readers.

Digital Book Readers

Digital editions of this book are available at all major retailers, at libraries upon request and with many subscription services. If you have a digital edition of this book that you downloaded elsewhere, such as a file sharing site, you should know that the author doesn't receive any royalties or income from such downloads. Already downloaded this book or others? Donate here to ensure William can keep writing the books you need:

https://www.paypal.com/cgi-bin/webscr?cmd=_s-xclick&hosted_button_id=CPSBGLZ35AB26

Support Information

Every effort has been made to ensure the accuracy of the contents of this book. As corrections are received or changes are made, they will be added to the online page for the book available at:

http://www.williamrstanek.com/exchangeserver/

If you have comments, questions, or ideas regarding the book, or questions that are not answered by visiting the site above, send them via e-mail to:

williamstanek@aol.com

Other ways to reach the author:

Facebook: http://www.facebook.com/William.Stanek.Author

Twitter: http://twitter.com/williamstanek

It's important to keep in mind that Microsoft software product support is not offered. If you have questions about Microsoft software or need product support, please contact Microsoft.

Microsoft also offers software product support through the Microsoft Knowledge Base at:

http://support.microsoft.com/

Conventions & Features

This book uses a variety of elements to help keep the text clear and easy to follow. You'll find code terms and listings in monospace, except when I tell you to actually enter or type a command. In that case, the command appears in **bold**. When I introduce and define a new term, I put it in *italics*.

The first letters of the names of menus, dialog boxes, user interface elements, and commands are capitalized. Example: the New Mail Contact dialog box. This book also has notes, tips and other sidebar elements that provide additional details on points that need emphasis.

Keep in mind that throughout this book, where William has used click, right-click and double-click, you can also use touch equivalents, tap, press and hold, and double tap. Also, when using a device without a physical keyboard, you are able to enter text by using the onscreen keyboard. If a device has no physical keyboard, simply touch an input area on the screen to display the onscreen keyboard.

Share & Stay in Touch

The marketplace for technology books has changed substantially over the past few years. In addition to becoming increasingly specialized and segmented, the market has been shrinking rapidly, making it extremely difficult for books to find success. If you want William to be able to continue writing and write the books you need for your career, raise your voice and support his work.

Without support from you, the reader, future books by William will not be possible. Your voice matters. If you found the book to be useful, informative or otherwise helpful, please take the time to let others know by sharing about the book online.

To stay in touch with William, visit him on Facebook or follow him on Twitter. William welcomes messages and comments about the book, especially suggestions for improvements and additions. If there is a topic you think should be covered in the book, let William know.

Chapter 1. Welcome to Exchange 2016

Before getting to the specifics of working with Exchange 2016, take a few moments to familiarize yourself with the configuration options available. Microsoft Exchange is available in on-premises, online and hybrid implementations.

With an on-premises implementation, you deploy Exchange server hardware on your network and manage all aspects of the implementation. Here, you control the servers and determine which version of Exchange those servers will run. Exchange Server 2016 is the current version of Exchange, and was released in its original implementation in October 2015. Like other releases of Exchange, Exchange Server 2016 is updated periodically with software updates which may change or enhance the options available.

With an online implementation, you manage the service-level settings, organization configuration, and recipient configuration while relying on Microsoft for hardware and other services. Microsoft determines which version of Exchange those servers will run. Online implementations always use the most current release version of Exchange, which at present is Exchange Server 2016. As with any on-premises implementation, Microsoft's servers are updated periodically with software updates which may change or enhance the options available.

Although either an on-premises or online implementation can be your only solution for all your enterprise messaging needs, a hybrid implementation gives you an integrated online and on-premises solution. Here, your organization controls the on-premises servers and Microsoft controls the online servers. The on-premises servers and online servers can run the same, or different, versions of Exchange.

Understanding the various implementation scenarios will help you work through the rest of this book and will also help you navigate Exchange 2016 and its management options on your own. This chapter covers the basics. You'll learn about Exchange Admin Center and Exchange Management Shell, the essential tools for managing Exchange 2016.

As you get started with Exchange 2016, it's important to point out that with this version, Microsoft has completed the consolidation of server roles begun with Exchange 2013. Thus, Mailbox and Edge Transport are now the only server roles available. Mailbox servers now perform all messaging and client access tasks except for perimeter security, which can be handled by servers running the Edge Transport role.

Getting Started with Exchange Admin Center

Exchange Admin Center replaces Exchange Management Console and Exchange Control Panel (ECP) used in early releases of Exchange and there is no longer a separate graphical administration tool. Exchange Admin Center is a browser-based application designed for managing on-premises, online, and hybrid Exchange organizations.

For on-premises management, you access Exchange Admin Center through the Mailbox servers deployed in your Exchange organization. For online management, you access Exchange Admin Center through the Mailboxes servers hosted by Microsoft. Although the application can be configured with an internal access URL and a separate external access URL, only an internal access URL is configured by default in on-premises configurations. This means that by default you can access Exchange Admin Center only when you are on the corporate network.

Navigating Exchange Admin Center Options

After you log in to Exchange Admin Center, you'll see the list view with manageable features listed in the left pane, also called the Features pane (see Figure 1-1). When you select a feature in the Features pane, you'll then see the related topics or "tabs" for that feature. The manageable items for a selected topic or tab are displayed in the main area of the browser window. For example, when you select Recipients in the Features pane, the topics or tabs that you can work with are: Mailboxes, Groups, Resources, Contacts, Shared and Migration.

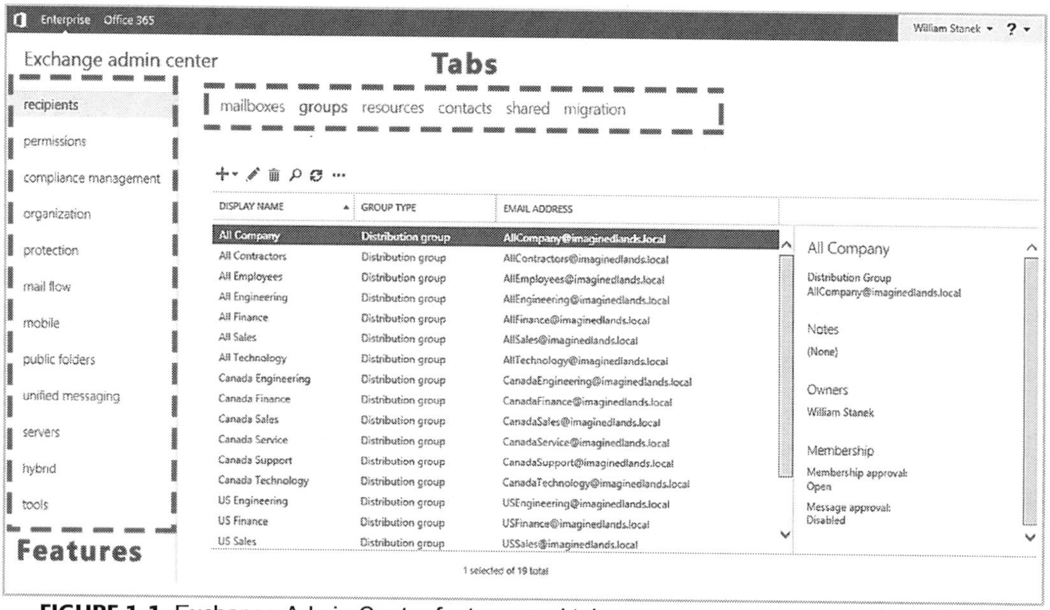

FIGURE 1-1 Exchange Admin Center features and tabs

As shown in Figure 1-2, the navigation bar at the top of the window has several important options. You use the Enterprise and Office 365 options for cross-premises navigation.

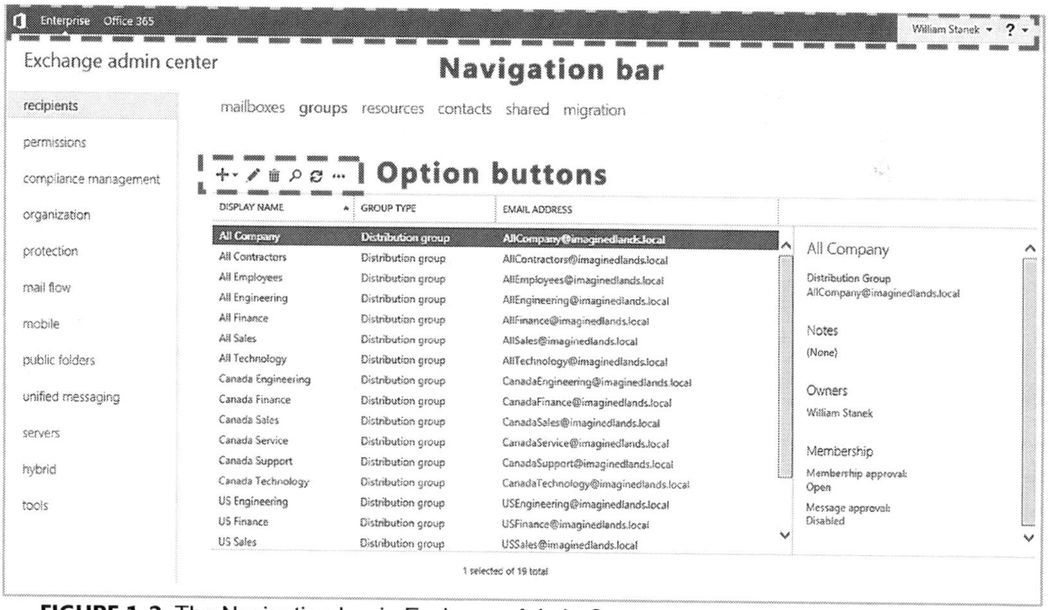

FIGURE 1-2 The Navigation bar in Exchange Admin Center

If there are notifications, you'll see a Notification icon on the Navigation bar. Clicking this icon displays notifications, such as alerts regarding automated or batch processes. The User button shows the currently logged on user. Clicking the User button allows you to logout or sign in as another user.

Below the tabs, you'll find a row of Option buttons:

 New – Allows you to create a new item.

 Edit – Allows you to edit a selected item.

Delete – Deletes a selected item.

Search – Performs a search within the current context.

Refresh – Refreshes the display so you can see changes.

••• **More** – If available, displays additional options.

When working with recipients, such as mailboxes or groups, you can click the More button (•••) to display options to:

- Add or remove columns
- Export data for the listed recipients to a .csv file
- Perform advanced searches

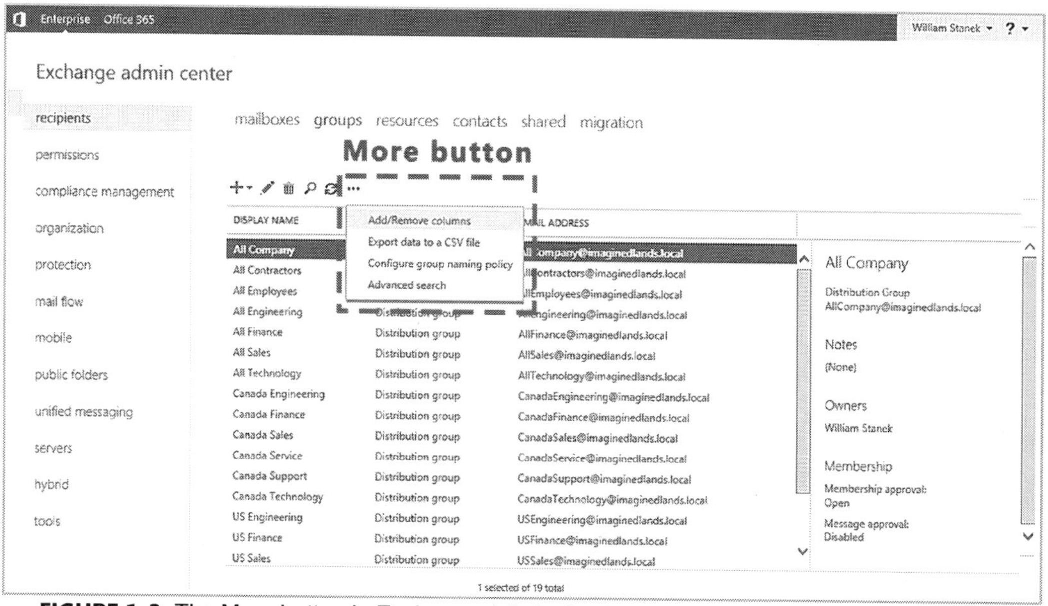

FIGURE 1-3 The More button in Exchange Admin Center

If you customize the view by adding or removing columns, the settings are saved for the computer that you are using to access Exchange Admin Center. However, because the settings are saved as browser cookies, clearing the browser history will remove the custom settings.

When working with recipients, you typically can select multiple items and perform bulk editing as long as you select like items, such as mailbox users or mail-enabled contacts. Select multiple items using the Shift or Ctrl key and then use bulk editing options in the Details pane to bulk edit the selected items.

> **NOTE**   Although ECP for Exchange 2010 would return only 500 recipients at a time, Exchange Admin Center for Exchange 2016 doesn't have this limitation. Results are paged so that you can go through results one page at a time and up to 20,000 recipients can be returned in the result set.

Accessing Exchange Admin Center

Exchange Admin Center is designed to be used with Windows, Windows Server and other operating systems. When you are working with Windows or Windows Server, you can use Internet Explorer or the Edge browser. With other operating systems, such as Linux, you can use Firefox or Chrome. On Mac OS X 10.5 or later, you can also use Safari.

You access Exchange Admin Center by following these steps:

1. Open your web browser and enter the secure URL for Exchange Admin Center. If you are outside the corporate network, enter the external URL, such as *https://mail.imaginedlands.com/ecp*. If you are inside the corporate network, enter the internal URL, such as https://mailserver23/ecp.

2. If your browser displays a security alert stating there's a problem with the site's security certificate or that the connection is untrusted, proceed anyway. This alert is displayed because the browser does not trust the self-signed certificate that was created when the Exchange server was installed.

- With Internet Explorer, the error typically states "There's a problem with this website's security certificate." Proceed by selecting the Continue To This Web Site (Not Recommended) link.
- With Google Chrome, the error typically states "The site's security certificate is not trusted." Continue by clicking Proceed Anyway.
- With Mozilla Firefox, the error typically states "This connection is untrusted." Proceed by selecting I Understand The Risks and then selecting Add Exception. Finally, in the Add Security Exception dialog box, select Confirm Security Exception.

3. You'll see the logon page for Exchange Admin Center (as shown in Figure 1-4). Enter your user name and password, then click **Sign In**.

Be sure to specify your user name in DOMAIN\username format. The domain can either be the DNS domain, such as imaginedlands.com, or the NetBIOS domain name, such as pocket-consulta. For example, the user AnneW could specify her logon name as imaginedlands.com\annew or imaginedlands\annew.

4. If you are logging on for the first time, select your preferred display language and time zone, and then click **Save**.

FIGURE 1-4 Signing in to Exchange Admin Center

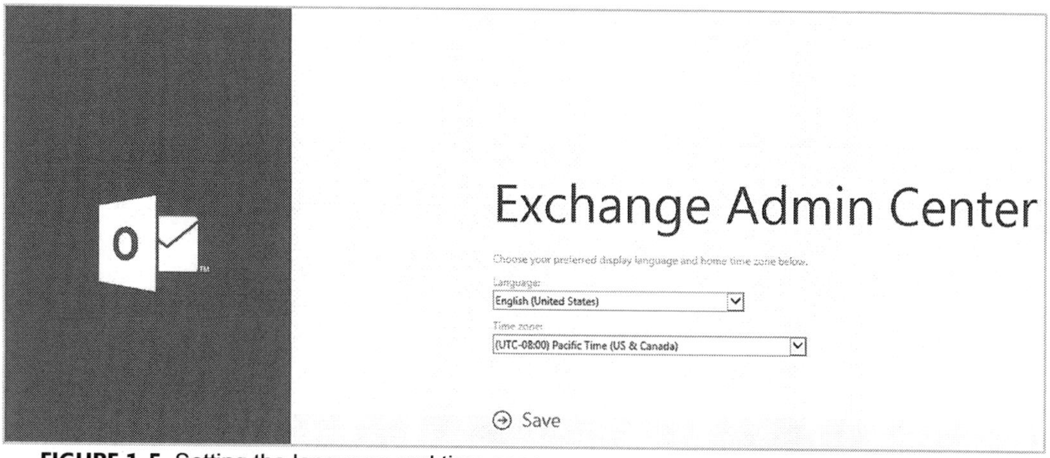

FIGURE 1-5 Setting the language and time zone.

To ensure all features are available you should only use Exchange Admin Center with the most recent version of the browser available for your operating system. The version of Exchange Admin Center you see depends on the version of Exchange running on the Mailbox server hosting your personal mailbox. Exchange 2016 runs version 15.1, and you can specify this version explicitly by appending **?ExchClientVer=15** to the internal or external URL. By default, you must use HTTPS to connect. Using HTTPS ensures data transmitted between the client browser and the server is encrypted and secured.

Authenticating and Proxying Connections

When you access Exchange Admin Center in a browser, a lot is happening in the background that you don't see. Although you access the application using a specific server in your organization, the Client Access service running on the server acts as a front-end proxy that authenticates and proxies the connection to the Exchange back end using Internet Information Services (IIS). Thus, although Mailbox server functions perform the actual back-end processing, the front-end IIS configuration is essential to proper operations.

As shown in Figure 1-6, you can examine the configuration settings for Exchange Admin Center and other applications using Internet Information Services (IIS) Manager. The server to which you connect processes your remote actions via the ECP application running on the default website. The physical directory for this application is %ExchangeInstallPath%\FrontEnd\HttpProxy\Ecp. This application runs in the context of an application pool named MSExchangeECPAppPool. In the

%ExchangeInstallPath%\FrontEnd\HttpProxy\Ecp directory on your server, you'll find a web.config file that defines the settings for the ECP application.

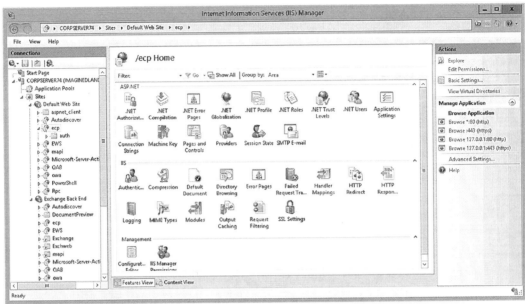

FIGURE 1-6 Viewing the applications that handle Exchange processing.

The Mailbox server where your mailbox resides performs its tasks and processing via the ECP application running on the Exchange Back End website. The physical directory for this application is %ExchangeInstallPath%\ClientAccess\Ecp. This application also runs in the context of an application pool named MSExchangeECPAppPool. In the %ExchangeInstallPath%\ClientAccess\Ecp directory on your server, you'll find a web.config file that defines the settings for the ECP application.

Getting Started with Exchange Management Shell

Microsoft Exchange Server 2016 includes Exchange Management Shell, which is an extensible command-line environment for Exchange Server that builds on the existing framework provided by Windows PowerShell. When you install Exchange Server 2016 on a server, or when you install the Exchange Server management tools on a workstation, you install Exchange Management Shell as part of the process.

When you start Exchange Management Shell, the working environment is loaded automatically with many of the working environment features coming from profiles, which are a type of script that runs automatically when you start the shell. However, the working environment is also determined by other imported elements.

Running and Using Cmdlets

A cmdlet (pronounced *commandlet*) is the smallest unit of functionality when working with command shells. You can think of a cmdlet as a built-in command. Rather than being highly complex, most cmdlets are quite simple and have a small set of associated properties.

You use cmdlets the same way you use any other commands and utilities. Cmdlet names are not case sensitive. This means you can use a combination of both uppercase and lowercase characters. After starting the shell, you can type the name of the cmdlet at the prompt, and it will run in much the same way as a command-line command.

For ease of reference, cmdlets are named using verb-noun pairs. The verb tells you what the cmdlet does in general. The noun tells you what specifically the cmdlet works with. For example, the Get-Variable cmdlet gets a named environment variable and returns its value. If you don't specify which variable to get as a parameter, Get-Variable returns a list of all environment variables and their values.

You can work with cmdlets in several ways:

- Executing commands directly at the shell prompt
- Running commands from scripts
- Calling them from C# or other .NET Framework languages

You can enter any command or cmdlet you can run at the shell prompt into a script by copying the related command text to a file and saving the file with the .ps1 extension. You can then run the script in the same way you would any other command or cmdlet. Keep in mind that when you are working with Windows PowerShell, the current directory is not part of the environment path in most instances. Because of this, you typically need to use "./" when you run a script in the current directory, such as:

```
./runtasks
```

> **NOTE** Windows PowerShell includes a rich scripting language and allows the use of standard language constructs for looping, conditional execution, flow control, and variable assignment. Discussion of these features is beyond the scope of this book. A good resource is *Windows PowerShell: The Personal Trainer*.

Running and Using Other Commands and Utilities

Because the shell runs within the context of the Windows command prompt, you can run all Windows command-line commands, utilities, and graphical applications from within the shell. However, remember that the shell interpreter parses all commands before passing off the command to the command prompt environment. If the shell has a like-named command or a like-named alias for a command, this command, and not the expected Windows command, is executed.

Non–shell commands and programs must reside in a directory that is part of the PATH environment variable. If the item is found in the path, it is run. The PATH variable also controls where the shell looks for applications, utilities, and scripts. In the shell, you can work with Windows environment variables using $env. To view the current settings for the PATH environment variable, type **$env:path**. To add a directory to this variable, use the following syntax:

```
$env:path += ";DirectoryPathToAdd"
```

where *DirectoryPathToAdd* is the directory path you want to add to the path, such as:

```
$env:path += ";C:\Scripts"
```

To have this directory added to the path every time you start the shell, you can add the command line as an entry in your profile. Profiles store frequently used elements, including aliases and functions. Generally speaking, profiles are always loaded when you work with the shell. Keep in mind that cmdlets are like built-in commands rather than standalone executables. Because of this, they are not affected by the PATH environment variable.

Using Cmdlet Parameters and Errors

You use parameters to control the way cmdlets work. All cmdlet parameters are designated with an initial dash (–). As some parameters are position-sensitive, you sometimes can pass parameters in a specific order without having to specify the parameter name. For example, with Get-Service, you don't have to specify the – Name parameter and can simply type:

```
get-service ServiceName
```

where ServiceName is the name of the service you want to examine, such as:

```
get-service MSExchangeIS
```

Here, the command returns the status of the Microsoft Exchange Information Store service. Because you can use wildcards, such as *, with name values, you can also type get-service mse* to return the status of all Microsoft Exchange–related services.

When you work with cmdlets, you'll encounter two standard types of errors: terminating errors and nonterminating errors. While terminating errors halt execution, nonterminating errors cause error output to be returned but do not halt execution. With either type or error, you'll typically see error text that can help you resolve the problem that caused it. For example, an expected file might be missing or you might not have sufficient permissions to perform a specified task.

Using Cmdlet Aliases

For ease of use, the shell lets you create aliases for cmdlets. An alias is an abbreviation for a cmdlet that acts as a shortcut for executing the cmdlet. For example, you can use the alias *gsv* instead of the cmdlet name Get-Service.

At the shell prompt, enter **get-alias** to list all currently defined aliases. Define additional aliases using the Set-Alias cmdlet. The syntax is:

```
set-alias aliasName cmdletName
```

where *aliasName* is the alias you want to use and *cmdletName* is the cmdlet for which you are creating an alias. The following example creates a "go" alias for the Get-Process cmdlet:

```
set-alias go get-process
```

To use your custom aliases whenever you work with the shell, enter the related command line in your profile.

Working with Exchange Management Shell

The Exchange Management Shell is a command-line management interface built on Windows PowerShell. You use the Exchange Management Shell to manage any aspect of an Exchange Server 2016 configuration that you can manage in the Exchange Admin Center. This means that you can typically use either tool to configure Exchange Server 2016. However, only the Exchange Management Shell has the full complement of available commands, and this means that some tasks can be performed only at the shell prompt.

Starting Exchange Management Shell

After you've installed the Exchange management tools on a computer, the Exchange Management Shell, shown in Figure 1-7, is available. On desktop computers running Windows 8.1 or Windows 10, one way to start the shell is by using the Apps Search box. Type **shell** in the Apps Search box, and then select Exchange Management Shell. Or click Start, click All Apps and then choose Exchange Management Shell.

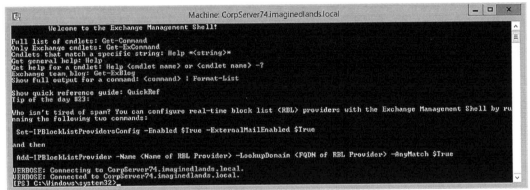

FIGURE 1-7 Exchange Management Shell

Starting Exchange Management Shell on Windows Server 2012 R2 or Windows Server 2016 is a little different. Here, click Start and then click the More button (•••) to display the Apps screen. On the Apps screen, choose Exchange Management Shell. While you are working with the Apps screen, right-click the tile for Exchange Management Shell and then select Pin To Start or Pin To Taskbar. This will make it easier to access the shell in the future.

Exchange Management Shell is designed to be run only on domain-joined computers. Whether you are logged on locally to an Exchange server or working remotely, starting the shell opens a custom Windows PowerShell console. The console does the following:

1. Connects to the closest Exchange 2016 server using Windows Remote Management (WinRM).

2. Performs authentication checks that validate your access to the Exchange 2016 server and determine the Exchange role groups and roles your account is a member of. You must be a member of at least one management role.

3. Creates a remote session with the Exchange 2016 server. A remote session is a runspace that establishes a common working environment for executing commands on remote computers.

> **NOTE**   It's important to note that selecting the shell in this way starts the Exchange Management Shell using your user credentials. This enables you to perform any administrative tasks allowed for your user account and in accordance with the Exchange role groups and management roles you're assigned. As a result, you don't need to run the Exchange Management Shell in administrator mode, but you can. To do so, right-click Exchange Management Shell shortcut, and then click Run As Administrator.

Using Exchange Cmdlets

When you are working with the Exchange Management Shell, additional Exchange-specific cmdlets are available. As with Windows PowerShell cmdlets, you can get help information on Exchange cmdlets:

* To view a list of all Exchange cmdlets, enter **get-excommand** at the shell prompt.
* To view a list of Exchange cmdlets for a particular item, such as a user, contact or mailbox, enter **get-help *ItemName***, where *ItemName* is the name of the item you want to examine.

When you work with the Exchange Management Shell, you'll often work with Get, Set, Enable, Disable, New, and Remove cmdlets (the groups of cmdlets that begin with these verbs). These cmdlets all accept the –Identity parameter, which identifies the unique object with which you are working.

Typically, a cmdlet that accepts the –Identity parameter has this parameter as its first parameter, allowing you to specify the identity, with or without the parameter name. When identities have names as well as aliases, you can specify either value as the identity. For example, you can use any of the following techniques to retrieve the mailbox object for the user William Stanek with the mail alias Williams:

```
get-mailbox –identity william
get-mailbox –identity 'William Stanek'
get-mailbox Williams
get-mailbox "William Stanek"
```

With Get cmdlets, you typically can return an object set containing all related items simply by omitting the identity. For example, if you type **get-mailbox** at the shell prompt without specifying an identity, you get a list of all mailboxes in the enterprise (up to the maximum permitted to return in a single object set).

By default, all cmdlets return data in table format. Because there are often many more columns of data than fit across the screen, you might need to switch to Format-List output to see all of the data. To change to the Format-List output, redirect the output using the pipe symbol (|) to the Format-List cmdlet, as shown in this example:

```
get-mailbox –identity williams | format-list
```

You can abbreviate Format-List as *fl*, as in this example:

```
get-mailbox –identity williams | fl
```

Either technique typically ensures that you see much more information about the object or the result set than if you were retrieving table-formatted data.

Working with Object Sets and Redirecting Output

When you are working with PowerShell or Exchange Management Shell, you'll often need to redirect the output of one cmdlet and pass it as input to another cmdlet. You can do this using the pipe symbol. For example, if you want to view mailboxes for a specific mailbox database rather than all mailboxes in the enterprise, you can pipe the output of Get-MailboxDatabase to Get-Mailbox, as shown in this example:

```
get-mailboxdatabase -Identity "Engineering" | get-mailbox
```

Here, you use Get-MailboxDatabase to get the mailbox database object for the Engineering database. You then send this object to the Get-Mailbox cmdlet as input, and Get-Mailbox iterates through all the mailboxes in this database. If you don't perform any other manipulation, the mailboxes for this database are listed as output, as shown here:

Name	Alias	Server	ProhibitSendQuota
Administrator	Administrator	mailboxsvr82	unlimited
William S	williams	mailboxsvr82	unlimited
Tom G	tomg	mailboxsvr82	unlimited
David W	davidw	mailboxsvr82	unlimited
Kari F	karif	mailboxsvr82	unlimited
Connie V	conniev	mailboxsvr82	unlimited
Mike D	miked	mailboxsvr82	unlimited

You can also pipe this output to another cmdlet to perform an action on each individual mailbox in this database. If you don't know the name of the mailbox database you want to work with, enter **get-mailboxdatabase** without any parameters to list all available mailbox databases.

Chapter 2. Working with Exchange Online

Exchange Online is available as part of an Office 365 plan and as a standalone service. Microsoft offers a variety of Office 365 plans that include access to Office Web Apps, the full desktop versions of Office, or both as well as access to Exchange Online. You'll likely want to use an Office 365 midsize business or enterprise plan to ensure Active Directory integration is included as you'll need this feature to create a hybrid Exchange organization. If you don't want to use Office 365, Microsoft offers plans specifically for Exchange Online. The basic plans are the cheapest but don't include in-place hold and data loss prevention features that large enterprises may need to meet compliance and regulatory requirements. That said, both basic and advanced plans support Active Directory integration for synchronization with on-premises Active Directory infrastructure and the creation of hybrid Exchange organizations.

In Exchange Online, email addresses, distribution groups, and other directory resources are stored in the directory database provided by Active Directory for Windows Azure. Windows Azure is Microsoft's cloud-based server operating system. Exchange Online fully supports the Windows security model and by default relies on this security mechanism to control access to directory resources. Because of this, you can control access to mailboxes and membership in distribution groups and perform other security administration tasks through the standard permission set.

Because Exchange Online uses Windows security, you can't create a mailbox without first creating a user account that will use the mailbox. Every Exchange mailbox must be associated with a user account—even those used by Exchange Online for general messaging tasks.

As you get started with Exchange Online, it's important to keep in mind that available features and options can change over time. Why? Microsoft releases cumulative updates for Exchange on a fixed schedule and applies these cumulative updates to their hosted Exchange servers prior to official release of an update for on-premises Exchange servers. Thus, when you see that an update has been released for the current Exchange Server product you know it has been applied to all Exchange Online servers and all of the mailboxes stored in the cloud as well.

Getting Started with Exchange Online

With Exchange Online, the tools you'll use most often for administration are Office Admin Center and Exchange Admin Center. Regardless of whether you use Exchange Online with Office 365, you'll use Office Admin Center as it's where you manage service-level settings, including the Office tenant domain, subscriptions, and licenses.

Navigating Exchange Online Services

When you sign up for Office 365 and Exchange Online, you'll be provided an access URL for Office Admin Center, such as https://portal.microsoftonline.com/admin/default.aspx. After you log in by entering your username and password, you'll see the Office Admin Center dashboard, shown in Figure 2-1.

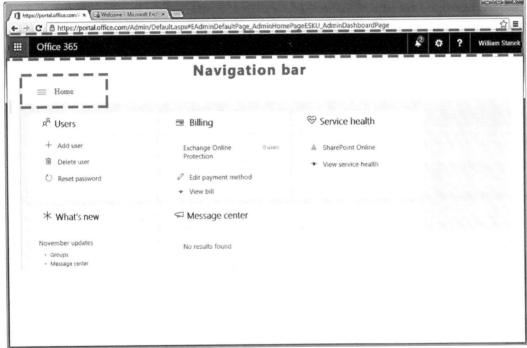

FIGURE 2-1 Use Office Admin Center to manage users and accounts

As with Exchange Admin Center, Office Admin Center has a Navigation bar with several options:

Apps – Displays a list of the available apps you can switch to, including Office Admin Center.

 Notifications – Displays notifications, such as alerts regarding licensing or subscription issues.

 Help – Displays help and feedback options.

 Settings – Displays options for accessing account settings.

 Account – Displays the name of the currently logged in user and provides options for accessing the account's profile page and signing out.

Below the Navigation bar, you'll find the Home button:

 – Click to display the Features pane. Click again to hide the Features pane.

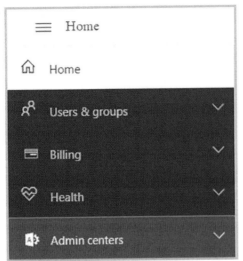

FIGURE 2-2 The Features pane in Office 365 Admin Center

From the Office Admin Center dashboard, you have full access to Office 365 and Exchange Online. Like Office Admin Center, Exchange Admin Center for Exchange Online is a web application. You use Exchange Admin Center for Exchange Online to manage:

- **Organization configuration data.** This type of data is used to manage policies, address lists, and other types of organizational configuration details.
- **Recipient configuration data.** This type of data is associated with mailboxes, mail-enabled contacts, and distribution groups.

Although Exchange Admin Center for on-premises installations and Exchange Admin Center for Exchange Online are used in the same way and have many similarities, they also have many differences. These differences include limitations that apply to the online environment but do not apply to on-premises environments.

The easiest way to access Exchange Admin Center for Exchange Online, shown in Figure 2-3, is via Office Admin Center:

1. In Office Admin Center, click **Home** (☰) to display the Features pane. If the Admin Centers panel is closed, click it to see the related options.
2. Click Exchange under the Admin Centers heading. This opens the Exchange Admin Center dashboard.

If you are using a mixed or hybrid environment with on-premises and online services, you can also access Office Admin Center and Exchange Admin Center for Exchange Online from your on-premises installation:

1. Access Exchange Admin Center for your on-premises installation and then click Office 365 on the Navigation bar.

2. After your browser connects to Office.com, click Sign In on the Navigation bar and then select Work, School Or University as your account type.

3. Provide the email address and password for your Microsoft account and then click Sign In. This opens Office Admin Center.

4. In Office Admin Center, click Menu and then click Exchange under the Admin Centers heading. This opens the Exchange Admin Center dashboard.

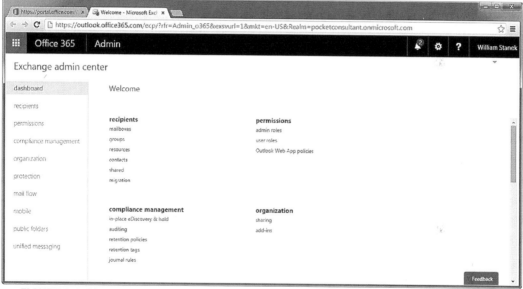

FIGURE 2-3 Use the Exchange Admin Center to manage recipients, permissions and more.

The dashboard is unique to Exchange Admin Center for Exchange Online and serves to provide quick access to commonly used features. These features are also available via the Features pane and the related tabs.

Other than the dashboard, Exchange Admin Center for Exchange Online works just like Exchange Admin Center for on-premises installations. Manageable features are listed in the Features pane. After you select a feature in the Features pane, you'll see the related topics or "tabs" for that feature. The manageable items for a selected topic or tab are displayed in the main area of the browser window. For example, when you select Organization in the Features pane, the topics or tabs that you can work with are: Sharing and Apps.

Understanding Office 365 Licensing

With Exchange Online, you perform administration using either Exchange Admin Center or Windows PowerShell—not Exchange Management Shell, which is meant to be used only with on-premises installations of Exchange. Regardless of which approach you use to create new users in Exchange Online, you must license mailbox users in Office 365. You do this by licensing mailbox plans and associating a mailbox plan with each mailbox user.

Using Exchange Admin Center, you can associate mailbox plans when you create mailbox users or afterward by editing the account properties. In PowerShell, you use the New-Mailbox cmdlet with the –MailboxPlan parameter to do the same.

When you assign mailbox plans, you need to ensure you have enough licenses. You purchase and assign licenses using Office 365 Admin Center:

1. If the Billing options aren't currently displayed in the Features pane, expand Billing by clicking it in the Features pane and then click Licensing to see the number of valid, expired and assigned licenses.
2. Click Subscriptions under Billing in the Features pane to display subscription and licensing options.
3. Click Add Subscriptions to purchase additional services. For example, if you scroll down the list of purchasable services, you'll see the Exchange Online plans.
4. While viewing plans, click Buy Now to purchase a particular plan. As shown in Figure 2-4, you'll have the option to specify how many user licenses you want for the selected plan before you check out.

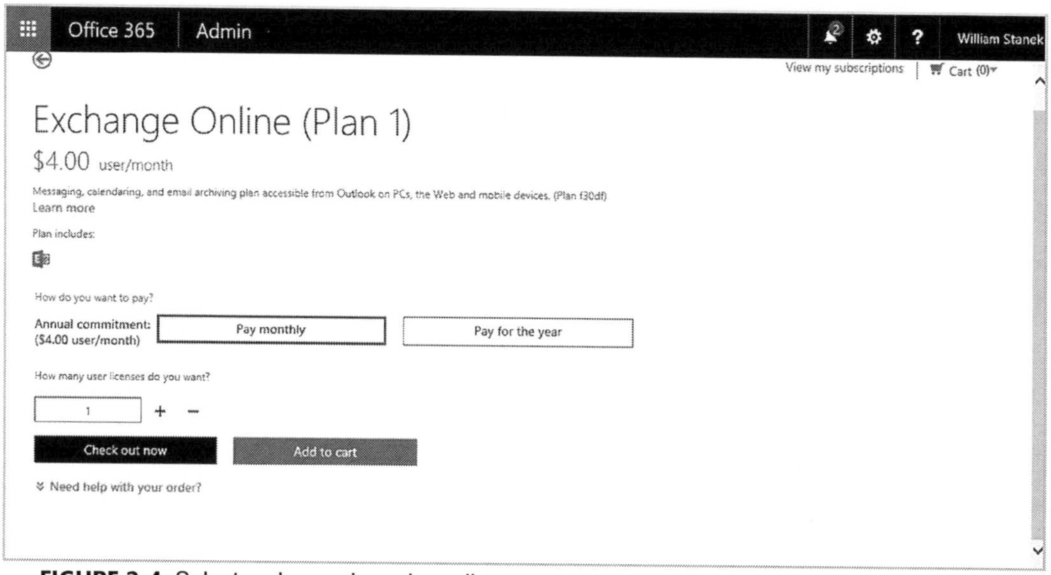

FIGURE 2-4 Select a plan and purchase licenses.

Although Office 365 will allow you to assign more mailbox plans than you have licenses for, you shouldn't do this. After the initial grace period, problems will occur. For example, mail data for unlicensed mailboxes may become unavailable. Remember, the number of valid licenses shouldn't exceed the number of assigned licenses.

You activate and license synced users in Office 365 as well. Under Users And Groups > Active Users, select the check boxes for the users you want to activate and license and then select Activate Synced Users. Next, specify the work location for the users, such as United States. Under Assign Licenses, select the mailbox plan to assign. Finally, select Activate.

Using Windows PowerShell with Exchange Online

Although Office Admin Center and Exchange Admin Center provide everything you need to work with Exchange Online, there may be times when you want to work from the command line, especially if you want to automate tasks with scripts. Enter Windows PowerShell.

Getting Started with Windows PowerShell

Windows PowerShell is built into Windows and Windows Server. Windows PowerShell supports cmdlets, functions and aliases. Cmdlets are built-in commands. Functions provide basic functionality. Aliases are abbreviations for cmdlet names. As cmdlet, function and alias names are not case sensitive, you can use a combination of both uppercase and lowercase characters to specify cmdlet, function and alias names.

Although Windows PowerShell has a graphical environment called Windows PowerShell ISE (powershell_ise.exe), you'll usually work with the command-line environment. The PowerShell console (powershell.exe) is available as a 32-bit or 64-bit environment for working with PowerShell at the command line. On 32-bit versions of Windows, you'll find the 32-bit executable in the %SystemRoot%\System32\WindowsPowerShell\v1.0 directory.

On 64-bit versions of Windows and Windows Server, a 64-bit and a 32-bit console are available. The default console is the 64-bit console, which is located in the %SystemRoot%\System32\WindowsPowerShell\v1.0 directory. The 32-bit executable in the %SystemRoot%\SysWow64\WindowsPowerShell\v1.0 directory and is labeled as Windows PowerShell (x86).

With Windows 8.1 or later, you can start the PowerShell console by using the Apps Search box. Type **powershell** in the Apps Search box, and then press Enter. Or you can select Start and then choose Windows PowerShell. From Mac OS X or Linux, you can run either Windows 7 or later in a virtual environment to work with Windows PowerShell.

In Windows, you also can start Windows PowerShell from a command prompt (cmd.exe) by typing **powershell** and pressing Enter. To exit Windows PowerShell and return to the command prompt, type exit.

When the shell starts, you usually will see a message similar to the following:

```
Windows PowerShell
Copyright (C) 2012 Microsoft Corporation.
All rights reserved.
```

You can disable this message by starting the shell with the –Nologo parameter, such as:

```
powershell -nologo
```

By default, the version of scripting engine that starts depends on the operating system you are using. With Windows 8.1 and Windows Server 2012 R2, the default scripting engine is version 4.0. With Windows 10 and Windows Server 2016, the default scripting engine is version 4.0. To confirm the version of Windows PowerShell installed, enter the following command:

```
Get-Host | Format-List Version
```

Because you can abbreviate Format-List as FL, you also could enter:

```
Get-Host | fl Version
```

> **NOTE** Letter case does not matter with Windows PowerShell. Thus, Get-Host, GET-HOST and get-host are all interpreted the same.

Figure 2-5 shows the PowerShell window. When you start PowerShell, you can set the version of the scripting engine that should be loaded. To do this, use the –Version parameter. In this example, you specify that you want to use PowerShell Version 3.0:

```
powershell -version 3
```

> **NOTE** Windows can only load available versions of the scripting engine. For example, you won't be able to run the version 5.0 scripting engine if only PowerShell Version 4.0 is available.

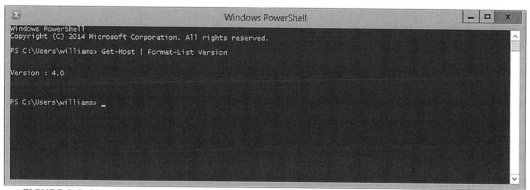

FIGURE 2-5 Use the PowerShell console to manage Exchange remotely at the prompt.

By default, the PowerShell window displays 50 lines of text and is 120 characters wide. When additional text is to be displayed in the window or you enter commands and the PowerShell console's window is full, the current text is displayed in the window and prior text is scrolled up. To temporarily pause the display when a command is writing output, press Ctrl+S. You can then press Ctrl+S to resume or Ctrl+C to terminate execution.

Understanding the Default Working Environment

When you run Windows PowerShell, a default working environment is loaded automatically. The features for this working environment come primarily from profiles, which are a type of script that run automatically whenever you start PowerShell. The working environment also is determined by imported snap-ins, providers, modules, command paths, file associations, and file extensions.

To start Windows PowerShell without loading profiles, use the –Noprofile parameter, such as:

```
powershell -noprofile
```

Whenever you work with scripts, you need to keep in mind the current execution policy and whether signed scripts are required. Execution policy is a built-in security feature of Windows PowerShell that controls whether and how you can run configuration files and scripts. Although the default configuration depends on which operating system and edition are installed, policy is always set on either a per-user or per-computer basis in the Windows registry.

You can display the execution policy currently being applied, using the Get-ExecutionPolicy cmdlet. The available execution policies, from least secure to most secure, are:

- **Bypass.** Bypasses warnings and prompts when scripts run. Use with programs that have their own security model or when a PowerShell script is built into a larger application.
- **Unrestricted.** Allows all configuration files and scripts to run whether they are from local or remote sources and regardless of whether they are signed or unsigned. When you run a configuration file or script from a remote resource, you are prompted with a warning that the file comes from a remote resource before the configuration file is loaded or the script runs.

- **RemoteSigned.** Requires all configuration files and scripts from remote sources to be signed by a trusted publisher. However, configuration files and scripts on the local computer do not need to be signed. PowerShell does not prompt you with a warning before running scripts from trusted publishers.
- **AllSigned.** Requires all configuration files and scripts from all sources—whether local or remote—to be signed by a trusted publisher. Thus, configuration files and scripts on the local computer and remote computers must be signed. PowerShell prompts you with a warning before running scripts from trusted publishers.
- **Restricted.** Prevents PowerShell from loading configuration files and scripts. Effects all configuration files and scripts, regardless of whether they are signed or unsigned. Because a profile is a type of script, profiles are not loaded either.
- **Undefined.** Removes the execution policy that is set for the current user scope and instead applies the execution policy set in Group Policy or for the LocalMachine scope. If execution policy in all scopes is set to Undefined, the default execution policy, Restricted, is the effective policy.

By default, when you set execution policy, you are using the LocalMachine scope, which is applied to all users of the computer. You also can set the scope to CurrentUser so that the execution policy level is only applied to the currently logged on user.

Using Set-ExecutionPolicy, you can change the preference for the execution policy. Normally, changes to execution policy are written to the registry. However, if the Turn On Script Execution setting in Group Policy is enabled for the computer or user, the user preference is written to the registry, but it is not effective. Windows PowerShell will display a message explaining that there is a conflict. Finally, you cannot use Set-ExecutionPolicy to override a group policy, even if the user preference is more restrictive than the policy setting. For example, you can set the execution policy to run scripts regardless of whether they have a digital signature and work in an unrestricted environment by entering:

```
set-executionpolicy unrestricted
```

When you change execution policy, the change occurs immediately and is applied to the local console or application session. Because the change is written to the registry, the new execution policy normally will be used whenever you work with PowerShell.

Learning About Cmdlets and Functions

When you are working with Windows PowerShell, you can get a complete list of cmdlets and functions available by entering **get-command**. The output lists cmdlets and functions by name and associated module.

Another way to get information about cmdlets is to use Get-Help. When you enter **get-help *-***, you get a list of all cmdlets, including a synopsis that summarizes the purpose of the cmdlet. Rather than listing help information for all commands, you can get help for specific commands by following Get-Help with the name of the cmdlet you want to work with, such as:

```
get-help clear-history
```

Because Windows PowerShell V3 and later use online and updatable help files, you may see only basic syntax for cmdlets and functions when you use Get-Help. To get full help details, you'll have to either use online help or download the help files to your computer. For online help, add the –online parameter to your Get-Help command, such as:

```
get-help get-variable –online
```

You can use the Update-Help cmdlet to download and install the current help files from the Internet. Without parameters, Update-Help updates the help files for all modules installed on the computer. When you are working with Update-Help, keep the following in mind:

- Update-Help downloads files only once a day
- Update-Help only installs help files when they are newer than the ones on the computer
- Update-Help limits the total size of uncompressed help files to 1 GB

You can override these restrictions using the –Force parameter.

Connecting to Exchange Online Using PowerShell

The way you use Windows PowerShell to manage Exchange Server and Exchange Online are different. With Exchange Server installations, you manage Exchange using Exchange Management Shell, which is a command-line management interface built on Windows PowerShell that you can use to manage any aspect of an Exchange Server configuration that you can manage in the Exchange Admin Center. With Exchange Online installations, you manage Exchange using a remote session and the built-in functions and capabilities of Exchange Management Shell are not available.

Exploring How the Shell Uses Remote Sessions

The Exchange Management Shell is designed to be run only on domain-joined computers and is available when you have installed the Exchange management tools on a management computer or server. Whether you are logged on locally to an Exchange server or working remotely, starting Exchange Management Shell opens a custom Windows PowerShell console that runs in a remote session with an Exchange server.

A remote session is a runspace that establishes a common working environment for executing commands on remote computers. Before creating the remote session, this custom console connects to the closest Exchange server using Windows Remote Management (WinRM) and then performs authentication checks that validate your access to the Exchange server and determine the Exchange role groups and roles your account is a member of. You must be a member of at least one management role.

Because the Exchange Management Shell uses your user credentials, you are able to perform any administrative tasks allowed for your user account and in accordance with the Exchange role groups and management roles you're assigned. You don't need to run the Exchange Management Shell in elevated, administrator mode, but you can by right-clicking Exchange Management Shell, and then selecting Run As Administrator.

By examining the properties of the shortcut that starts the Exchange Management Shell, you can see the actual command that runs when you start the shell is:

```
C:\Windows\System32\WindowsPowerShell\v1.0\powershell.exe -noexit -command
". 'C:\Program Files\Microsoft\Exchange Server\V15\bin\RemoteExchange.ps1';
Connect-ExchangeServer -auto -ClientApplication:ManagementShell "
```

Here, the command starts PowerShell, runs the RemoteExchange.ps1 profile file, and then uses the command Connect-ExchangeServer to establish the remote session.

The –Auto parameter tells the cmdlet to automatically discover and try to connect to an appropriate Exchange server. The –ClientApplication parameter specifies that client-side application is the Exchange Management Shell. When you run the shell in this way, Windows Powershell loads a profile script called RemoteExchange.ps1 that sets aliases, initializes Exchange global variables, and loads .NET assemblies for Exchange. The profile script also modifies the standard PowerShell prompt so that it is scoped to the entire Active Directory forest and defines Exchange-specific functions, including:

- **Get-Exbanner.** Displays the Exchange Management Shell startup banner.
- **Get-Exblog.** Opens Internet Explorer and accesses the Exchange blog.
- **Get-Excommand.** Lists all available Exchange commands.
- **Get-Pscommand.** Lists all available PowerShell commands.
- **Get-Tip.** Displays the tip of the day.
- **Quickref.** Opens Internet Explorer and accesses the Exchange Management Shell quick start guide.

All of these processes simplify the task of establishing an interactive remote session with Exchange server. As implemented in the default configuration, you have a one-to-one, interactive approach for remote management, meaning you establish a session with a specific remote server and work with that specific server whenever you execute commands.

Establishing Remote Sessions

When you are working with PowerShell outside of Exchange Management Shell, you must manually establish a remote session with Exchange. As the RemoteExchange.ps1 profile file and related scripts are not loaded, the related cmdlets and functions are not available. This means you cannot use Get-Exbanner, Get-Exblog, Get-Excommand, Get-PScommand, Get-Tip or Quickref. Further, when you are working with an online installation of Exchange, the cmdlets available are different from when you are working with Exchange Server.

PowerShell provides several cmdlets for establishing remote sessions, including Enter-PSSession and New-PSSession. The difference between the two options is subtle but important.

Using an Interactive Remote Session

You can use the Enter-PSSession cmdlet to start an interactive session with Exchange or any other remote computer. The basic syntax is Enter-PSSession ComputerName, where ComputerName is the name of the remote computer, such as the following:

```
enter-pssession Server58
```

When the session is established, the command prompt changes to show that you are connected to the remote computer, as shown in the following example:

```
[Server58]: PS C:\Users\wrstanek.cpand1\Documents>
```

While working in a remote session, any commands you enter run on the remote computer just as if you had typed them directly on the remote computer. Generally, to perform administration, you need to use an elevated, administrator shell and pass credentials along in the session. Establishing a connection in this way uses the standard PowerShell remoting configuration.

However, you cannot connect to Exchange Online using the standard PowerShell remoting configuration. You must go through a PowerShell application running on ps.outlook.com or another appropriate web server. Typically, when you work with Exchange Online, you use the connection URI https://ps.outlook.com/powershell/ and the actual session is redirected to your specific online server. To ensure redirection doesn't fail, you must add the –AllowRedirection parameter.

As shown in the following example, you use the –ConnectionURI parameter to specify the connection URI, the –ConfigurationName parameter to specify the configuration namespace, and the –Authentication parameter to set the authentication type to use:

```
Enter-PSSession -ConfigurationName Microsoft.Exchange
-ConnectionUri https://ps.outlook.com/powershell/
-Authentication Basic -AllowRedirection
```

Here, you set the configuration namespace as Microsoft.Exchange, establish a connection to the Exchange Online URL provided by Microsoft, and use Basic authentication. As you don't specify credentials, you will be prompted to provide credentials.

You also can pass in credentials as shown in this example:

```
Enter-PSSession -ConfigurationName Microsoft.Exchange
-ConnectionUri https://ps.outlook.com/powershell/
-Authentication Basic -Credential
wrstanek@imaginedlands.onmicrosoft.com
-AllowRedirection
```

Here, you pass in credentials and are prompted for the associated password.

Alternatively, you can store credentials in a Credential object and then use Get-Credential to prompt for the required credentials, as shown here:

```
$Cred = Get-Credential
Enter-PSSession -ConfigurationName Microsoft.Exchange
-ConnectionUri https://ps.outlook.com/powershell/
-Authentication Basic -Credential
$Cred -AllowRedirection
```

When you are finished working with Exchange Online, you can end the interactive session by using Exit-PSSession or by typing exit. Although Enter-PSSession provides a quick and easy way to establish a remote session, the session ends when you use Exit-PSSession or exit the PowerShell prompt and there is no way to reestablish the original session. Thus, any commands you are running and any command context is lost when you exit the session.

Thus, as discussed in this section, the basic steps for using a standard interactive remote session are:

1. Open an administrator Windows PowerShell prompt.
2. Use Enter-PSSession to establish a remote session.
3. Work with Exchange Online.
4. Exit the remote session using Exit-PSSession or by exiting the PowerShell window.

Creating and Importing a Remote Session

Instead of using a standard interactive session, you may want to create a session that you disconnect and reconnect. To do this, you establish the session using New-PSSession and then import the session using Import-PSSession. The basic syntax:

```
$Session = New-PSSession -ConfigurationName
Microsoft.Exchange -ConnectionUri
https://ps.outlook.com/powershell/
-Authentication Basic -Credential
wrs@imaginedlands.onmicrosoft.com
-AllowRedirection
```

In this example, you use New-PSSession to create a session and store the related object in a variable called $Session. You create the session by setting the configuration namespace as Microsoft.Exchange, establishing a connection to the Exchange Online URL provided by Microsoft, which typically is https://ps.outlook.com, and using HTTPS with Basic authentication for the session. You also allow redirection. Allowing redirection is important as otherwise the session will fail when the Microsoft web servers redirect the session to the actual location of your Exchange Online installation.

To establish the connection, you must always pass in your Exchange Online user name and password. In the previous example, you specify the user name to use and are prompted for the related password. You also could specify the credentials explicitly, as shown here:

```
$Cred = Get-Credential
$Session = New-PSSession -ConfigurationName Microsoft.Exchange
-ConnectionUri https://ps.outlook.com/powershell/
-Authentication Basic -Credential $Cred
-AllowRedirection
```

Here, you store credentials in a Credential object and then use Get-Credential to prompt for the required credentials.

After you establish a session with Exchange Online, you must import the server-side PowerShell session into your client-side session. To do this, you enter the following command:

```
Import-PSSession $Session
```

Where $Session is the name of the variable in which the session object is stored. You can then work with the remote server and Exchange Online.

When you are finished working remotely, you should disconnect the remote shell. It's important to note that, beginning with Windows PowerShell 3.0, sessions are persistent by default. When you disconnect from a session, any command or scripts that are running in the session continue running, and you can later reconnect to the session to pick up where you left off. You also can reconnect to a session if you were disconnected unintentionally, such as by a temporary network outage.

Exchange Online allows each administrative account to have up to three simultaneous connections to sever-side sessions. If you close the PowerShell window without disconnecting from the session, the connection remains open for 15 minutes and then disconnects automatically.

To disconnect a session manually without stopping commands or releasing resources, you can use Disconnect-PSSession, as shown in this example:

```
Disconnect-PSSession $Session
```

Here, the $Session object was instantiated when you created the session and you disconnect while the session continues to be active. As long as you don't exit the PowerShell window in which this object was created, you can use this object to reconnect to the session by entering:

```
Connect-PSSession $Session
```

Later, when you are finished working with Exchange Online, you should remove the session. Removing a session stops any commands or scripts that are running, ends the session, and releases the resources the session was using. You can remove a session by running the following command:

```
Remove-PSSession $Session
```

Thus, as discussed in this section, the basic steps for working with an imported session are:

1. Open an administrator Windows PowerShell prompt.
2. Use New-PSSession to establish the remote session.
3. Import the session using Import-PSSession.
4. Work with Exchange Online. Optionally, disconnect from the session using Disconnect-PSSession and reconnect to the session using Connect-PSSession.
5. Remove the remote session using Remove-PSSession.

Connecting to Windows Azure

You can manage the Office 365 service, its settings and accounts using either Office Admin Center or Windows PowerShell. Every account you create in the online environment is in fact created in the online framework within which Office 365 and Exchange Online operate. This framework is called Windows Azure, and like Windows Server, it uses directory services provided by Active Directory.

Before you can manage Office 365, its settings, and accounts from Windows PowerShell, you must install the Windows Azure Active Directory module (which is available at the Microsoft Download Center: http://go.microsoft.com/fwlink/p/?linkid=236297). Any computer capable of running Exchange or acting as a management computer can run this module. However, there are several prerequisites, including .NET framework 3.51 and the Microsoft Online Services Sign-in Assistant version 7.0 or later. At the time of this writing, the sign-in assistant was available at http://go.microsoft.com/fwlink/?LinkId=286152. Be sure to download and install only the 64-bit versions of the module and the sign-in assistant.

After you download and install the required components, the Windows Azure Active Directory module is available for your use in any PowerShell window. This module also is referred to as the Microsoft Online module. Although Windows PowerShell 3.0 and later implicitly import modules, you may need to explicitly import this module in some configurations. After you import the module, if necessary, you can connect to the Windows Azure and Microsoft Online Services using the Connect-MSOLService cmdlet.

Because you'll typically want to store your credentials in a Credential object rather than be prompted for them, the complete procedure to connect to Microsoft Online Services by using Windows PowerShell is:

```
import-module msonline
$cred = get-credential
connect-msolservice -credential:$cred
```

Or, with Windows PowerShell 3.0 or later, use:

```
$cred = get-credential
connect-msolservice -credential:$cred
```

After connecting to the service, you can use cmdlets for Windows Azure Active Directory to manage online settings and objects. For example, if you want to get a list of user accounts that have been created in the online service along with their licensing status, enter **get-msoluser**. The results will be similar to the following:

```
UserPrincipalName           DisplayName      isLicensed
-----------------           -----------      ----------
wrstanek@imaginedlands.onm... William Stanek    True
tonyv@imaginedlands.onm...   Tony Vidal        False
```

Cmdlets for Windows Azure Active Directory

Exchange Online runs on Windows Azure rather than Windows Server. As the two operating environments have different directory services, you must use cmdlets specific to Active Directory for Windows Azure if you want to work with users, groups and related objects.

You'll find complete information about these cmdlets online at http://msdn.microsoft.com/library/azure/jj151815.aspx. The available cmdlets include:

Cmdlets for managing groups and roles

Add-MsolGroupMember
Add-MsolRoleMember
Get-MsolGroup
Get-MsolGroupMember
Get-MsolRole
Get-MsolRoleMember
Get-MsolUserRole
New-MsolGroup
Redo-MsolProvisionGroup
Remove-MsolGroup
Remove-MsolGroupMember
Remove-MsolRoleMember
Set-MsolGroup

Cmdlets for managing licenses and subscriptions

Get-MsolAccountSku
Get-MsolSubscription
New-MsolLicenseOptions
Set-MsolUserLicense

Cmdlets for managing service principals

Get-MsolServicePrincipal
Get-MsolServicePrincipalCredential
New-MsolServicePrincipal
New-MsolServicePrincipalAddresses
New-MsolServicePrincipalCredential
Remove-MsolServicePrincipal
Remove-MsolServicePrincipalCredential
Set-MsolServicePrincipal

- **Cmdlets for managing users**

Convert-MsolFederatedUser

Get-MsolUser

New-MsolUser

Redo-MsolProvisionUser

Remove-MsolUser

Restore-MsolUser

Set-MsolUser

Set-MsolUserPassword

Set-MsolUserPrincipalName

- **Cmdlets for managing the Azure service**

Add-MsolForeignGroupToRole

Connect-MsolService

Get-MsolCompanyInformation

Get-MsolContact

Get-MsolPartnerContract

Get-MsolPartnerInformation

Redo-MsolProvisionContact

Remove-MsolContact

Set-MsolCompanyContactInformation

Set-MsolCompanySettings

Set-MsolDirSyncEnabled

Set-MsolPartnerInformation

- **Cmdlets for managing domains**

Confirm-MsolDomain

Get-MsolDomain

Get-MsolDomainVerificationDns

Get-MsolPasswordPolicy

New-MsolDomain

Remove-MsolDomain

Set-MsolDomain

Set-MsolDomainAuthentication

Set-MsolPasswordPolicy

- **Cmdlets for managing single sign-on**

Convert-MsolDomainToFederated
Convert-MsolDomainToStandard
Get-MsolDomainFederationSettings
Get-MsolFederationProperty
New-MsolFederatedDomain
Remove-MsolFederatedDomain
Set-MsolADFSContext
Set-MsolDomainFederationSettings
Update-MsolFederatedDomain

You also can enter **get-help *msol*** to get a list of commands specific to Microsoft Online Services.

Working with Exchange Online Cmdlets

When you work with Exchange Online, the operating environment is different from when you are working with on-premises Exchange Server installations. As a result, different cmdlets and options are available.

Cmdlets Specific to Exchange Online

Because the operating environment for Exchange Online is different from on-premises Exchange, Exchange Online has cmdlets that aren't available when you are working with on-premises Exchange. You'll find complete information about these cmdlets online at https://technet.microsoft.com/library/jj200780(v=exchg.160).aspx. The additional cmdlets include:

- **Cmdlets for working with online recipients**

Add-RecipientPermission
Get-LinkedUser
Get-RecipientPermission
Get-RemovedMailbox
Get-SendAddress

Import-ContactList

Remove-RecipientPermission

Set-LinkedUser

Undo-SoftDeletedMailbox

- **Cmdlets for working with connected accounts**

Get-ConnectSubscription

Get-HotmailSubscription

Get-ImapSubscription

Get-PopSubscription

Get-Subscription

New-ConnectSubscription

New-HotmailSubscription

New-ImapSubscription

New-PopSubscription

New-Subscription

Remove-ConnectSubscription

Remove-Subscription

Set-ConnectSubscription

Set-HotmailSubscription

Set-ImapSubscription

Set-PopSubscription

- **Cmdlets for working with antispam and anti-malware**

Disable-HostedContentFilterRule

Enable-HostedContentFilterRule

Get-HostedConnectionFilterPolicy

Get-HostedContentFilterPolicy

Get-HostedContentFilterRule

Get-HostedOutboundSpamFilterPolicy

Get-QuarantineMessage

New-HostedConnectionFilterPolicy

New-HostedContentFilterPolicy

New-HostedContentFilterRule

Release-QuarantineMessage

Remove-HostedConnectionFilterPolicy

Remove-HostedContentFilterPolicy

Remove-HostedContentFilterRule

Set-HostedConnectionFilterPolicy

Set-HostedContentFilterPolicy

Set-HostedContentFilterRule

Set-HostedOutboundSpamFilterPolicy

- **Cmdlets for working with connectors**

Get-InboundConnector

Get-OutboundConnector

New-InboundConnector

New-OutboundConnector

Remove-InboundConnector

Remove-OutboundConnector

Set-InboundConnector

Set-OutboundConnector

- **Cmdlets for working with messaging policy and compliance**

Get-DataClassificationConfig

Get-RMSTrustedPublishingDomain

Import-RMSTrustedPublishingDomain

Remove-RMSTrustedPublishingDomain

Set-RMSTrustedPublishingDomain

- **Cmdlets for organization and perimeter control**

Enable-OrganizationCustomization

Get-PerimeterConfig

Set-PerimeterConfig

- **Cmdlets for online reporting**

Get-ConnectionByClientTypeDetailReport

Get-ConnectionByClientTypeReport

Get-CsActiveUserReport

Get-CsAVConferenceTimeReport

Get-CsConferenceReport

Get-CsP2PAVTimeReport

Get-CsP2PSessionReport

Get-GroupActivityReport

Get-MailboxActivityReport

Get-MailboxUsageDetailReport

Get-MailboxUsageReport

Get-MailDetailDlpPolicyReport

Get-MailDetailMalwareReport

Get-MailDetailSpamReport

Get-MailDetailTransportRuleReport

Get-MailFilterListReport

Get-MailTrafficPolicyReport

Get-MailTrafficReport

Get-MailTrafficSummaryReport

Get-MailTrafficTopReport

Get-MessageTrace

Get-MessageTraceDetail

Get-MxRecordReport

Get-OutboundConnectorReport

Get-RecipientStatisticsReport

Get-ServiceDeliveryReport

Get-StaleMailboxDetailReport

Get-StaleMailboxReport

Although cmdlets specific to Windows Azure Active Directory and Exchange Online itself are available, many of the cmdlets associated with on-premises Exchange continue to be available as well. Primarily, these cmdlets include those that are specific to recipients and mailboxes and do not include those specific to Exchange on-premises configurations or to Exchange server configurations. For example, you can continue to use cmdlets for working with mailboxes, including Disable-Mailbox,

Enable-Mailbox, Get-Mailbox, New-Mailbox, Remove-Mailbox, and Set-Mailbox. However, you cannot use cmdlets for working with mailbox databases. In Exchange Online, mailbox databases are managed automatically as part of the service.

Working with Exchange Online Cmdlets

When you work with the Exchange Online, you'll often use Get, Set, Enable, Disable, New, and Remove cmdlets. The groups of cmdlets that begin with these verbs all accept the –Identity parameter, which identifies the unique object with which you are working. Generally, these cmdlets have the –Identity parameter as the first parameter, which allows you to specify the identity, with or without the parameter name.

For identities that have names as well as aliases, you can specify either value as the identity. For example, to retrieve the mailbox object for the user William Stanek with the mail alias Williams, you can use any of the following techniques:

```
get-mailbox Williams
get-mailbox –identity williams
get-mailbox "William Stanek"
get-mailbox –identity 'William Stanek'
```

Typically, Get cmdlets return an object set containing all related items when you omit the identity. For example, if you enter get-mailbox without specifying an identity, PowerShell displays a list of all mailboxes available (up to the maximum permitted to return in a single object set).

Cmdlets can display output is several different formats. Although all cmdlets return data in table format by default, there are often many more columns of data than fit across the screen. For this reason, you might need to output data in list format.

To output in list format, redirect the output using the pipe symbol (|) to the Format-List cmdlet, as shown in this example:

```
get-mailbox "William Stanek" | format-list
```

Because fl is an alias for Format-List, you also can use fl, as in this example:

```
get-mailbox "William Stanek" | fl
```

With a list format output, you should see much more information about the object or the result set than if you were retrieving table-formatted data.

Note also the pipe symbol (|) used in the examples. When you are working with Windows PowerShell, you'll often need to use the pipe symbol (|) to redirect the output of one cmdlet and pass it as input to another cmdlet. For example, access to remote PowerShell is a privilege for an online user that can be viewed with Get-User and managed with Set-User. To determine whether a particular user has remote shell access, you can enter:

```
Get-User UserID | fl RemotePowerShellEnabled
```

where UserID is the identity of the user to view, such as:

```
Get-User WilliamS | fl RemotePowerShellEnabled
```

If the user should have remote PowerShell access but doesn't currently, you can enable access using the –RemotePowerShellEnabled parameter of Set-User, as shown in this example:

```
Set-User WilliamS -RemotePowerShellEnabled $true
```

If the user has remote PowerShell access but shouldn't, you can disable access by setting the –RemotePowerShellEnabled to $false, as shown in this example:

```
Set-User TonyG -RemotePowerShellEnabled $false
```

When you work with list- or table-formatted data, you may want to specify the exact data to display. For example, with Get-User, you can display only the user name, display name and remote PowerShell status using:

```
Get-User | Format-Table Name, DisplayName,
RemotePowerShellEnabled
```

If your organization has a lot of users you can prevent the result set from getting truncated by allowing an unlimited result set to be returned, as shown in this example:

```
Get-User -ResultSize Unlimited | Format-Table
Name,DisplayName,RemotePowerShellEnabled
```

With cmdlets that have many properties, you may want to filter the output based on a specific property. For example, to display a list of all users who have remote PowerShell access, you can filter the result set on the RemotePowerShellEnabled property, as shown in the following example:

```
Get-User -ResultSize unlimited -Filter {RemotePowerShellEnabled -eq $true}
```

Alternatively, you may want to see a list of users who don't have remote PowerShell access. To do this, filter the results by looking for users who have the RemotePowerShellEnabled property set to $False:

```
Get-User -ResultSize unlimited -Filter {RemotePowerShellEnabled -eq $false}
```

Chapter 3. Getting Started with Users and Contacts

User and contact management is a key part of Exchange administration. User accounts enable individual users to log on to the network and access network resources. In Active Directory, users are represented by User and InetOrgPerson objects.

User objects represent standard user accounts; InetOrgPerson objects represent user accounts imported from non-Microsoft Lightweight Directory Access Protocol (LDAP) or X.500 directory services. User and InetOrgPerson are the only Active Directory objects that can have Exchange mailboxes associated with them.

In contrasts, contacts, are people who you or others in your organization want to get in touch with. Contacts can have street addresses, phone numbers, fax numbers, and email addresses associated with them. Unlike user accounts, contacts don't have network logon privileges.

Working with Users and Contacts

In Active Directory, users are represented as objects that can be mailbox-enabled or mail-enabled. A *mailbox-enabled* user account has an Exchange mailbox associated with it. Mailboxes are private storage areas for sending and receiving mail. A user's display name is the name Exchange presents in the global address list.

Another important identifier for mailbox-enabled user accounts is the Exchange alias. The alias is the name that Exchange associates with the account for addressing mail. When your mail client is configured to use Microsoft Exchange Server, you can type the alias or display name in the To, Cc, or Bcc text boxes of an email message and have Exchange Server resolve the alias or name to the actual email address.

Although you'll likely configure most Windows user accounts as mailbox-enabled, user accounts don't have to have mailboxes associated with them. You can create user accounts without assigning a mailbox. You can also create user accounts that are *mail-enabled* rather than mailbox-enabled, which means that the account has an off-site email address associated with it but doesn't have an actual mailbox. Mail-enabled users have Exchange aliases and display names that Exchange Server can resolve to actual email addresses. Internal users can send a message to the mail-enabled user account using the Exchange display name or alias, and the message will be directed to the external address. Users outside the organization can use the Exchange alias to send mail to the user.

It's not always easy to decide when to create a mailbox for a user. To better understand the decision-making process, consider the following scenario:

1. You've been notified that two new users, Elizabeth and Joe, will need access to the domain.

2. Elizabeth is a full-time employee who starts on Tuesday. She'll work on site and needs to be able to send and receive mail. People in the company need to be able to send mail directly to her.

3. Joe, on the other hand, is a consultant who is coming in to help out temporarily. His agency maintains his mailbox, and he doesn't want to have to check mail in two places. However, people in the company need to be able to contact him, and he wants to be sure that his external address is available.

4. You create a mailbox-enabled user account for Elizabeth. Afterward, you create a mail-enabled user account for Joe, ensuring that his Exchange information refers to his external email address.

Mail-enabled users are one of several types of custom recipients that you can create in Exchange Server. Another type of custom recipient is a *mail-enabled* contact. You create a mail-enabled contact so that users can more easily send email to that contact. A mail-enabled contact has an external email address.

Microsoft Exchange Server 2016 has in-place archiving for user mailboxes, which is designed to replace the need for personal stores in Outlook. An in-place archive is an alternative storage location for historical message data that is seamlessly accessible to a user in Microsoft Outlook 2010 or later and Outlook Web App.

The in-place archive is created as an additional mailbox and is referred to as an archive mailbox. Users can easily move and copy mail data between a primary mailbox and an archive mailbox. Because in-place archiving is a premium feature, an enterprise license is required for each user with an archive mailbox. For more information, see "Working with Archive Mailboxes" in Chapter 6 "Adding Special-Purpose Mailboxes."

How Email Routing Works: The Essentials

Exchange uses email addresses to route messages to mail servers inside and outside the organization. When routing messages internally, Mailbox servers use mail connectors to route messages to other Exchange servers, as well as to other types of mail servers that your company might use. Two standard types of connectors are used:

* **Send connectors**   Control the flow of outbound messages
* **Receive connectors**   Control the flow of inbound messages

Send and Receive connectors use Simple Mail Transfer Protocol (SMTP) as the default transport and provide a direct connection among Mailbox servers in an on-premises Exchange organization. Edge Transport servers can also receive mail from and send mail to other types of mail servers.

You can use these connectors to connect Mailbox servers in an organization. When routing messages outside the company, Mailbox servers and Edge Transport servers use mail gateways to transfer messages. The default gateway is SMTP.

Online-only deployments work in much the same way, except that mail is routed through the Exchange Online organization. Here, Exchange Online Protection handles transport.

In hybrid deployments, mailboxes can reside in the on-premises Exchange organization and in an Exchange Online organization. Messages are sent between the organizations transparently and appear as internal messages. To enhance security, messages are encrypted and transferred between the organizations using Transport Layer Security (TLS).

Exchange Server 2016 uses directory-based recipient resolution for all messages that are sent from and received by users throughout an Exchange organization. The Exchange component responsible for recipient resolution is the Categorizer. The Categorizer must be able to associate every recipient in every message with a corresponding recipient object in Active Directory.

All senders and recipients must have a primary SMTP address. If the Categorizer discovers a recipient that does not have a primary SMTP address, it will determine what the primary SMTP address should be or replace the non-SMTP address. Replacing a non-SMTP address involves encapsulating the address in a primary SMTP address that will be used while transporting the message.

> **IMPORTANT** Non-SMTP email address formats include fax, X.400, and the legacy Exchange format (EX). The Categorizer encapsulates email addresses using non-SMTP formats in the Internet Mail Connector Encapsulated Addressing (IMCEA) format. For example, the Categorizer encapsulates the fax address, FAX:888-555-1212, as IMCEA-FAX-888-555-1212@yourdomain.com. Any email address that is longer than what SMTP allows is transmitted as an extended property in the XExch50 field, provided the name part of the address and domain part of the address don't exceed the allowed limits. The maximum allowed length for an email address in Exchange is 571 characters, 315 characters for the name part of the address, 255 characters for the domain name, and the @ sign character that separates the two name parts.

In addition to primary SMTP email addresses, you can configure alternative recipients and forwarding addresses for users and public folders. If there is an alternative recipient or forwarding address, redirection is required during categorization. You specify the addresses to which messages will be redirected in Active Directory, and redirection history is maintained with each message.

Managing Recipients: The Fundamentals

Exchange Management Shell provides many commands for working with mailbox-enabled users, mail-enabled users, and contacts. The main commands you'll use are shown in the following list:

MAILBOX-ENABLED USER	MAIL-ENABLED USERS	CONTACTS
Connect-Mailbox	Disable-MailUser	Disable-MailContact
Disable-Mailbox	Enable-MailUser	Enable-MailContact
Enable-Mailbox	Get-MailUser	Get-MailContact
Get-Mailbox	New-MailUser	New-MailContact

MAILBOX-ENABLED USER	MAIL-ENABLED USERS	CONTACTS
New-Mailbox	Remove-MailUser	Remove-MailContact
Remove-Mailbox	Set-MailUser	Set-MailContact
Set-Mailbox		

Because Exchange organizations can be on-premises, online, or a hybrid of the two, working with recipients is more complex than it used to be, especially when it comes to creating recipients. Normally, to work with the recipient you access the organization where the recipient should be or has been created. For example, if a mailbox was created in the on-premises Exchange organization, you connect to the on-premises organization and work with the mailbox using the on-premises implementation of Exchange Admin Center or Exchange Management Shell. If a mailbox was created in the online Exchange organization, you connect to the online organization and work with the mailbox using the online implementation of Exchange Admin Center or Exchange Management Shell.

With hybrid deployments, however, you can synchronize users from on-premises Active Directory to Exchange Online. You do this using the hybrid deployment tools. When you run the sync tool for the first time, it copies all of the user accounts, contacts, and groups from Active Directory to Exchange Online. The domains in your organization are then synchronized automatically, so you need to re-run the sync tool only if you add, remove, or rename domains.

Although accounts for synced users are created in the Exchange Online organization, they are not activated for online use, which means they don't have access to the online features and also haven't been licensed. If you want to create an online mailbox for a synced user, you also must activate the account before the grace period expires. If the user has a local mailbox and you want to move it to Exchange Online, you run the Mailbox Migration Wizard. This wizard configures forwarding of the user's local mailbox to Exchange Online and then copies the user's mailbox data to Exchange Online. Moving and migrating mailboxes is discussed in more detail in Chapter 7 "Managing Mailboxes."

To create a new synced mailbox user, you have several options. One option is as follows:

1. Create the user account in Active Directory Users And Computers.
2. Wait for the account to be synchronized with Exchange Online.
3. Access the Exchange Online organization. Next, either create the mailbox for the user or migrate the user's existing mailbox to Exchange Online. If you create a mailbox for the user, keep the following in mind:

- For Exchange Admin Center, this means using the online console for administration. In a synchronized hybrid deployment, you can access the online console from an on-premises console. Click the **Office 365** option. After your browser connects to Office.com, click **Sign In** on the Navigation bar and then select **Work, School Or University** as your account type. Next, provide the email address and password for your Microsoft account and then click **Sign In** to open

  Office Admin Center. In Office Admin Center, click **Home** (▤) to display the Features pane and then click **Exchange** under the Admin Centers heading. This opens the Exchange Admin Center dashboard.
- For Exchange Online, you access the Exchange Online organization by establishing a remote session as discussed in "Connecting to Exchange Online Using PowerShell" in Chapter 2 "Working with Exchange Online."

4. Using Office 365 Admin Center, activate the synced user and assign a license. When you assign a license, a mailbox is created automatically.

The second option for creating a new synced mailbox user is to use the New-RemoteMailbox cmdlet. In this method, you access the on-premises Exchange organization in Exchange Management Shell and then use New-RemoteMailbox to create an enabled and synced mailbox user, which means:

- A mail-enabled user is created in on-premises Active Directory.
- An associated mailbox is created in Exchange Online.

> **NOTE** Don't forget, you'll also need to assign the user a mailbox plan.

The basic syntax for the RemoteMailbox cmdlets are as follows:

- **New-RemoteMailbox**   Creates a mail-enabled user in on-premises Active Directory and a mailbox in Exchange Online.

```
New-RemoteMailbox -Name CommonName [-Alias ExchangeAlias]
[-ArbitrationMailbox ModeratorMailbox] [-Archive <$true
| $false>] [-DisplayName Name] [-DomainController FullyQualifiedName]
[-FirstName FirstName] [-Initials Initials] [-LastName LastName]
[-ModeratedBy Moderators] [-ModerationEnabled <$true | $false>]
[-OnPremisesOrganizationalUnit OUName] [-OverrideRecipientQuotas <$true |
$false>] [-Password Password] [-PrimarySmtpAddress SmtpAddress]
[-RemotePowerShellEnabled <$true |$false>] [-RemoteRoutingAddress
ProxyAddress] [-ResetPasswordOnNextLogon <$true | $false>]
[-SamAccountName PreWin2000Name] [-SendModerationNotifications <Never |
Internal | Always>] [-UserPrincipalName LoginName]
```

- **Enable-RemoteMailbox**   Creates an online mailbox for a user already created in on-premises Active Directory.

```
Enable-RemoteMailbox -Identity UserId [-Alias ExchangeAlias]
[-DisplayName DisplayName] [-DomainController DomainControllerName]
[-PrimarySmtpAddress SmtpAddress] [-RemoteRoutingAddress ProxyAddress]
```

- **Disable-RemoteMailbox**   Removes an online mailbox but keeps the user account in on-premises Active Directory.

```
Disable-RemoteMailbox -Identity UserId [-Archive <$true | $false>]
[-DomainController DomainControllerName] [-IgnoreDefaultScope<$true |
$false>] [-IgnoreLegalHold <$true | $false>]
```

- **Remove-RemoteMailbox**   Removes an online mailbox and the related account in on-premises Active Directory.

```
Remove-RemoteMailbox -Identity UserId [-Archive <$true | $false>]
[-DomainController DomainControllerName] [-IgnoreDefaultScope<$true |
$false>] [-IgnoreLegalHold <$true | $false>]
```

Regardless of which approach you use to create new mailbox users in Exchange Online, you must license these mailbox users in Office 365. You do this by associating a mailbox plan with each mailbox user. Using the graphical tools, you can associate mailbox plans when you are creating mailbox users or afterward by editing the account properties. In a remote session with Exchange Online, you can use the -

MailboxPlan parameter with the New-Mailbox cmdlet to do the same. However, at the time of this writing, there are no mailbox plan parameters for any of the RemoteMailbox cmdlets. (Hopefully, this oversight will be corrected by the time you read this.)

When you assign mailbox plans, you need to ensure you have enough licenses. You purchase and assign licenses using the billing and subscription optins in Office 365 Admin Center. Select **Billing** on the dashboard or click **Subscriptions** under the Billing heading in the Features pane to see the subscription and licensing options.

Office 365 will allow you to assign more mailbox plans than you have licenses for. However, after the initial grace period, problems will occur. For example, mail data for unlicensed mailboxes may become unavailable. Remember, the number of valid licenses shouldn't exceed the number of assigned licenses.

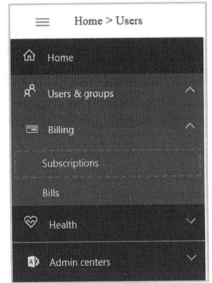

FIGURE 3-1 Accessing subscriptions in Office 365 Admin Center.

You activate and license synced users in Office 365 as well:

1. Select **Users** on the dashboard or click **Active Users** under the Users & Groups heading in the Features pane to display active users.

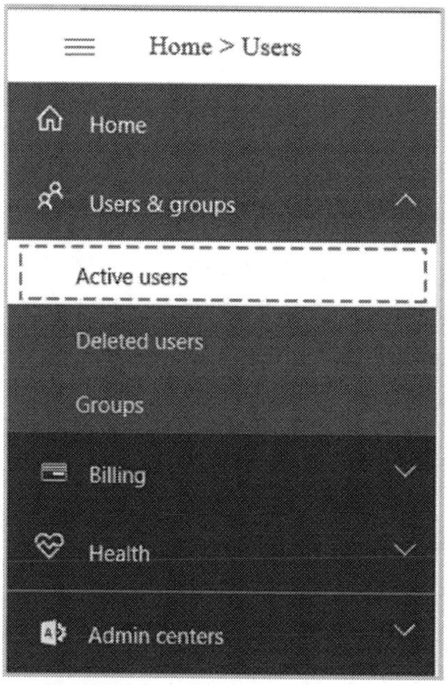

FIGURE 3-2 Accessing active users in Office 365 Admin Center.

2. On the Users page, click a user that you want to activate and license to display account settings.

3. Click **Edit** on the Products panel.

4. As shown in Figure 3-3, specify the work location for the user.

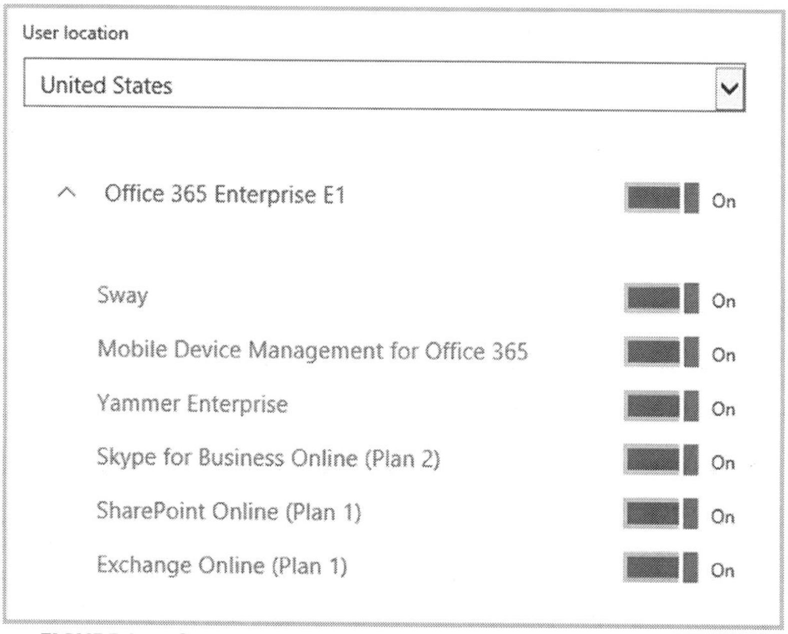

FIGURE 3-3 Switch the plan on and configure its options.

5. Select the mailbox plan to assign by clicking it to the On position.

6. Optionally, click to switch individual plan options on or off.

7. Select **Activate** or **Save** as appropriate.

The Office 365 service, its settings and accounts are all manageable from Windows PowerShell. Every account you create in the online environment is in fact created in the online framework within which Office 365 and Exchange Online operate. This framework is called Windows Azure, and like Windows Server, it uses Active Directory to provide its directory services. You can manage Office 365 from Windows PowerShell as discussed in "Connecting to Windows Azure" in Chapter 2.

Finding Existing Mailboxes, Contacts, And Groups

You work with recipients where they were created, which can be either in an on-premises Exchange organization or in Exchange Online. You can view current mailboxes, mail-enabled users, contacts, and groups by following these steps:

1. Open Exchange Admin Center using one of the following techniques:

- For on-premises Exchange, open your Web browser and then enter the secure URL for Exchange Admin Center, such as *https://mailserver16.imaginedlands.com/ecp*.
- For online Exchange, open your Web browser and then enter the secure URL for Office 365 Admin Center, such as *https://portal.microsoftonline.com/admin/default.aspx*. In Office 365 Admin Center, click Home to display the Features pane and then click **Exchange** under the Admin Centers heading to open the Exchange Online version of Exchange Admin Center.

2. As shown in Figure 3-4, select **Recipients** in the Features pane and then select the related Mailboxes, Groups, or Contacts tab, as appropriate for the type of recipient you want to work with.

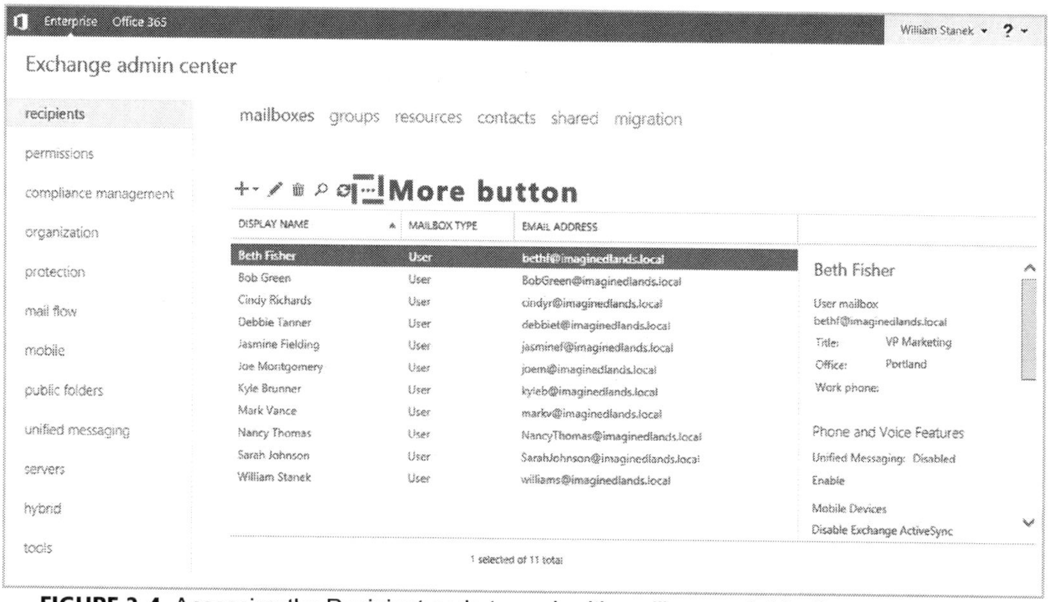

FIGURE 3-4 Accessing the Recipient node to work with mailboxes, distribution groups, and mail contacts.

By default, all recipients of the selected type are displayed. With mailboxes this means that user mailboxes, linked user mailboxes, legacy user mailboxes, and remote user mailboxes are displayed.

By default, Exchange Admin Center displays only three columns of information for each recipient, including the display name, mailbox type, and email address. To customize the columns of information displayed, click the More button (•••) and then select **Add/Remove Columns**. Use the options provided in the Add/Remove Columns dialog box, shown in Figure 3-5, to configure the columns to use, and then click **OK**.

add/remove columns

DISPLAY	COLUMN
☑	DISPLAY NAME
☑	MAILBOX TYPE
☑	EMAIL ADDRESS
☑	RECIPIENT TYPE
☐	EXCHANGE ACTIVESYNC POLICY
☐	ALIAS
☐	ARCHIVE DATABASE
☐	ARCHIVE STATE
☐	CITY
☐	COMPANY
☐	COUNTRY/REGION
☐	DATABASE
☐	DEPARTMENT

reset view

OK   Cancel

FIGURE 3-5 Customizing the list of columns to display using the options provided.

In large organizations, you may need to filter based on attributes to locate recipients you want to work with. To do this, click the More button (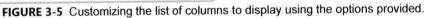) and then select **Advanced Search**. Next, use the Advanced Search dialog box, shown in Figure 3-6 to filter by alias, display name, department, email addresses, first name, last name, and recipient type. The Recipient Types condition allows you to filter the results for specific recipient subtypes, such as only remote mailbox users.

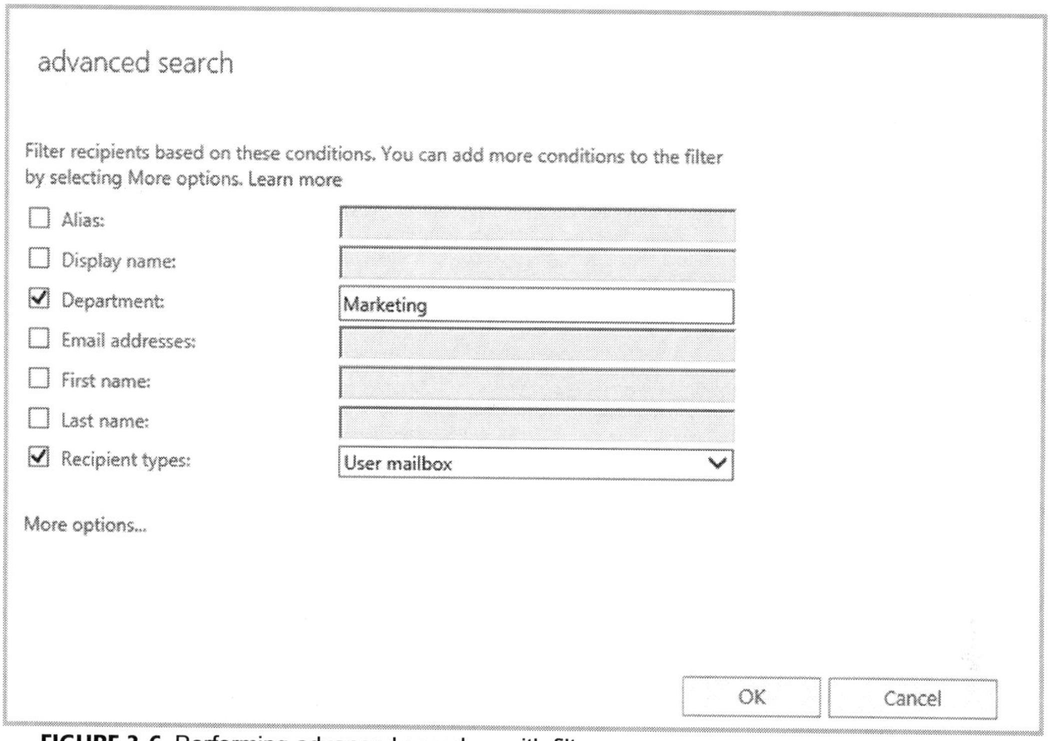

FIGURE 3-6 Performing advanced searches with filters.

You can add conditions that allow you to filter results based on city, state, country, office, title, group membership, and more:

1. Select **More Options** and then select **Add Condition**.
2. Click in the selection list and then select the condition, such as City.
3. Type the search word or phrase and then click **OK**.
4. Repeat this process to add other conditions.

In Exchange Management Shell, you can find mailboxes, contacts, and groups by using the following commands:

* **Get-User** Use the Get-User cmdlet to retrieve all users in the forest that match the specified conditions.

```
Get-User [-Identity UserId | -Anr Identifier] [-AccountPartition PartitionId]
[-Arbitration <$true | $false>] [-Credential Credential]
[-DomainController DomainControllerName] [-Filter FilterString]
[-IgnoreDefaultScope <$true | $false>] [-Organization OrgName]
[-OrganizationalUnit OUName] [-PublicFolder <$true | $false>]
```

```
[-ReadFromDomainController <$true | $false>] [-RecipientTypeDetails
Details] [-ResultSize Size] [-SortBy String]
```

- **Get-Contact** Use the Get-Contact cmdlet to retrieve information about a specified contact or contacts.

```
Get-Contact [-Identity ContactId | -Anr ContactID] [-AccountPartition
PartitionId] [-Credential Credential] [-DomainController
DomainControllerName] [-Filter FilterString] [-IgnoreDefaultScope <$true
| $false>] [-Organization OrgName] [-OrganizationalUnit OUName]
[-ReadFromDomainController <$true | $false>]
[-RecipientTypeDetails Details] [-ResultSize Size] [-SortBy Value]
```

- **Get-Group** Use the Get-Group cmdlet to query for existing groups.

```
Get-Group [-Identity GroupId | -Anr GroupID]
[-AccountPartition PartitionId] [-Credential Credential]
[-DomainController FullyQualifiedName] [-Filter FilterString]
[-IgnoreDefaultScope <$true | $false>] [-Organization OrgName]
[-OrganizationalUnit OUName] [-ReadFromDomainController <$true |
$false>] [-RecipientTypeDetails {"Contact" | "MailContact" |
"MailUser" | "RoleGroup" | "User" | "UserMailbox" | ... }]
[-ResultSize Size] [-SortBy Value]
```

- **Get-RemoteMailbox** Use the Get-RemoteMailbox cmdlet to get details for mail-enabled users in on-premises Active Directory that have mailboxes in Exchange Online.

```
Get-RemoteMailbox [-Identity UserId | -Anr Identifier] [-Alias
ExchangeAlias] [-Archive <$true | $false>] [-DomainController
DomainControllerName] [-OnPremisesOrganizationalUnit OUName]
[-ReadFromDomainController DomainControllerName]
[-ResultSize NumResults]
```

Finding Synced, Unlicensed, Inactive, and Blocked Users

When you are working with hybrid organizations, users can be synced from Active Directory to Exchange Online. These synced users can have mailboxes on-premises or in Exchange Online. If you need to view all the synced users, determine where a synced user's mailbox is located, or perform other tasks with synced users, complete the following steps:

1. Open Office 365 Admin Center. Select **Users & Groups** in the Features pane, and then click **Active Users**.

2. On the Filters drop-down list, select **Synced Users**.

3. You should now see a list of synced users.

A synced user is only one type of user you may want to find in an Exchange Online organization. You also may want to find:

- **Unlicensed users**   These users haven't been assigned an Exchange Online license. Although there is a grace period for licensing after creating a mailbox user online, the user may lose mailbox data after the grace period expires.
- **Inactive users**   These users have been deleted by an admin, which puts them in inactive status for a period of 30 days. When the recovery period expires, the account and any unprotected data is removed.
- **Sign-in Allowed users**   These users can sign in and the related accounts are active.
- **Sign-in Blocked users**   These users cannot sign in and the related accounts are blocked, such as may happen when a user's password expires.
- **Users with errors**   These users have errors associated with their accounts.

You can find allowed users, blocked users, unlicensed users, or users with errors by completing the following steps:

1. Open Office 365 Admin Center. Select **Users & Groups** in the Features pane, and then click **Active Users**.

2. On the Filters drop-down list, select Sign-in Allowed Users, Sign-in Blocked Users, Unlicensed Users, or Users With Errors as appropriate.

In Office 365 Admin Center, you can find inactive users by selecting Users And Groups in the Features pane and then selecting the Deleted Users tab.

Chapter 4. Managing Users

In Exchange Server 2016, Exchange Admin Center and Exchange Management Shell are the primary administration tools you use to manage mailboxes and mail contacts. You can use these tools to create and manage mail-enabled user accounts, mailbox-enabled user accounts, and mail-enabled contacts, as well as any other configurable aspect of Exchange Server.

The sections that follow examine techniques to manage user accounts and the related Exchange features of those accounts whether you are working with either on-premises Exchange organizations or Exchange Online. In a hybrid environment, you always manage domain user accounts and their mailboxes using the on-premises Exchange tools. Your changes are then synced to the online environment.

> **NOTE** Domain administrators can create user accounts and contacts using Active Directory Users And Computers. If any existing user accounts need to be mail-enabled or mailbox-enabled, you perform these tasks using the Exchange management tools. If existing contacts need to be mail-enabled, you also perform this task using the Exchange management tools.

Creating Mailbox-Enabled and Mail-Enabled User Accounts

Generally speaking, you need to create a user account for each user who wants to use network resources. The following sections explain how to create domain user accounts that are either mailbox-enabled or mail-enabled, and how to add a mailbox to an existing user account. If a user needs to send and receive email, you need to create a new mailbox-enabled account for the user or add a mailbox to the user's existing account. Otherwise, you can create a mail-enabled account.

Working with Logon Names and Passwords

Before you create a domain user account, you should think for a moment about the new account's logon name and password. You identify all domain user accounts with a logon name. This logon name can be (but doesn't have to be) the same as the user's email address. In Windows domains, logon names have two parts:

* **User name** The account's text label
* **User domain** The domain where the user account exists

For the user Williams whose account is created in imaginedlands.com, the full logon name for Windows is williams@imaginedlands.com.

User accounts can also have passwords and public certificates associated with them. *Passwords* are authentication strings for an account. *Public certificates* combine a public and private key to identify a user. You log on with a password by typing the password. You log on with a public certificate by using a smart card and a smart card reader.

Although Windows displays user names to describe privileges and permissions, the key identifiers for accounts are security identifiers (SIDs). SIDs are unique identifiers that Windows generates when you create accounts. SIDs consist of the domain's security ID prefix and a unique relative ID. Windows uses these identifiers to track accounts independently from user names. SIDs serve many purposes; the two most important are to allow you to easily change user names and to allow you to delete accounts without worrying that someone could gain access to resources simply by re-creating an account with the same user name.

When you change a user name, you tell Windows to map a particular SID to a new name. When you delete an account, you tell Windows that a particular SID is no longer valid. Afterward, even if you create an account with the same user name, the new account won't have the same privileges and permissions as the previous one because the new account will have a new SID.

Mail-Enabling New User Accounts

Mail-enabled users are defined as custom recipients in Exchange Server. They have an Exchange alias and an external email address, but they do not have an Exchange mailbox. All email messages sent to a mail-enabled user are forwarded to the remote email address associated with the account.

In Exchange Admin Center, mail-enabled users are listed as Mail Users under Recipients > Contacts. You can manage mail-enabled users through Exchange Admin Center and Exchange Management Shell.

> **NOTE** With on-premises Exchange, you have two options for mail-enabled users and contacts that are no longer needed. You can disable the mail-enabled user or contact, or you can delete the mail-enabled user or contact.

> With Exchange online, your only option is to delete the mail-enabled user or contact.

You can create a new mail-enabled user by completing the following steps:

1. In Exchange Admin Center, select **Recipients** in the Features pane and then select **Contacts**.

2. Click **New** ( ) and then select **Mail User**. This opens the New Mail User dialog box, shown in Figure 4-1.

3. If you are working with on-premises Exchange, Existing User is selected by default and you'll need to select **New User** instead.

4. Type the user's first name, middle initial, and last name in the text boxes provided. These values are used to create the Display Name entry (as well as the Active Directory name with on-premises Exchange).

5. The Display Name and Name properties can't exceed 64 characters. As necessary, make changes to the Display Name, Name, or both text boxes. For example, you might want to type the name in LastName FirstName MiddleInitial format or in FirstName MiddleInitial LastName format.

> **IMPORTANT** The difference between the Display Name and the Name properties is subtle but important. The Display Name property sets the name displayed in Exchange and Outlook. The Name property sets the display name in Active Directory and is the Common Name (CN) value associated with the user.

6. In the Alias text box, type an alias for the mail-enabled user. This alias should uniquely identify the mail-enabled user in the Exchange organization. Alias names cannot contain spaces.

7. In the External Email Address text box, type the mail user's external email address. By default, the address is configured as a standard SMTP email address. If you are working with on-premises Exchange, you can specify a custom address type by selecting the related option and then entering a prefix that identifies the custom type. Use X.400, GroupWise or Lotus Notes for X.400, GroupWise and Lotus Notes address types respectively.

8. With on-premises Exchange, the user account is created in the default user container, which typically is the Users container. Because you'll usually need to create new user accounts in a specific organizational unit rather than in the Users container, click **Browse** to the right of the Organizational Unit text box. In the Select Organizational Unit dialog box, choose the location where you want to store the account and then click **OK**.

9. In the User ID or User Logon Name text box, type the user's logon name. Use the drop-down list to select the domain with which you want to associate the account. This sets the fully qualified logon name, such as williams@imaginedlands.com.

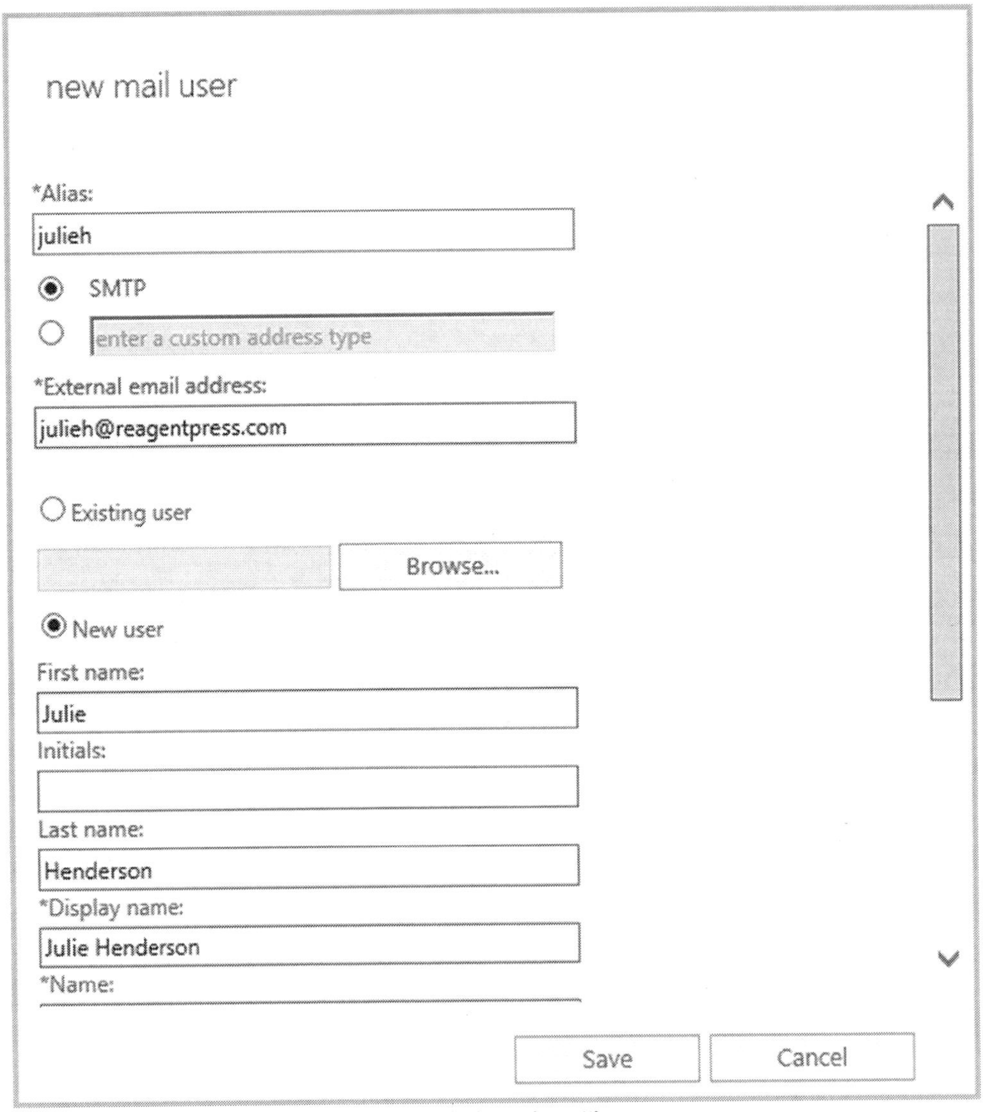

---

new mail user

*Alias:

julieh

⦿ SMTP

◯ enter a custom address type

*External email address:

julieh@reagentpress.com

◯ Existing user

[   ]   Browse...

⦿ New user

First name:

Julie

Initials:

[   ]

Last name:

Henderson

*Display name:

Julie Henderson

*Name:

Save   Cancel

FIGURE 4-1 Configuring the mail-enabled user's settings.

10. Type and then confirm the password for the account. This password must follow the conventions of your organization's password policy. Typically, this means that the password must include at least eight characters and must use three of the four available character types: lowercase letters, uppercase letters, numbers, and symbols.

11. With on-premises Exchange you can select Require Password Change On Next Logon check box to ensure that the user changes the password at next logon.

12. Click **Save**. Exchange Admin Center creates the new mail-enabled user.

If an error occurs, the user will not be created. You will need to click OK, correct the problem, and then click Save again. Consider the error example shown in Figure 4-2. In this instance, the user logon name/user ID was already in use so the user couldn't be created.

FIGURE 4-2 An error occurs when a user's principal name is already in use.

You can list all mail-enabled users by typing **get-mailuser** at the Exchange Management Shell prompt. Sample 4-1 provides the full syntax and usage for Get-MailUser.

SAMPLE 4-1 Get-MailUser cmdlet syntax and usage

Syntax

```
Get-MailUser [-Identity Identifier | -Anr Name] [-AccountPartition PartitionId]
[-Credential Credential] [-DomainController FullyQualifiedName] [-Filter
FilterString] [-IgnoreDefaultScope {$true | $false}] [-Organization OrgName]
[-OrganizationalUnit OUName] [-ReadFromDomainController {$true | $false}]
[-ResultSize Size] [-SortBy Value]
```

Usage

```
Get-MailUser -Identity "aaron1" | fl


Get-MailUser -OrganizationalUnit "marketing" | fl
```

> **NOTE** By default, Get-MailUser lists the name and recipient type for matches. In the example, fl is an alias for Format-List and is used to get detailed information about matching entries.

You can create a new mail-enabled user account using the New-MailUser cmdlet. Sample 4-2 shows the syntax and usage. When prompted, provide a secure password for the user account.

> **NOTE** The syntax and usage are entered on multiple lines for ease of reference. You must enter the command-line values for a cmdlet on a single line.

SAMPLE 4-2 New-MailUser cmdlet syntax and usage

Syntax

```
New-MailUser -Name CommonName -ExternalEmailAddress EmailAddress
[-Password Password] [-UserPrincipalName LoginName] {AddtlParams1}


New-MailUser -Name CommonName -FederatedIdentity FederatedId
-WindowsLiveID WindowsLiveId [-EvictLiveId <$true | $false>]
[-ExternalEmailAddress EmailAddress] [-NetID NetID] {AddtlParams2}


New-MailUser -Name CommonName -FederatedIdentity FederatedId
-MicrosoftOnlineServicesID WindowsLiveId [-NetID NetID] {AddtlParams2}


New-MailUser -Name CommonName -ImportLiveId <$true | $false>
-WindowsLiveID WindowsLiveId [-ExternalEmailAddress EmailAddress]
[-UsageLocation CountryInfo] {AddtlParams2}


New-MailUser -Name CommonName [-MicrosoftOnlineServicesID WindowsLiveId]
{AddtlParams2}


New-MailUser -Name CommonName -MicrosoftOnlineServicesID WindowsLiveId
```

```
-Password Password [-ExternalEmailAddress EmailAddress] [-UsageLocation
CountryInfo] {AddtlParams2}


New-MailUser -Name CommonName -Password Password -WindowsLiveID
WindowsLiveId [-EvictLiveId <$true | $false>] [-ExternalEmailAddress
EmailAddress] [-UsageLocation CountryInfo] {AddtlParams2}


New-MailUser -Name CommonName -UseExistingLiveId <$true | $false>
-WindowsLiveID WindowsLiveId [-BypassLiveId <$true | $false>]
[-ExternalEmailAddress EmailAddress] [-NetID NetID]
[-UsageLocation CountryInfo] {AddtlParams2}


{AddtlParams1}
[-Alias ExchangeAlias] [-ArbitrationMailbox ModeratorMailbox]
[-DisplayName Name] [-DomainController FullyQualifiedName] [-FirstName
FirstName] [-Initials Initials] [-LastName LastName]
[-MacAttachmentFormat <BinHex | UuEncode | AppleSingle | AppleDouble>]
[-MessageBodyFormat <Text | Html | TextAndHtml>] [-MessageFormat <Text |
Mime>] [-ModeratedBy Moderators] [-ModerationEnabled <$true | $false>]
[-Organization OrgName] [-OrganizationalUnit OUName] [-PrimarySmtpAddress
}SmtpAddress] [-ResetPasswordOnNextLogon <$true | $false>]
}[-SamAccountName PreWin2000Name] [-SendModerationNotifications <Never |
Internal | Always>] [-UsageLocation CountryInfo] [-UsePreferMessageFormat
<$true | $false>]


{AddtlParams2}
[-Alias ExchangeAlias] [-ArbitrationMailbox ModeratorMailbox]
[-DisplayName Name] [-DomainController FullyQualifiedName] [-FirstName
FirstName] [-Initials Initials] [-LastName LastName] [-ModeratedBy
Moderators] [-ModerationEnabled <$true | $false>] [-Organization OrgName]
[-OrganizationalUnit OUName] [-PrimarySmtpAddress SmtpAddress]
[-RemotePowerShellEnabled <$true | $false>] [-ResetPasswordOnNextLogon
<$true | $false>] [-SamAccountName PreWin2000Name]
[-SendModerationNotifications <Never | Internal | Always>]
```

```
New-MailUser -Name "Frank Miller" -Alias "Frankm"
-OrganizationalUnit "imaginedlands.local/Technology"
-UserPrincipalName "Frankm@imaginedlands.local" -SamAccountName "Frankm"
-FirstName "Frank" -Initials "" -LastName "Miller"
-ResetPasswordOnNextLogon $false
-ExternalEmailAddress "SMTP:Frankm@hotmail.com"
```

Mail-Enabling Existing User Accounts

When a user already has an account in Active Directory, you can mail-enable the account using Exchange Admin Center and Exchange Management Shell. In Exchange Admin Center for your on-premises organization, you can mail-enable an existing user account by completing the following steps:

1. Select **Recipients** in the Features pane and then select **Contacts**.

2. Click **New** () and then select **Mail User**. This opens the New Mail User dialog box.

3. In the Alias text box, type an alias for the mail-enabled user. This alias should uniquely identify the mail-enabled user in the Exchange organization. Alias names cannot contain spaces.

4. In the External Email Address text box, type the mail user's external email address. By default, the address is configured as a standard SMTP email address. If you are working with on-premises Exchange, you can specify a custom address type by selecting the related option and then entering a prefix that identifies the custom type. Use X.400, GroupWise or Lotus Notes for X.400, GroupWise and Lotus Notes address types respectively.

5. The Existing User option is selected by default, as shown in Figure 4-3. Click **Browse**. This displays the Select User dialog box.

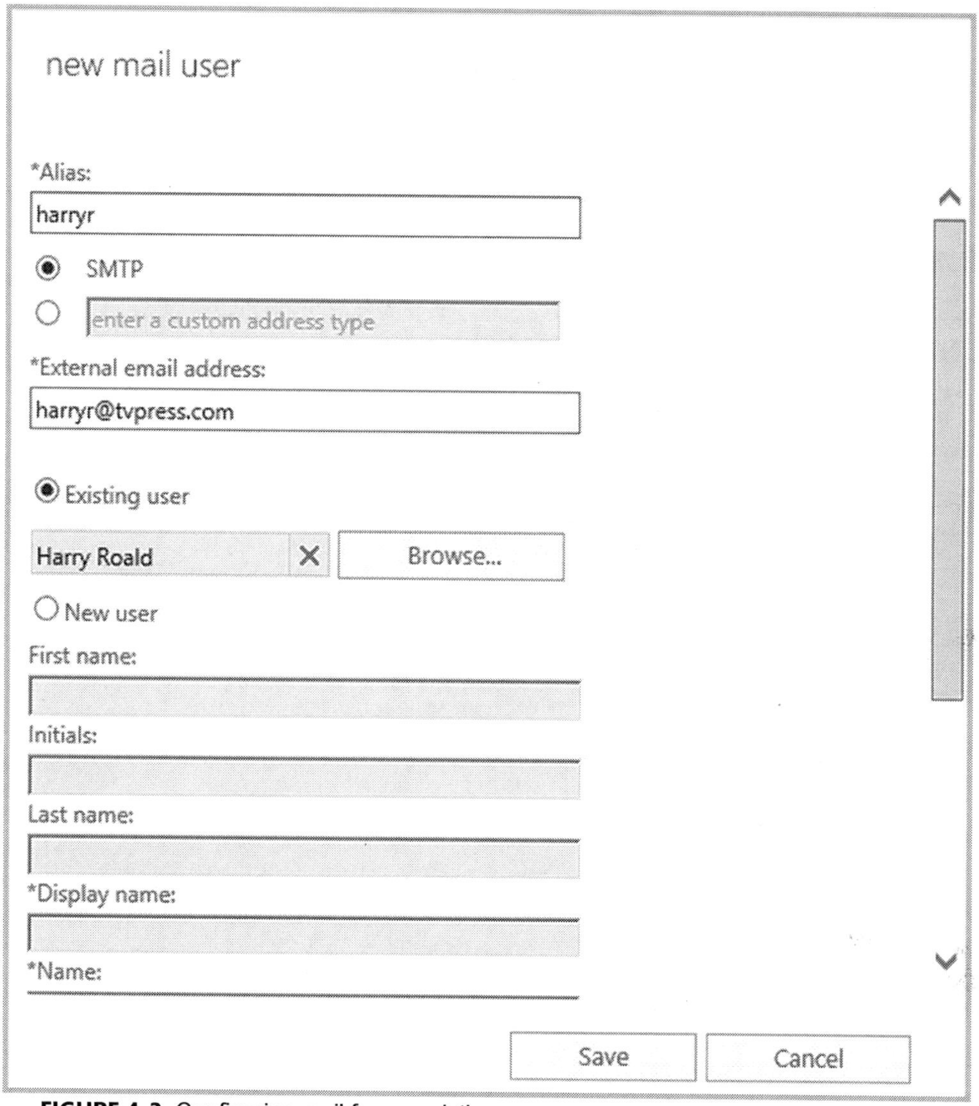

new mail user

*Alias:

harryr

◉ SMTP

○ enter a custom address type

*External email address:

harryr@tvpress.com

◉ Existing user

Harry Roald ✕   Browse...

○ New user

First name:

Initials:

Last name:

*Display name:

*Name:

Save   Cancel

FIGURE 4-3 Configuring mail for an existing user.

6. In the Select User dialog box, select the user account you want to mail-enable and then click **OK**. User accounts that are not yet mail-enabled or mailbox-enabled for the current domain are listed by name and organizational unit.

7. Click **Save**. Exchange Admin Center mail-enables the user account you previously selected. If you're working in a synced, hybrid organization, the mail-enabled user will be synced to Exchange Online as well. If an error occurs, the user account will not be mail-enabled. You will need to correct the problem and repeat this procedure. Click **Finish**.

You can mail-enable an existing user account using the Enable-MailUser cmdlet. Sample 4-3 shows the syntax and usage. For the identity parameter, you can use the user's display name, logon name, or user principal name.

SAMPLE 4-3 Enable-MailUser cmdlet syntax and usage

Syntax

```
Enable-MailUser -Identity Identity -ExternalEmailAddress EmailAddress
[-Alias ExchangeAlias] [-DisplayName Name] [-DomainController
FullyQualifiedName] [-MacAttachmentFormat <BinHex | UuEncode |
AppleSingle | AppleDouble>] [-MessageBodyFormat <Text | Html |
TextAndHtml>] [-MessageFormat <Text | Mime>] [-PrimarySmtpAddress
SmtpAddress] [-UsePreferMessageFormat <$true | $false>]
```

Usage

```
Enable-MailUser -Identity "imaginedlands.local/Marketing/Frank Miller"
-Alias "Frankm" -ExternalEmailAddress "SMTP:Frankm@hotmail.com"
```

Managing Mail-Enabled User Accounts

You can manage mail-enabled users in several ways. If a user account should no longer be mail-enabled, you can disable mail forwarding. To disable mail forwarding in Exchange Admin Center for your on-premises organization, select Recipients in the Features pane and then select the Contacts tab. Next, select the user you want to disable. Click the More button (•••) and then select **Disable**. When prompted to confirm, select **Yes**. If you're working in a synced, hybrid organization, this change will be synced to Exchange Online as well.

At the Exchange Management Shell prompt, you can disable mail forwarding using the Disable-MailUser cmdlet, as shown in Sample 4-4.

SAMPLE 4-4 Disable-MailUser cmdlet syntax and usage

Syntax

```
Disable-MailUser -Identity Identity [-DomainController
FullyQualifiedName] [-IgnoreDefaultScope {$true | $false}]
```

Usage

```
Disable-MailUser -Identity "Frank Miller"
```

If you no longer need a mail-enabled user account, you can permanently remove it from Active Directory. To remove a mail-enabled user account in Exchange Admin Center for your on-premises organization, select the mail user and then select the Delete option. When prompted to confirm, click Yes. If you're working in a synced, hybrid organization, this change will be synced to Exchange Online as well.

At the Exchange Management Shell prompt, you can remove a mail-enabled user account by using the Remove-MailUser cmdlet, as shown in Sample 4-5.

SAMPLE 4-5 Remove-MailUser cmdlet syntax and usage

Syntax

```
Remove-MailUser -Identity "Identity" [-DomainController DCName]
[-IgnoreDefaultScope {$true | $false}]
[-KeepWindowsLiveID {$true | $false}]
```

Usage

```
Remove-MailUser -Identity "Frank Miller"
```

Creating Domain User Accounts with Mailboxes

You can create a new domain user account with a mailbox in several ways. If you are using a hybrid configuration and want the user created in Active Directory and the mailbox created in Exchange online, you can use the techniques discussed earlier under "Understanding on-premises and online recipient management." Otherwise, you can create a new domain user account and a mailbox for that account using only your on-premises Exchange administration tools. To do this, complete the following steps:

1. In Exchange Admin Center, select **Recipients** in the Features pane and then select **Mailboxes**.

2. Click **New** ( ) and then select **User Mailbox**. This opens the New User Mailbox dialog box, shown in Figure 4-4.

3. In the Alias text box, type an alias for the mailbox user. This alias should uniquely identify the user in the Exchange organization. Alias names cannot contain spaces.

> **NOTE** The alias and domain suffix are combined to create the email address for the user. For example, if the alias is tedc and the domain suffix is imaginedlands.com, the email address is set as tedc@imaginedlands.com.

4. Select **New User**. Type the user's first name, middle initial, and last name in the text boxes provided. These values are used to create the Display Name entry as well as the Active Directory name with on-premises Exchange.

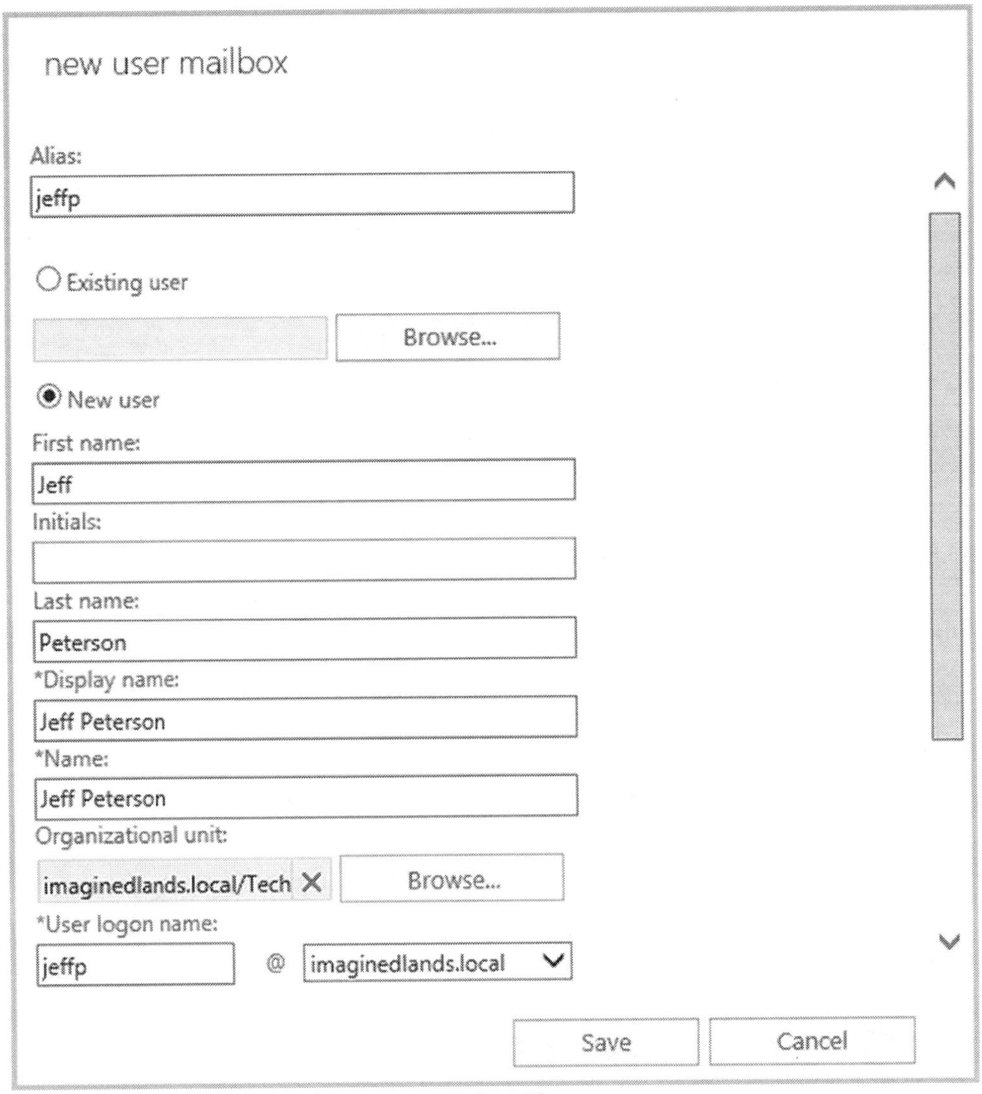

new user mailbox

Alias:

`jeffp`

○ Existing user

| | Browse... |

◉ New user

First name:

`Jeff`

Initials:

| |

Last name:

`Peterson`

*Display name:

`Jeff Peterson`

*Name:

`Jeff Peterson`

Organizational unit:

`imaginedlands.local/Tech` ✕   Browse...

*User logon name:

`jeffp` @ `imaginedlands.local` ⌄

| Save | Cancel |

FIGURE 4-4 Configuring the mailbox user's settings.

5. The Display Name and Name properties can't exceed 64 characters. As necessary, make changes to the Display Name, Name, or both text boxes. For example, you might want to type the name in LastName FirstName MiddleInitial format or in FirstName MiddleInitial LastName format.

> **IMPORTANT** The difference between the Display Name and the Name properties is subtle but important. The Display Name property sets the name displayed in Exchange and Outlook. The Name property sets the display name in Active Directory and is the Common Name (CN) value associated with the user.

6. Unless you specify otherwise, the user account is created in the default user container, which typically is the Users container. Because you'll usually need to create new user accounts in a specific organizational unit rather than in the Users container, click **Browse** to the right of the Organizational Unit text box. In the Select An Organizational Unit dialog box, shown in Figure 4-5, choose the location to store the account and then click **OK**.

7. In the User Logon Name text box, type the user's logon name. Use the drop-down list to select the domain with which you want to associate the account. This sets the fully qualified logon name, such as jeffp@imaginedlands.local.

8. Type and then confirm the password for the account. This password must follow the conventions of your organization's password policy. Typically, this means that the password must include at least eight characters and must use three of the four available character types: lowercase letters, uppercase letters, numbers, and symbols.

9. You can select the Require Password Change On Next Logon check box to ensure that the user changes the password at next logon.

10. Click **More Options**. At this point, you can do the following:

- **Specify the mailbox database** Exchange uses the mailbox provisioning load balancer to select a database to use when you create a mailbox and do not specify the mailbox database to use. If you want to specify the database to use, click Browse to the right of the Mailbox Database box. In the Select Mailbox Database dialog box, you'll see a list of available mailbox databases listed by name, server, and Exchange version. Select the mailbox database to use and then select OK.
- **Create an archive mailbox** If you want to create an archive mailbox for the user, select the related check box. Items in the user's mailbox will be moved automatically to the archive mailbox based on the default retention policy. Using the related Browse option, you also can choose a mailbox database for the archive. If you don't chose a mailbox database for the archive, Exchange chooses one for you.

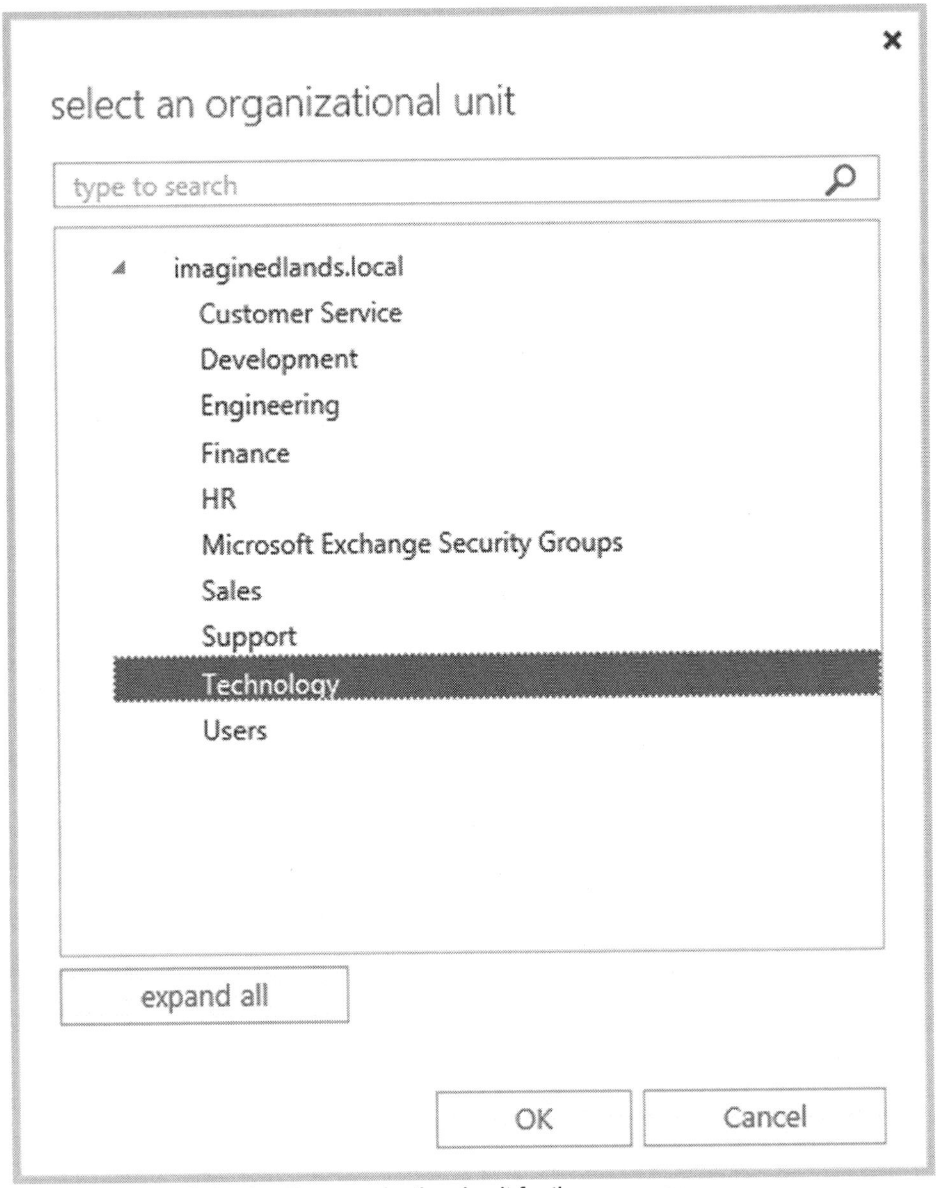

FIGURE 4-5 Selecting the organizational unit for the new user.

- **Assign an address book policy**   By default, a user has access to the full address book information in the organization. Using address book policies, you can create customized address books. To apply an available policy, select it from the drop-down list.

  11. Click **Save**. Exchange Admin Center creates the new mailbox user. If an error occurs, neither the user nor the mailbox will be created. You will need to click OK, correct the problem, and then click Save again.

Creating the user account and mailbox isn't necessarily the final step. You might also want to do the following:

* Add detailed contact information for the user, such as a business phone number and title
* Add the user to security and distribution groups
* Enable or disable mailbox features for the account
* Modify the user's default delivery options, storage limits, and restrictions on the account
* Associate additional email addresses with the account

> **NOTE** For all mailbox-enabled accounts, an SMTP email address is configured automatically. You can also add more addresses of the same type. For example, if Brian Johnson is the company's human resources administrator, he might have the primary SMTP address of brianj@imaginedlands.com and an alternate SMTP address of resumes@imaginedlands.com.

You may also want to apply appropriate policies to the mailbox. Various types of policies control how users access their mailboxes and how mailbox data is stored. These policies include:

* **Address book policy** Controls access to the address book information in the organization and allows you to create custom views for various users. A default address book policy is not created when you install Exchange 2016. You can check to see if any address book policies have been created by entering **get-addressbookpolicy** in Exchange Management Shell.
* **Mobile device mailbox policy** Controls security settings for mobile devices. When you install Exchange Server, a default mobile device mailbox policy is created and applied automatically to all new mailboxes you create unless you specify a different policy to use. To view the settings for the default policy, enter **get-mobiledevicemailboxpolicy –identity "Default"** in Exchange Management Shell.
* **Retention policy** Specifies the delete and move-to-archive rules that are applied to items in mailboxes. Exchange Server 2016 uses retention policies and retention tags as part of the Messaging Records Management feature. When you install Exchange 2016 a default retention policy is created but is not applied to new mailboxes by default. Therefore, you must explicitly assign a retention policy. To view the settings for the default policy, enter **get-retentionpolicy –identity "Default MRM Policy" | fl** in Exchange Management Shell.
* **Role assignment policy** Controls management roles assigned to users. When you install Exchange Server, a default role assignment policy is created and applied automatically to all new mailboxes you create unless you specify a different policy to use. To view the settings for the default policy, enter **get-**

roleassignmentpolicy –identity "Default Role Assignment Policy" in Exchange Management Shell.

- **Sharing policy** Controls how users can share calendar and contact information with users outside your organization. When you install Exchange Server, a default sharing policy is created and applied automatically to all new mailboxes you create unless you specify a different policy to use. To view the settings for the default policy, enter **get-sharingpolicy –identity "Default Sharing Policy"** in Exchange Management Shell.

In Exchange Management Shell, you can create a user account with a mailbox by using the New-Mailbox cmdlet. Sample 4-6 provides the syntax and usage. When you are prompted, enter a secure password for the new user account.

SAMPLE 4-6 New-Mailbox cmdlet syntax and usage

Syntax

```
New-Mailbox -Name Name -Password Password -UserPrincipalName
UserNameAndSuffix {AddtlParams} {CommonParams} {ModParams}


New-Mailbox -Name Name -Room <$true | $false> [-Office OfficeName]
[-Password Password] [-Phone PhoneNumber] [-ResourceCapacity Capacity]
[-UserPrincipalName UserNameAndSuffix] {CommonParams} {ModParams}


New-Mailbox -Name Name -Password Password -WindowsLiveID WindowsLiveId
[-EvictLiveId <$true | $false>] {AddtlParams} {CommonParams}
{ModParams}


New-Mailbox -Name Name -UseExistingLiveId <$true | $false> -WindowsLiveID
WindowsLiveId [-BypassLiveId <$true | $false>] [-NetID NetID]
{AddtlParams} {CommonParams} {ModParams}


New-Mailbox -Name Name -UserPrincipalName UserNameAndSuffix [-MailboxPlan
MailboxPlanId] {CommonParams} {ModParams}


New-Mailbox -Name Name -AccountDisabled <$true | $false> [-MailboxPlan
MailboxPlanId] [-Password Password] [-UsageLocation Location]
[-UserPrincipalName UserNameAndSuffix] {CommonParams} {ModParams}
```

```
New-Mailbox -Name Name -ImportLiveId <$true | $false> -WindowsLiveID
WindowsLiveId {AddtlParams} {CommonParams} {ModParams}


New-Mailbox -Name Name -RemovedMailbox RemovedMailboxId [-MailboxPlan
MailboxPlanId] [-Password Password] {CommonParams} {ModParams}


New-Mailbox -Name Name -FederatedIdentity FederatedId -WindowsLiveID
WindowsLiveId [-EvictLiveId <$true | $false>] [-NetID NetID]
{AddtlParams} {CommonParams}


New-Mailbox -Name Name -FederatedIdentity FederatedId
-MicrosoftOnlineServicesID WindowsLiveId [-NetID NetID]
{AddtlParams} {CommonParams}


New-Mailbox -Name Name -ArchiveDomain SmtpDomain -Password Password
-UserPrincipalName UserNameAndSuffix [-MailboxPlan MailboxPlanId]
[-RemoteArchive <$true | $false>] [-RemovedMailbox RemovedMailboxId]
{CommonParams} {ModParams}


New-Mailbox -Name Name -MicrosoftOnlineServicesID WindowsLiveId -Password
Password {AddtlParams} {CommonParams} {ModParams}


New-Mailbox -Name Name [-UserPrincipalName UserNameAndSuffix] {CommonParams}
{ModParams}


New-Mailbox -Name Name -LinkedDomainController DCName -LinkedMasterAccount
Identity [-LinkedCredential Credential] [-UserPrincipalName UserNameAndSuffix]
{CommonParams} {ModParams}


New-Mailbox -Name Name -Equipment <$true | $false> [-Password Password]
[-UserPrincipalName UserNameAndSuffix] {CommonParams} {ModParams}


New-Mailbox -Name Name -Shared <$true | $false> [-Password Password]
[-UserPrincipalName UserNameAndSuffix] {CommonParams} {ModParams}


New-Mailbox -Name Name [-Password Password] [-UserPrincipalName
```

UserNameAndSuffix] {CommonParams} {ModParams}

New-Mailbox -Name **Name** -Arbitration <$true | $false> -UserPrincipalName
UserNameAndSuffix [-Password **Password**] {CommonParams}

New-Mailbox -Name **Name** [-Password **Password**] [-UserPrincipalName
UserNameAndSuffix] {CommonParams} {ModParams}

New-Mailbox -Name **Name** -Discovery <$true | $false> [-Password **Password**]
[-UserPrincipalName **UserNameAndSuffix]** {CommonParams}

New-Mailbox -Name **Name** -EnableRoomMailboxAccount <$true | $false>
-Room <$true | $false> [-MicrosoftOnlineServicesID **WindowsLiveId**]
[-RoomMailboxPassword **Password**] [-UserPrincipalName **UserNameAndSuffix**]
{CommonParams}

New-Mailbox -Name **Name** -PublicFolder <$true | $false> [-HoldForMigration
<$true | $false>] [-IsExcludedFromServingHierarchy <$true | $false>]
{CommonParams}

{AddtlParams}
[-MailboxPlan **PlanID**] [-RemovedMailbox **RemovedMailboxId**]
[-UsageLocation **Location**]

{ModParams}
[-ArbitrationMailbox **ModeratorMailbox**] [-ModeratedBy **Moderators**]
[-ModerationEnabled <$true | $false>] [-SendModerationNotifications
<Never | Internal | Always>]

{CommonParams}
[-ActiveSyncMailboxPolicy **MailboxPolicyId**] [-AddressBookPolicy **ABPolicyId**]
[-Alias **ExchangeAlias**] [-Archive {$true | $false}] [-ArchiveDatabase
DatabaseId] [-Database **DatabaseId**] [-DisplayName **Name**]
[-DomainController **FullyQualifiedName**] [-ExternalDirectoryObjectID **ObjectID**]
[-FirstName **FirstName**] [-ImmutableId **Id**] [-Initials **Initials**] [-LastName
LastName] [-ManagedFolderMailboxPolicy **MailboxPolicyId**]

```
[-ManagedFolderMailboxPolicyAllowed {$true | $false}]
[-Organization OrgName] [-OrganizationalUnit OUName]
[-OverrideRecipientQuotas {$true | $false}] [-PrimarySmtpAddress
SmtpAddress] [-QueryBaseDNRestrictionEnabled <$true | $false>]
[-RemoteAccountPolicy PolicyId] [-RemotePowershellEnabled
<$true | $false>] [-ResetPasswordOnNextLogon <$true | $false>]
[-RetentionPolicy PolicyId] [-RoleAssignmentPolicy PolicyId]
[-SamAccountName PreWin2000Name] [-SharingPolicy PolicyId]
[-TargetAllMDBs <$true | $false>] [-ThrottlingPolicy PolicyId]
```

Usage

```
New-Mailbox -Name "Shane S. Kim" -Alias "shanek"
-OrganizationalUnit "imaginedlands.local/Engineering"
-Database "Engineering Primary"
-UserPrincipalName "shanek@imaginedlands.local" -SamAccountName "shanek"
-FirstName "Shane" -Initials "S" -LastName "Kim"
-ResetPasswordOnNextLogon $true -Archive $true
```

Creating Online User Accounts with Mailboxes

You can create user accounts with mailboxes in Exchange Online. These accounts are then available in the online organization.

To create an online user account, follow these steps:

1. From the dashboard in Office 365 Admin Center, select **Add User**. This opens the Add User window, shown in Figure 4-6.

2. Type the user's first name and last name in the text boxes provided. These values are used to create the Display Name entry.

3. The Display Name and Name properties can't exceed 64 characters. As necessary, make changes to the Display Name. For example, you might want to type the name in LastName FirstName format or in FirstName LastName format.

4. In the User Name text box, type the user's logon name. Use the drop-down list to select the domain with which you want to associate the account. This sets the fully qualified logon name, such as mikejackson@imaginedlands.onmicrosoft.com (which is referred to as the logon ID with Exchange Online).

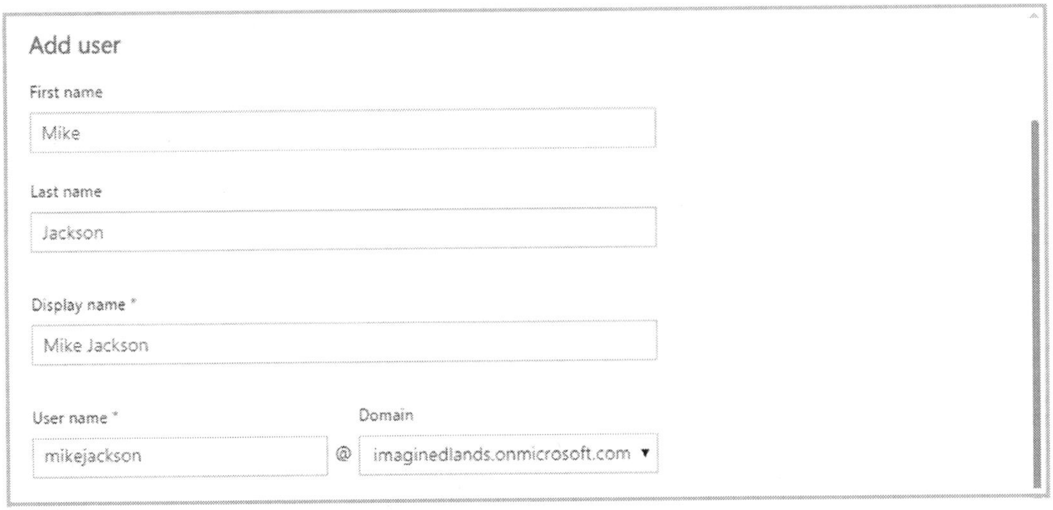

Add user

First name

Mike

Last name

Jackson

Display name *

Mike Jackson

User name *

mikejackson

Domain

@ imaginedlands.onmicrosoft.com ▼

FIGURE 4-6 Providing the details for the new user.

5. Expand the Contact Information panel by clicking on it and add contact information, such as Job Title and Department, as appropriate.

6. By default, Exchange Online will generate a temporary password for the user and email the account information along with the password to the email address associated with your logon. Exchange Online will also make the user change the password when the first sign in. To change these settings, expand the Password panel by clicking on it and then specify the desired options. You can create a password for the user, specify an alternative address for emailing the account information or both.

7. By default, the user account is created with no administrator access. If you are creating an account for an administrator, expand the Roles panel by clicking on it and then specify the desired options. You can specify that the user is a global administrator or create a custom administrator role.

8. Expand the Products panel by clicking on it and select a product plan, license or both to assign to the user. Click **Save** to create the user account and mailbox.

IMPORTANT   The available licenses will depend on the license types previously purchased for your organization. If you don't have available subscriptions, the appropriate subscriptions and licenses will be purchased for you automatically.

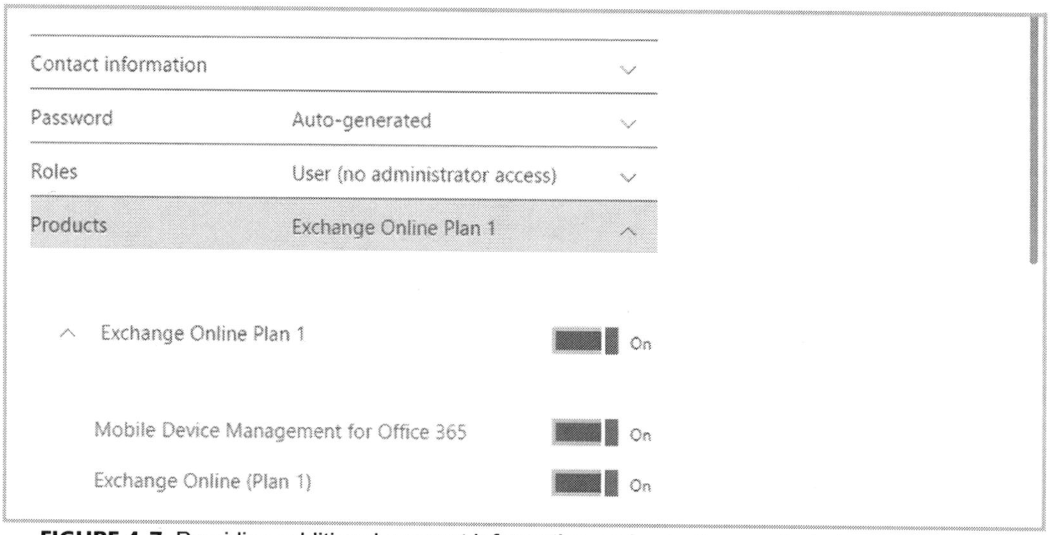

FIGURE 4-7 Providing additional account information and selecting product plans.

Creating the online user account and mailbox isn't necessarily the final step. You might also want to do the following:

- Add the user to security and distribution groups
- Enable or disable mailbox features for the account
- Modify the user's default delivery options, storage limits, and restrictions on the account
- Associate additional email addresses with the account

In Exchange Management Shell, you can create an online user account using the New-Mailbox cmdlet. Keep in mind that a mailbox is created only when you use the -MailboxPlan parameter to assign a mailbox plan to the new user.

Adding Mailboxes to Existing Domain User Accounts

You don't have to create an Exchange mailbox when you create a domain user account. You can create a mailbox for a domain user account any time you determine the mailbox is needed.

You can add a mailbox to an existing domain user account in several ways. If you are using a hybrid configuration and want the mailbox created in Exchange online, you can use the techniques discussed earlier under "Understanding on-premises and online recipient management." Otherwise, you can add a mailbox to a domain user account using only your on-premises Exchange administration tools. To do this, complete the following steps:

1. In Exchange Admin Center, select **Recipients** in the Features pane and then select **Mailboxes**.

2. Click **New** (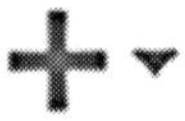) and then select **User Mailbox**. This opens the New User Mailbox dialog box, shown in Figure 4-8.

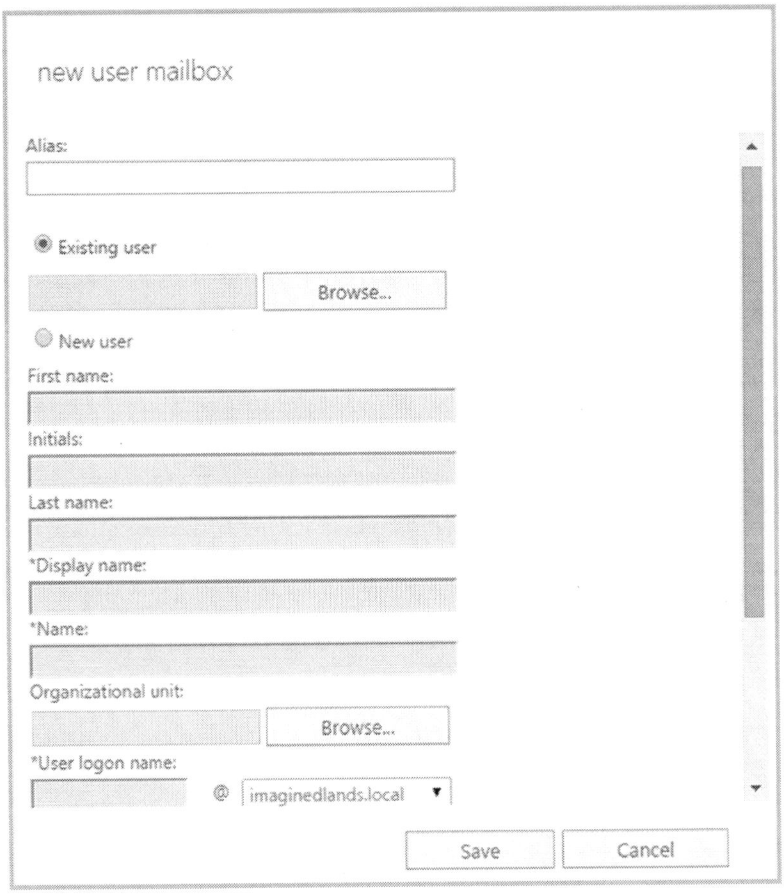

FIGURE 4-8 **Adding a mailbox to an existing domain user account.**

3. In the Alias text box, type an alias for the mailbox user. This alias should uniquely identify the user in the Exchange organization. Alias names cannot contain spaces.

> **NOTE** The alias and domain suffix are combined to create the email address for the user. For example, if the alias is tedc and the domain suffix is imaginedlands.com, the email address is set as tedc@imaginedlands.com.

4. The Existing User option is selected by default. Click **Browse**. This displays the Select User dialog box.

5. In the Select User dialog box, shown in Figure 4-9, select the user account you want to mailbox-enable and then click **OK**. User accounts that are not yet mail-enabled or mailbox-enabled for the current domain are listed by name and organizational unit.

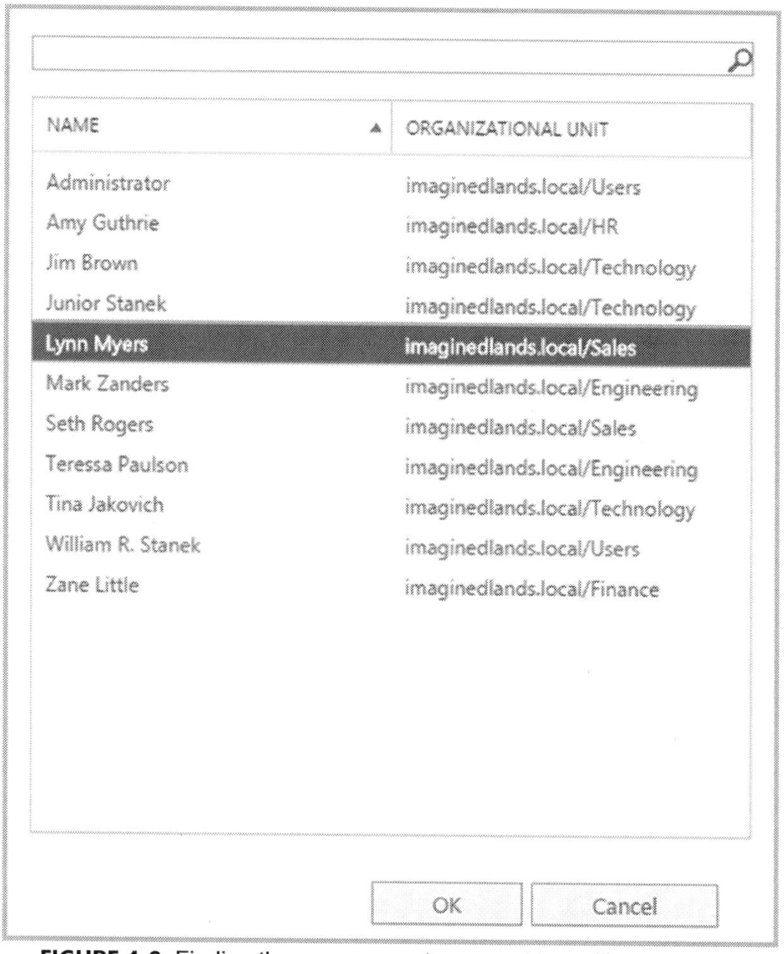

NAME	ORGANIZATIONAL UNIT
Administrator	imaginedlands.local/Users
Amy Guthrie	imaginedlands.local/HR
Jim Brown	imaginedlands.local/Technology
Junior Stanek	imaginedlands.local/Technology
Lynn Myers	imaginedlands.local/Sales
Mark Zanders	imaginedlands.local/Engineering
Seth Rogers	imaginedlands.local/Sales
Teressa Paulson	imaginedlands.local/Engineering
Tina Jakovich	imaginedlands.local/Technology
William R. Stanek	imaginedlands.local/Users
Zane Little	imaginedlands.local/Finance

OK   Cancel

FIGURE 4-9 Finding the user account you want to mailbox-enable.

6. Click More Options. You can now:

- **Specify the mailbox database**   Exchange uses the mailbox provisioning load balancer to select a database to use when you create a mailbox and do not specify the mailbox database to use. If you want to specify the database to use, click Browse to the right of the Mailbox Database box. In the Select Mailbox Database dialog box, you'll see a list of available mailbox databases listed by name, server, and Exchange version. Select the mailbox database to use and then click OK.

- **Create an archive mailbox** If you want to create an archive mailbox for the user, select the related check box. Items in the user's mailbox will be moved automatically to the archive mailbox based on the default retention policy. You also can choose a mailbox database for the archive. If you don't choose a mailbox database for the archive, Exchange chooses one for you.
- **Assign an address book policy** By default, a user has access to the full address book information in the organization. Using address book policies, you can create customized address books. To apply an available policy, select it from the drop-down list.

7. Click **Save**. Exchange Admin Center creates the mailbox for the selected user. If an error occurs, the mailbox will not be created. You will need to click OK, correct the problem, and then click Save again.

In Exchange Management Shell, you can add a mailbox to individual user accounts using the Enable-Mailbox cmdlet. Sample 4-7 provides the syntax and usage. If you want to create mailboxes for multiple accounts, you need to enter a separate command for each account.

SAMPLE 4-7 Enable-Mailbox cmdlet syntax and usage

Syntax

```
Enable-Mailbox [-AccountDisabled <$true | $false>] [-MailboxPlan
MailboxPlanId] [-UsageLocation Location] {AddtlParams} {CommonParams}


Enable-Mailbox -LinkedDomainController DCName -LinkedMasterAccount Identity [-
Database DatabaseId] [-LinkedCredential Credential]
[-TargetAllMDBs <$true | $false>] {CommonParams}


Enable-Mailbox -Discovery <$true | $false> [-Database DatabaseId]
[-TargetAllMDBs <$true | $false>] {CommonParams}


Enable-Mailbox [-AccountDisabled <$true | $false>] [-MailboxPlan
MailboxPlanId] [-UsageLocation Location] {AddtlParams} {CommonParams}


Enable-Mailbox -Equipment <$true | $false> [-AccountDisabled <$true |
$false>] {AddtlParams} {CommonParams}


Enable-Mailbox -Room <$true | $false> [-AccountDisabled <$true | $false>]
```

```
{AddtlParams} {CommonParams}


Enable-Mailbox -PublicFolder <$true | $false> [-Database DatabaseId]
[-HoldForMigration <$true | $false>] {CommonParams}


Enable-Mailbox -Arbitration <$true | $false> [-Database DatabaseId]
[-TargetAllMDBs <$true | $false>] {CommonParams}


Enable-Mailbox -Shared <$true | $false> [-AccountDisabled <$true | $false>]
{AddtlParams} {CommonParams}


Enable-Mailbox [-Archive <$true | $false>] [-ArchiveDatabase DatabaseId]
[-ArchiveGuid <Guid>] [-ArchiveName <MultiValuedProperty>]
[-BypassModerationCheck <$true | $false>] {CommonParams}


Enable-Mailbox -ArchiveDomain SmtpDomain [-RemoteArchive <$true |
 $false>] {CommonParams}


{AddtlParams}


[-BypassModerationCheck <$true | $false>] [-Database DatabaseId] [-
TargetAllMDBs <$true | $false>]


{CommonParams}
[-ActiveSyncMailboxPolicy MailboxPolicyId] [-Alias ExchangeAlias]
[-DisplayName Name] [-DomainController FullyQualifiedName]
[-ManagedFolderMailboxPolicy MailboxPolicyId]
[-ManagedFolderMailboxPolicyAllowed {$true | $false}]
[-OverrideRecipientQuotas {$true | $false}]
[-PrimarySmtpAddress SmtpAddress]
[-RetentionPolicy PolicyId] [-RoleAssignmentPolicy PolicyId]
```
Usage

```
Enable-Mailbox -Identity "imaginedlands.local/Engineering/Oliver Lee"
-Alias "Oliverl" -Database "Engineering Primary"
```

Setting or Changing the Common Name and Logon Name for Domain User Accounts

All domain user accounts have a common name stored in Active Directory and a logon name used for logging on to the domain. These names can be different from the mailbox display name and mailbox alias used by Exchange Server.

You can set this information for a domain user account by completing the following steps:

1. In Exchange Admin Center, select **Recipients** in the Features pane and then select **Mailboxes**.

2. Double-click the mailbox entry for the user with which you want to work. This opens a properties dialog box for the user.

3. On the General page, shown in Figure 4-10, use the following text boxes to set the user's common name and logon name:

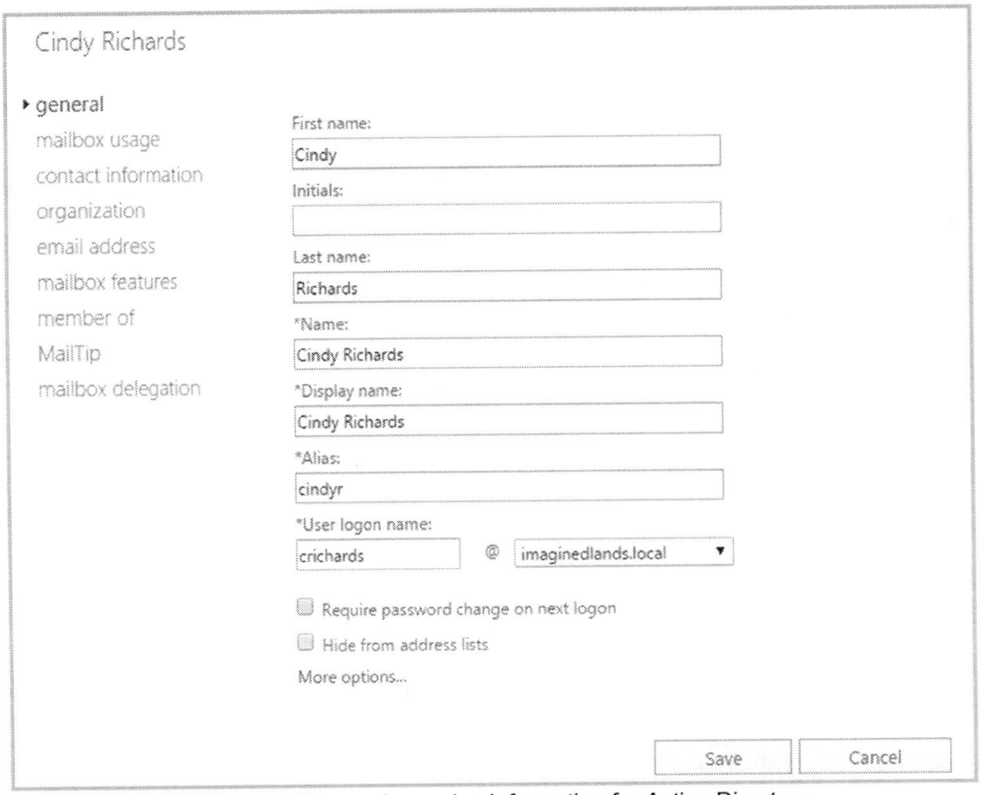

FIGURE 4-10 Changing the user's naming information for Active Directory.

- **First Name, Initials, Last Name**   Sets the user's full name.
- **Name**   Sets the user's display name as seen in logon sessions and in Active Directory.
- **User Logon Name**   Sets the user's logon name.

    4.   Click **Save** to apply your changes.

Setting or Changing Contact Information for User Accounts

You can set contact information for a user account by completing the following steps:

1.   In Exchange Admin Center, select **Recipients** in the Features pane and then select **Mailboxes**.

2.   Double-click the mailbox entry for the user with which you want to work.

3.   On the Contact Information page, shown in Figure 4-11, use the text boxes provided to set the user's business address or home address. Normally, you'll want to enter the user's business address. This way, you can track the business locations and mailing addresses of users at various offices.

NOTE   You need to consider privacy issues before entering private information, such as home addresses and home phone numbers, for users. Discuss the matter with the appropriate groups in your organization, such as the human resources and legal departments. You might also want to get user consent before releasing home addresses.

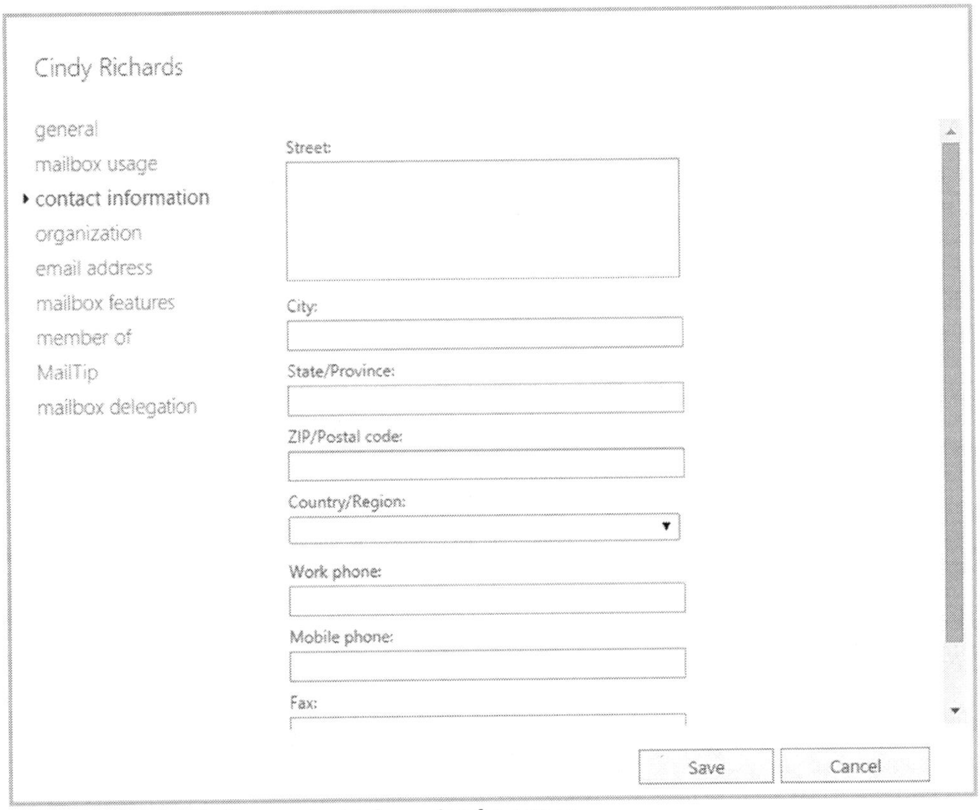

FIGURE 4-11 Setting contact information for a user.

4. Use the Work Phone, Mobile Phone, and Fax text boxes to set the user's primary business telephone, mobile phone, and fax numbers.

5. Click More Options. Use the Office text box to set the user's office and the Web Page text box to set the URL of the user's home page, which can be on the Internet or the company intranet.

6. On the Organization page, shown in Figure 4-12, as appropriate, type the user's title, department, and company.

7. To specify the user's manager, click **Browse**. In the Manager dialog box, select the user's manager and then click **OK**. When you specify a manager, the user shows up as a direct report in the manager's account. Click **Save** to apply the changes.

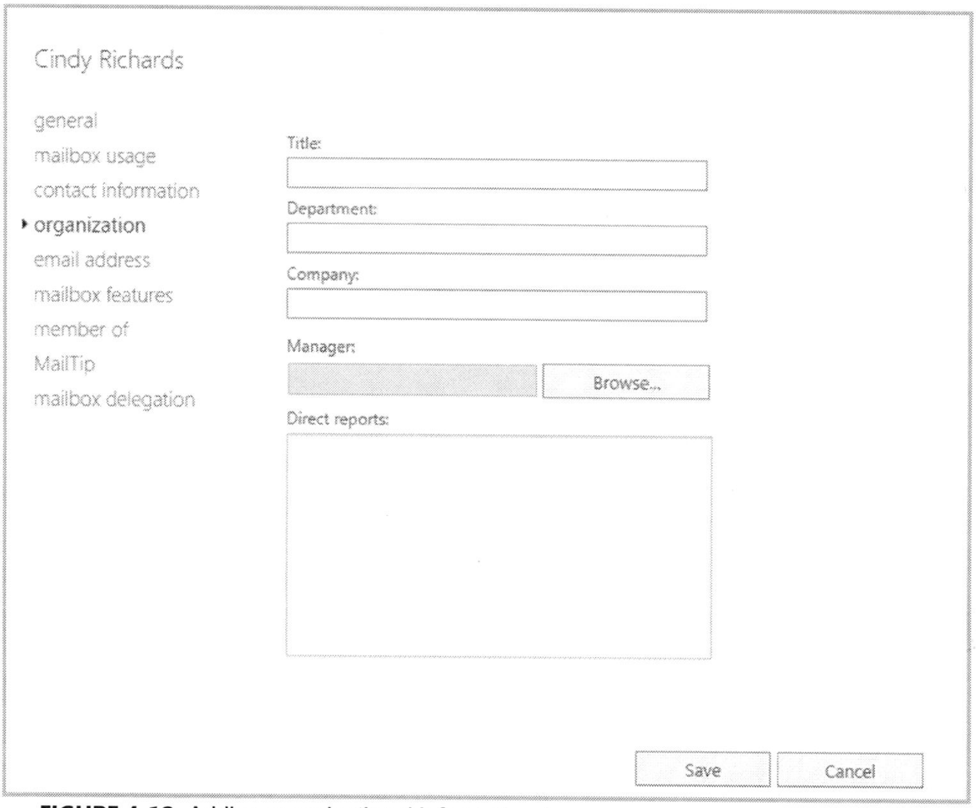

FIGURE 4-12 Adding organizational information for a user.

Changing Logon ID or Logon Domain for Online Users

For Exchange Online, the fully-qualified logon ID is the user's name followed by the @ symbol and the user's logon domain. You can modify this information for an online user account by completing the following steps:

1. In the dashboard for Office 365 Admin Center, select **Users & Groups** in the Features pane and then select **Active Users**.

2. Click the mailbox entry for the user with which you want to work. This opens a properties dialog box for the user.

3. Click **Edit** on the Email Addresses panel and then use the User Name and Domain text boxes to set the user's logon name and domain.

4. Click **Save** to apply your changes.

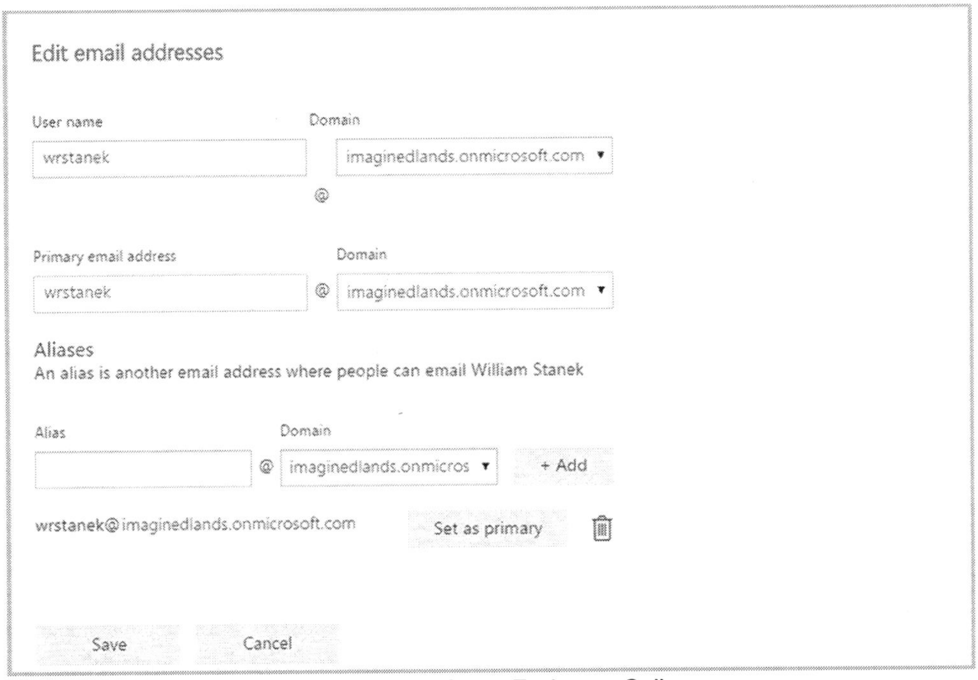

FIGURE 4-13 Updating the user name for an Exchange Online user.

Changing a User's Exchange Server Alias and Display Name

Each mailbox has an Exchange alias and display name associated with it. The Exchange alias is used with address lists as an alternative way of specifying the user in the To, Cc, or Bcc text boxes of an email message. The alias also sets the primary SMTP address associated with the account.

> **TIP** Whenever you change the Exchange alias in the on-premises organization, a new email address is generated and set as the default address for SMTP. The previous email addresses for the account aren't deleted. Instead, these remain as alternatives to the defaults. To learn how to change or delete these additional email addresses, see "Adding, changing, and removing email and other addresses" later in this chapter.
>
> With Exchange Online, changing a user's Exchange alias doesn't normally change the primary SMTP address for the user.

To change the Exchange alias and mailbox name on a user account, complete the following steps:

1. In Exchange Admin Center, select **Recipients** in the Features pane and then select **Mailboxes**.

2. Double-click the mailbox entry for the user with which you want to work.

3. On the General page, the Display Name text box sets the mailbox name. Change this text box if you'd like the mailbox to have a different display name.

4. The Alias text box sets the Exchange alias. If you'd like to assign a new alias, enter the new Exchange alias in this text box.

5. Click **Save**.

> **NOTE** Often, the user logon name and the Exchange alias are set to the same value. If you've implemented this practice in your organization, you may also want to modify the user logon name. However, this is not a best practice when security is a concern.

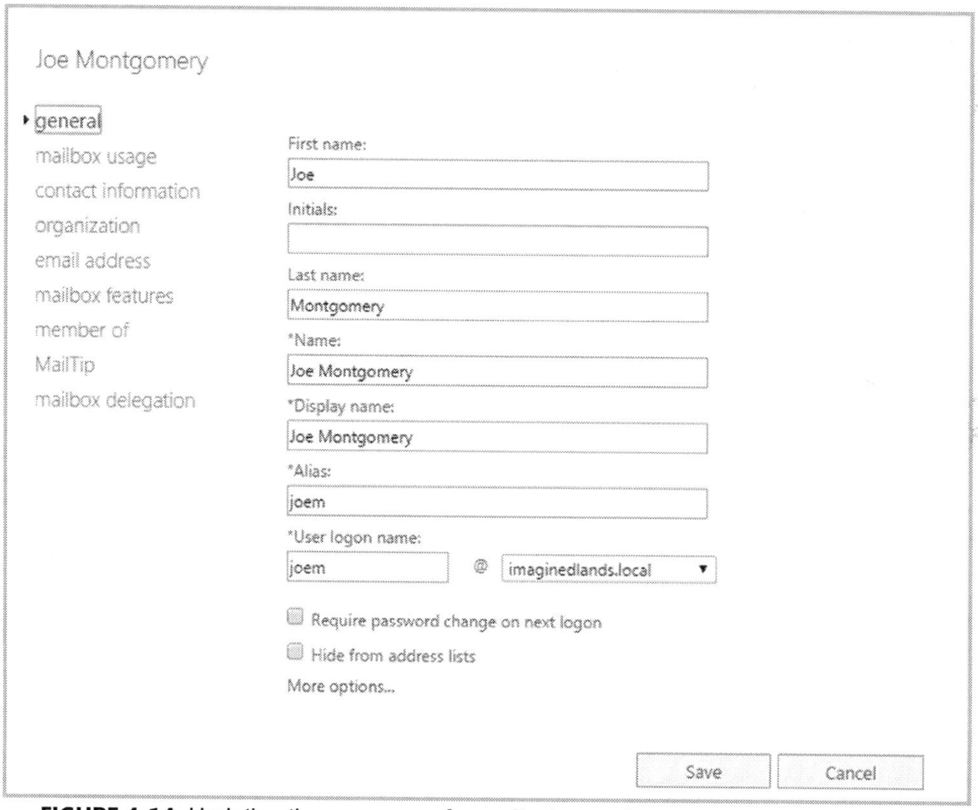

Joe Montgomery

▸ general
 mailbox usage
 contact information
 organization
 email address
 mailbox features
 member of
 MailTip
 mailbox delegation

First name:
Joe

Initials:

Last name:
Montgomery

*Name:
Joe Montgomery

*Display name:
Joe Montgomery

*Alias:
joem

*User logon name:
joem @ imaginedlands.local ▾

☐ Require password change on next logon

☐ Hide from address lists

More options...

Save   Cancel

FIGURE 4-14 Updating the user name for an Exchange Server user.

Adding, Changing, and Removing Email and Other Addresses

When you create a mailbox-enabled user account, default email addresses are created. Any time you update the user's Exchange alias in the on-premises Exchange organization, a new default email address is created. However, the old addresses aren't deleted. They remain as alternative email addresses for the account.

With Exchange Online, changing a user's Exchange alias doesn't normally change the email address for the user. You can, however, modify the primary SMTP address or add additional SMTP addresses.

Exchange also allows you to create non-SMTP addresses for users:

- Exchange Unified Messaging (EUM) addresses used by the Unified Messaging service to locate UM-enabled users within the Exchange organization
- Custom addresses for legacy Exchange (Ex) as well as these non-Exchange mail organizations: X.400, X.500, MSMail, CcMail, Lotus Notes, and Novell GroupWise

To add, change, or remove an email or other address, follow these steps:

1. In Exchange Admin Center, select **Recipients** in the Features pane and then select **Mailboxes**.
2. Double-click the mailbox entry for the user you want to work with.
3. On the Email Address page, shown in Figure 4-15, you can use the following techniques to manage the user's email addresses:

- **Create a new SMTP address** Click Add (✚). Because the address type SMTP is selected by default, enter the SMTP email address, and then click OK to save your changes.

- **Create a new EUM address** Click Add (✚), and then select the EUM option. Enter the custom address or extension. Next, click Browse and then select a dial plan Click OK to save your changes.

- **Create a custom address** Click Add (✚), and then select the Custom Address Type option. Enter the custom address type in the text box provided. Valid types include: X.400, X.500, EUM, MSMail, CcMail, Lotus Notes, and

NovellGroupWise. Next, enter the custom address. This address must comply with the format requirements for the address type. Click OK to save your changes.

> **TIP** Use SMTP as the address type for standard Internet email addresses. For custom address types, such as X.400, you must enter the address in the proper format.

- **Edit an existing address** Double-click the address entry, or select the entry and then select Edit on the toolbar. Modify the settings in the Address dialog box, and then click OK.
- **Delete an existing address** Select the address, and then click Remove.

> **NOTE** You can't delete the primary SMTP address without first promoting another email address to the primary position. Exchange Server uses the primary SMTP address to send and receive messages.

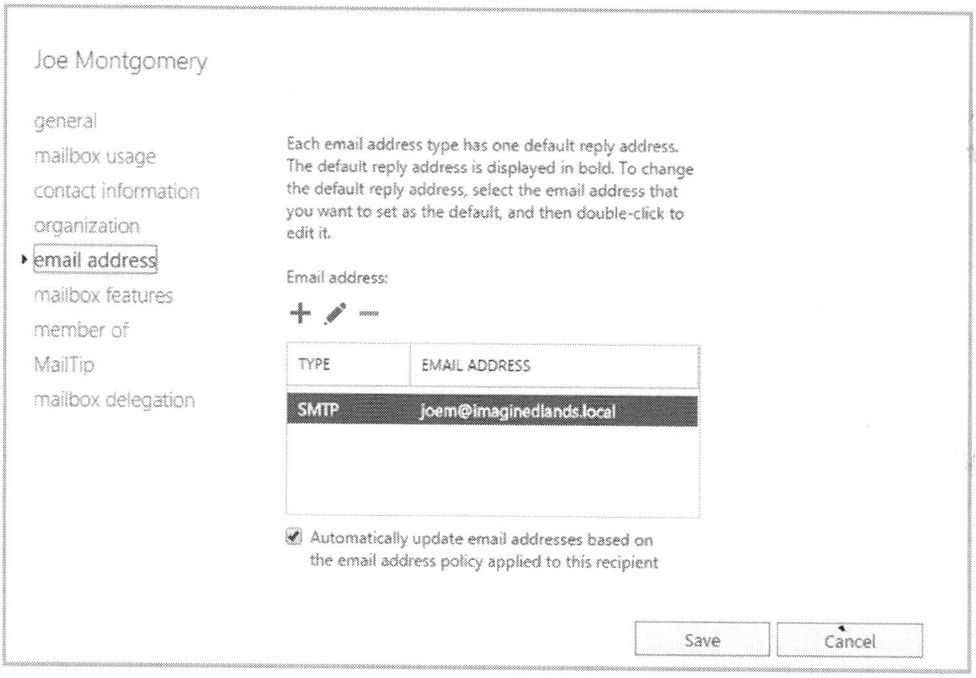

Joe Montgomery

general

mailbox usage

contact information

organization

▶ email address

mailbox features

member of

MailTip

mailbox delegation

Each email address type has one default reply address. The default reply address is displayed in bold. To change the default reply address, select the email address that you want to set as the default, and then double-click to edit it.

Email address:

＋ ✎ －

TYPE	EMAIL ADDRESS
SMTP	joem@imaginedlands.local

☑ Automatically update email addresses based on the email address policy applied to this recipient

Save   Cancel

FIGURE 4-15 Configuring the email addresses for the user account.

Setting a Default Reply Address for a User Account

Each email address type has one default reply address. This email address sets the value of the Reply To text box. To change the default reply address, follow these steps:

1. In Exchange Admin Center, select **Recipients** in the Features pane and then select **Mailboxes**.

2. Double-click the mailbox entry for the user with which you want to work.

3. On the Email Address page, current default email addresses are highlighted with bold text. Email addresses that aren't highlighted are used only as alternative addresses for delivering messages to the current mailbox. To change the current default settings, select an email address that isn't highlighted and then click **Edit** (✏).

4. In the Email Address dialog box, select the **Make This The Reply Address** checkbox. Click **OK** to save the changes.

Changing A User's Web, Wireless Service, And Protocol Options

When you create user accounts with mailboxes, global settings determine the web, wireless services, and protocols that are available. You can change these settings for individual users at any time by completing the following steps:

1. In Exchange Admin Center, select **Recipients** in the Features pane and then select **Mailboxes**.

2. Double-click the mailbox entry for the user with which you want to work.

3. Click the **Mailbox Features** tab. As shown in Figure 4-16, configure the following web, wireless services, and protocols for the user:

- **Exchange ActiveSync**   Allows the user to synchronize the mailbox and to browse wireless devices. Properties allow you to specify an Exchange ActiveSync policy. When you enable Exchange ActiveSync, the account users the default mobile device mailbox policy. To set an alternative policy, click the related View Details option.
- **Outlook Web App**   Permits the user to access the mailbox with a web browser. Properties allow you to specify an Outlook Web App mailbox policy.
- **Unified Messaging**   Allows the user to access unified messaging features, such as the voice browser. In a standard configuration of Exchange 2016, all new mailbox users have unified messaging enabled. However, a default UM Mailbox policy is required to fully activate the feature. If one hasn't been assigned, click Enable to display a dialog box that will allow you to specify the required policy.
- **MAPI**   Permits the user to access the mailbox with a Messaging Application Programming Interface (MAPI) email client.

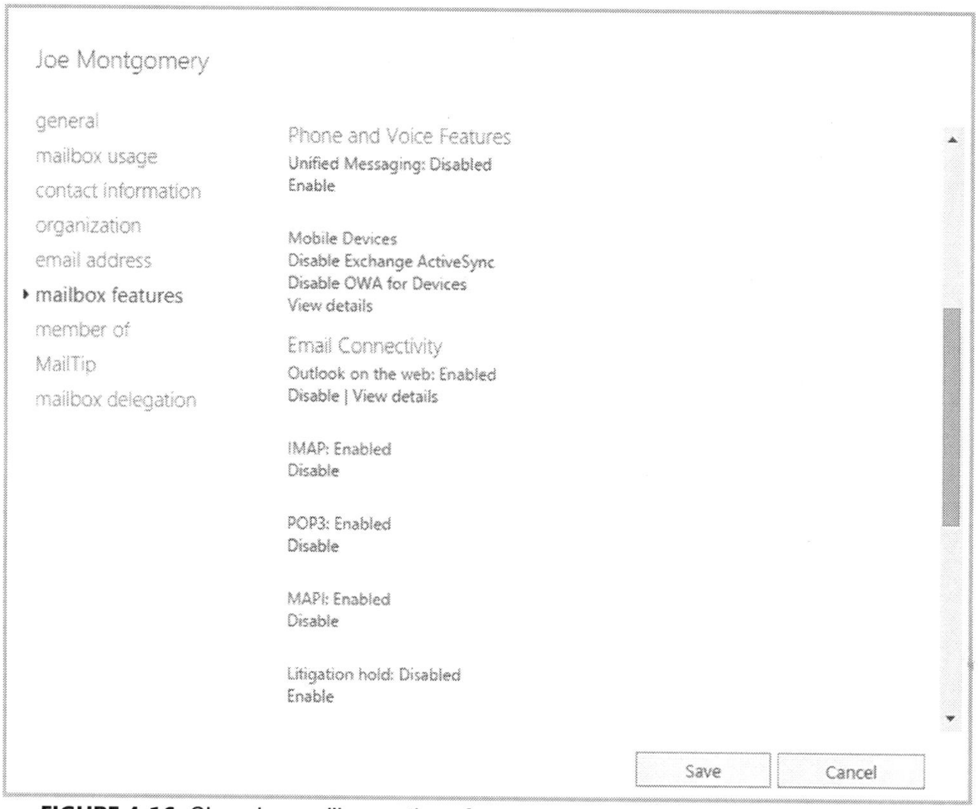

FIGURE 4-16 Changing mailbox options for users.

- **POP3**   Permits the user to access the mailbox with a Post Office Protocol version 3 (POP3) email client.
- **IMAP4**   Permits the user to access the mailbox with an Internet Message Access Protocol version 4 (IMAP4) email client.
- **Litigation Hold**   Indicates whether a mailbox is subject to litigation hold where users can delete mail items but the items are retained by Exchange. Properties allow you to provide a note to users about litigation hold and the URL of a webpage where they can learn more.
- **Archive**   Indicates whether an in-place archive mailbox has been created for the user. When you enable an in-place archive, you can specify the mailbox database to use. Properties allow you to specify the name of the folder in the user's mailbox that contains the archive as well as to set archive quota limit and warning values.

4. Select an option and then click **Enable** or **Disable**, as appropriate, to change the status. If an option has required properties, you'll be prompted to configure these properties when you enable the option. If an option has additional configurable properties, click the related View Details option to configure them.

5. Click **Save** to close the Properties dialog box.

Requiring Domain User Accounts to Change Passwords

Group Policy settings typically require users to periodically change their passwords. Sometimes, you might have to ensure that a user changes her password the next time she logs on. For example, if you have to reset a password and give it to the user over the phone, you might want the user to change the password the next time she logs on.

You can set a user account to require the password to be changed on next logon by completing the following steps:

1. In Exchange Admin Center, select **Recipients** in the Features pane and then select **Mailboxes**.
2. Double-click the mailbox entry for the user with which you want to work.
3. On the General page, select the **Require Password Change On Next Logon** check box. Click **OK**.

You can use the Set-User cmdlet to perform the same task, following the syntax shown in Sample 4-8.

SAMPLE 4-8 Requiring a user password change

Syntax

```
Set-User -Identity UserIdentity
-ResetPasswordOnNextLogon <$false|$true>
```

Usage

```
Set-User -Identity "Oliver Lee" -ResetPasswordOnNextLogon $true
```

Deleting Mailboxes from User Accounts

When you disable a mailbox for a domain user account using the Exchange management tools, you permanently remove all Exchange attributes from the user object in Active Directory and mark the primary mailbox for deletion. Exchange Server then deletes the mailbox according to the retention period you set on the account or on the mailbox database. Because you only removed the user account's Exchange attributes, the user account still exists in Active Directory.

In Exchange Admin Center, you can delete a mailbox from a domain user account and all related Exchange attributes by completing the following steps:

1. In Exchange Admin Center, select **Recipients** in the Features pane and then select **Mailboxes**.

2. Select the mailbox entry for the user with which you want to work with.

3. Select the **More** button (•••) and then select **Disable**.

4. When prompted to confirm this action, select **Yes**. The mailbox is then in the disconnected state and will be removed when the retention period expires. If the account was subject to litigation hold, mail items subject to litigation hold are preserved as recoverable items until the litigation hold period expires.

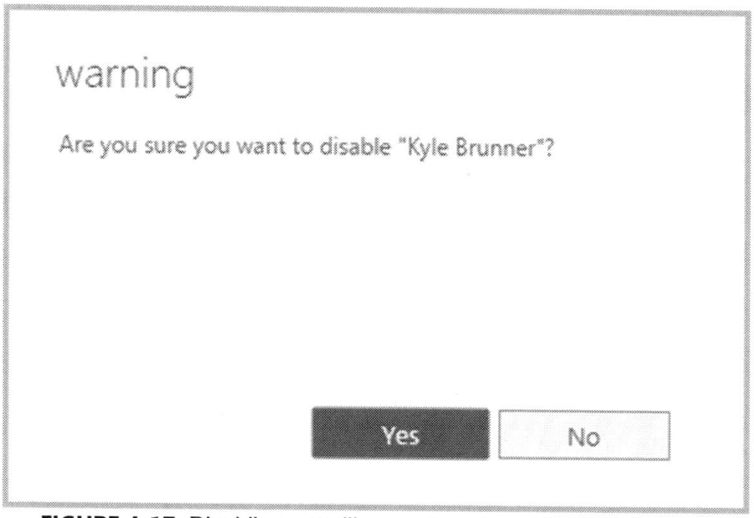

FIGURE 4-17 Disabling a mailbox and marking it for deletion.

If you remove the Exchange Online license for an online user account, the user's account is marked as an unlicensed account. Exchange Online deletes mailboxes from unlicensed accounts automatically after the grace period expires. By default, this grace period is 30 days. As with on-premises Exchange, retention hold, archiving and litigation hold settings determine whether some or any mailbox data is held.

You can remove a license from an online user account by completing the following steps:

1. In the dashboard for Office 365 Admin Center, select **Users & Groups** in the Features pane and then select **Active Users**.

2. Next, click the user whose license you want to remove.

3. Click **Edit** on the Products panel and then click the toggle to Off for the plan or license you want to remove.

4. Click **Assign**. The license that was previously assigned to this user will become available to be assigned to another user.

You can use the Disable-Mailbox cmdlet to delete mailboxes while retaining the user accounts as well. Sample 4-9 shows the syntax and usage.

SAMPLE 4-9 Disable-Mailbox cmdlet syntax and usage

Syntax

```
Disable-Mailbox -Identity Identifier [-DomainController DCName]
```

Usage

```
Disable-Mailbox -Identity "Oliver Lee"
```

Deleting User Accounts and Their Mailboxes

When you delete a domain user account and its mailbox using the Exchange management tools, you permanently remove the account from Active Directory and mark the primary mailbox for deletion. Exchange Server then deletes the mailbox according to the retention period you set on the account or on the mailbox database. Further, if the account was subject to litigation hold, mail items subject to litigation hold are preserved as recoverable items until the litigation hold period expires.

After you delete an account, you can't create an account with the same name and have the account automatically retain the same permissions as the original account. This is because the SID for the new account won't match the SID for the old account. However, that doesn't mean that after you delete an account, you can never again create an account with that same name. For example, a person might leave the company only to return a short while later. You can create an account using the same naming convention as before, but you'll have to redefine the permissions for that account.

Because deleting built-in accounts could have far-reaching effects on the domain, Windows doesn't let you delete built-in user accounts. In Exchange Admin Center, you can remove other types of accounts and the mailboxes associated with those accounts by following these steps:

1. In Exchange Admin Center, select **Recipients** in the Features pane and then select **Mailboxes**.

2. Select the user to delete and then click **Delete** (🗑).

3. When prompted to confirm this action, select **Yes**.

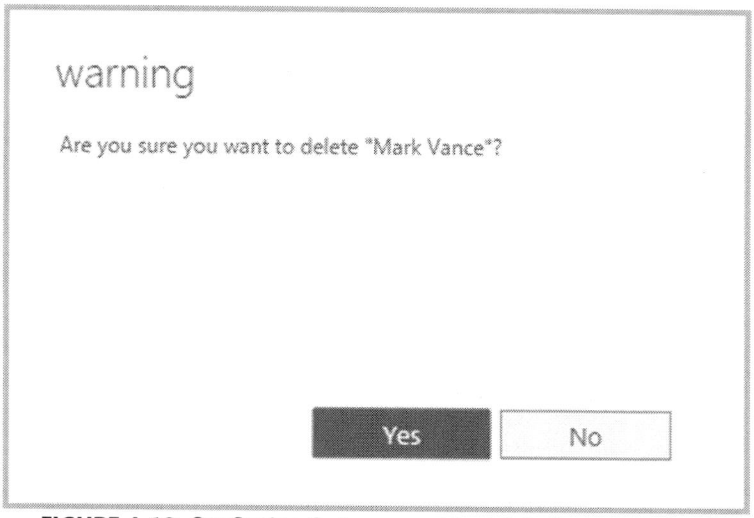

warning

Are you sure you want to delete "Mark Vance"?

[Yes] [No]

FIGURE 4-18 Confirming that you want to delete the account and mailbox.

> **NOTE** Because Exchange security is based on domain authentication, you can't have a mailbox without an account. If you still need the mailbox for an account you want to delete, you can disable the account using Active Directory Users And Computers. Disabling the account in Active Directory prevents the user from logging on, but you can still access the mailbox if you need to. To disable an account, Right-click the account in Active Directory Users And Computers and then select Disable Account. If you don't have permissions to use Active Directory Users And Computers, ask a domain administrator to disable the account for you.
>
> **IMPORTANT** If your organization synchronizes user accounts to Exchange Online from your on-premises Active Directory environment, you must delete and restore synced user accounts using the on-premises tools. You can't delete or restore them in the online organization.

If you delete the corresponding Office 365 user account for a mailbox, the online user's mailbox is marked for deletion and the account is marked as a deleted account.

Deleted online users aren't removed immediately. Instead, the accounts are inactivated and marked for deletion. By default, the retention period is 30 days. When the retention period expires, a user and all related data is permanently deleted and is not recoverable. As with on-premises Exchange, retention hold, archiving, and litigation hold settings determine whether some or any mailbox data is held.

You can delete an online user account by completing the following steps:

1. In the dashboard for Office 365 Admin Center, select **Users & Groups** in the Features pane and then select **Active Users**.

2. Click the user whose license you want to remove and then click **Delete User**.

3. When prompted to confirm this action, select **Delete**. The license that was previously assigned to this user will become available to be assigned to another user.

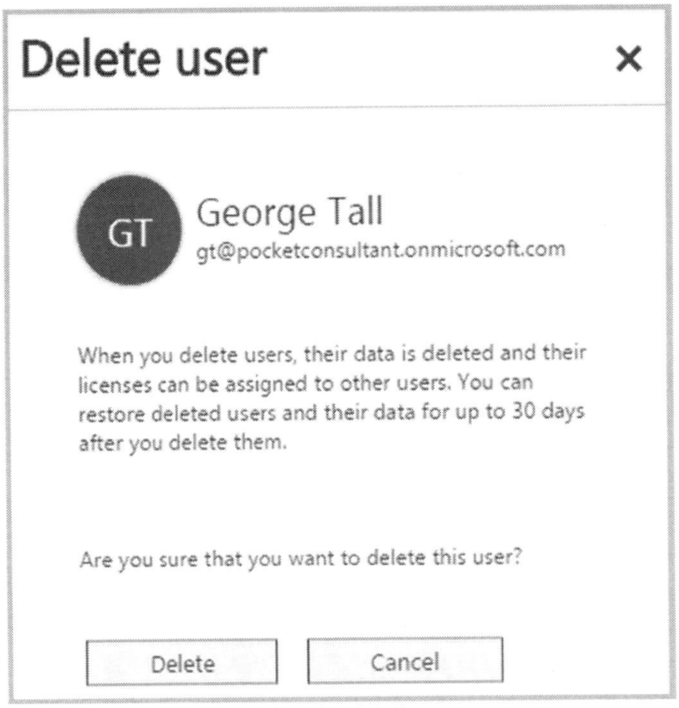

Delete user   ✕

GT George Tall
gt@pocketconsultant.onmicrosoft.com

When you delete users, their data is deleted and their licenses can be assigned to other users. You can restore deleted users and their data for up to 30 days after you delete them.

Are you sure that you want to delete this user?

| Delete | Cancel |

FIGURE 4-19 Confirming the deletion.

You also can use the Remove-Mailbox cmdlet to delete user accounts. Sample 4-10 shows the standard syntax. By default, the –Permanent flag is set to $false and mailboxes are retained in a disconnected state according to the mailbox retention policy. Otherwise, set the –Permanent flag to $true to remove the mailbox from Exchange.

SAMPLE 4-10 Remove-Mailbox cmdlet syntax and usage

Syntax

```
Remove-Mailbox -Identity UserIdentity {AddtlParams}
```

```
Remove-Mailbox -Database DatabaseId -StoreMailboxIdentity StoreMailboxId
{AddtlParams}
```

```
{AddtlParams}
[-Arbitration <$false|$true>] [-DomainController DCName]
[-IgnoreDefaultScope {$true | $false}] [-KeepWindowsLiveID {$true |
$false}] [-Permanent <$false | $true>]
[-RemoveLastArbitrationMailboxAllowed {$true | $false}]
```

Usage

```
Remove-Mailbox -Identity "Oliver Lee"
```

```
Remove-Mailbox -Identity "Oliver Lee" -Permanent $true
```

Chapter 5. Managing Contacts

Contacts represent people with whom you or others in your organization want to get in touch. Contacts can have directory information associated with them, but they don't have network logon privileges.

The only difference between a standard contact and a mail-enabled contact is the presence of email addresses. A mail-enabled contact has one or more email addresses associated with it; a standard contact doesn't. When a contact has an email address, you can list the contact in the global address list or other address lists. This allows users to send messages to the contact.

In Exchange Admin Center, mail-enabled contacts and mail-enabled users are both listed in the Mail Contact node. Mail-enabled contacts are listed with the recipient type Mail Contact, and mail-enabled users are listed with the recipient type Mail User.

Creating Mail-Enabled Contacts

You can create and mail-enable a new contact by completing the following steps:

1. In Exchange Admin Center, select **Recipients** in the Features pane and then select **Contacts**.

2. Click **New** ( ) and then select **Mail Contact**. This opens the New Mail Contact dialog box, shown in Figure 5-1.

new mail contact

First name:

Neal

Initials:

Last name:

Osterman

*Display name:

Neal Osterman

*Name:

Neal Osterman

*Alias:

nealosterman

*External email address:

nealo@reagentpress.com

Organizational unit:

imaginedlands.local/Develo ✕ | Browse...

Save | Cancel

FIGURE 5-1 Creating a new mail contact for the Exchange organization

3. Type the contact's first name, middle initial, and last name in the text boxes provided. These values are used to automatically create the following entries:

- **Name** The common name is displayed in Active Directory (and only applies with on-premises Exchange).
- **Display Name** The Display Name is displayed in the global address list and other address lists created for the organization. It is also used when addressing email messages to the contact.

4. Enter the Exchange alias for the contact. Aliases provide an alternative way of addressing users and contacts in To, Cc, and Bcc text boxes of email messages.

5. In the External Email Address text box, enter the address to associate with the contact. With on-premises Exchange, you can use both SMTP and non-SMTP addresses. With online Exchange, only standard SMTP addresses are accepted.

> **NOTE** For non-SMTP addresses, the dialog box requires that you use a prefix that identifies the address type and that the address format comply to the rules for that type. Use the prefix X400: for X.400 addresses, the prefix X500: for X.500 addresses, the prefix MSMAIL: for MSMail addresses, the prefix CCMAIL: for CcMail addresses, the prefix LOTUSNOTES: for Lotus Notes, and the prefix NOVELLGROUPWISE: for NovellGroupWise.

6. The Organizational Unit text box shows where in Active Directory the contact will be created. By default, this is the Users container in the current domain. Because you'll usually need to create new contacts in a specific organizational unit rather than in the Users container, click **Browse**. Use the Select An Organizational Unit dialog box to choose the location in which to store the contact, and then click **OK**.

7. Click **Save**. Exchange Admin Center creates the new contact and mail-enables it. If an error occurs, the contact will not be created. You will need to correct the problem and repeat this procedure.

In Exchange Management Shell, you can create a new mail-enabled contact using the New-MailContact cmdlet. Sample 5-1 provides the syntax and usage.

SAMPLE 5-1 New-MailContact cmdlet syntax and usage

Syntax

```
New-MailContact –Name Name –ExternalEmailAddress TYPE:EmailAddress
[-ArbitrationMailbox ModeratorMailbox] [-Alias ExchangeAlias]
[-DisplayName Name] [-DomainController DCName] [-FirstName FirstName]
[-Initials Initials] [-LastName LastName] [-MacAttachmentFormat <BinHex |
UuEncode | AppleSingle | AppleDouble>] [-MessageBodyFormat <Text | Html |
TextAndHtml>] [-MessageFormat <Text | Mime>] [-ModeratedBy Moderators]
[-ModerationEnabled <$true | $false>] [-Organization OrgName]
[-OrganizationalUnit OUName] [-PrimarySmtpAddress
SmtpAddress] [-SendModerationNotifications <Never | Internal | Always>]
[-UsePreferMessageFormat <$true | $false>]
```

Usage

```
New-MailContact -ExternalEmailAddress "SMTP:wendywheeler@msn.com"
 -Name "Wendy Wheeler" -Alias "WendyWheeler"
 -OrganizationalUnit "imaginedlands.local/Corporate Services"
 -FirstName "Wendy" -Initials "" -LastName "Wheeler"
```

In Exchange Management Shell, you can mail-enable an existing contact using the Enable-MailContact cmdlet. Sample 5-2 provides the syntax and usage.

SAMPLE 5-2 Enable-MailContact cmdlet syntax and usage

Syntax

```
Enable-MailContact -Identity ContactId -ExternalEmailAddress EmailAddress
[-Alias ExchangeAlias] [-DisplayName Name] [-DomainController
FullyQualifiedName] [-MacAttachmentFormat <BinHex | UuEncode |
AppleSingle | AppleDouble>] [-MessageBodyFormat <Text | Html |
TextAndHtml>] [-MessageFormat <Text | Mime>] [-PrimarySmtpAddress
SmtpAddress] [-UsePreferMessageFormat <$true | $false>]
```

Usage

```
Enable-MailContact -Identity "cpand.com/Sales/John Smith"
 -ExternalEmailAddress "SMTP:johnsmith@imaginedlands.com"
 -Alias "JohnSmith" -DisplayName "John Smith"
```

Setting or Changing a Contact's Name and Alias

Mail-enabled contacts can have the following name components:

* **First Name, Initials, Last Name**   The first name, initials, and last name of the contact
* **Common Name**   The name used in Active Directory, for on-premises contacts
* **Display Name**   The name displayed in the global address list
* **Alias**   The Exchange alias for the contact

You can set or change name and alias information for a mail-enabled contact or user by completing the following steps:

1. In Exchange Admin Center, select **Recipients** in the Features pane and then select **Contacts**.

2. Double-click the name of the mail-enabled contact or user you want to work with. The Properties dialog box appears.

3. On the General tab, use the textboxes provided to update the first name, middle initial, and last name as necessary. Changes you make will update the display name but not the common name. Therefore, as necessary, use the Name text box to update the common name.

4. With mail-enabled contacts, the Alias text box sets the Exchange alias. If you'd like to assign a new alias, enter the new Exchange alias in this text box.

5. With mail-enabled users, the User Logon Name text box sets the name used to log on to the domain as well as the domain suffix.

6. Click **Save** to apply your changes.

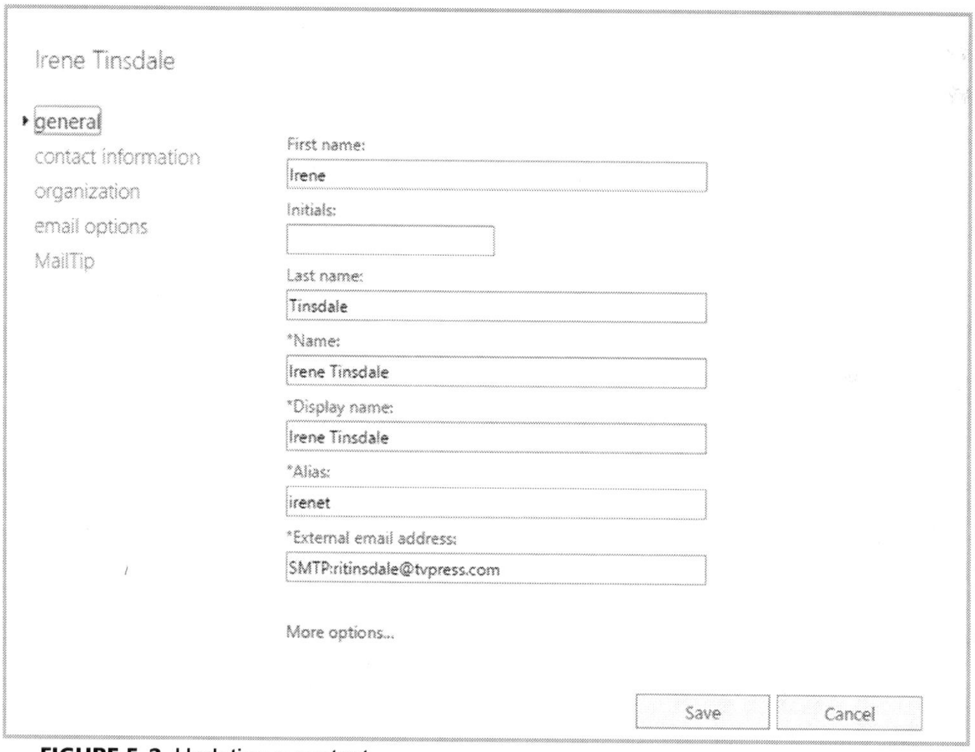

FIGURE 5-2 Updating a contact.

Setting Additional Directory Information for Contacts

You can set additional directory information for a mail-enabled contact or user by completing the following steps:

1. In Exchange Admin Center, select **Recipients** in the Features pane and then select **Contacts**.

2. Double-click the name of the mail-enabled contact or user you want to work with. The Properties dialog box appears.

3. On the Contact Information page, use the text boxes provided to set the contact's business address or home address. Normally, you'll want to enter the contact's business address. This way, you can track the business locations and mailing addresses of contacts at various offices.

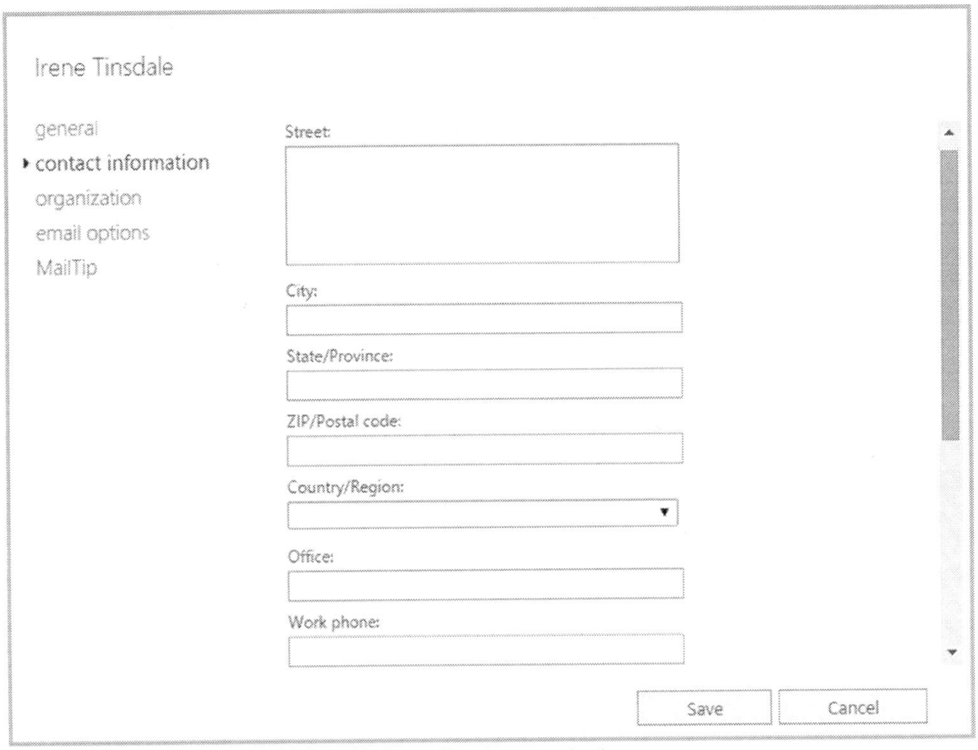

FIGURE 5-3 Adding additional information to a contact.

NOTE You need to consider privacy issues before entering private information, such as home addresses and home phone numbers, for users. Discuss the matter with the appropriate groups in your organization, such as the human resources and legal departments. You might also want to get user consent before releasing home addresses.

4. Use the Work Phone, Mobile Phone, and Fax text boxes to set the contact or user's primary business telephone, mobile phone, and fax numbers.

5. Use the Office text box to set the user's Office and the Notes text box to add any important notes about the contact.

6. On the Organization page, as appropriate, type the contact or user's title, department, and company.

7. To specify the contact or user's manager, click **Browse**. In the Manager dialog box, select the manager and then click **OK**. When you specify a manager, the contact or user shows up as a direct report in the manager's account. Click **Save** to apply the changes.

Changing Email Addresses Associated with Contacts

Mail-enabled contacts and users have several types of email addresses associated with them:

- An internal, automatically generated email address used for routing within the organization
- An external email address to which mail routed internally is forwarded for delivery

With mail-enabled contacts, you can only use SMTP email addresses. You can change the SMTP email addresses associated with a mail-enabled contact by completing the following steps:

1. In Exchange Admin Center, select **Recipients** in the Features pane and then select **Contacts**.

2. Double-click the name of the mail-enabled contact you want to work with. The Properties dialog box appears.

3. On the General page, the external SMTP email address of the mail-enabled contact is listed. This is the primary SMTP email address for the mail-enabled contact. As necessary, enter a new email address.

> **NOTE** The primary email address is listed with the prefix SMTP:. When you enter a new email address, you aren't required to enter this prefix. Thus, you could enter SMTP:williams@treyresearch.net or williams@treyresearch.net.

4. On the Email Options page, the primary SMTP email address is listed along with the internal email address. You can use the following techniques to manage the internal addresses:

- **Create an alternative internal address**   Click Add (+). Specify the internal email address to use by entering the Exchange alias and then selecting the domain for this internal address. Click OK.

- **Edit an existing address** Double-click the address, or click **Edit** () on the toolbar. Modify the address settings as necessary, and then click OK.
- **Delete an existing address** Select the address, and then click Remove.

5. Click **Save** to apply your changes.

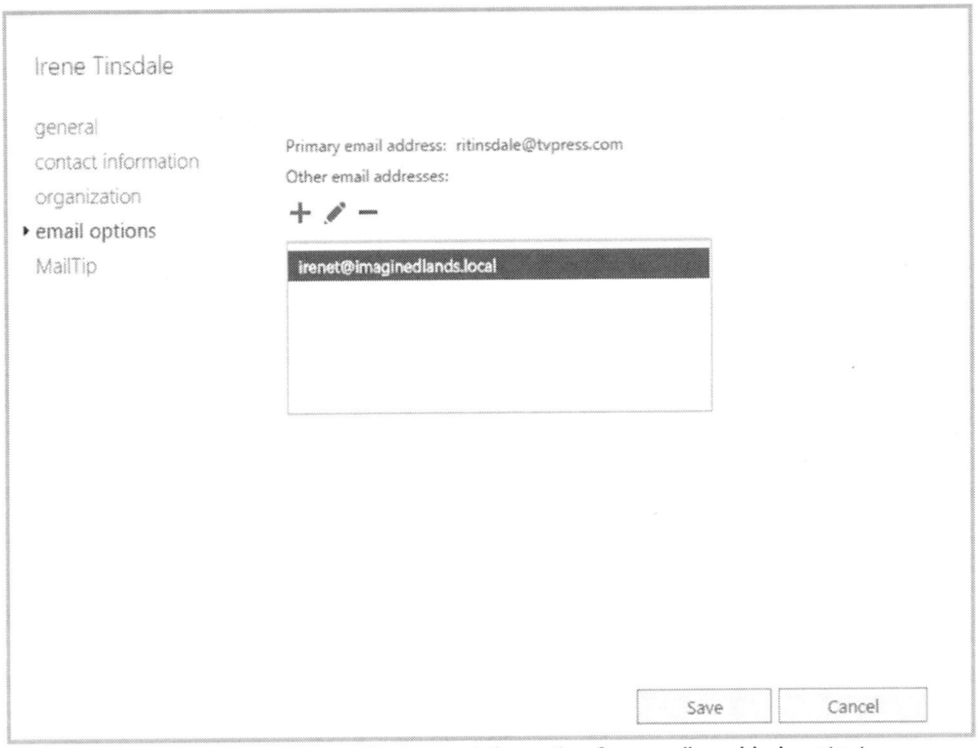

Irene Tinsdale

general

contact information

organization

▸ email options

MailTip

Primary email address: ritinsdale@tvpress.com

Other email addresses:

\+ ✎ \-

irenet@imaginedlands.local

Save   Cancel

FIGURE 5-4 Modifying the email address information for a mail-enabled contact.

With mail-enabled users, you can use SMTP and non-SMTP email addresses. You can change the email addresses associated with a mail-enabled user by completing the following steps:

1. In Exchange Admin Center, select **Recipients** in the Features pane and then select **Contacts**.

2. Double-click the name of the mail-enabled user you want to work with. The Properties dialog box appears.

3. On the Email Addresses page, you can use the following techniques to manage the mail-enabled user's email addresses:

- **Create a new SMTP address** Click Add ( ). Because the address type SMTP is selected by default, enter the SMTP email address, and then click OK to save your changes.

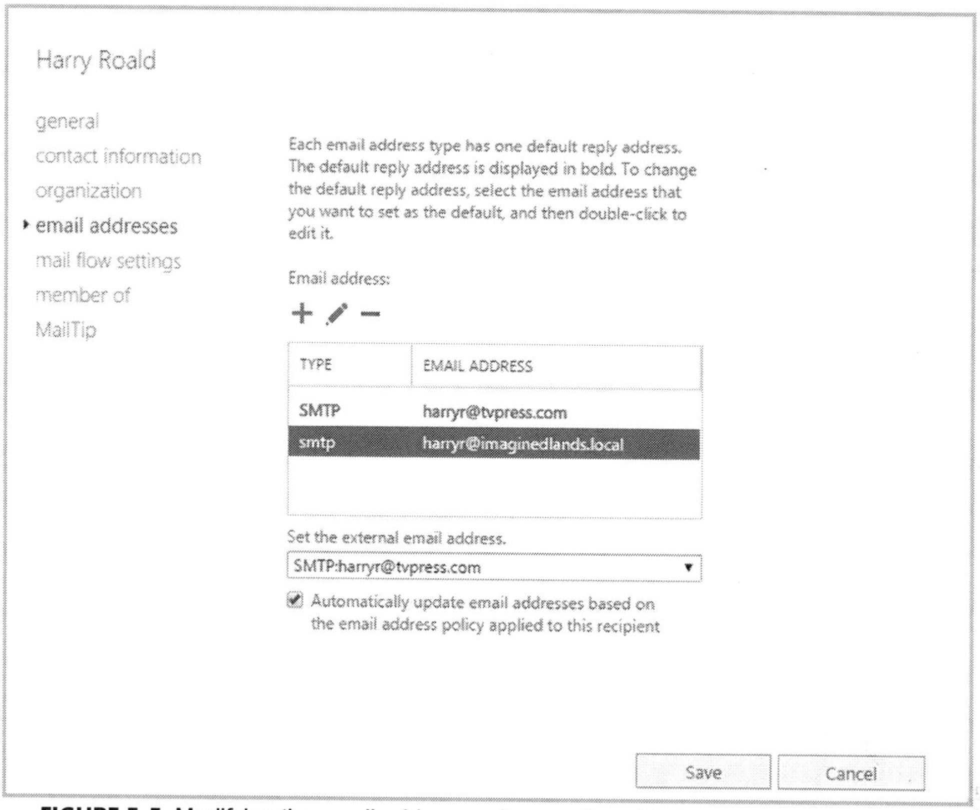

FIGURE 5-5 Modifying the email addresses for a mail-enabled user.

- **Create a custom address** Click Add ( ), and then select the Custom Address Type option. Enter the custom address type in the text box provided. Valid types include: X.400, X.500, EUM, MSMail, CcMail, Lotus Notes, and NovellGroupWise. Next, enter the custom address. This address must comply with the format requirements for the address type. Click OK to save your changes.
- **Edit an existing address** Double-click the address entry, or select the entry and then select Edit on the toolbar. Modify the settings in the Address dialog box, and then click OK.
- **Delete an existing address** Select the address, and then click Remove.

> **NOTE** You can't delete the primary SMTP address without first promoting another email address to the primary position. Exchange Server uses the primary SMTP address to send and receive messages.

4. The external email address of the mail-enabled user is also listed on the Email Addresses page. This is the primary email address for the mail user or contact. As necessary, select an alternative email address to be the primary.

5. Click **Save** to apply your changes.

Disabling Contacts and Removing Exchange Attributes

With on-premises Exchange, you have two options for mail-enabled users and contacts that are no longer needed. You can disable the mail-enabled user or contact, or you can delete the mail-enabled user or contact. With Exchange online, your only option is to delete the mail-enabled user or contact.

When you disable a contact using the on-premises Exchange management tools, you permanently remove the contact from the Exchange database, but you do not remove it from Active Directory.

In Exchange Admin Center, you can disable mail-enabled contacts by following these steps:

1. In Exchange Admin Center, select **Recipients** in the Features pane and then select **Contacts**.

2. Select the contact that you want to disable.

3. Click the More button (•••) and then select **Disable**.

4. When prompted to confirm this action, select **Yes**.

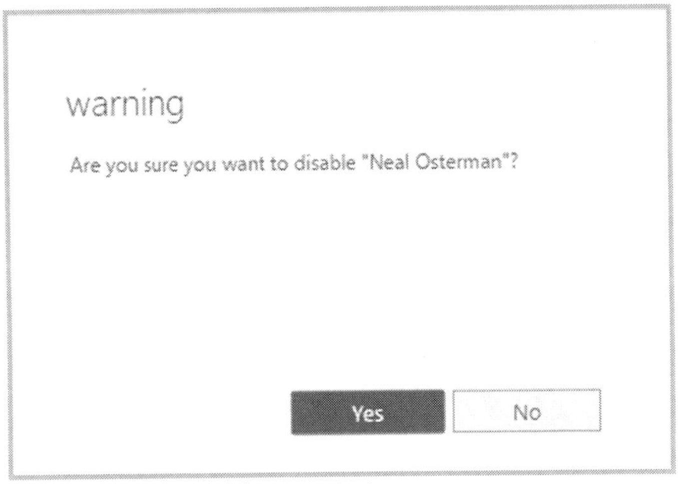

warning

Are you sure you want to disable "Neal Osterman"?

Yes   No

FIGURE 5-6 Disabling a contact.

You can use the Disable-MailContact cmdlet to remove Exchange attributes from contacts while retaining the contact in Active Directory. Sample 5-3 shows the syntax and usage.

SAMPLE 5-3 Disable-MailContact cmdlet syntax and usage

Syntax

```
Disable-MailContact -Identity ContactIdentity
```

Usage

```
Disable-MailContact -Identity "David So"
```

Later, if you want to re-enable the contact, you can do this using the Enable-MailContact cmdlet.

Deleting Contacts

When you delete a mail-enabled user or contact from Exchange Online, the mail-enabled user or contact is permanently removed from Exchange Online. When you delete a contact using the on-premises Exchange management tools, you permanently remove it from Active Directory and from the Exchange database. In Exchange Admin Center, you can delete contacts by following these steps:

1. In Exchange Admin Center, select **Recipients** in the Features pane and then select **Contacts**.

2. Select the contact that you want to delete and then click **Delete**.

3. When prompted to confirm this action, select **Yes**.

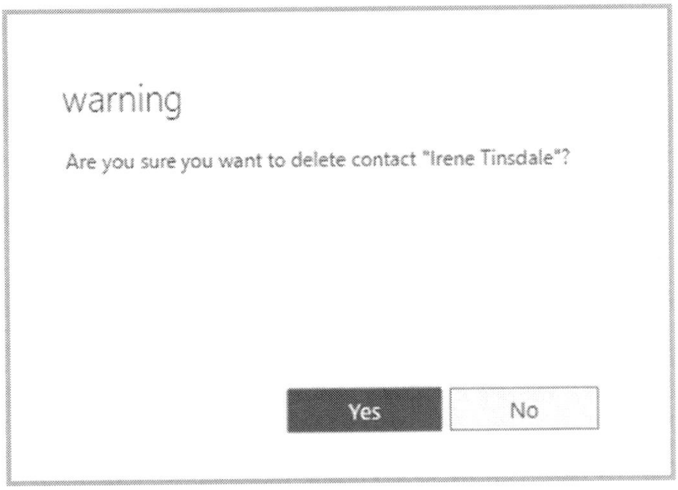

FIGURE 5-7 Deleting a contact.

You can use the Remove-MailContact cmdlet to delete contacts as well. Sample 5-4 shows the syntax and usage.

SAMPLE 5-4 Remove-MailContact cmdlet syntax and usage

Syntax

```
Remove-MailContact -Identity ContactIdentity
```

Usage

```
Remove-MailContact -Identity "Henrik Larsen"
```

Chapter 6. Adding Special-Purpose Mailboxes

Exchange Server 2016 and Exchange Online make it easy to create several special-purpose mailbox types, including:

- **Room mailbox** A room mailbox is a mailbox for room scheduling.
- **Equipment mailbox** An equipment mailbox is a mailbox for equipment scheduling.
- **Linked mailbox** A linked mailbox is a mailbox for a user from a separate, trusted forest.
- **Forwarding mailbox** A forwarding mailbox is a mailbox that can receive mail and forward it off site.
- **Archive mailbox** An archive mailbox is used to store a user's messages, such as might be required for executives and needed by some managers.
- **Arbitration mailbox** An arbitration mailbox is used to manage approval requests, such as may be required for handling moderated recipients and distribution group membership approval.
- **Discovery mailbox** A Discovery mailbox is the target for Discovery searches and can't be converted to another mailbox type after it's created. In-Place eDiscovery is a feature of Exchange 2016 that allows authorized users to search mailboxes for specific types of content as might be required to meet legal discovery requirements.
- **Shared mailbox** A shared mailbox is a mailbox that is shared by multiple users, such as a general mailbox for customer inquiries.
- **Public folder mailbox** A public folder mailbox is a shared mailbox for storing public folder data.

The sections that follow discuss techniques for working with these special-purpose mailboxes.

Using Room and Equipment Mailboxes

You use room and equipment mailboxes for scheduling purposes only. You'll find that

- Room mailboxes are useful when you have conference rooms, training rooms, and other rooms for which you need to coordinate the use.
- Equipment mailboxes are useful when you have projectors, media carts, or other items of equipment for which you need to coordinate the use. Every room and equipment mailbox must have a separate user account associated with it. Although these accounts are required so that the mailboxes can be used for scheduling, the accounts are disabled by default so that they cannot be used for

logon. To ensure that the resource accounts do not get enabled accidentally, you need to coordinate closely with other administrators in your organization.

> **IMPORTANT** Each room or piece of equipment must have a separate user account. This is necessary to track the unique free/busy data for each resource.
>
> **NOTE** The Exchange Admin Center doesn't show the enabled or disabled status of user accounts. The only way to check the status is to use domain administration tools.

Because the number of scheduled rooms and amount of equipment grows as your organization grows, you'll want to carefully consider the naming conventions you use with rooms and equipment:

* With rooms, you may want to use display names that clearly identify the rooms' physical locations. For example, you might have rooms named "Conference Room B on Fifth Floor" or "Building 83 Room 15."
* With equipment, you may want the display name to identify the type of equipment, the equipment's characteristics, and the equipment's relative location. For example, you might have equipment named "Dell LED Projector at Seattle Office" or "Fifth Floor Media Cart."

As with standard user mailboxes, room and equipment mailboxes have contact information associated with them (see Figure 6-1). To make it easier to find rooms and equipment, you should provide as much information as possible. If a room has a conference or call-in phone, be sure to provide this phone number. Also, provide location details that help people find the conference room and specify the room capacity. The phone, location, and capacity are displayed in Microsoft Office Outlook.

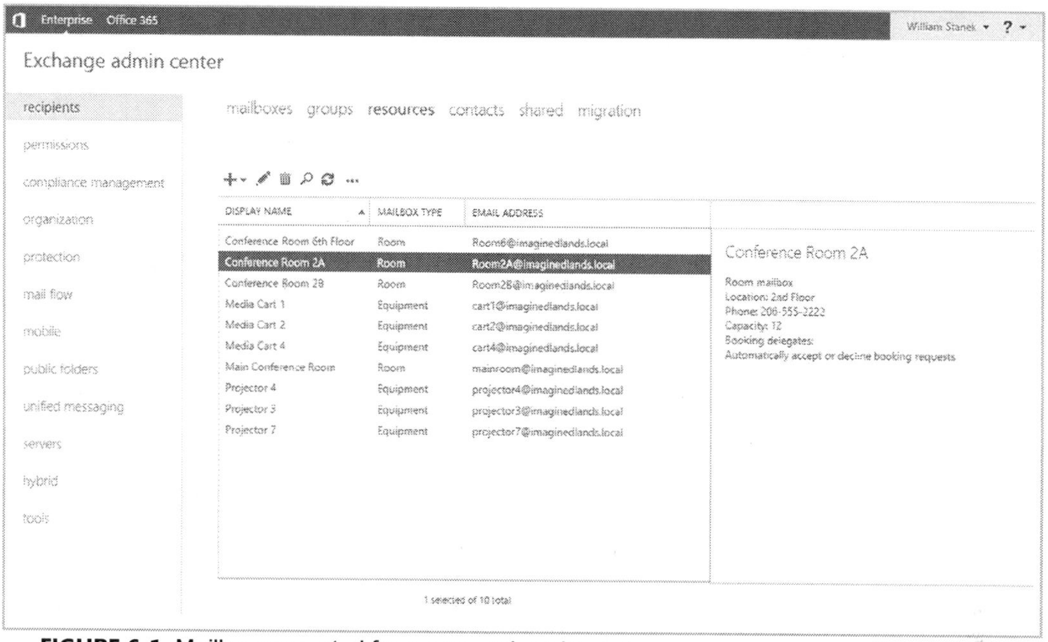

FIGURE 6-1 Mailboxes created for rooms and equipment.

After you've set up mailboxes for your rooms and equipment, scheduling the rooms and equipment is straightforward. In Exchange, room and equipment availability is tracked using free/busy data. In Outlook, a user who wants to reserve rooms, equipment, or both simply makes a meeting request that includes the rooms and equipment that are required for the meeting.

The steps to schedule a meeting and reserve equipment are as follows:

1. Create a meeting request. In Outlook 2010 or later, click **New Items**, and then select **Meeting**. Or press Ctrl+Shift+Q.

2. In the To text box, invite the individuals who should attend the meeting by typing their display names, Exchange aliases, or email addresses, as appropriate (see Figure 6-2).

3. Type the display name, Exchange alias, or email address for any equipment you need to reserve.

4. Click Rooms to the right of the Location text box. The Select Rooms dialog box appears, as shown in Figure 6-3. By default, the Select Rooms dialog box uses the All Rooms address book. Rooms are added to this address book automatically when you create them.

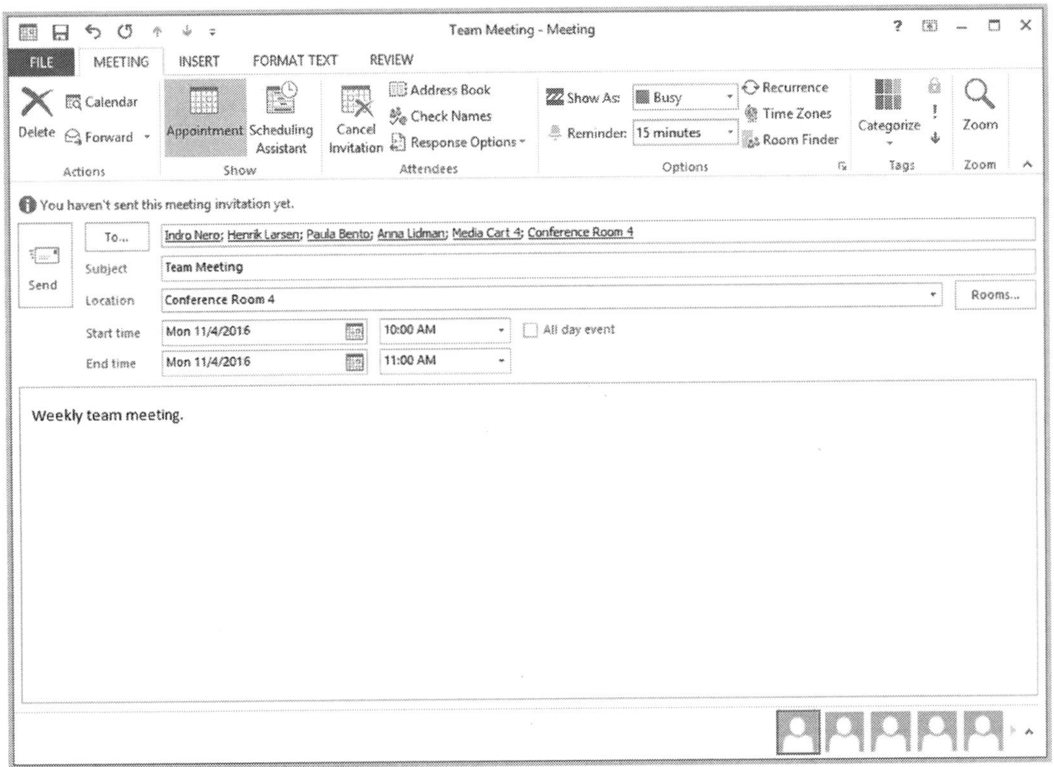

FIGURE 6-2 You can schedule a meeting with a reserved room and reserved equipment.

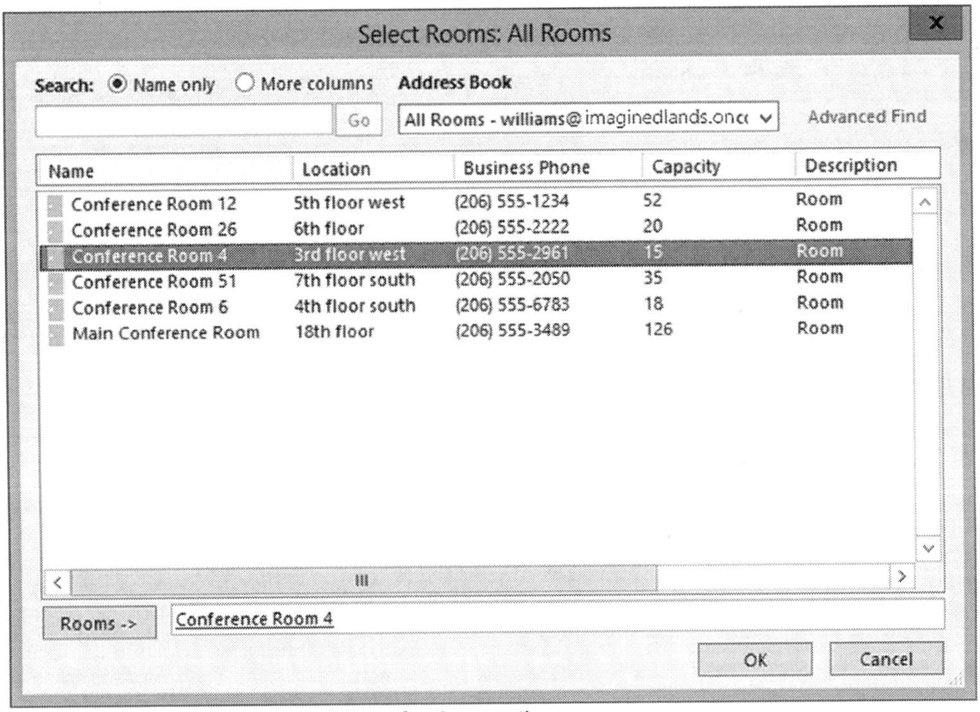

FIGURE 6-3 Select a room to use for the meeting.

5. Double-click the room you'd like to use. This adds the room to the Rooms list. Click **OK** to close the Select Rooms dialog box.

6. In the Subject text box, type the meeting subject.

7. Use the Start Time and End Time options to schedule the start and end times for the meeting.

8. Click **Scheduling Assistant** to view the free/busy data for the invited users and the selected resources. Use the free/busy data to make changes if necessary.

9. After you type a message to accompany the meeting request, click **Send**.

Exchange can be configured to accept booking requests automatically, based on availability, or to route requests through delegates, such as office administrators, who review requests. Although small organizations might not need coordinators for rooms and equipment, most large organizations will need coordinators to prevent conflicts.

Both on-premises Exchange and Exchange Online provide additional booking options that can help to reduce conflicts (see Figure 6-4). The booking options are the same for both rooms and equipment. The options allow you to:

* Specify whether repeat bookings are allowed. By default, repeat bookings are allowed. If you disable the related settings, users won't be able to schedule repeating meetings.
* Specify whether the room or equipment can be scheduled only during working hours. By default, this option is disabled, which allows rooms and equipment to be scheduled for use at any time. The standard working hours are defined as 8:00 AM to 5:00 PM Monday through Friday but can be changed using the Calendaring options in Outlook.
* Specify the maximum number of days in advance the room or equipment can be booked. By default, rooms and equipment can be booked up to 180 days in advance. You can change the default to any value from 0 to 1080. A value of 0 removes the lead time restriction completely.
* Specify the maximum duration that the room or equipment can be reserved. By default, rooms and equipment can be reserved for up to 24 hours, which allows for preparation and maintenance that may be required. You can change the default to any value from 0 to 35791394.1. A value of 0 removes the duration restriction completely.

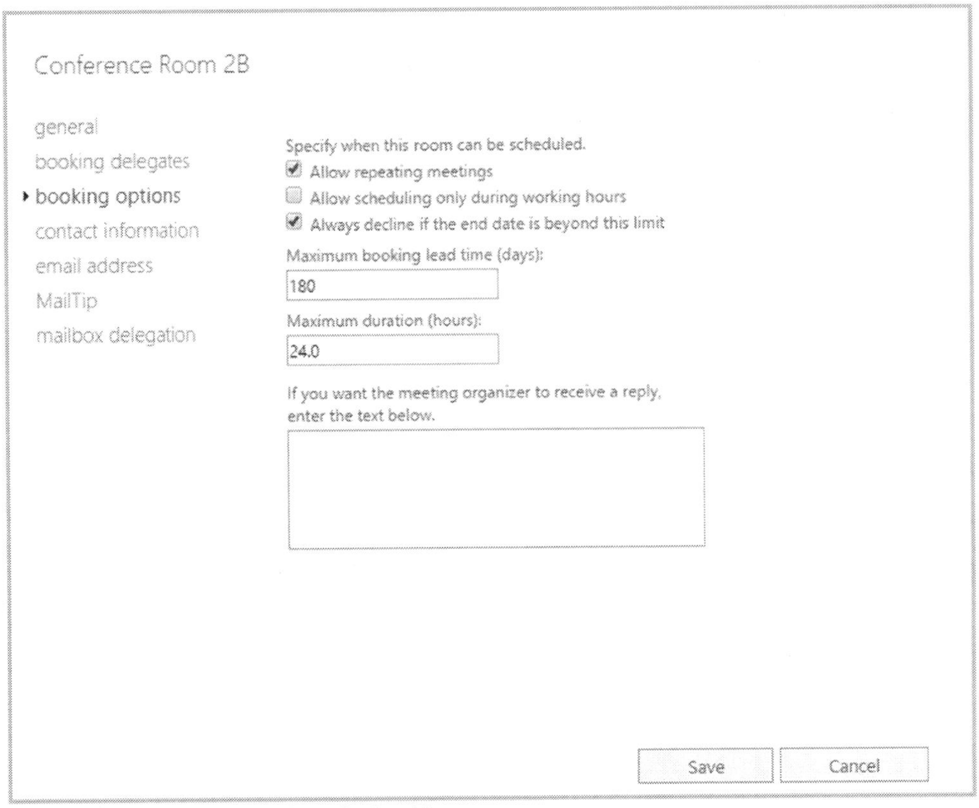

Conference Room 2B

general
booking delegates
▸ booking options
contact information
email address
MailTip
mailbox delegation

Specify when this room can be scheduled.
☑ Allow repeating meetings
☐ Allow scheduling only during working hours
☑ Always decline if the end date is beyond this limit
Maximum booking lead time (days):
180
Maximum duration (hours):
24.0

If you want the meeting organizer to receive a reply, enter the text below.

Save   Cancel

FIGURE 6-4 Set restrictions for booking rooms.

You can configure booking options after you create the room or equipment mailbox. In Exchange Admin Center, navigate to Recipients > Resources and then double-click the resource you want to configure. Next, in the properties dialog box for the resource, select Booking Options. After you change the booking options, click Save to apply the changes.

Adding Room Mailboxes

In Exchange Admin Center, room mailboxes are displayed under Recipients > Resources. In Exchange Management Shell, you can find all room mailboxes in the organization by entering:

```
Get-Mailbox -ResultSize unlimited -Filter {(RecipientTypeDetails
-eq 'RoomMailbox')}
```

You can create room mailboxes by completing the following steps:

1. In Exchange Admin Center, select **Recipients** in the Features pane and then select **Resources**.

2. Click **New** (![plus icon]), and then select **Room Mailbox**. This opens the New Room Mailbox dialog box, shown in Figure 6-5.

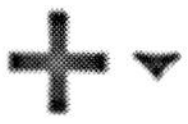

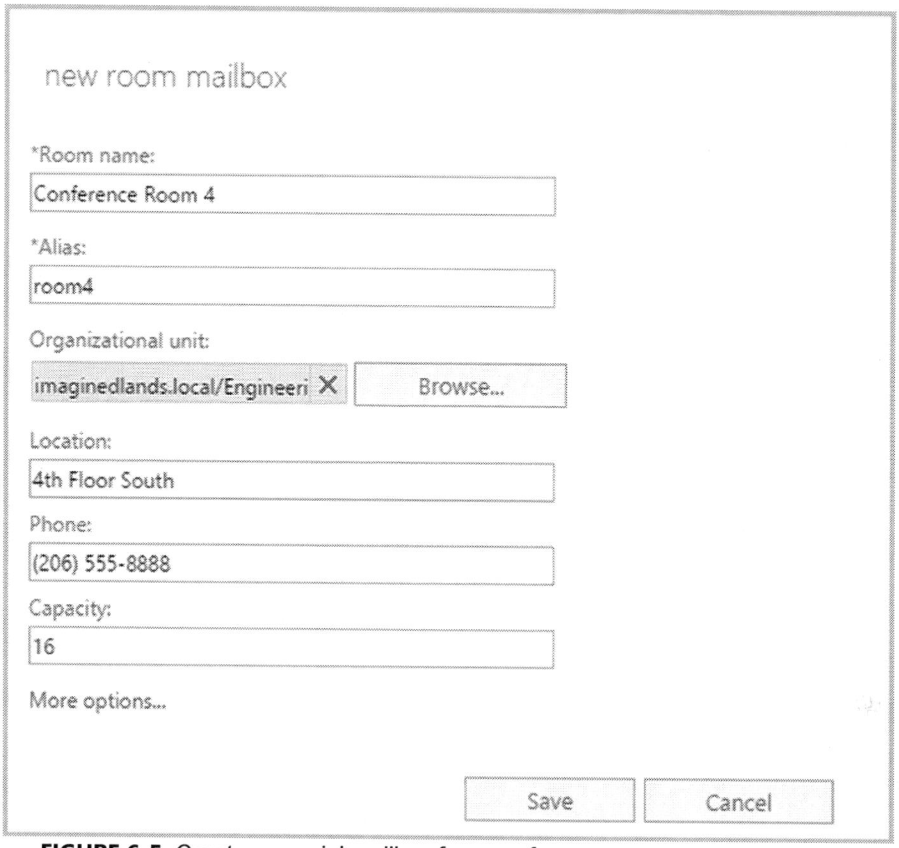

new room mailbox

*Room name:

Conference Room 4

*Alias:

room4

Organizational unit:

imaginedlands.local/Engineeri ✕   Browse...

Location:

4th Floor South

Phone:

(206) 555-8888

Capacity:

16

More options...

Save   Cancel

FIGURE 6-5 Create a special mailbox for a conference room.

3. Type a descriptive display name in the Room Name text box.

4. For on-premises Exchange, enter the Exchange alias in the Alias text box. The Exchange alias is used to set the default email address.

5. For Exchange Online, enter the Exchange alias in the Email Address text box and then use the drop-down list to select the domain with which the room is to be associated. The Exchange Alias and the domain name are combined to set the fully qualified name, such as room4@imaginedlands.onmicrosoft.com.

6. For on-premises Exchange, the Organizational Unit text box shows where in Active Directory the user account will be created. By default, this is the Users

container in the current domain. Because you'll usually need to create room and equipment accounts in a specific organizational unit rather than in the Users container, click Browse to the right of the Organizational Unit text box. Use the Select Organizational Unit dialog box to choose the location in which to store the account, and then click OK.

7. Specify the room location, phone number and capacity using the text boxes provided.

8. With on-premises Exchange, click More Options to configure these additional options:

- **Mailbox Database**   If you want to specify a mailbox database rather than use an automatically selected one, click Browse to the right of the Mailbox Database text box. In the Select Mailbox Database dialog box, choose the mailbox database in which the mailbox should be stored. Mailbox databases are listed by name as well as by associated server and Exchange version running on the server.
- **Address Book Policy**   If you've implemented address book policies to provide customized address book views, select the address book policy to associate with the equipment mailbox.

9. Click Save to create the room mailbox. If an error occurs during account or mailbox creation, neither the account nor the related mailbox will be created. You need to correct the problem before you can complete this procedure.

By default, booking requests are accepted or declined automatically based on availability. Here, the first person to reserve the room gets the reservation. If your organization has resource coordinators, you can change the booking options by completing the following steps:

1. Double-click the room mailbox with which you want to work.

2. On the Booking Delegates page, choose the Select Delegates option.

3. Next, use the options under Delegates to specify the coordinator. Click the Add button, use the Select Delegates dialog box to select coordinators for the room. Simply double-click to add a name to the list of delegates.

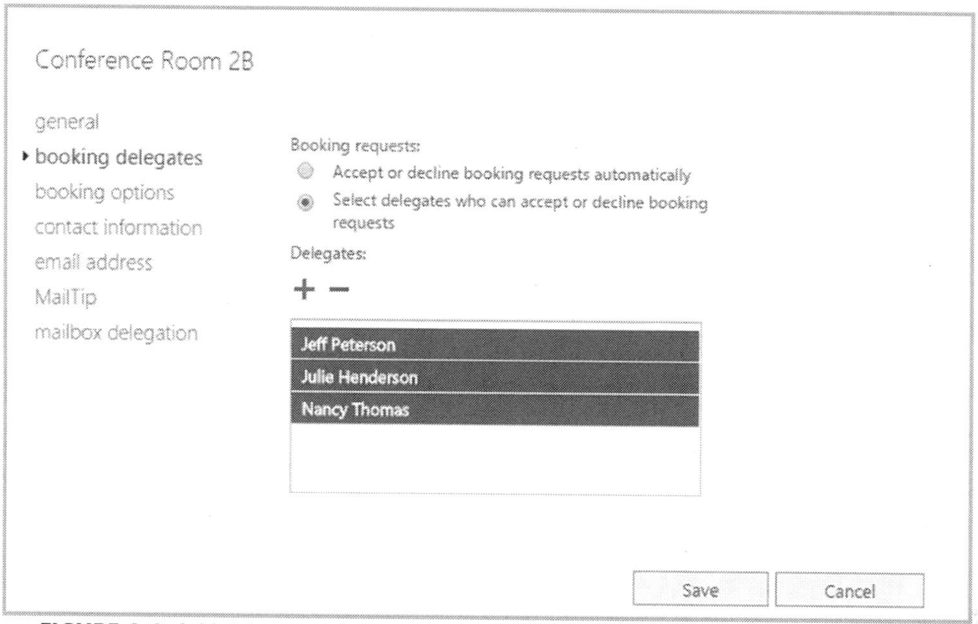

FIGURE 6-6 Add delegates if you don't want booking requests to be handled automatically.

In Exchange Management Shell, you can create a user account with a mailbox for rooms by using the New-Mailbox cmdlet. Sample 6-1 provides the syntax and usage.

> **NOTE** For rooms, you must use the –Room parameter. For equipment, you must use the –Equipment parameter. By default, when you use either parameter, the related value is set as $true. Additionally, although with earlier releases of Exchange you needed to set a password for the related user account, this is no longer required. When you create mailboxes for Exchange Online, you cannot specify a database.

SAMPLE 6-1 Creating room mailboxes

Syntax

```
New-Mailbox -Name 'DisplayName' -Alias 'ExchangeAlias'
  -OrganizationalUnit 'OrganizationalUnit'
  -UserPrincipalName 'LogonName' -SamAccountName 'prewin2000logon'
  -FirstName '' -Initials '' -LastName ''
  -Database 'Server\MailboxDatabase'
  -Room
```

Usage

```
New-Mailbox -Name 'Conference Room 27' -Alias 'room27'
  -OrganizationalUnit 'imaginedlands.com/Sales'
```

```
-UserPrincipalName 'room27@imaginedlands.com' -SamAccountName 'room27'
-FirstName '' -Initials '' -LastName ''
-Database 'Sales Primary'
-Room
```

Adding Equipment Mailboxes

In Exchange Admin Center, equipment mailboxes are displayed under Recipients >
Resources. In Exchange Management Shell, you can find all equipment mailboxes in
the organization by entering:

```
Get-Mailbox -ResultSize unlimited -Filter {(RecipientTypeDetails
-eq 'EquipmentMailbox')}
```

You can create equipment mailboxes by completing the following steps:

1. In Exchange Admin Center, select **Recipients** in the Features pane and then
    select **Resources**.

2. Click **New** (   ), and then select **Equipment Mailbox**. This opens the
    New Equipment Mailbox dialog box, shown in Figure 6-7.

3. Type a descriptive display name in the Equipment Name text box.

4. For on-premises Exchange, enter the Exchange alias in the Alias text box.
    The Exchange alias is used to set the default email address.

5. For Exchange Online, enter the Exchange alias in the Email Address text box
    and then use the drop-down list to select the domain with which the room is
    to be associated. The Exchange Alias and domain name are combined to set
    the full name, such as projector5@imaginedlands.onmicrosoft.com.

6. For on-premises Exchange, the Organizational Unit text box shows where in
    Active Directory the user account will be created. By default, this is the Users
    container in the current domain. Because you'll usually need to create room
    and equipment accounts in a specific organizational unit rather than in the
    Users container, click **Browse** to the right of the Organizational Unit text
    box. Use the Select Organizational Unit dialog box to choose the location in
    which to store the account, and then click **OK**.

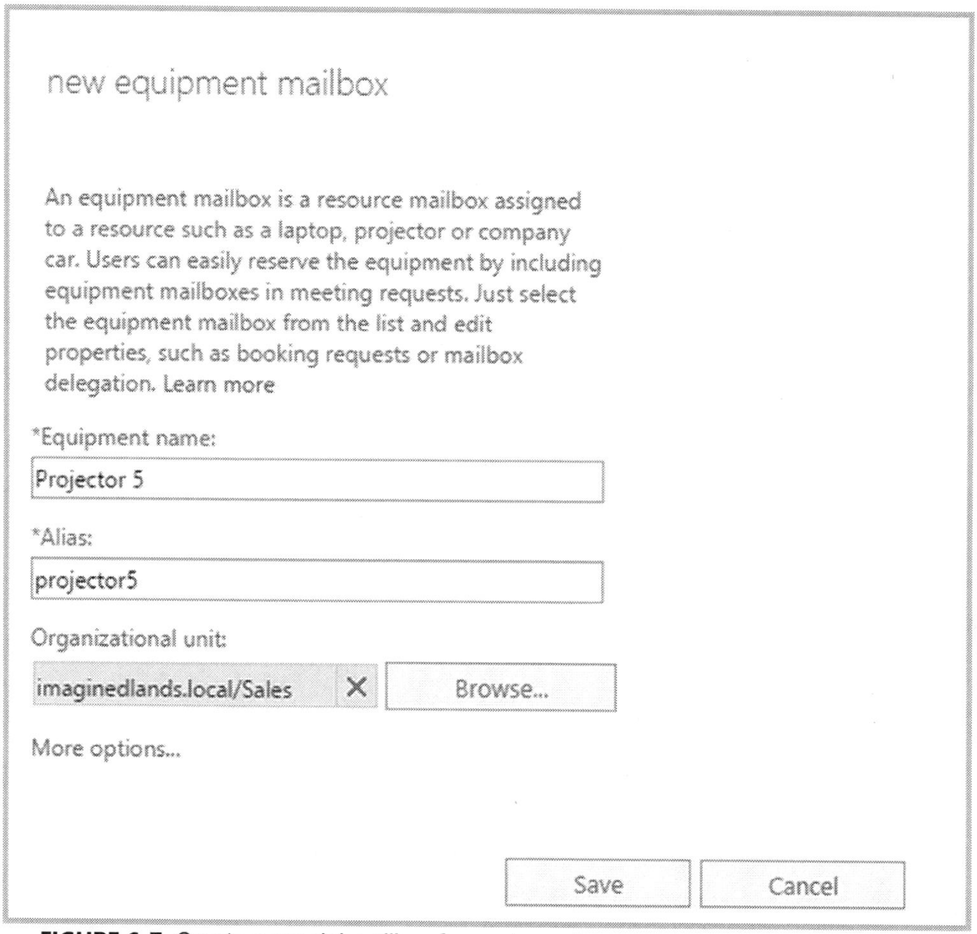

FIGURE 6-7 Create a special mailbox for equipment.

7. With on-premises Exchange, click **More Options** to configure these additional options:

- **Mailbox Database** If you want to specify a mailbox database rather than use an automatically selected one, click the Browse button to the right of the Mailbox Database text box. In the Select Mailbox Database dialog box, choose the mailbox database in which the mailbox should be stored. Mailbox databases are listed by name as well as by associated server and Exchange version running on the server.

- **Address Book Policy** If you've implemented address book policies to provide customized address book views, select the address book policy to associate with the equipment mailbox.

8. Click **Save** to create the equipment mailbox. If an error occurs during account or mailbox creation, neither the account nor the related mailbox will

be created. You need to correct the problem before you can complete this procedure.

By default, booking requests are accepted or declined automatically based on availability. Here, the first person to reserve the equipment gets the reservation. If your organization has resource coordinators, you can change the booking options by completing the following steps:

1. Double-click the room mailbox with which you want to work.
2. On the Booking Delegates page, choose the Select Delegates option.
3. Next, use the options under Delegates to specify the coordinator. Click the Add button, use the Select Delegates dialog box to select coordinators for the room. Simply double-click to add a name to the list of delegates.

In Exchange Management Shell, you can create a user account with a mailbox for equipment by using the New-Mailbox cmdlet. Sample 6-2 provides the syntax and usage. Although with earlier releases of Exchange you needed to set a password for the related user account, this is no longer required. When you create mailboxes for Exchange Online, you cannot specify a database.

SAMPLE 6-2 Creating equipment mailboxes

Syntax

```
New-Mailbox -Name 'DisplayName' -Alias 'ExchangeAlias'
  -OrganizationalUnit 'OrganizationalUnit'
  -UserPrincipalName 'LogonName' -SamAccountName 'prewin2000logon'
  -FirstName '' -Initials '' -LastName ''
  -Database 'Server\MailboxDatabase'
  -Equipment
```

Usage

```
New-Mailbox -Name 'Media Cart 3' -Alias 'cart3'
  -OrganizationalUnit 'imaginedlands.com/Marketing'
  -UserPrincipalName 'cart3@imaginedlands.com' -SamAccountName 'cart3'
  -FirstName '' -Initials '' -LastName ''
  -Database 'Marketing Primary'
  -Equipment
```

Adding Linked Mailboxes

A linked mailbox is a mailbox that is accessed by a user in a separate, trusted forest. Typically, you use linked mailboxes when your organization's mailbox servers are in a separate resource forest and you want to ensure that users can access free/busy data across these forests. You use linked mailboxes with on-premises Exchange organizations.

All linked mailboxes have two user account associations:

- A unique user account in the same forest as the Mailbox server. The same forest user account is disabled automatically so that it cannot be used for logon.
- A unique user account in a separate forest for which you are creating a link. The separate forest user account is enabled so that it can be used for logon.

In Exchange Admin Center, linked mailboxes are displayed under Recipients > Mailboxes. In Exchange Management Shell, you can find all linked mailboxes in the organization by entering:

```
Get-Mailbox -ResultSize unlimited -Filter {(RecipientTypeDetails -eq
'LinkedMailbox')}
```

You can create a linked mailbox by completing the following steps:

1. In Exchange Admin Center, select **Recipients** in the Features pane, and then select **Mailboxes**.

2. Click **New** ( ), and then select **Linked Mailbox**. This starts the New Linked Mailbox Wizard. A linked mailbox cannot be created without a forest or domain trust in place between the source and target forests.

3. On the New Linked Mailbox page, click **Browse** to the right of the Linked Forest text box. In the Select Trusted Forest Or Domain dialog box, select the linked forest or domain in which the user's original account is located, and then click **OK**. This is the separate forest that contains the user account that you want to create the linked mailbox for in the current forest. Click **Next**.

4. If your organization has configured a one-way outgoing trust where the current forest trusts the linked forest, you're prompted for administrator credentials in the linked forest so that you can gain access to a domain

controller in that forest. Type the user name and password for an administrator account in the account forest, and then click Next.

5. Click **Browse** to the right of the Linked Domain Controller text box. In the Select Domain Controller dialog box, select a domain controller in the linked forest, and then click **OK**.

6. Click **Browse** to the right of the Linked Master Account text box. Use the options in the Select User dialog box to select the original user account in the linked forest, and then click OK.

7. Click **Next**. On the General Information page, the Organizational Unit text box shows where in Active Directory the user account will be created. By default, this is the Users container in the current domain. Select the Specify The Organizational Unit check box and then click Browse to create the new user account in a different container. Use the Select Organizational Unit dialog box to choose the location in which to store the account, and then click OK.

8. In the User Logon Name text box, type the user's logon name. Use the drop-down list to select the domain with which the account is to be associated. This sets the fully qualified logon name.

9. Click **More Options**. Type the user's first name, middle initial, and last name in the text boxes provided. These values are used to create the Name entry, which is the user's display name.

10. Optionally, enter an Exchange alias for the user. The alias must be unique in the forest. If you don't specify an alias, the logon name is used as the alias.

11. If you want to specify a mailbox database rather than use an automatically selected one, click Browse to the right of the Mailbox Database text box. In the Select Mailbox Database dialog box, choose the mailbox database in which the mailbox should be stored. Mailbox databases are listed by name as well as by associated server and Exchange version running on the server.

12. Click **Save** to create the account and the related mailbox. If an error occurs during account or mailbox creation, neither the account nor the related mailbox will be created. You will need to correct the problem.

In Exchange Management Shell, you can create a user account with a linked mailbox by using the New-Mailbox cmdlet. Sample 6-3 provides the syntax and usage. You'll be prompted for the credentials of an administrator account in the linked forest. Although with earlier releases of Exchange you needed to set a password for the related user account, this is no longer required.

Syntax

```
New-Mailbox -Name 'DisplayName' -Alias 'ExchangeAlias'
  -OrganizationalUnit 'OrganizationalUnit'
  -Database 'Database'
  -UserPrincipalName 'LogonName' -SamAccountName 'prewin2000logon'
  -FirstName 'FirstName' -Initials 'Initial' -LastName 'LastName'
  -ResetPasswordOnNextLogon State
  -LinkedDomainController 'LinkedDC'
  -LinkedMasterAccount 'domain\user'
  -LinkedCredential:(Get-Credential 'domain\administrator')
```

Usage

```
New-Mailbox -Name 'Wendy Richardson' -Alias 'wendyr'
  -OrganizationalUnit 'imaginedlands.com/Sales'
  -Database 'Corporate Services Primary'
  -UserPrincipalName 'wendyr@imaginedlands.com' -SamAccountName 'wendyr'
  -FirstName 'Wendy' -Initials '' -LastName 'Richardson'
  -ResetPasswordOnNextLogon $true
  -LinkedDomainController 'TvpressDC58'
  -LinkedMasterAccount 'tvpress\wrichardson'
  -LinkedCredential:(Get-Credential 'tvpress\williams')
```

Adding Forwarding Mailboxes

Custom recipients, such as mail-enabled users, don't normally receive mail from users outside the organization because a custom recipient doesn't have an email address that resolves to a specific mailbox in your organization. At times, though, you might want external users, applications, or mail systems to be able to send mail to an address within your organization and then have Exchange forward this mail to an external mailbox.

> **TIP** You can send and receive text messages using Outlook Web App in Exchange 2016, or you can send text messages the old-fashioned way. In my organization, I've created forwarding mailboxes for text-messaging alerts. This simple solution lets managers (and monitoring systems) within the organization quickly and easily send text messages to IT personnel. In this

case, I've set up mail-enabled users for each text messaging email address, such as 8085551212@tvpress.com, and then created a mailbox that forwards email to the custom recipient. Generally, the display name of the mail-enabled user is in the form Alert *User Name*, such as Alert William Stanek. The display name and email address for the mailbox are in the form Z *LastName* and AE-*MailAddress*@myorg.com, such as Z Stanek and AE-WilliamS@tvpress.com, respectively. Afterward, I hide the mailbox so that it isn't displayed in the global address list or in other address lists; this way, users can see only the Alert William Stanek mailbox.

To create a user account to receive mail and forward it off site, follow these steps:

1. Using Exchange Admin Center, create a mail-enabled user. Name the account Alert *User Name*, such as Alert William Stanek. Be sure to establish an external email address that refers to the user's Internet address.

2. Using Exchange Admin Center, create a mailbox-enabled user account in the domain. Name the account with the appropriate display name, such as Z Stanek, William. Be sure to create an Exchange mailbox for the account, but don't grant any special permission to the account. You might want to restrict the account so that the user can't log on to any servers in the domain. Optionally, hide this mailbox from address lists.

3. Using Exchange Admin Center, access the properties dialog box for the mailbox user account.

4. On the Mailbox Features page, select the View Details option under Mail Flow. This displays the Delivery Options dialog box.

5. In the Delivery Options dialog box, select the Enable Forwarding check box and then click Browse.

6. In the Select Recipient dialog box, select the mail-enabled user you created earlier and then click OK twice. Click Save. You can now use the user account to forward mail to the external mailbox.

Z William Stanek

general

mailbox usage   POP3: Enabled
                             Disable
contact information

organization   MAPI: Enabled
                             Disable
email address

▸ **mailbox features**   Litigation hold: Disabled
                             Enable
member of

MailTip   Archiving: Disabled
                             Enable
mailbox delegation

Mail Flow

Delivery Options
Delivery options control forwarding and recipient limits.
View details

Message Size Restrictions
Message size restrictions control the maximum size of
messages that the recipient can send and receive.
View details

[Save]   [Cancel]

---

delivery options

Forwarding Address
Forward email to the following recipient. Learn more

☑ Enable forwarding
Forward email to the following recipient:

| Alert William Stanek   ✕ | [Browse...]

☐ Deliver message to both forwarding address and
   mailbox
Recipient limit
☐ Maximum recipients:

[OK]   [Cancel]

Working with Archive Mailboxes

Each user can have an alternate mailbox for archives. An archive mailbox is used to store a user's old messages, such as might be required for executives and needed by some managers and users. In Outlook and Outlook Web App, users can access archive mailboxes in much the same way as they access a regular mailbox.

Archive mailboxes are created in one of two ways. The standard approach is to create an in-place archive. Both on-premises Exchange and Exchange Online use in-place archives by default. With hybrid organizations, you also can use online archives. With an online archive, the archive for an on-premises mailbox is created in the online service.

Adding In-Place Archives

You can create an in-place archive mailbox at the same time you create the user's standard mailbox. To create an in-place archive mailbox, complete the following steps:

1. In Exchange Admin Center, select Recipients in the Features pane and then select Mailboxes. Double-click the entry for the user's standard mailbox. Any user that already has an archive mailbox has "User (Archive)" as the mailbox type.

2. On the Mailbox Features page, the status of archiving is listed under the Archiving heading. If archiving is disabled, select **Enable** under the Archiving heading and continue with this procedure.

3. With on-premises Exchange, if the mailbox had an archive previously and that archive still exists, this archive is used in its original location. Otherwise, the Create In-Place Archive dialog box is displayed. If you want to specify a mailbox database rather than use an automatically selected one, click Browse to the right of the Mailbox Database text box. In the Select Mailbox Database dialog box, choose the mailbox database in which the mailbox should be stored and then click **OK**. Mailbox databases are listed by name as well as by associated server and Exchange version running on the server.

4. Click **Save**. If an error occurs during mailbox creation, the archive mailbox will not be created. You need to correct the problem before you can complete this procedure and create the archive mailbox.

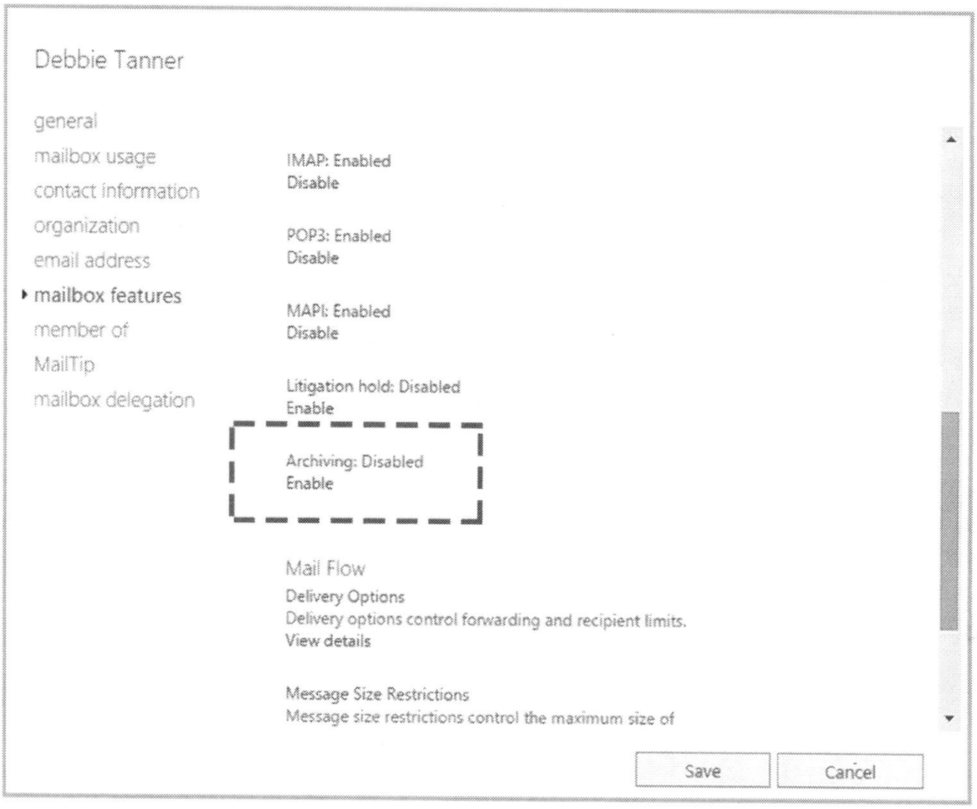

Debbie Tanner

general

mailbox usage

contact information

organization

email address

▸ mailbox features

member of

MailTip

mailbox delegation

IMAP: Enabled
Disable

POP3: Enabled
Disable

MAPI: Enabled
Disable

Litigation hold: Disabled
Enable

Archiving: Disabled
Enable

Mail Flow

Delivery Options
Delivery options control forwarding and recipient limits.
View details

Message Size Restrictions
Message size restrictions control the maximum size of

Save   Cancel

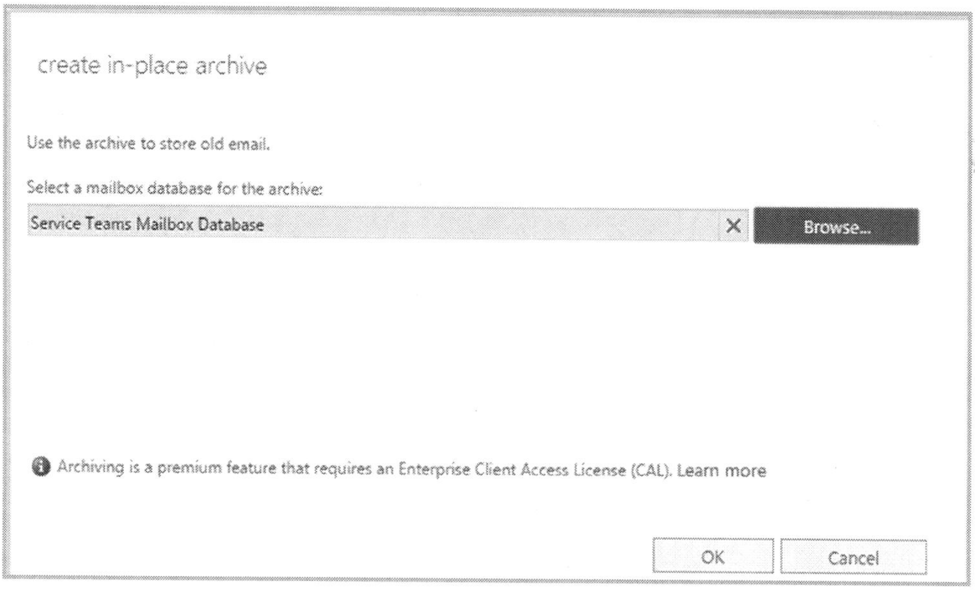

create in-place archive

Use the archive to store old email.

Select a mailbox database for the archive:

Service Teams Mailbox Database   ✕   Browse...

🛈 Archiving is a premium feature that requires an Enterprise Client Access License (CAL). Learn more

OK   Cancel

When you are working with Exchange Admin Center, you can enable in-place archiving for multiple mailboxes as well. When you select multiple mailboxes using the Shift or Ctrl keys, the Details pane displays bulk editing options. Scroll down the list of options and then click **More Options**. Next, under Archive, click **Enable**.

The Bulk Enable Archive dialog box is displayed. If you want to specify a mailbox database for the archives rather than use an automatically selected one, click

Browse to the right of the Mailbox Database text box. In the Select Mailbox Database dialog box, choose the mailbox database in which the archive mailboxes should be stored and then click **OK**.

Using Exchange Management Shell, you can create an archive mailbox using the Enable-Mailbox cmdlet. The basic syntax is as follows:

```
Enable-Mailbox [-Identity] Identity -Archive [-Database DatabaseID]
```

such as:

```
Enable-Mailbox imaginedlands.com/engineering/tonyg -archive
```

Because each user can have only one archive mailbox, you get an error if the user already has an archive mailbox. Items in the user's mailbox will be moved automatically to the archive mailbox based on the archive and retention policy. When you install Exchange Server, a default archive and retention policy is created for all archive mailboxes. This policy is named Default MRM Policy. Because of this policy, email messages from the entire mailbox are moved to the archive after two years by default.

For bulk editing, you can use various techniques. Generally, you'll want to:

* Ensure you are working with mailboxes for regular users and not mailboxes for rooms, equipment, and so on. To do this, filter the results based on the RecipientTypeDetails.
* Ensure the mailbox doesn't already have an on-premises or online archive. To do this, filter the results based on whether the mailbox has an associated ArchiveGuid and the ArchiveDomain.
* Ensure you don't enable archives on mailboxes that shouldn't have them, such as the Discovery Search Mailbox. To do this, filter based on the name or partial name of mailboxes to exclude.

Consider the following example:

```
Get-Mailbox -Database Sales -Filter {RecipientTypeDetails -eq 'UserMailbox'
-AND ArchiveGuid -eq $null -AND ArchiveDomain -eq $null -AND Name -NotLike
"DiscoverySearchMailbox*"} | Enable-Mailbox -Archive
```

In this example, Get-Mailbox retrieves all mailboxes for regular users in the Sales database that don't have in-place or online archiving enabled and that also don't have a name starting with: DiscoverySearchMailbox. The results are then piped through Enable-Mailbox to add an archive mailbox to these mailboxes.

Adding Online Archives

In hybrid organizations, several features, including online archives, are enabled by default. If you are unsure whether online archives have been enabled for your hybrid deployment, enter **Get-HybridConfiguration | fl** at a PowerShell prompt and then verify that the OnlineArchive flag is set on the Features parameter. To modify the hybrid configuration, you can use Set-HybridConfiguration. However, do not use Set-HybridConfiguration without a solid understanding of hybrid configurations. Keep in mind that when you use the -Features parameter with Set-HybridConfiguration, you must explicitly specify all the features that you want enabled. Any feature that you omit will be disabled.

In Exchange Management Shell, you create online archives using the Enable-Mailbox cmdlet with the -RemoteArchive, -ArchiveDatabase, and -ArchiveDomain parameters. The required -RemoteArchive parameter is a flag that specifies you want to create the archive online. The optional -ArchiveDatabase sets the name or GUID of the archive database in the online organization. The optional -ArchiveDomain sets the fully qualified domain name of the domain for the online organization. Consider the following examples:

```
Enable-Mailbox -Identity issan@contoso.com -RemoteArchive


Enable-Mailbox -Identity issan@contoso.com -RemoteArchive -ArchiveDatabase
"D919BA05-46A6-415f-80AD-7E09334BB852" -ArchiveDomain
"imaginedlands.onmicrosoft.com"
```

The first example creates the online archive using the default database and online domain. The second example explicitly sets the GUID of the database and domain parameters.

Managing Archive Settings

Whether you use Exchange Admin Center or Exchange Management Shell, several other parameters are set for archive mailboxes. The default name for the archive mailbox is set as In-Place Archive – *UserDisplayName,* such as In-Place Archive – Henrik Larsen. With on-premises Exchange, the default quota and warning quota are set as 50 GB and 45 GB respectively. With Exchange Online, the default quota and warning quota are set as 25 GB and 22.5 GB, respectively.

You can confirm the details for a user's archive mailbox by entering the following command:

```
Get-Mailbox "Name" | fl name, alias, servername, *archive*
```

where *name* is the display name or alias of the user you want to work with, such as:

```
Get-Mailbox "Henrik Larsen" | fl name, alias, servername, *archive*
```

You can change the archive name and set quotas by using Set-Mailbox. The basic syntax is as follows:

```
Set-Mailbox [-Identity] Identity –ArchiveName Name
–ArchiveQuota Quota –ArchiveWarningQuota Quota
```

When you set a quota, specify the value with MB (for megabytes), GB (for gigabytes), or TB (for terabytes), or enter 'Unlimited' to remove the quota. Here is an example:

```
set-mailbox imaginedlands.com/engineering/tonyg
–ArchiveQuota '28GB' –ArchiveWarningQuota '27GB'
```

For bulk editing, you can use Get-Mailbox to retrieve the user mailboxes you want to work with and then apply the changes by piping the results to Set-Mailbox. If you do so, ensure that you filter the results appropriately. Consider the following example:

```
Get-Mailbox -ResultSize unlimited -Filter {RecipientTypeDetails -eq
'UserMailbox' -AND ArchiveGuid -ne $null} | Set-Mailbox –ArchiveQuota
'20GB' –ArchiveWarningQuota '18GB'
```

In this example, Get-Mailbox retrieves all mailboxes for regular users in the entire organization that have archiving enabled. The results are then piped through Set-Mailbox to modify the quota and quota warning values.

In Exchange Admin Center, you manage archive settings by completing these steps:

1. In Exchange Admin Center, select Recipients in the Features pane and then select Mailboxes. Double-click the entry for the user's standard mailbox. Any user that already has an archive mailbox has "User (Archive)" as the mailbox type.

2. On the Mailbox Features page, click **View Details** under the Archiving heading.

3. To change the name of the archive mailbox, enter the new name in the Name text box.

4. To set a quota, enter the desired value in gigabytes in the Archive Quota combo box.

5. To set a quota warning, enter a quota warning in gigabytes in the Issue Warning At combo box.

archive mailbox

Status:

Local archive created

Database:

Mailbox Database

Name:

In-Place Archive - Jeff Peterson

Archive usage:

Archive usage displays the archive storage limit and current usage. Learn more

10 GB used 10% of 100 GB.

*Archive quota (GB):

100 ▼

*Issue warning at (GB):

90 ▼

ⓘ Archiving is a premium feature that requires an Enterprise Client Access License (CAL).
Learn more

OK   Cancel

To disable an archive mailbox, open the properties dialog box for the user to the Mailbox Features page and then select **Disable** under the Archiving heading. Click **Yes** when prompted to confirm.

warning

If you disable this person's archive, you'll have 30 days to enable it again and retain the existing content. After 30 days, all information in their archive will be permanently deleted. If you enable the archive again after this time, a new archive mailbox is created. Are you sure you want to disable this archive?

Yes   No

> **REAL WORLD** When you disable an archive mailbox for a user, the archive mailbox is marked for deletion and disconnected from the user account. The archive mailbox is retained according to the mailbox retention policy. To connect the disabled archive mailbox to the existing mailbox, you must use the Connect-Mailbox cmdlet with the -Archive parameter. Otherwise, if you disable an archive mailbox for a user mailbox and then enable an archive mailbox for that same user, a new archive mailbox is created for the user.

When you are working with Exchange Admin Center, you can disable in-place archiving for multiple mailboxes as well. When you select multiple mailboxes using the Shift or Ctrl keys, the Details pane displays bulk editing options. Scroll down the list of available options and then click **More Options**.

Next, under Archive, click **Disable**. When the Bulk Disable Archive dialog box is displayed, click **OK**.

In Exchange Management Shell, you can disable an archive mailbox by using Disable-Mailbox. The basic syntax is as follows:

```
Disable-Mailbox [-Identity] Identity -Archive
```

such as:

```
disable-mailbox imaginedlands.com/engineering/tonyg -archive
```

For bulk editing, you can use a technique similar to the one discussed for enabling archives. Consider the following example:

```
Get-Mailbox -Database Sales -Filter {RecipientTypeDetails -eq 'UserMailbox'
-AND ArchiveGuid -ne $null} | Disable-Mailbox -Archive
```

In this example, Get-Mailbox retrieves all mailboxes for regular users in the Sales database that have archiving enabled. The results are then piped through Disable-Mailbox to remove the archive mailbox from these mailboxes.

Adding Arbitration Mailboxes

Exchange moderated transport requires all email messages sent to specific recipients to be approved by moderators. You can configure any type of recipient as a moderated recipient, and Exchange will ensure that all messages sent to those recipients go through an approval process.

Distribution groups are the only types of recipients that use moderation by default. Membership in distribution groups can be closed, owner approved, or open. While any Exchange recipient can join or leave an open distribution group, joining or leaving a closed group requires approval. Group owners receive join and remove requests and can either approve or deny those requests.

Distribution groups can also be unmoderated or moderated. With unmoderated groups, any approved sender (which is all senders by default) can send messages to the group. With moderated groups, messages are sent to moderators for approval before being distributed to members of the group. The only exception is for a message sent by a moderator. A message from a moderator is delivered immediately because a moderator has the authority to determine what is and isn't an appropriate message.

> **NOTE** The default moderator for a distribution group is the group's owner.

Arbitration mailboxes are used to store messages that are awaiting approval. When you install Exchange Server 2016, a default arbitration mailbox is created. For the purposes of load balancing or for other reasons, you can convert other mailboxes to the arbitration mailbox type by using the Enable-Mailbox cmdlet. The basic syntax is as follows:

```
Enable-Mailbox [-Identity] Identity -Arbitration
```

such as:

```
enable-mailbox imaginedlands.com/users/moderatedmail -Arbitration
```

You can create an arbitration mailbox by using New-Mailbox as shown in this example:

```
New-Mailbox ModeratedMail -Arbitration -UserPrincipalName
ModeratedMail@imaginedlands.com
```

Adding Discovery Mailboxes

Exchange Discovery helps organizations comply with legal discovery requirements and can also be used as an aid in internal investigations or as part of regular monitoring of email content. Exchange Discovery uses content indexes created by Exchange Search to speed up the search process.

> **NOTE** By default, Exchange administrators do not have sufficient rights to perform Discovery searches. Only users with the Discovery Management role can perform Discovery searches. If a user is not a member of the role, she doesn't have access to the related options. This means she can't access the In-Place eDiscovery & Hold interface in Exchange Admin Center or the In-Place eDiscovery & Hold cmdlets in PowerShell.

Whether you are working in an online, on-premises, or hybrid organization, you use Exchange Admin Center to perform searches. With hybrid configurations, an on-premises search will return results from the online organization.

Discovery searches are performed against designated mailboxes or all mailboxes in the Exchange organization. Items in mailboxes that match the Discovery search are copied to a target mailbox. Only mailboxes specifically designated as Discovery mailboxes can be used as targets. In a hybrid configuration, you must copy items to an on-premises mailbox, regardless of whether the items are from the online or on-premises organization.

> **TIP** By default, Discovery search does not include items that cannot be indexed by Exchange Search. To include such items in the search results, select the Include Items That Can't Be Searched check box in Exchange Admin Center.

In Exchange Admin Center, you can access the discovery and hold settings by selecting Compliance Management in the Features pane and then selecting In-Place eDiscovery & Hold. While working with In-Place eDiscovery & Hold, you can create searches across mailboxes by specifying filters and hold options for search results.

When you install Exchange Server 2016, a default Discovery mailbox is created. You can convert other mailboxes to the Discovery mailbox type by using the Enable-Mailbox cmdlet. The basic syntax is as follows:

```
Enable-Mailbox [-Identity] Identity –Discovery
```

such as:

```
enable-mailbox imaginedlands.com/hr/legalsearch –discovery
```

You can create a Discovery mailbox by using New-Mailbox as shown in this example:

```
New-Mailbox LegalSearch –Discovery –UserPrincipalName
LegalSearch@imaginedlands.com
```

Once a Discovery mailbox is established, you can't convert it to another mailbox type. You can't use Exchange Admin Center to create Discovery mailboxes.

Adding Shared Mailboxes

Shared mailboxes are mailboxes that are shared by multiple users. Although shared mailboxes must have an associated user account, this account is not used for logon in the domain and is disabled by default. Users who access the shared mailbox do so using access permissions.

You can create a shared mailbox by using New-Mailbox, as shown in this example:

```
New-Mailbox -Shared -Name "Customer Service" -DisplayName
"Customer Service" -Alias Service -UserPrincipalName
customerservice@imaginedlands.com
```

In this example, a user account named CustomerService is created for this mailbox. This user account is disabled by default to prevent logon using this account. After creating the mailbox, you need to grant Send On Behalf Of permission to the appropriate users or security groups by using Set-Mailbox and the -GrantSendOnBehalfTo parameter. Finally, you need to add access rights that allow these users or security groups to log on to the mailbox by using Add-MailboxPermission and the -AccessRights parameter. Ensure these rights are inherited at all levels of the mailbox using -InheritanceType All as well. One way this would all come together is shown in the following example:

```
New-Mailbox -Shared -Name "Customer Service" -DisplayName
"Customer Service" -Alias Service -UserPrincipalName
customerservice@imaginedlands.com | Set-Mailbox -GrantSendOnBehalfTo
CustomerServiceGroup | Add-MailboxPermission -User CustomerServiceGroup
-AccessRights FullAccess -InheritanceType All
```

In Exchange Admin Center, you can create a shared mailbox by following these steps:

1. Select **Recipients** in the Features pane and then select **Shared**.

2. Click **New** (➕). This opens the New Shared Mailbox dialog box, shown in Figure 6-8.

3. In the Display Name text box, type a descriptive name for the shared mailbox.

4. For on-premises Exchange, the Organizational Unit text box shows where in Active Directory the associated user account will be created. By default, this is the Users container in the current domain. If you want to use a different container, click Browse to the right of the Organizational Unit text box. Use the Select Organizational Unit dialog box to choose the location in which to store the account, and then click OK.

5. For on-premises Exchange, enter the Exchange alias in the Alias text box. The Exchange alias is used to set the default email address.

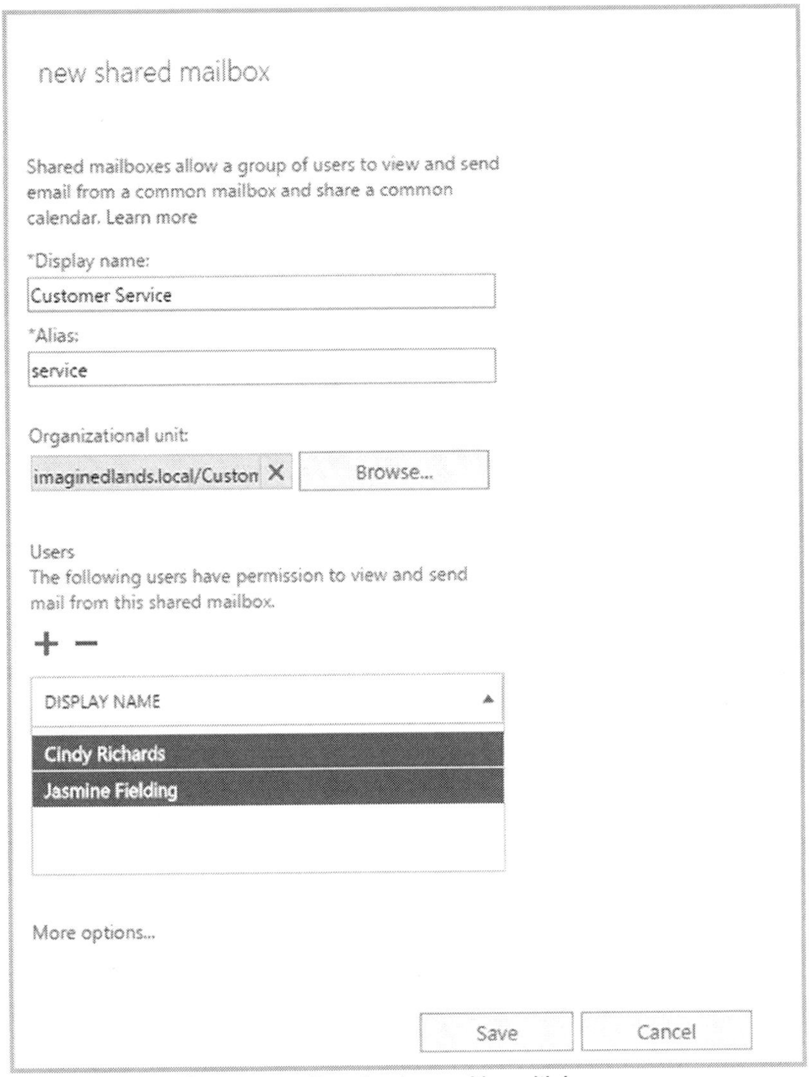

FIGURE 6-8 Create a mailbox to share with multiple users.

6. For Exchange Online, enter the Exchange alias in the Email Address text box and then use the drop-down list to select the domain with which the room is to be associated. The Exchange Alias and domain name are combined to set the fully qualified name, such as service@imaginedlands.onmicrosoft.com.

7. Under Users, click Add (   ). In the Select Full Access dialog box, select users, security groups, or both that should be able to view and send email from the shared mailbox. Select multiple users and groups using the Shift or Ctrl keys.

8. Click **More Options** to configure these additional options:

- **Alias**   For Exchange Onilne, sets the Exchange alias and overrides the default value you set previously using the Email Address text box. This allows a resource to have an alias that is different from the name portion of its email address.
- **Mailbox Database**   For on-premises Exchange, if you want to specify a mailbox database rather than use an automatically selected one, click Browse to the right of the Mailbox Database text box. In the Select Mailbox Database dialog box, choose the mailbox database in which the mailbox should be stored. Mailbox databases are listed by name as well as by associated server and Exchange version running on the server.
- **Archive**   For on-premises Exchange, if you want to create an on-premises archive mailbox as well, select the related checkbox. Optionally, click Browse to choose the mailbox database for the archive.
- **Address Book Policy**   For on-premises Exchange, if you've implemented address book policies to provide customized address book views, select the address book policy to associate with the equipment mailbox.

9. Click **Save** to create the shared mailbox. If an error occurs during account or mailbox creation, neither the account nor the related mailbox will be created. You need to correct the problem before you can complete this procedure.

Mailbox database:

| Service Teams Mailbo: X | Browse... |

Archive
Use the archive to store old email.
☑ Create an on-premises archive mailbox for this user

| | Browse... |

Address book policy:

| [No Policy] ▼ |

Save   Cancel

Adding Public Folder Mailboxes

Public folders are used to share messages and files in an organization. Public folder trees define the structure of an organization's public folders. You can make the default public folder tree accessible to users based on criteria you set, and then users can create folders and manage their content.

Each public folder in the default public folder tree can have specific access permissions. For example, you can create public folders called CompanyWide, Marketing, and Engineering. Whereas you would typically make the CompanyWide folder accessible to all users, you would make the Marketing folder accessible only to users in the marketing department and the Engineering folder accessible only to users in the engineering department.

Users access public folders from Outlook clients, including Outlook Web App and Outlook 2010 or later. With Outlook Web App and Outlook 2010 or later, users can add and remove favorite public folders and perform item-level operations, such as creating and managing posts. However, users can create or delete public folders only from Outlook 2010 or later. As an administrator, you can manage public folders in Exchange Admin Center.

Unlike Exchange 2010 and earlier versions of Exchange, current Exchange servers no longer use public folder databases or store public folder data separately from mailbox data. Instead, Exchange Server and Exchange Online store public folder data in mailboxes. This significant architecture change greatly simplifies public folder management.

In Exchange Admin Center, you work with public folders by selecting Public Folders in the Features pane and then selecting either Public Folder Mailboxes or Public Folders as appropriate. You use the options under Public Folder Mailboxes to create and manage the mailboxes that store public folder data. You use the options under Public Folders to view and manage the public folder hierarchy.

An Exchange organization can have one or more public folder mailboxes and those mailboxes can be created on one or more Mailbox servers throughout the organization. While each public folder mailbox can contain public folder content, only the first public folder mailbox created in an Exchange organization contains the writable copy of the public folder hierarchy. This mailbox is referred to as the hierarchy mailbox. Any additional public folder mailboxes contain read-only copies of the public-folder hierarchy.

Because there's only one writeable copy of the public folder hierarchy, proxying is used to relay folder changes to the hierarchy mailbox. This means that any time users working with folders in an additional mailbox create new subfolders, the folder creation, modification, or removal is proxied to the hierarchy mailbox by the content mailbox users are connected to.

In Exchange Admin Center, you can create a public folder mailbox by following these steps:

1. Select **Public Folders** in the Features pane and then select **Public Folder Mailboxes**.

2. Click **New** (╋). This opens the New Public Folder Mailbox dialog box, shown in Figure 6-9.

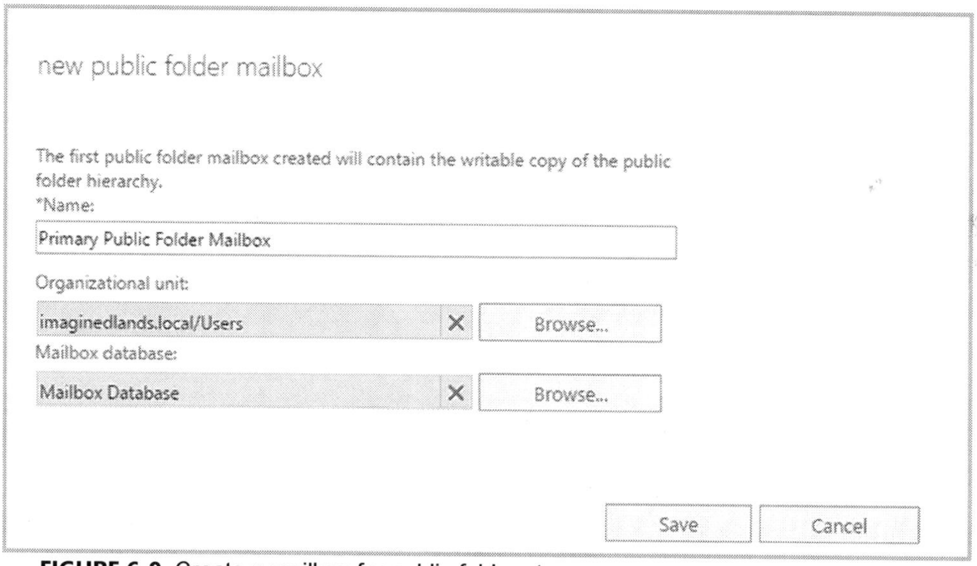

---

new public folder mailbox

The first public folder mailbox created will contain the writable copy of the public folder hierarchy.
*Name:

| Primary Public Folder Mailbox |

Organizational unit:

| imaginedlands.local/Users | × | Browse... |

Mailbox database:

| Mailbox Database | × | Browse... |

| Save | Cancel |

FIGURE 6-9 Create a mailbox for public folder storage.

3. Type a descriptive name for the mailbox.

4. With on-premises Exchange, you can associate the mailbox with a specific organizational unit. Click Browse to the right of the Organizational Unit text box. Use the Select Organizational Unit dialog box to choose the location in

which to store the account, and then click **OK**. A user account for the mailbox is created in the selected organizational unit (with the account disabled for login).

5. With on-premises Exchange, you can specify a mailbox database rather than use an automatically selected one, click Browse to the right of the Mailbox Database text box. In the Select Mailbox Database dialog box, choose the mailbox database in which the mailbox should be stored and then click **OK**.

6. Click **Save** to create the public folder mailbox. If an error occurs during account or mailbox creation, neither the account nor the related mailbox will be created. You need to correct the problem before you can complete this procedure.

Public folder content can include email messages, documents, and more. The content is stored in the public folder mailbox but isn't replicated across multiple public folder mailboxes. Instead, all users access the same public folder mailbox for the same set of content.

When you create the first public folder in the organization, you establish the root of the public folder hierarchy. You can then create subfolders and assign access permissions on folders. In Exchange Admin Center, select Public Folders > Public Folders and then use the available options to create subfolders and set permissions on those folders.

When you create public folder mailboxes, they inherit the quota limits of the mailbox database in which they are stored. You can modify the quota limits using the properties dialog for the mailbox.

Double-click the mailbox entry. In the Public Folder Mailbox dialog box, on the Mailbox Usage page, click **More Options** and then select **Customize The Settings For This Mailbox**. Next, use the selection lists provided to specify when warnings are issued, what posts are prohibited, and the maximum size of items. Apply the changes by clicking **Save**.

Primary Public Folder Mailbox

general

▸ mailbox usage

The mailbox usage displays the quota and usage information of every public folder mailbox. Click 'More options' to edit the quotas.

0 B used, 0% of 2 GB

More options... ①

Save   Cancel

Primary Public Folder Mailbox

general

▸ mailbox usage

○ Use the default quota settings from the mailbox database

◉ Customize the quota settings for this mailbox ②

*Issue a warning at (GB):
210

*Prohibit post at (GB):
250

*Maximum item size (GB):
unlimited

Save   Cancel

When users are connected to public folder mailboxes and make routine changes to an Exchange store hierarchy or content, the changes are synchronized every 15 minutes using Incremental Change Synchronization (ICS). Immediate syncing is used for non-routine changes, such as folder creation. If no users are connected to public folder mailboxes, synchronization occurs once every 24 hours by default.

Chapter 7. Managing Mailboxes

The difference between a good Microsoft Exchange Server administrator and a great one is the attention he or she pays to mailbox administration. Mailboxes are private storage places for messages you've sent and received, and they are created as part of private mailbox databases in Exchange. Mailbox settings control mail delivery, permissions, and storage limits.

You can configure most mailbox settings on a per-mailbox basis. However, with Exchange Online, some settings are configured for all users of the service while other settings are fixed as part of the service and cannot be changed. With on-premises Exchange, you cannot change some settings without moving mailboxes to another mailbox database or changing the settings of the mailbox database itself. For example, with on-premises Exchange, you set the storage location on the file system, the storage limits, the deleted item retention, and the default offline address book on a per-mailbox-database basis. Keep this in mind when performing capacity planning and when deciding which mailbox location to use for a particular mailbox.

Managing Mailboxes: The Essentials

You often need to manage user mailboxes the way you do user accounts. Some of the management tasks are intuitive and others aren't. If you have questions, be sure to read the sections that follow.

Whether you are working with on-premises Exchange or Exchange Online, you can use bulk editing techniques to work with multiple user mailboxes at the same time. To select multiple user mailboxes not in sequence, hold down the Ctrl key and then click the left mouse button on each user mailbox you want to select. To select a series of user mailboxes, select the first mailbox, hold down the Shift key, and then click the last mailbox.

The actions you can perform on multiple resources depend on the types of recipients you've selected. The actions you can perform on multiple user mailboxes include:

* Updating contact information, organization information, or custom attributes
* Changing mailbox quotas or deleted item retention settings
* Enabling or disabling Outlook Web App, POP3, IMAP, MAPI, or ActiveSync

- Managing policy for Outlook Web App, ActiveSync, Address Books, Retention, Role Assignment, or Sharing
- Enabling or disabling mailbox archives
- Moving mailboxes to another database

Although you cannot bulk edit room or equipment mailboxes, you can perform these actions on shared mailboxes.

Viewing Current Mailbox Size, Message Count, and Last Logon

You can use Exchange Admin Center to view the last logon date and time, the mailbox size, and how much of the total mailbox quota has been used by completing these steps:

1. Select **Recipients** in the Features pane and then select **Mailboxes**.

2. Double-click the mailbox with which you want to work.

3. On the Mailbox Usage page, review the Last Logon text box to see the last logon date and time (see Figure 7-1). If a user hasn't logged on to her mailbox, you can't get mailbox statistics and will get an error when you view this page.

4. Under the last logon time, notice the mailbox usage statistics, depicted in a bar graph and numerically as a percentage of the total mailbox quota that has been used.

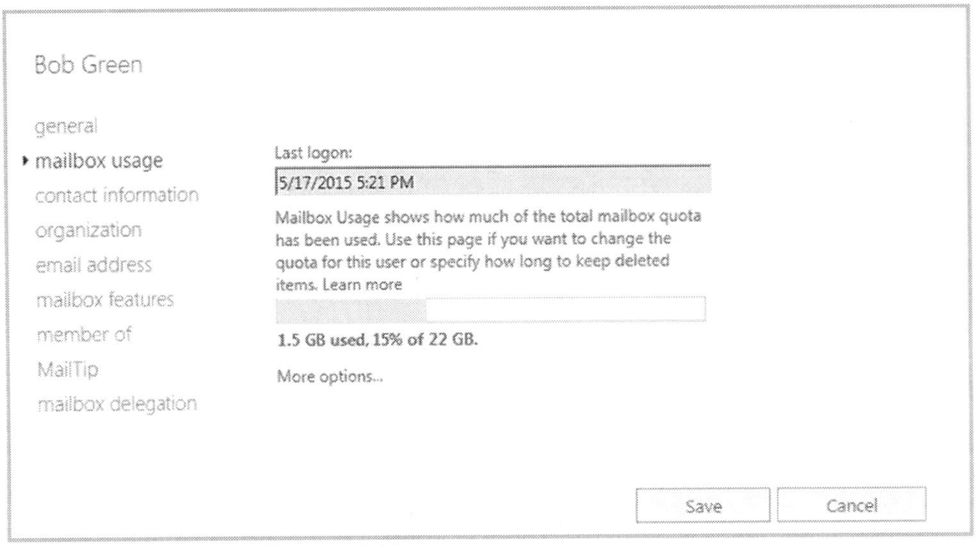

Bob Green

general
▸ mailbox usage
contact information
organization
email address
mailbox features
member of
MailTip
mailbox delegation

Last logon:

5/17/2015 5:21 PM

Mailbox Usage shows how much of the total mailbox quota has been used. Use this page if you want to change the quota for this user or specify how long to keep deleted items. Learn more

1.5 GB used, 15% of 22 GB.

More options...

Save   Cancel

FIGURE 7-1 View mailbox statistics.

If you want to view similar information for all mailboxes on a server, the easiest way is to use the Get-MailboxStatistics cmdlet with the -Server or -Database parameter. Sample 7-1 shows examples using Get-MailboxStatistics. Use the –Archive parameter to return mailbox statistics for the archive mailbox associated with a specified mailbox.

SAMPLE 7-1 Getting statistics for multiple mailboxes

```
Get-MailboxStatistics -Identity 'Identity' [-Archive <$true|$false>]
[-DomainContoller DomainController] [-IncludeMoveHistory <$true|$false>]
[-IncludeMoveReport <$true|$false>]


Get-MailboxStatistics -Server 'Server' | -Database 'Database'
[-DomainContoller DomainController]
```

Usage

```
Get-MailboxStatistics -Server 'corpsvr127'


Get-MailboxStatistics -Database 'Engineering Primary'


Get-MailboxStatistics -Identity 'imaginedlands\williams'
```

When you are working with Exchange Management Shell, the standard output won't necessarily provide all the information you are looking for. Often, you need to format the output as a list or table using Format-List or Format-Table, respectively, to get the additional information you are looking for. Format-List is useful when you are working with a small set of resources or want to view all the properties that are available. Once you know what properties are available for a particular resource, you can format the output as a table to view specific properties. For example, if you format the output of Get-MailboxStatistics as a list, you see all the properties that are available for mailboxes, as shown in this example and sample output:

```
get-mailboxstatistics -identity "imaginedlands\denises" | format-list
```

```
AssociatedItemCount     : 21622
DeletedItemCount        : 1211
DisconnectDate          :
DisplayName             : Denise Strong
```

```
ItemCount                : 20051
LastLoggedOnUserAccount  : NT AUTHORITY\SYSTEM
LastLogoffTime           : 3/17/2016 11:51:42 PM
LastLogonTime            : 3/17/2016 12:14:22 PM
LegacyDN                 : /O=FIRST ORGANIZATION/OU=EXCHANGE ADMINISTRATIVE
GROUP/CN=RECIPIENTS/CN=ERIK ANDERSEN
MailboxGuid              : b7fb0ca8-936b-410f-a2a1-59825eebbdfe
MailboxType              : Private
ObjectClass              : Mailbox
StorageLimitStatus       :
TotalDeletedItemSize     : 1927 KB (1927,535 bytes)
TotalItemSize            : 191121.2 KB (191,121,225 bytes)
Database                 : Customer Service Primary
ServerName               : MAILSERVER92
DatabaseName             : Customer Service Primary
IsQuarantined            : False
IsArchiveMailbox         : False
IsMoveDestination        : False
DatabaseIssueWarningQuota      : 1.899 GB (2,039,480,320 bytes)
DatabaseProhibitSendQuota      : 2 GB (2,147,483,648 bytes)
DatabaseProhibitSendReceiveQuota : 2.3 GB (2,469,396,480 bytes)
Identity                       : b7fb0ca8-936b-410f-a2a1-59825eebbdfe
MapiIdentity                   : b7fb0ca8-936b-410f-a2a1-59825eebbdfe
OriginatingServer              : mailserver92.imaginedlands.com
IsValid                        : True
ObjectState                    : Unchanged
```

Once you know the available properties, you can format the output as a table to get exactly the information you want to see. The following example gets information about all the mailboxes in the Engineering Primary database and formats the output as a table:

```
Get-MailboxStatistics -Database 'Engineering Primary' | format-table
DisplayName, TotalItemSize, TotalDeletedItemSize, Database, ServerName
```

Configuring Apps for Mailboxes

With both on-premises Exchange and Exchange Online, you can add apps to the Outlook Web App interface to add functionality. Several apps are installed and made available to users by default, including the following apps created by Microsoft:

- **Action Items**   Makes action item suggestions based on message content
- **Bing Maps**   Allows users to map addresses found in their messages
- **My Templates**   Allows users to save text and images to insert into messages.
- **Suggested Meetings**   Shows meeting suggestions found in messages and allows users to add the meetings to their calendars.
- **Unsubscribe**   Allows users to block or unsubscribe from email subscription feeds.

Other apps can be added from the Office Store, from a URL, or from a file. All of these apps have various levels of read, read/write, or other permissions on user mailboxes. Because apps also may send data to a third-party service, you may want to consider carefully whether apps should be enabled in your organization. Where strict, high security is a requirement, my recommendation is to disable all apps.

In Exchange Admin Center, you manage apps as part of the organization configuration. Select Organization in the Features pane and then select Apps. As shown in Figure 7-2, you'll then see the installed apps and their status. To work with Apps for Outlook, you must have View-Only Organization Management, Help Desk or Organization Management permissions.

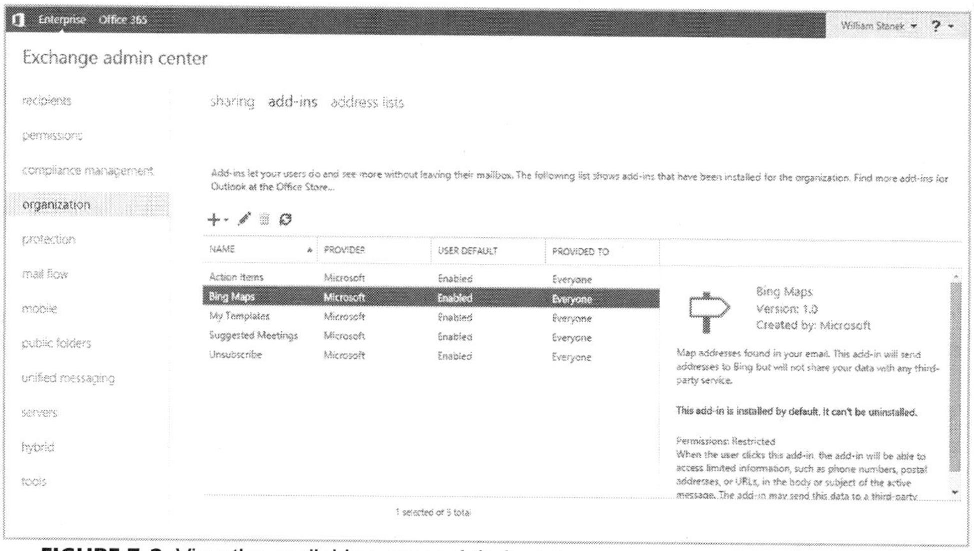

FIGURE 7-2 View the available apps and their status.

To add an app, do one of the following:

- To add an app from the Office store, click New ( ), select **Add From The Office Store** to open a new browser window to the Office store, and then select an app to add. When you select the app's Add option, review the app details and then click Add. When prompted to confirm, select Yes.
- If you know the URL of the manifest file for the app you want to add, click New and then select Add From URL. In the Add From URL dialog box, enter the URL and then click Install. Be sure to use the full path.
- If you've copied the manifest file to a local server, click New and then select Add From File. In the Add From File dialog box, select Browse. In the Choose File To Upload dialog box, locate and select the manifest file and then select Open. Manifest files end with the .xml extension.

All apps have two status values:

- **User Default**   Reflects whether the app is disabled by default, enabled by default, or enabled and mandatory.
- **Provided To**   Reflects whether the app is available to all users in the organization (everyone) or to no users in the organization (nobody).

The default apps are made available to all users and enabled by default. This is reflected in the status of Enabled for User Default and Everyone for Provided To by default.

When you install a new app, the app is made available to all users but disabled by default. This is reflected in the status of Disabled for User Default and Everyone for Provided To.

If you have appropriate permissions, you can manage app status by clicking the app and then clicking Edit. In the Action Items dialog box, shown in Figure 7-3, do one of the following:

- If you don't want the app to be available to users, clear the Make This App Available checkbox and then click Save.
- If you want the app to be available to users, select the Make This App Available checkbox and then specify the app status as optional and enabled by default, optional and disabled by default, or mandatory and always enabled. Finally, click Save.

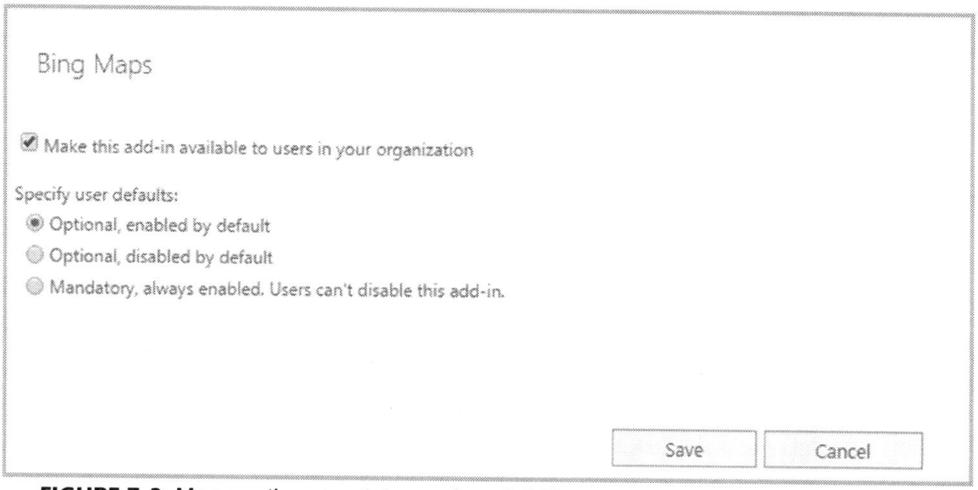

FIGURE 7-3 Manage the app status and availability.

Any app you install can be removed by selecting it and then selecting the Delete option. Although you can't uninstall the defaults apps, you can make any or all of the default apps unavailable to users.

Hiding Mailboxes from Address Lists

Occasionally, you might want to hide a mailbox so that it doesn't appear in the global address list or other address lists. One reason for doing this is if you have administrative mailboxes that you use only for special purposes. To hide a mailbox from the address lists, follow these steps:

1. Open the Properties dialog box for the mailbox-enabled user account by double-clicking the user name in Exchange Admin Center.

2. On the General page, select **Hide From Address Lists**.

3. Click **Save**.

Z William Stanek

> general
mailbox usage
contact information
organization
email address
mailbox features
member of
MailTip
mailbox delegation

First name:

Z William

Initials:

Last name:

Stanek

*Name:

William Stanek

*Display name:

Z William Stanek

*Alias:

williams

*User logon name:

williams @ imaginedlands.local ▼

☐ Require password change on next logon

☑ Hide from address lists

More options...

Save   Cancel

Defining Custom Mailbox Attributes for Address Lists

Address lists, such as the global address list, make it easier for users and administrators to find available Exchange resources, including users, contacts, distribution groups, and public folders. The fields available for Exchange resources are based on the type of resource. If you want to add more values that should be displayed or searchable in address lists, such as an employee identification number, you can assign these values as custom attributes.

Exchange provides 15 custom attributes—labeled Customer Attribute 1, Custom Attribute 2, and so on through Custom Attribute 15. You can assign a value to a custom attribute by completing the following steps:

1. Open the Properties dialog box for the mailbox-enabled user account by double-clicking the user name in Exchange Admin Center.

Z William Stanek

▸ **general**

mailbox usage

contact information

organization

email address

mailbox features

member of

MailTip

mailbox delegation

*User logon name:

williams   @   imaginedlands.local ▼

☐ Require password change on next logon

☑ Hide from address lists

Organizational unit:

imaginedlands.local/Users

Mailbox database:

Mailbox Database

Custom attributes:

NUMBER ▲	VALUE

Save   Cancel

2. On the General page, click **More Options**. Under the Custom Attributes heading, you'll see any currently defined custom attributes. Click **Edit** (

) to display the Custom Attributes dialog box.

3. Enter attribute values in the text boxes provided. Click **OK** and then click **Save**.

Restoring On-Premises Users and Mailboxes

When you disable or delete a mailbox, on-premises Exchange retains the deleted mailbox in the mailbox database and puts the mailbox in a disabled state. There is, however, an important distinction between disabling and deleting a mailbox, and this difference affects recovery. When you disable a mailbox, the Exchange attributes are removed from the user account and the mailbox is marked for removal, but the user account is retained. When you delete a mailbox, the Exchange attributes are removed from the user account, the mailbox is marked for removal, and the user account itself is either marked for deletion or deleted entirely. Additionally, with either, if the mailbox has an in-place archive, the in-place archive will also be marked for removal. However, if the mailbox has a remote archive, the remote archive is removed permanently.

Disabled and deleted mailboxes are referred to as disconnected mailboxes. Disconnected mailboxes are retained in a mailbox database until the deleted mailbox retention period expires, which is 30 days by default. Deleted users may be retained as well.

In Exchange Admin Center, you can find disconnected mailboxes and reconnect them by completing these steps:

1. Select **Recipients** in the Features pane and then select **Mailboxes**.

2. Click the More button (●●●) and then select **Connect A Mailbox**. The Connect A Mailbox dialog box shows all mailboxes marked for deletion but currently retained regardless of whether those mailboxes were disabled, deleted, or soft deleted.

> **IMPORTANT**   When you move mailboxes between databases, mailboxes in the original (source) database are soft deleted. This means they are disconnected, marked as soft deleted, but retained in the original database until the deleted mailbox retention period expires. In Exchange Management Shell, you can use a DisconnectReason of "SoftDeleted" to find soft-deleted mailboxes.

3. In the Connect A Mailbox dialog box, shown in Figure 7-4, use the selection list provided to select the server where you want to look for disconnected mailboxes.

4. Click the mailbox to restore it and then click Connect (▣⤳).

5. Connect the mailbox to the user account to which it was connected previously or to a different user account. If the original user account is available, select the Yes option to reconnect the mailbox to the original user account. If the original user isn't available or you want to associate the mailbox with a different user, select the No option and follow the prompts.

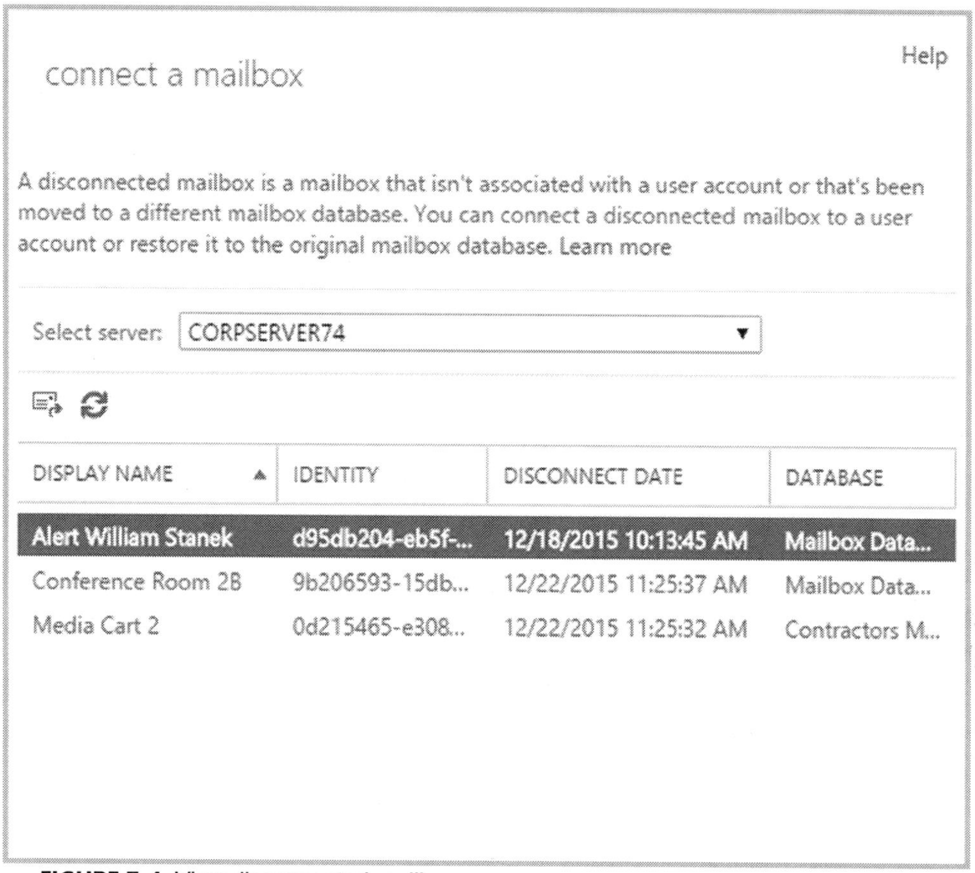

FIGURE 7-4 View disconnected mailboxes.

You can find all disabled mailboxes in an on-premises Exchange organization by entering the following command:

```
Get-MailboxDatabase | Get-MailboxStatistics | Where { $_.DisconnectReason
-eq "Disabled" } | ft DisplayName,Database,DisconnectDate,DisconnectReason
```

Or you can find disabled mailboxes in a particular database using the following command:

```
Get-MailboxStatistics -Database DatabaseName | Where { $_.DisconnectReason
-eq "Disabled" } | ft DisplayName,Database,DisconnectDate,DisconnectReason
```

> **NOTE** You can't use this technique with Exchange Online. See "Restoring online users and mailboxes" later in this chapter.

If you find that you need a mail-enabled or mailbox user account that was deleted, you may be able to restore the deleted account. For on-premises Exchange, you can restore user accounts from Active Directory. When Active Directory Recycle Bin is enabled, you can recover deleted objects using Active Directory Administrative Center (as long as the deleted object and recycled object lifetimes have not expired).

In Active Directory Administrative Center, select the Deleted Object container to see the available deleted objects. When you select a deleted user by clicking it, you can use the Restore option to restore the user to its original container. For example, if the user account was deleted from the Users container, the user account is restored to this container. Once the user account is restored, you can restore the Exchange settings and data. You can use Connect-Mailbox to connect the user account to its disconnected mailbox.

When you connect a disconnected mailbox using Connect-Mailbox, you associate the mailbox with a user account that isn't mail-enabled, which means the user account cannot have an existing mailbox associated with it. Connect-Mailbox has a slightly different syntax for standard mailboxes, shared mailboxes, and linked mailboxes. For standard mailbox users, the basic syntax for Connect-Mailbox is:

```
Connect-Mailbox -Identity ExchangeId -Database DatabaseName -User ADUserId
-Alias ExchangeAlias
```

where ExchangeID identifies the disconnected mailbox in the Exchange organization, DatabaseName is the name of the database where the disconnected mailbox resides, ADUserID identifies the Active Directory user account to reconnect the mailbox to, and ExchangeAlias sets the desired Exchange Alias. Consider the following example:

```
Connect-Mailbox -Identity "Thomas Axen" -Database "Sales Database"
-User "Thomas Axen" -Alias ThomasA
```

This example reconnects the Exchange mailbox for Thomas Axen with the related user account in Active Directory and sets the Exchange alias as ThomasA. The alias is combined with the user logon domain to set the User Principal Name (referred to in the UI as the User Logon Name). The User Principal Name must be unique within the organization. If another user account has the same User Principal Name, you'll see a warning about a user name conflict. You will need to resolve this conflict before you can connect the mailbox.

When you disable or remove an archive mailbox from a mailbox, the archive mailbox is disconnected from the source mailbox, marked for deletion, and retained according to the retention settings. To connect a disabled archive mailbox to the original source mailbox, you use the Connect-Mailbox cmdlet with the -Archive parameter.

Although Connect-Mailbox has restrictions, you can connect a disconnected mailbox to a user account that already has a mailbox. When you restore the mailbox, its contents are copied into the target user's existing mailbox while the deleted mailbox itself is retained in the mailbox database until the retention period expires (or it is purged by an administrator).

You use New-MailboxRestoreRequest to restore mailboxes to accounts with existing mailboxes. The basic syntax is:

```
New-MailboxRestoreRequest -SourceMailbox MailboxID -SourceDatabase
DatabaseName -TargetMailbox ExchangeID
```

where MailboxID is the display name or GUID of the disconnected mailbox to restore, DatabaseName is the name of the database where the disconnected mailbox resides, and ExchangeID is an Exchange alias or name for the account where the mailbox should be added. Consider the following example:

```
New-MailboxRestoreRequest -SourceMailbox "Karen Berg" -SourceDatabase
"Marketing Database" -TargetMailbox "Dag Rovik"
```

You can restore archive mailboxes to users with existing accounts as well. Use the -TargetIsArchive parameter as shown in this example:

```
New-MailboxRestoreRequest -SourceMailbox "In-Place Archive - Karen Berg"
-SourceDatabase "Marketing Database" -TargetMailbox "Dag Rovik"
-TargetIsArchive
```

Restoring Online Users and Mailboxes

If you remove the Exchange Online license for an online user account, the user's account is marked as an unlicensed account. Exchange Online deletes mailboxes from unlicensed accounts automatically after the grace period expires. By default, this grace period is 30 days. If you delete a user account in the online organization, the user account is marked as deleted but retained until the retention period expires, which is 30 days by default.

In Office 365 Admin Center, you can find deleted users and restore them by completing these steps:

1. Select Users & Groups, Deleted Users to view deleted users, as shown in Figure 7-5. If the online organization has available licenses, you can restore the deleted users.

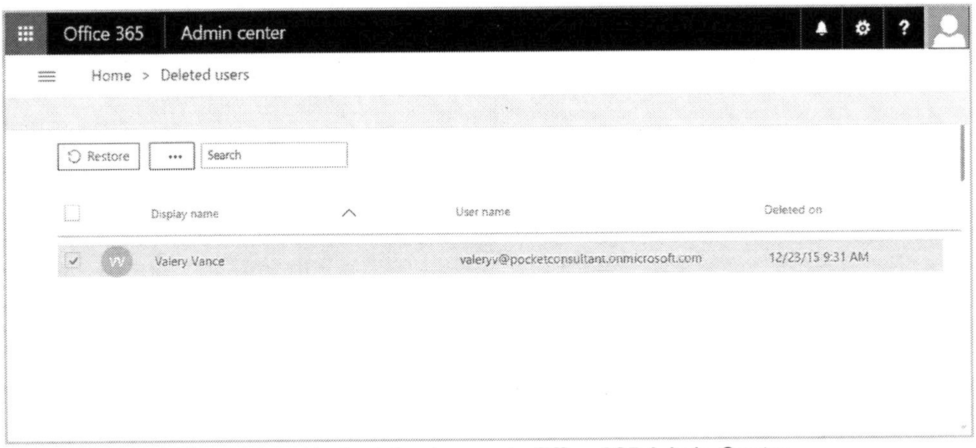

FIGURE 7-5 View deleted but retained users in Office 365 Admin Center.

2. Select the accounts to restore and then click **Restore**. As shown in Figure 7-6, you'll then be prompted to confirm the action by clicking Restore again.

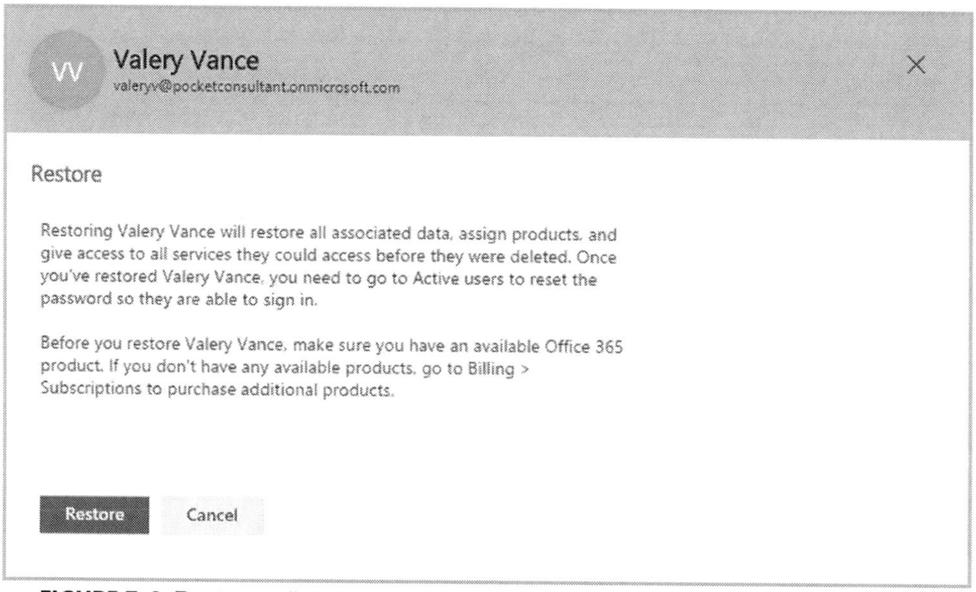

FIGURE 7-6 Resture online users in Office 365 Admin Center.

3. Each user account successfully restored will be confirmed. Click **Close**.

4. After you restore accounts, you'll need to select Users & Groups, Active Users and then reset the passwords to allow login.

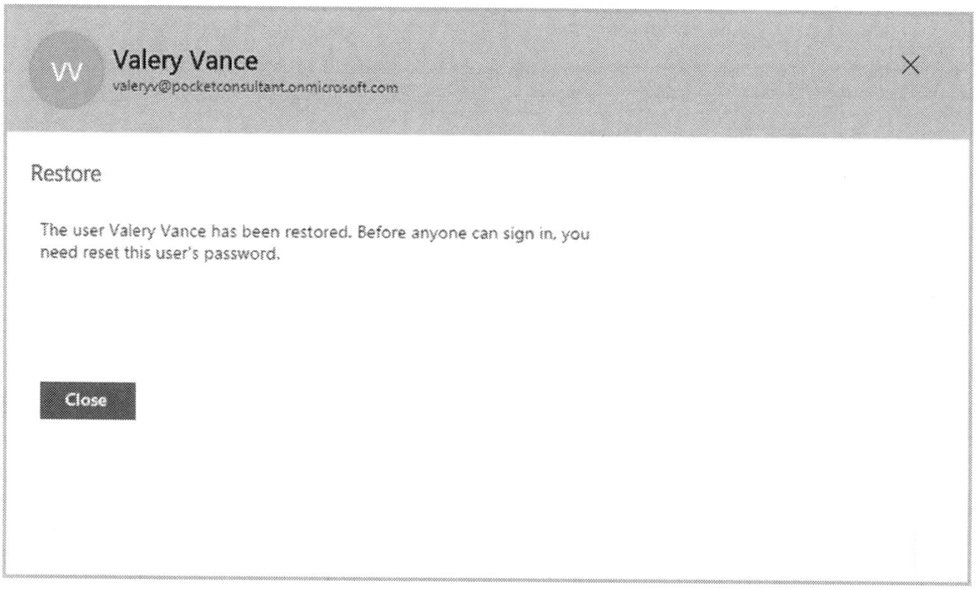

NOTE Keep in mind that account restoration will fail if there are any naming or other conflicts. The User Principal Name must be unique within the organization. If another user account has the same the User Principal Name, you'll see a warning about a user name conflict. You'll then be able to edit the user name or replace the active user with the deleted user.

When you connect to Microsoft Online Services as discussed in Chapter 2 "Working with Exchange Online," you can get information about accounts in Windows PowerShell. Enter **Get-MsolUser** to get a list of active user accounts. As shown in the following example the default output shows the User Principal Name, display name, and licensing status of user accounts:

```
UserPrincipalName                            DisplayName         isLicensed
-----------------                            -----------         ----------
cart3@imaginedlands.onmicrosoft.com          Media Cart 3        False
wrstanek@imaginedlands.onmicrosoft.com       William Stanek      True
room3@imaginedlands.onmicrosoft.com          Conference Room 3   False
georges@imaginedlands.onmicrosoft.com        George Schaller     False
room42@imaginedlands.onmicrosoft.com         Conference Room 42  False
```

The output shows the user accounts associated with all types of users, including the user accounts associated with room and equipment mailboxes. Although room and equipment mailboxes don't need to be licensed, standard user accounts require licenses.

You can get a list of users whose accounts have been marked for deletion by entering **Get-MsolUser –ReturnDeletedUsers**. Accounts marked for deletion are listed by User Principal Name, display name, and licensing status. To restore a deleted account, use Restore-MsolUser. The basic syntax for this command is:

```
Restore-MsolUser -UserPrincipalName OnlineId
```

where OnlineId is the User Principal Name of the account to restore:

```
Restore-MsolUser -UserPrincipalName valv@imaginedlands.onmicrosoft.com
```

The account restore will fail if there are any naming or other conflicts. To resolve a name conflict, use the -NewUserPrincipalName parameter to set a new User Principal Name for the user.

Repairing Mailboxes

You can use New-MailboxRepairRequest to detect and repair mailbox corruption. By default, the command attempts to repair all types of mailbox corruption issues, including issues associated with search folders, aggregate counts, provisioned folders, and folder views.

The basic syntax for New-MailboxRepairRequest is:

```
New-MailboxRepairRequest -Mailbox ExchangeID
```

where ExchangeID identifies the mailbox to repair, such as:

```
New-MailboxRepairRequest -Mailbox TonyS
```

```
New-MailboxRepairRequest -Mailbox tonys@imaginedlands.com
```

```
New-MailboxRepairRequest -Mailbox "Tony Smith"
```

During the repair process, the mailbox cannot be accessed. Once started, the detect and repair process cannot be stopped, unless you dismount the associated database. Add the -Archive parameter to repair the archive mailbox associated with an Exchange identifier rather than the primary mailbox.

You also can use New-MailboxRepairRequest to examine and repair all mailboxes in a database. As the repair process works its way through all the mailboxes in the database, only the mailbox being repaired is locked and inaccessible. All other mailboxes in the database remain accessible to users.

Moving Mailboxes

Exchange Server 2016 supports online mailbox moves. To complete an upgrade, balance the server load, manage drive space, or relocate mailboxes, you can move mailboxes from one server or database to another server or database. The process you use to move mailboxes depends on where the mailbox or mail data is stored:

* When you want to work with mail data stored on a user's computer, you can use the import or export process to move mail data.
* When a user's mailbox is stored on an on-premises Exchange server and you want to move the mailbox to a database on the same server or another server in the same forest, you can use an online mailbox move or batch migration to move the mailbox.

- When a user's mailbox is stored on an on-premises Exchange server in one Active Directory forest and you want to move the mailbox to an on-premises Exchange server in another forest, you can use a cross-forest move to move the mailbox.
- When a user's mailbox is stored on-premises and you want to move the mailbox to Exchange Online or vice versa, you can use a remote move to move the mailbox.

Importing and Exporting Mail Data

When Microsoft Outlook uses Exchange Server, a user's mail data can be delivered in one of two ways:

- Server mailbox with local copies
- Personal folders

With server mailboxes, messages are delivered to mailboxes on the Exchange server and users can view or receive new mail only when they are connected to Exchange. A local copy of the user's mail data is stored in an .ost file on her computer.

Personal folders are alternatives to server mailboxes. Personal folders are stored in a .pst file on the user's computer. With personal folders, you can specify that mail should be delivered to the user's inbox and stored on the server or that mail should be delivered only to the user's inbox. Users have personal folders when Outlook is configured to use Internet email or other email servers. Users might also have personal folders if the auto-archive feature is used to archive messages.

When you are working with on-premises Exchange, you can:

- Import mail data from .pst files using mailbox import request cmdlets
- Export mail data to .pst files using mailbox export request cmdlets

> **IMPORTANT** You must have the Mailbox Import Export role to be able to import or export mailbox data. As this role isn't assigned to any role group, you must be explicitly assigned this role.

The import and export processes are asynchronous. They are queued and processed independently of Exchange Management Shell. The related commands are shown in the following list:

IMPORT MAILBOX DATA	EXPORT MAILBOX DATA
Get-MailboxImportRequest	Get-MailboxExportRequest
New-MailboxImportRequest	New-MailboxExportRequest
Set-MailboxImportRequest	Set-MailboxExportRequest
Suspend-MailboxImportRequest	Suspend-MailboxExportRequest
Resume-MailboxImportRequest	Resume-MailboxExportRequest
Remove-MailboxImportRequest	Remove-MailboxExportRequest
Get-MailboxImportRequestStatistics	Get-MailboxExportRequestStatistics

Mailbox imports and exports are initiated with Mailbox Import and Mailbox Export requests respectively. These requests are sent to the Microsoft Exchange Mailbox Replication Service (MRS) running on a Mailbox server in the source forest. The MRS queues the request for processing, handling all requests on a first-in, first-out basis. When a request is at the top of the queue, the replication service begins importing or exporting mail data.

Before you can import or export data, you need to create a shared network folder that is accessible to your Exchange servers, and the Exchange Trusted Subsystem group must have read/write access to this share.

You use New-MailboxImportRequest to import data from a .pst file to a mailbox or personal archive. Keep in mind you can't import data to a user account that doesn't have a mailbox and that the destination mailbox must be already available. The import process will not create a mailbox. By default, all mail folders are imported. However, you can specifically include or exclude folders. You also can import mail data to only the user's personal archive.

You use New-MailboxExportRequest to export mailbox data to a .pst file. The command allows you to export one or more mailboxes, with each mailbox export handling a separate request. When exporting mail data, you can specify folders to include or exclude and export mail data from the user's archive. You also can filter the messages so only messages that match your content filter are exported.

Performing On-Premises Mailboxes Moves and Migrations

The destination database for an on-premises mailbox move can be on the same server, on a different server, in a different domain, or in a different Active Directory site. Exchange Server 2016 performs move operations as a series of steps that allows a mailbox to remain available to a user while the move operation is being completed. When the move is completed, the user begins accessing the mailbox in the new location. Because users can continue to access their email account during the move, you can perform online moves at any time.

The online move process hasn't changed substantially since it was introduced with Exchange Server 2010:

* On-premises mailbox moves are initiated with a Move Mailbox request that is sent to the Microsoft Exchange MRS running on a Mailbox server in the source forest. The MRS queues the request for processing, handling all requests on a first-in, first-out basis. When a request is at the top of the queue, the replication service begins replicating mailbox data to the destination database.
* When the replication service finishes its initial replication of a mailbox, it marks the mailbox as Ready To Complete and periodically performs data synchronization between the source and destination database to ensure that the contents of a mailbox are up to date. After a mailbox has been moved, you can complete the move request and finalize the move.

When you are working with PowerShell, you initiate a move using New-MoveRequest and then start the actual move using Start-MoveRequest. Although the online move process allows you to move multiple mailboxes, with each move handled as a separate request, the process isn't ideal for batch moves of multiple mailboxes, and this is where mailbox migrations come in. With mailbox migration, you can move multiple mailboxes in an Exchange on-premises organization, migrate on-premises mailboxes to Exchange Online, or migrate Exchange Online mailboxes back to an on-premises Exchange organization.

> **NOTE**   You can use the batch migration process to move a single or multiple mailboxes within on-premises Exchange. With a single mailbox, the batch migration is handled as a local move.

From a high level, the standard batch migration process is similar to a mailbox move:

- Batch mailbox migration is initiated with a Migration Batch request that is sent to the Microsoft Exchange MRS running on a Mailbox server in the source forest. The MRS queues the request for processing, handling all requests on a first-in, first-out basis. When a request is at the top of the queue, the replication service begins replicating mailbox data to the destination database.
- When the replication service finishes its initial replication of a mailbox, it marks the mailbox as Ready To Complete and periodically performs data synchronization between the source and destination database to ensure that the contents of a mailbox are up to date. After a mailbox has been migrated, you can complete the migration request and finalize the migration.

Where things get complicated are on cross-forest batch migrations and remote migrations. With a cross-forest migration, you perform a batch mailbox migration from an Exchange server in one Active Directory forest to an Exchange server in another Active Directory forest. With a remote migration, you perform a batch mailbox migration from on-premises Exchange to Exchange Online or vice versa.

Cross-forest and remote migrations use migration endpoints. You create a migration endpoint in the target environment. The endpoint identifies the source environment where the mailboxes are currently located. You then initiate the migration in the target environment. With a cross-forest migration, this means you:

1. Create a migration endpoint in the target domain.
2. Initiate the migration in the target domain.

With a migration from on-premises Exchange to Exchange Online, this means you:

1. Create a migration endpoint in Exchange Online.
2. Initiate the migration from Exchange Online.

With a migration from Exchange Online to on-premises Exchange, this means you:

1. Create a migration endpoint in on-premises Exchange.
2. Initiate the migration from on-premises Exchange.

A complete cross-forest or remote migration has four parts. You create a migration endpoint using New-MigrationEndpoint and then create the migration batch using New-MigrationBatch. You start the migration using Start-MigrationBatch. When the migration has finished initial synchronization, you can finalize the migration using Complete-MigrationBatch.

In Exchange Admin Center, you can initiate move and migration requests using the options on the Migration page. To access this page, select **Recipients** in the Features pane and then select **Migration** (see Figure 7-7). Although the PowerShell commands for moves and migrations give you complete control over the process, you'll find that Exchange Admin Center greatly simplifies the process:

- For local moves, you log on to a Mailbox server in the Active Directory forest where the source mailboxes are located. On the Migration page, select New (✚ ˅) and then select **Move To A Different Database**. Follow the prompts in the New Local Mailbox Move dialog box to perform the move.
- For remote migrations, you can use the options in Exchange Admin Center for Exchange Online to initiate the process, whether migrating from or to Exchange Online. On the Migration page, select **More** (•••), select **Migration Endpoints**, and then follow the prompts to create the required migration endpoint. Next, select New and then select either **Migrate To Exchange Online** or **Migrate From Exchange Online** as appropriate. Follow the prompts in the New Migration Batch dialog box to perform the migration.
- For cross-forest moves, you log on to a Mailbox server in the target Active Directory forest. On the Migration page, select **More** (•••), select **Migration Endpoints**, and then follow the prompts to create the required migration endpoint. Next, select **New** (✚ ˅) and then select **Move To This Forest**. Follow the prompts in the New Cross-Forest Mailbox Move dialog box to perform the move.

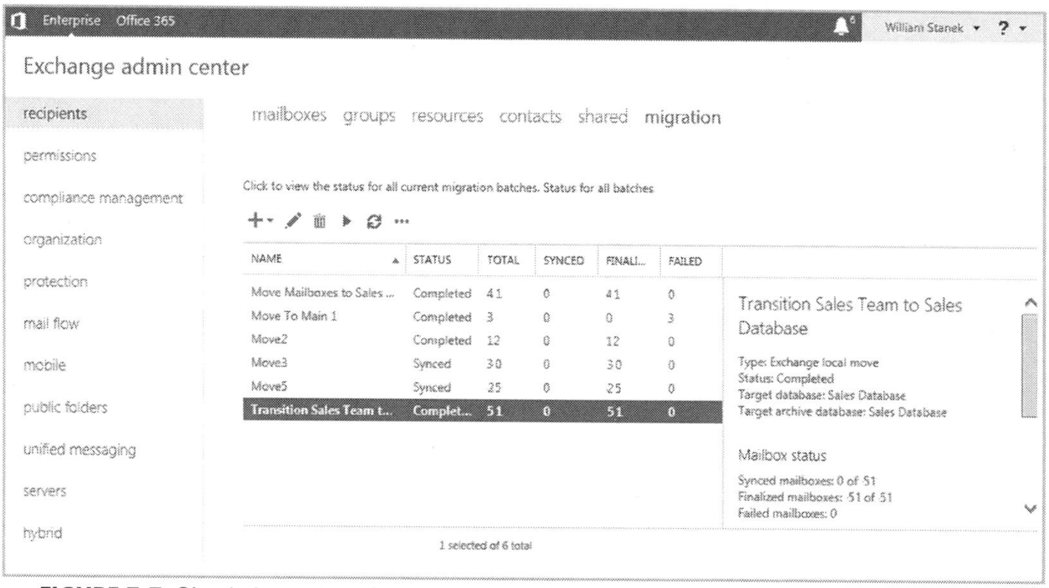

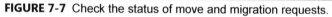

FIGURE 7-7 Check the status of move and migration requests.

On the Migration page, you also can track the status of move and migration requests. If a move or migration request fails, you can get more information about the failure by double-clicking the request and then clicking View to the right of the Failed Message entry.

When you move mailboxes from one server to another, to a different organization, or even to a different database on the same server, keep in mind that the Exchange policies of the new mailbox database might be different from the old one. Because of this, consider the following issues before you move mailboxes to a new server or database:

- **General policy** Changes to watch out for include the storage limits, the deleted item retention, and the default offline address book settings. The risk is that the users whose mailboxes you move could lose or gain access to public folders. They might have a different offline address book, which might have different entries. This address book will also have to be downloaded in its entirety the first time the user's mail client connects to Exchange after the move.
- **Database policy** Changes to watch out for pertain to the maintenance interval and automatic mounting. If Exchange performs maintenance when these users are accessing their mail, they might have slower response times. If the mailbox database is configured so that it isn't mounted at startup, restarting the Exchange services could result in the users not being able to access their mailboxes.
- **Limits** Changes to watch out for pertain to storage limits and deletion settings. Users might be prohibited from sending and receiving mail if their mailbox

exceeds the storage limits of the new mailbox database. Users might notice that deleted items stay in their Deleted Items folder longer or are deleted sooner than expected if the Keep Deleted Items setting is different.

Performing On-Premises Mailbox Moves

With online moves and batch migrations, you can move mailboxes between databases on the same server. You also can move mailboxes from a database on one server to a database on another server regardless of whether the servers are in a different Active Directory site or in another Active Directory forest.

Normally, when you perform online migrations, the move process looks like this:

1. You create a batch migration request for the mailboxes that you want to move using either Exchange Admin Center or Exchange Management Shell.

2. The request is sent to the Mailbox Replication Service running on a Mailbox server in the current Active Directory site. This server acts as the Mailbox Replication Service proxy.

3. MRS adds the mailboxes to the Request queue and assigns the status Created to the request. This indicates the move has been requested but not started.

4. When a request is at the top of the queue, MRS begins replicating the related mailboxes to the destination database and assigns the Syncing status to the request.

5. When MRS finishes its initial replication of the mailboxes, the service assigns the Synced status to the request.

6. The request remains in the Synced state until you or another administrator specifies that you want to complete the request. MRS performs a final data synchronization and then marks the request as Completed.

7. When the request is completed, the mailboxes are available in the new location. Because users can continue to access their email accounts during the move, you can perform online moves and migrations at any time.

One way to perform online mailbox moves and migrations is by using Exchange Management Shell. The commands for performing online mailbox moves include the following:

▪ **Get-MoveRequest** Displays the detailed status of an ongoing mailbox move that was initiated using the New-MoveRequest cmdlet.

- **New-MoveRequest**   Starts a mailbox move. You also can verify readiness to move by using the -WhatIf parameter. Use the -Priority parameter to set the relative priority of the request.
- **Resume-MoveRequest**   Resumes a move request that has been suspended or failed.
- **Set-MoveRequest**   Changes a move request after it has been started.
- **Suspend-MoveRequest**   Suspends a move request that has been started but has not yet been completed.
- **Remove-MoveRequest**   Cancels a mailbox move initiated using the New-MoveRequest cmdlet. You can use the Remove-MoveRequest command any time after initiating the move but only if the move request is not yet complete.

The commands for performing batch mailbox migrations include the following:

- **Get-MigrationBatch**   Displays the detailed status of an ongoing mailbox migration that was initiated using the New-MigrationBatch cmdlet.
- **Set-MigrationBatch**   Changes a migration request after it has been started.
- **New-MigrationBatch**   Submits a new mailbox migration request. You also can verify readiness to migrate by using the -WhatIf parameter. Use the -AutoStart parameter to allow immediate processing of the request. Use the -AutoComplete parameter to automatically finalize the batch when the initial synchronization is complete.
- **Start-MigrationBatch**   Submits a migration request for processing; required when the -AutoStart parameter is not used with New-MigrationBatch.
- **Stop-MigrationBatch**   Stops a migration request that has been started but has not yet been completed.
- **Complete-MigrationBatch**   Finalizes a migration request that has been synchronized; required when the -AutoComplete parameter is not used with New-MigrationBatch.
- **Remove-MigrationBatch**   Deletes a mailbox migration request that either isn't running or has been completed. If you created a new request but haven't submitted it, you can use this command to remove the request so that the mailboxes specified in the request aren't migrated. If the request is completed, the mailboxes are already migrated and you can use this command to remove the request from the queue.
- **Get-MigrationUser**   Retrieves information about the ongoing migration of a particular mailbox.
- **Remove-MigrationUser**   Allows you to remove a mailbox from a migration request.
- **Test-MigrationServerAvailability**   Ensures the target server for a cross-premises move is available and verifies the connection settings.

Other batch migration commands include: Get-MigrationStatistics, Get-MigrationUserStatistics, Get-MigrationConfig, Set-MigrationConfig, Get-MigrationEndpoint, Set-MigrationEndpoint, New-MigrationEndpoint, and Remove-MigrationEndpoint.

Moving Mailboxes Within a Single Forest

You perform online mailbox moves within a single forest by using Exchange Management Shell. To verify move readiness, use New-MoveRequest with the -WhatIf parameter for each mailbox you plan to move. The following examples show two different ways you can verify whether Morgan Skinner's mailbox can be moved:

```
New-MoveRequest -Identity 'morgans'
-TargetDatabase "Engineering Primary" -WhatIf
```

```
'imaginedlands.com/users/Morgan Skinner' | New-MoveRequest
-TargetDatabase 'Engineering Primary' -WhatIf
```

To initiate an online move, you use New-MoveRequest for each mailbox you want to move. The following examples show two different ways you can move Morgan Skinner's mailbox:

```
New-MoveRequest -Identity 'morgans' -Remote -RemoteHostName
'mailserver62.imaginedlands.com' -mrsserver
'mailserver19.imaginedlands.com' -TargetDatabase "Engineering Primary"
```

```
'imaginedlands.com/users/Morgan Skinner' | New-MoveRequest -Remote
-RemoteHostName 'mailserver62.imaginedlands.com' -mrsserver
'mailserver19.imaginedlands.com' -TargetDatabase 'Engineering Primary'
```

After you initiate a move, you can check the status of the online move using Get-MoveRequest. As shown in the following example, the key parameter to provide is the identity of the mailbox you want to check:

```
Get-MoveRequest -Identity 'morgans'
```

You can use Suspend-MoveRequest to suspend a move request that has not yet completed, and Resume-MoveRequest to resume a suspended move request. Resuming a suspended request allows it to complete.

You can cancel a move at any time prior to running the move request being completed by Exchange. To do this, run Remove-MoveRequest and specify the identity of the mailbox that shouldn't be moved. An example follows:

```
Remove-MoveRequest -Identity 'morgans'
```

When your source and destination Mailbox servers are running Exchange Server 2016 and are in the same forest, you can move mailboxes by completing these steps:

1. Log on to Exchange Admin Center via a Mailbox server in the domain or forest you want to work with. In Exchange Admin Center, select Recipients in the Features pane and then select Migration.

2. On the Migration page, you select New (✚ ▾) and then select **Move To A Different Database**. This starts the New Local Mailbox Move Wizard.

3. On the Select The Users page, shown in Figure 7-8, you can select the mailboxes to migrate by doing one of the following:

- Select the mailboxes that you want to migrate using the graphic interface. Click Add (✚). Use the Select Mailbox dialog box to select the mailboxes to move and then click Add. Next, click OK.

  You can select and move multiple mailboxes at the same time. To select multiple mailboxes individually, hold down the Ctrl key, and then click each mailbox that you want to select. To select a sequence of mailboxes, select the first mailbox, hold down the Shift key, and then click the last user mailbox.

- Select the mailboxes that you want to migrate using a file containing a list of comma-separated Exchange identifiers. Click **Specify The Users With A CSV File** and then click **Choose File**. Use the Open dialog box to select the .csv file and then click **OK**.

  The file you use should be named with the .CSV extension. The first line of the file should identify the column of data to import as: EmailAddress and each successive line in the file should be the email address of a mailbox to migrate, as shown in this example:

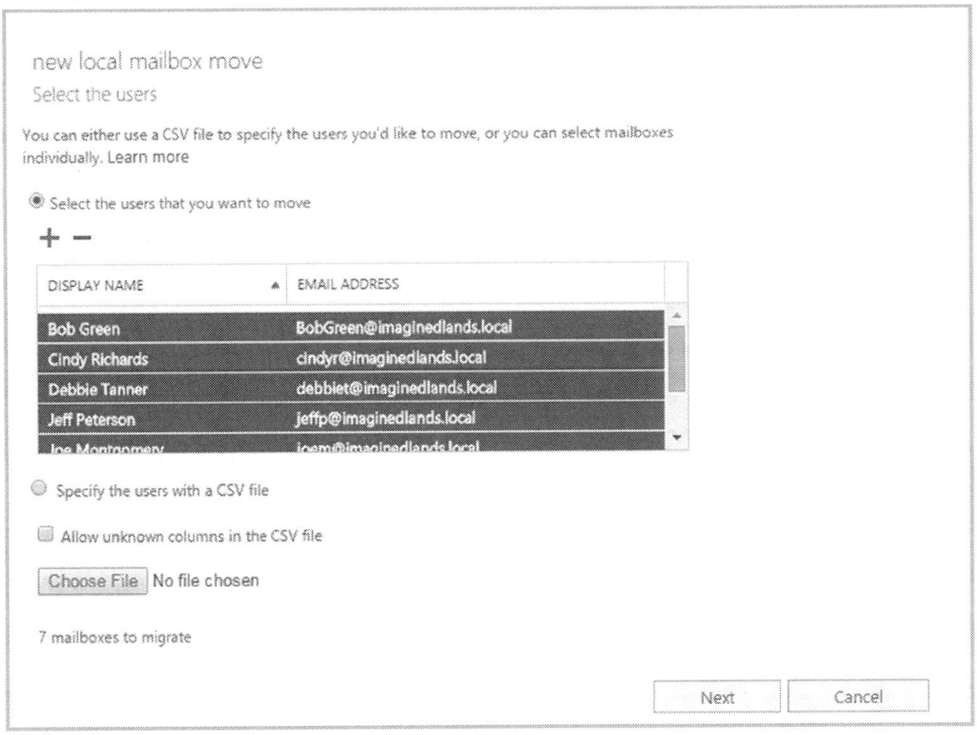

FIGURE 7-8 Select the mailboxes to migrate.

EmailAddress

annal@imaginedlands.com

deanh@imaginedlands.com

indron@imaginedlands.com

paulab@imaginedlands.com

williams@imaginedlands.com

4. Click **Next**. On the Move Configuration page, shown in Figure 7-9, enter a descriptive name for the migration batch.

5. Use the Archive options to specify whether you want to move only the primary mailbox for the selected recipients, only the archive mailbox for the selected recipients, or both.

6. If you are moving the primary mailboxes for recipients, click **Browse** to the right of the Target Database text box. In the Select Mailbox Database dialog box, choose the mailbox database to which the mailbox should be moved. Mailbox databases are listed by name as well as by associated server and Exchange version.

7. If you are moving the archive mailboxes for recipients, click **Browse** to the right of the Target Archive Database text box. In the Select Mailbox Database dialog box, choose the mailbox database to which the mailbox should be moved. Mailbox databases are listed by name as well as by associated server and Exchange version.

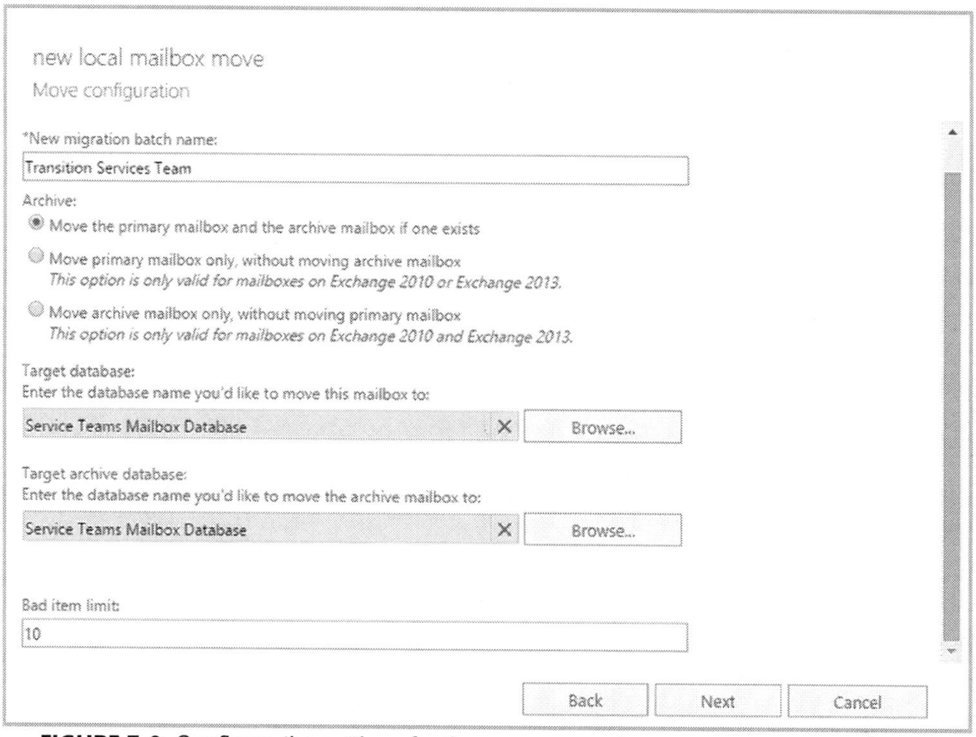

FIGURE 7-9 Configure the settings for the move request.

8. If corrupted messages are found in a mailbox that you are migrating, the messages are skipped automatically and not migrated as part of the mailbox. By default, the wizard skips a limited number of bad items in each mailbox and stops the migration if this value is exceeded. To specify the maximum number of bad items that can be skipped in each mailbox, enter a new value in the Bad Item Limit text box or enter 0 to allow an unlimited number of bad items to be skipped.

9. Click **Next**. On the Start The Batch page, your current login is selected as the recipient for the batch report. This report will contain details about errors encountered during the migration. To add or change recipients for this report, click **Browse**. Then use the Select Members dialog box to select the recipients that should receive the report and then click **OK**. You must select at least one recipient.

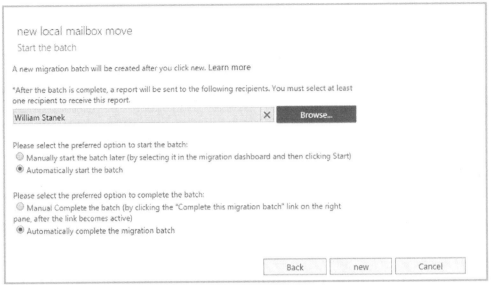

new local mailbox move

Start the batch

A new migration batch will be created after you click new. Learn more

*After the batch is complete, a report will be sent to the following recipients. You must select at least one recipient to receive this report.

| William Stanek | × | Browse... |

Please select the preferred option to start the batch:
- ○ Manually start the batch later (by selecting it in the migration dashboard and then clicking Start)
- ● Automatically start the batch

Please select the preferred option to complete the batch:
- ○ Manual Complete the batch (by clicking the "Complete this migration batch" link on the right pane, after the link becomes active)
- ● Automatically complete the migration batch

Back   new   Cancel

10. By default, Exchange Server creates and starts the batch migration request. When the request is completed, Exchange Server will also automatically finalize it. If you want to manually start the batch, select the Manual Start option. If you want to manually finalize the batch, select the Manual Complete option.

11. Click **New**. Migrating mailboxes can take several hours, depending on the size of the mailboxes you are moving. You can check the status of move requests by refreshing the view on the Migration page. While the request is in the Synced state, you can cancel the request by selecting it and then clicking Delete. You cannot cancel a request that has started syncing.

Moving Mailboxes Between Forests

You can perform online mailbox moves between different Exchange forests using Exchange Admin Center or Exchange Management Shell. When you are moving mailboxes between forests, verify that mailboxes are ready to be moved before you submit a move request. To verify readiness, the Microsoft Exchange Mailbox Replication service proxy in the source forest checks the status of each mailbox you are moving and also ensures you have the permissions required to move the mailboxes from the source forest to the target forest. If a user has an archive mailbox or subscriptions, you will likely need to remove the archive mailbox, the subscriptions, or both before you are able to move the mailbox.

You can verify move readiness in Exchange Management Shell by using New-MoveRequest with the -WhatIf parameter for each mailbox you plan to move. The following examples show two different ways you can verify whether Rob Carson's mailbox can be moved:

```
New-MoveRequest -Identity 'robc' -Remote
-RemoteHost 'mailserver62.imaginedlands.com'-mrsserver
'mailserver19.imaginedlands.com'
-TargetDatabase "Engineering Primary" -WhatIf


'imaginedlands.com/users/Rob Carson' | New-MoveRequest -Remote
-RemoteHost 'mailserver62.imaginedlands.com' -mrsserver
'mailserver19.imaginedlands.com'
-TargetDatabase 'Engineering Primary' -WhatIf
```

You can perform online mailbox moves between forests by following these steps:

1. Log on to Exchange Admin Center via a Mailbox server in the target forest. In Exchange Admin Center, select **Recipients** in the Features pane and then select **Migration**.

2. On the Migration page, select New ( ) and then select **Move To This Forest**. This starts the New Cross-Forest Mailbox Move Wizard.

3. On the Select The Users page, shown in Figure 7-10, you can select the mailboxes to migrate by doing one of the following:

- Select the mailboxes that you want to migrate using the graphic interface. Click Add ( ). Use the Select Mailbox dialog box to select the mailboxes to move and then click Add. Next, click OK.

    You can select and move multiple mailboxes at the same time. To select multiple mailboxes individually, hold down the Ctrl key, and then click each mailbox that you want to select. To select a sequence of mailboxes, select the first mailbox, hold down the Shift key, and then click the last user mailbox.

- Select the mailboxes that you want to migrate using a file containing a list of comma-separated Exchange identifiers. Click **Specify The Users With A CSV File** and then click **Choose File**. Use the Open dialog box to select the .csv file and then click **OK**.

    The file you use should be named with the .CSV extension. The first line of the file should identify the column of data to import as: EmailAddress and each successive line in the file should be the email address of a mailbox to migrate, as shown in this example:

```
EmailAddress
annal@imaginedlands.com
deanh@imaginedlands.com
indron@imaginedlands.com
paulab@imaginedlands.com
williams@imaginedlands.com
```

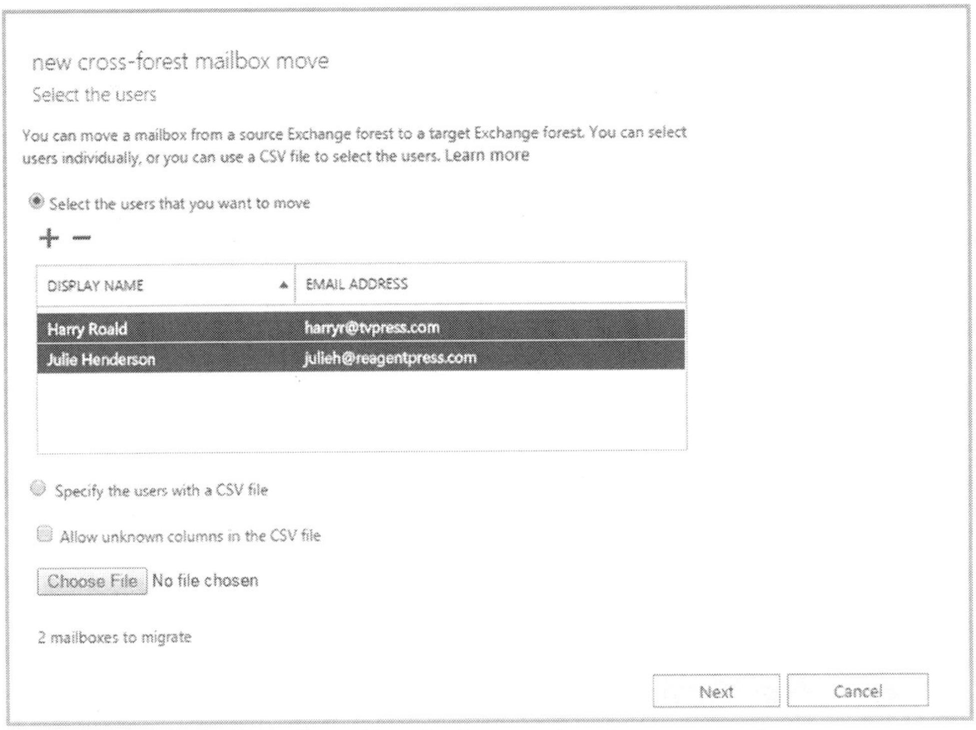

FIGURE 7-10 Configure the settings for the cross-forest move request.

4. Click **Next**. The target forest is the forest to which you are connected. The source forest is the forest where the mailboxes are located currently. In the Source Forest Administrator Name text box, enter the name of a user account that has appropriate administrative privileges in the source forest. Enter the name in Domain\UserName format, such as Imaginedlands\Williams.

```
new cross-forest mailbox move
Enter on-premises account credentials




Source forest administrator name (domain\administrator name):
tvpress\wrstanek

Source forest administrator password:
•••••••••••••••••


                                    Back          Next         Cancel
```

> **NOTE** The administrator must have sufficient permissions to create the required migration endpoint and move accounts. Typically, this means the account must be a member of both the Recipient Management and Server Management groups in the Exchange organization or have Organization Management permissions. However, if you previously migrated accounts between these forests, the migration endpoint created previously may still be available, in which case only Recipient Management permissions are required.

5. In the Source Forest Administrator Password text box, enter the password for the previously specified account.

6. When you click **Next**, Exchange uses the Autodiscover service to try to detect the availability of the migration endpoint as well as to test connectivity. If errors occur, the Confirm The Migration Endpoint page is displayed. At this point, you have several options. You can:

- Enter the fully qualified domain name of a Mailbox server in the source forest that can act as the remote MRS proxy server and then click Next to have Exchange try to connect to a migration endpoint on this server and then test connectivity.
- Click Back to provide alternate credentials and then click Next to retry the connection with those credentials. (Or simply click Back and then click Next to retry the connection with the original credentials.)
- Use the Exchange Remote Connectivity Analyzer (*https://testexchangeconnectivity.com*) to diagnose the connectivity issues. Once the issues are resolved, you can click Next to continue.

7. On the Start The Batch page, your current login is selected as the recipient for the batch report. This report will contain details about errors encountered during the migration. To add or change recipients for this

report, click **Browse**. Then use the Select Members dialog box to select the recipients that should receive the report and then click **OK**. You must select at least one recipient.

8. By default, Exchange Server creates and starts the batch migration request. When the request is completed, Exchange Server will also automatically finalize it. If you want to manually start the batch, select the Manual option. If you want to manually finalize the batch, clear the Automatically Complete check box.

9. Click **New**. Migrating mailboxes can take several hours, depending on the size and number of the mailboxes you are moving. You can check the status of move requests by refreshing the view on the Migration page. While the request is in the Synced state, you can cancel the request by selecting it and then clicking Delete. You cannot cancel a request that has started syncing.

You can perform online moves in Exchange Management Shell by using New-MoveRequest for each mailbox you plan to move. The following examples show two different ways you can move Adam Carpenter's mailbox:

```
New-MoveRequest -Identity 'adamc' -Remote
-RemoteHost 'mailserver62.imaginedlands.com' -mrsserver
'mailserver19.imaginedlands.com'
-TargetDatabase "Engineering Primary"


'imaginedlands.com/users/Adam Carpenter' | New-MoveRequest -Remote
-RemoteHost 'mailserver62.imaginedlands.com' -mrsserver
'mailserver19.imaginedlands.com'
-TargetDatabase 'Engineering Primary'
```

After you initiate a move, you can check the status of the online move by using Get-MoveRequest. As shown in the following example, the key parameters to provide are the identity of the mailbox you want to check and the name of the proxy server:

```
Get-MoveRequest -Identity 'adamc'
-mrsserver 'mailserver19.imaginedlands.com'
```

You can use Suspend-MoveRequest to suspend a move request that is not yet complete, and Resume-MoveRequest to resume a suspended move request. Resuming a suspended request allows it to complete.

At any time prior to running the move request completing, you can cancel the move by running Remove-MoveRequest and specifying the identity of the mailbox that shouldn't be moved, such as:

```
Remove-MoveRequest -Identity 'adamc' -mrsserver
'mailserver19.imaginedlands.com'
```

Managing Delivery Restrictions, Permissions, and Storage Limits

You use mailbox properties to set delivery restrictions, permissions, and storage limits. To change these configuration settings for mailboxes, follow the techniques discussed in this section.

Setting Message Size Restrictions for Contacts

You set message size restrictions for contacts in much the same way that you set size restrictions for users. Follow the steps listed in the next section.

Setting Message Size Restrictions on Delivery to and from Individual Mailboxes

Message size restrictions control the maximum size of messages that can be sent or received in the Exchange organization. With Exchange Online, the maximum size of messages that users can send is 35,840 KB and the maximum size of messages that users can receive is 36,864 KB by default. With on-premises Exchange, you can manage these settings in a variety of ways. Typically, you manage these restrictions for the organization as a whole using the Organization Transport Settings. To manage these settings complete these steps:

1. In Exchange Admin Center, select **Mail Flow** in the Features pane and then select **Receive Connectors**.

2. On the Receive Connectors page, click More (•••) and then select **Organization Transport Settings**.

3. By default, the maximum receive and send message size are both set to 10 MB. Use the options on the Limits page to set new defaults and then click **Save**.

organization transport settings

▸ limits
safety net
delivery

Maximum number of recipients:

500 ▾

Maximum receive message size (MB):

10 ▾

Maximum send message size (MB):

10 ▾

Save   Cancel

You also can manage these restrictions using transport rules that filter messages by size and have specific conditions that apply to the size of messages or attachments, including the Apply This Rule If The Message Size Is Greater Than Or Equal To condition and the Apply This Rule If Any Attachment Is Greater Than Or Equal To condition.

new rule

Name:

Message Size Filter

*Apply this rule if...

The message size is greater than or equal to...   ▾   '40.00 MB'

add condition

*Do the following...

Reject the message with the explanation...   ▾   'Message is too large, at 40 MB or larger.'

add action

Except if...

add exception

Properties of this rule:

☐ Audit this rule with severity level:

Low ▾

Choose a mode for this rule:

◉ Enforce

Save   Cancel

Using the Apply This Rule If The Message Size Is Greater Than Or Equal To condition, you can:

* Set restrictions regarding the size of messages that can be sent or received.
* Specify the action or actions to take if a message meets or exceeds this limit.
* Define exceptions for specific users and groups as well as for messages that have specifically-defined characteristics.

In Exchange Admin Center, you can create and manage transport rules, using the options found under Mail Flow > Rules. Click **New** and then select **Filter Messages By Size**.

The shell commands for working with transport rules include: Disable-TransportRule, Enable-TransportRule, Get-TransportRule, New-TransportRule, Remove-TransportRule, and Set-TransportRule.

When setting these types of organization-wide restrictions, you'll want to consider the global impact. Typically, you'll want to apply organization-wide restrictions only to prevent abuse of the mail system. For example, you may want to configure rules that block sending and receiving of very large files and provide a message that encourages senders to use a site mailbox configured as part of a Microsoft SharePoint site for sharing large documents instead.

Sometimes, you need to set exceptions for specific users. For example, some users might need to be able to send large files as part of their job.

While no delivery restrictions are set by default with on-premises Exchange, specific restrictions are set for online Exchange by default. For sending messages, the maximum message size is 35840 KB. For received messages, the maximum message size is 36864 KB. You can override these defaults by setting different maximum send and receive sizes, up to 153600 KB.

You set individual delivery restrictions by completing the following steps:

1. Open the Properties dialog box for the mailbox-enabled user account by double-clicking the user name in Exchange Admin Center under Recipients > Mailboxes.
2. On the Mailbox Features page, scroll down and then click **View Details** under Message Size Restrictions.

3. As shown in Figure 7-11, you can set the following send and receive restrictions:

    - **Sent Messages > Maximum Message Size**   Sets a limit on the size of messages the user can send. The value is set in kilobytes (KBs). If an outgoing message exceeds the limit, the message isn't sent and the user receives a non-delivery report (NDR).

    - **Received Messages > Maximum Message Size**   Sets a limit on the size of messages the user can receive. The value is set in KBs. If an incoming message exceeds the limit, the message isn't delivered and the sender receives an NDR.

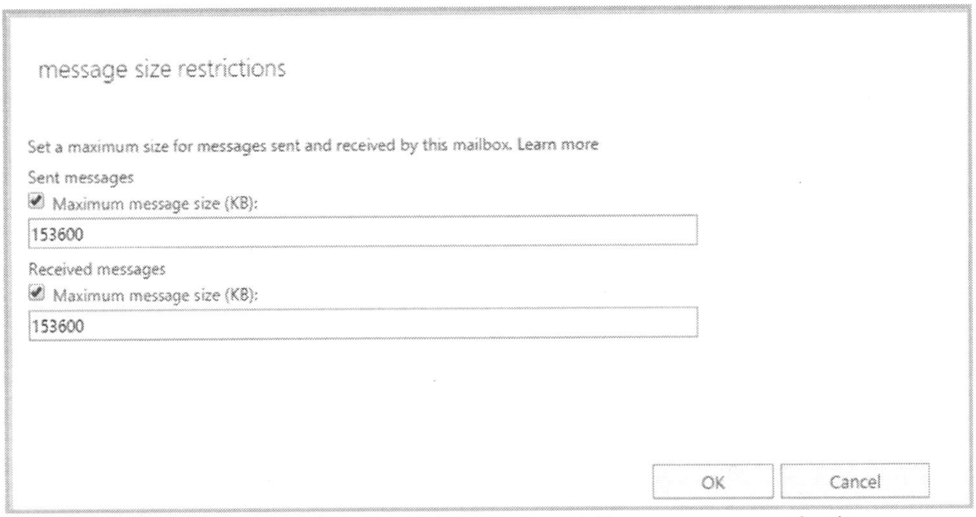

message size restrictions

Set a maximum size for messages sent and received by this mailbox. Learn more

Sent messages
☑ Maximum message size (KB):
153600

Received messages
☑ Maximum message size (KB):
153600

OK   Cancel

FIGURE 7-11 You can apply individual delivery restrictions on a per-user basis.

4. Click **OK** and then click **Save**. The restrictions that you set override the global default settings.

Setting Send and Receive Restrictions for Contacts

You set message send and receive restrictions for contacts in the same way that you set these restrictions for users. Follow the steps listed in the next section.

Setting Message Send and Receive Restrictions on Individual Mailboxes

By default, user mailboxes are configured to accept messages from anyone. To override this behavior, you can do the following:

- Specify that only messages from the listed users, contacts, or groups be accepted.
- Specify that messages from specific users, contacts, or groups be rejected.
- Specify that only messages from authenticated users—meaning users who have logged on to the Exchange system or the domain—be accepted.

With both on-premises Exchange and Exchange Online, you set message send and receive restrictions by completing the following steps:

1. Open the Properties dialog box for the mailbox-enabled user account by double-clicking the user name in Exchange Admin Center under Recipients > Mailboxes.

2. On the Mailbox Features page, scroll down and then click **View Details** under Message Delivery Restrictions. As shown in Figure 7-12, you can then set message acceptance restrictions.

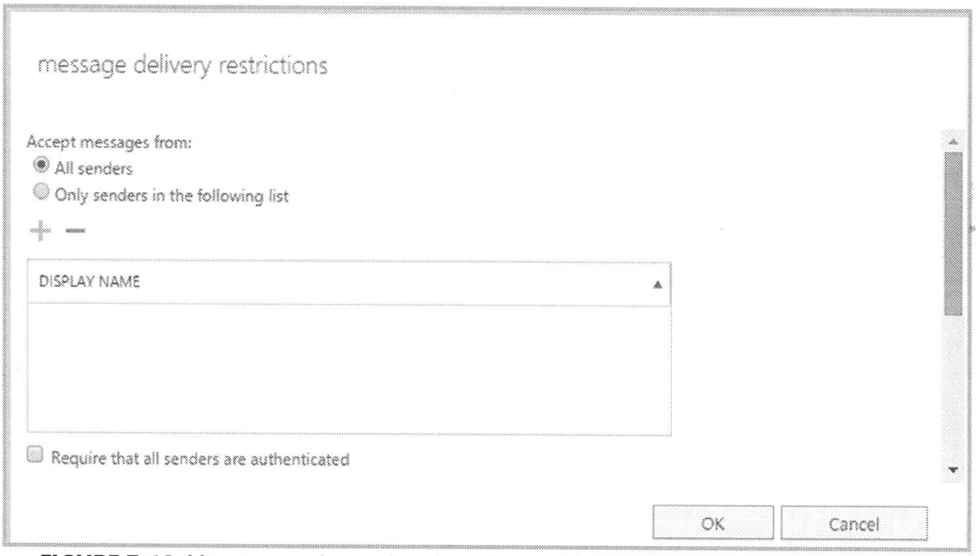

FIGURE 7-12 You can apply send and receive restrictions on messages on a per-user basis.

3. To accept messages from all email addresses except those on the reject list, under Accept Messages From, select **All Senders**.

4. To specify that only messages from the listed users, contacts, or groups be accepted, select the **Only Senders In The Following List** option and then add acceptable recipients by following these steps:

- Click Add (✚)to display the Select Members dialog box.
- Select a recipient, and then click OK. Repeat as necessary.

> **TIP** You can select multiple recipients at the same time. To select multiple recipients individually, hold down the Ctrl key and then click each recipient that you want to select. To select a sequence of recipients, select the first recipient, hold down the Shift key, and then click the last recipient.

5. If you want to ensure that messages are accepted only from authenticated users, select the **Require That All Senders Are Authenticated** check box.

6. To specify that no recipients should be rejected, under Reject Messages From, select **No Senders**.

7. To reject messages from specific recipients, under Reject Messages From, select **Senders In The Following List** and then add unacceptable recipients by following these steps:

- Click Add (✚) to display the Select Members dialog box.
- Select a recipient, and then click OK. Repeat as necessary

8. Click **OK**.

message delivery restrictions

Reject messages from:
- ● No senders
- ○ Senders in the following list

✚ ━

DISPLAY NAME

OK   Cancel

Permitting Others to Access a Mailbox

Occasionally, users need to access someone else's mailbox, and in certain situations, you should allow this. For example, if John is Susan's manager and Susan is going on vacation, John might need access to her mailbox while she's away. Another situation in which someone might need access to another mailbox is when you've set up special-purpose mailboxes, such as a mailbox for Webmaster@domain.com or a mailbox for Info@domain.com.

You can grant permissions for a mailbox in three ways:

- You can grant access to a mailbox and its content. If you want to grant access to a mailbox and its contents but not grant Send As permissions, use the Full Access settings. In Exchange Admin Center, open the Properties dialog box for the mailbox you want to work with and then select Mailbox Delegation. On the

  Mailbox Delegation page, under Full Access, click Add ( ), and then use the Select Full Access dialog box to choose the recipients who should have access to the mailbox. To revoke the authority to access the mailbox, select an existing user name in the Display Name list box and then click Remove.

Cindy Richards

general
mailbox usage
contact information
organization
email address
mailbox features
member of
MailTip
▸ mailbox delegation

Send As
The Send As permission allows a delegate to send email from this mailbox. The message will appear to have been sent by the mailbox owner.

+ –

DISPLAY NAME

Save   Cancel

- You can grant the right to send messages as the mailbox owner. If you want to grant Send As permissions, use the Send As settings. In Exchange Admin Center, open the Properties dialog box for the mailbox you want to work with and then select Mailbox Delegation. On the Mailbox Delegation page, under Send As, click

Add (**+**), and then use the Select Send As dialog box to choose the recipients who should have this permission. To revoke this permission, select an existing user name in the Display Name list box and then click Remove.

Cindy Richards

general

mailbox usage

contact information

organization

email address

mailbox features

member of

MailTip

▸ mailbox delegation

Send on Behalf
The Send on Behalf permission allows the delegate to send email on behalf of this mailbox. The From line in any message sent by a delegate indicates that the message was sent by the delegate on behalf of the mailbox owner.

+ —

DISPLAY NAME ▲

Save   Cancel

■ You can grant the right to send messages on behalf of the mailbox owner. If you want to allow a user to send messages from a user's mailbox but want recipients to know a message was sent on behalf of the mailbox owner (rather than by the mailbox owner), grant Send On Behalf Of permissions. In Exchange Admin Center, open the Properties dialog box for the mailbox, and then select Mailbox Delegation. On the Mailbox Delegation page, under Send On Behalf Of, click Add (

+), and then use the Select Send On Behalf Of dialog box to choose the recipients who should have this permission. To revoke this permission, select an existing user name in the Display Name list box and then click Remove.

Cindy Richards

general
mailbox usage
contact information
organization
email address
mailbox features
member of
MailTip
▸ mailbox delegation

Full Access
The Full Access permission allows a delegate to open
this mailbox and behave as the mailbox owner.

+ **–**

DISPLAY NAME ▲
Exchange Servers
Exchange Trusted Subsystem

Save   Cancel

In Exchange Management Shell, you can use the Add-MailboxPermission and
Remove-MailboxPermission cmdlets to manage full access permissions. Samples 7-2
and 7-3 show examples of using these cmdlets. In these examples, the AccessRights
parameter is set to FullAccess to indicate full access permissions on the mailbox.

SAMPLE 7-2 Adding full access permissions

Syntax

```
Add-MailboxPermission –Identity UserBeingGrantedPermission
 –User UserWhoseMailboxIsBeingConfigured –AccessRights 'FullAccess'
```

Usage

```
Add-MailboxPermission –Identity
'CN=Mike Lam,OU=Engineering,DC=pocket-consultant,DC=com'
–User 'IMAGINEDLANDS\boba' –AccessRights 'FullAccess'
```

SAMPLE 7-3 Removing full access permissions

Syntax

```
Remove-MailboxPermission –Identity 'UserBeingGrantedPermission'
 –User 'UserWhoseMailboxIsBeingConfigured' –AccessRights 'FullAccess'
–InheritanceType 'All'
```

Usage

```
Remove-MailboxPermission -Identity 'CN=Jerry Orman,
OU=Engineering,DC=pocket-consultant,DC=com'
 -User 'IMAGINEDLANDS\boba' -AccessRights 'FullAccess' -InheritanceType 'All'
```

In Exchange Management Shell, you can use the Add-ADPermission and Remove-ADPermission cmdlets to manage Send As permissions. Samples 7-4 and 7-5 show examples using these cmdlets. In these examples, the -ExtendedRights parameter is set to Send-As to indicate you are setting Send As permissions on the mailbox.

SAMPLE 7-4 Adding send as permissions

Syntax

```
Add-ADPermission -Identity UserBeingGrantedPermission
-User UserWhoseMailboxIsBeingConfigured -ExtendedRights 'Send-As'
```

Usage

```
Add-ADPermission -Identity 'CN=Jerry
Orman,OU=Engineering,DC=cpandl,DC=com'
-User 'IMAGINEDLANDS\boba' -ExtendedRights 'Send-As'
```

SAMPLE 7-5 Removing send as permissions

Syntax

```
Remove-ADPermission -Identity UserBeingRevokedPermission
-User UserWhoseMailboxIsBeingConfigured -ExtendedRights 'Send-As'
-InheritanceType 'All' -ChildObjectTypes $null
-InheritedObjectType $null -Properties $null
```

Usage

```
Remove-ADPermission -Identity 'CN=Jerry
Orman,OU=Engineering, DC=pocket-consultant,DC=com'
 -User 'IMAGINEDLANDS\boba' -ExtendedRights 'Send-As'
-InheritanceType 'All' -ChildObjectTypes $null -InheritedObjectTypes $null
-Properties $null
```

> **NOTE** Another way to grant access permissions to mailboxes is to do so through Outlook. Using Outlook, you have more granular control over permissions. You can allow a user to log on as the mailbox owner, delegate

mailbox access, and grant various levels of access. For more information on this issue, see the "Accessing Multiple Exchange Mailboxes" and "Granting Permission to Access Folders Without Delegating Access" sections in Chapter 10 "Configuring Exchange Clients. "

Forwarding Email to a New Address

Except when rights management prevents it, any messages sent to a user's mailbox can be forwarded to another recipient. This recipient can be another user or a mail-enabled contact. To configure mail forwarding, follow these steps:

1. Open the Properties dialog box for the mailbox-enabled user account by double-clicking the user name in Exchange Admin Center.

2. On the Mailbox Features page, scroll down and then click **View Details** under Mail Flow.

delivery options

Forwarding Address
Forward email to the following recipient. Learn more

☑ Enable forwarding
Forward email to the following recipient:

Mark Vance   ✕   Browse...

   ☑ Deliver message to both forwarding address and mailbox

Recipient limit
☐ Maximum recipients:

OK   Cancel

3. To remove forwarding, clear the Enable Forwarding check box.

4. To add forwarding, select the Enable Forwarding check box and then click **Browse**. Use the Select Mailbox User And Mailbox dialog box to choose the alternate recipient.

5. If you enabled forward, you can optionally specify that copies of forwarded messages should be retained in the original mailbox by selecting the **Deliver Message To Both Forwarding Address And Mailbox** checkbox.

If you use Exchange Management Shell to configure forwarding, you can specify that messages should be delivered to both the forwarding address and the current mailbox by setting the -DeliverToMailboxAndForward parameter to $true when using Set-Mailbox.

Setting Storage Restrictions on Mailbox and Archives

In a standard configuration of Exchange Online, each licensed user gets 25 GB of mailbox storage and a storage warning is issued when the mailbox reaches 22.5 GB. Similarly, if user has a licensed in-place archive, the archive can have up to 25 GB of storage; a storage warning is issued when the archive mailbox reaches 22.5 GB. Other licensing options are available that may grant additional storage rights.

With on-premises Exchange, you can set storage restrictions on multiple mailboxes using global settings for each mailbox database or on individual mailboxes using per-user restrictions. Global restrictions are applied when you create a mailbox and are reapplied when you define new global storage restrictions. Per-user storage restrictions are set individually for each mailbox and override the global default settings. By default, users can store up to 2 GB in their mailboxes. The quotas are set to:

- Issue a warning when the mailbox reaches 1.9 GB
- Prohibit send when the mailbox reaches 2 GB
- Prohibit send and receive when the mailbox reaches 2.3 GB

In contrast, the default settings for archive mailboxes allow users to store up to 50 GB in their archive mailboxes, and a warning is issued when the archive mailbox reaches 45 GB.

> **NOTE** Storage restrictions apply only to mailboxes stored on the server. They don't apply to personal folders. Personal folders are stored on the user's computer

To configure global storage restrictions, you edit the properties of mailbox databases. In Exchange Admin Center, navigate to Servers > Databases. Open the Properties dialog box for the mailbox database by double-clicking the database name. On the Limits page, set the desired storage restrictions using the options provided.

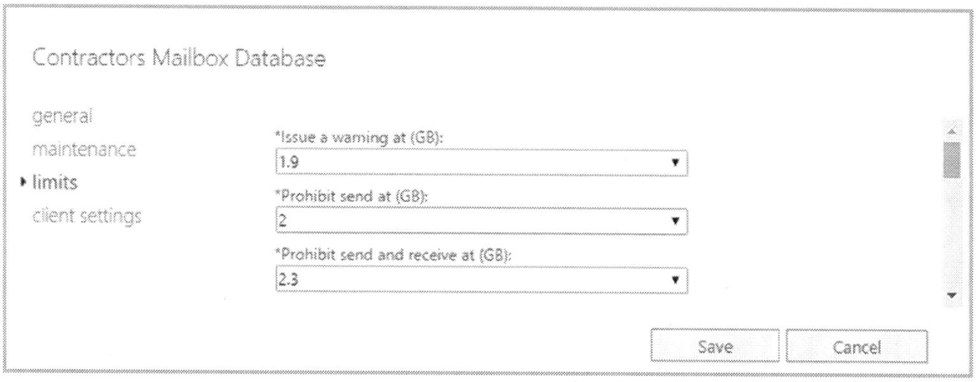

Contractors Mailbox Database

general

maintenance

▸ limits

client settings

*Issue a warning at (GB):
1.9

*Prohibit send at (GB):
2

*Prohibit send and receive at (GB):
2.3

Save   Cancel

You set individual storage restrictions for mailboxes by completing the following steps:

1. Open the Properties dialog box for the mailbox-enabled user account by double-clicking the user name in Exchange Admin Center.

2. On the Mailbox Usage page, click **More Options**. You'll then see the storage restrictions as shown in Figure 7-13.

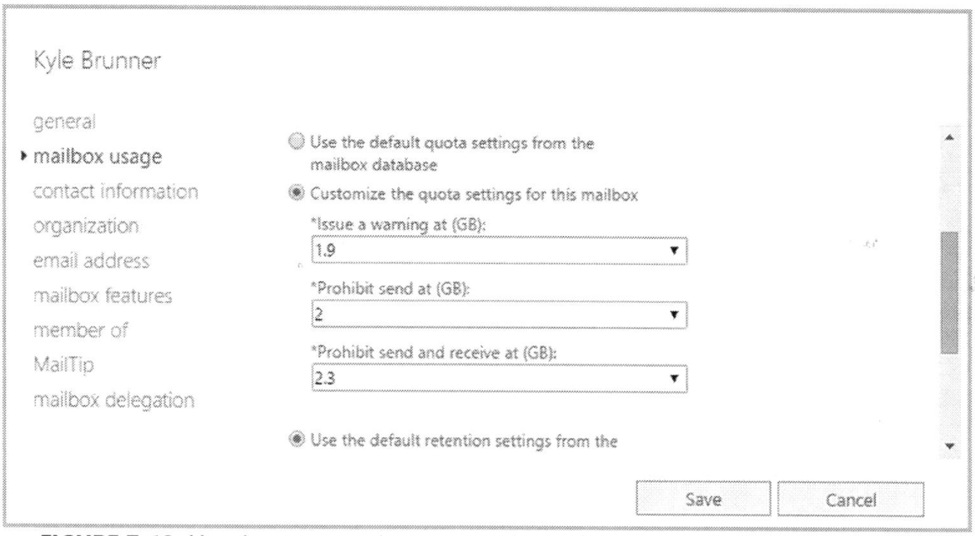

Kyle Brunner

general

▸ mailbox usage

contact information

organization

email address

mailbox features

member of

MailTip

mailbox delegation

○ Use the default quota settings from the mailbox database

◉ Customize the quota settings for this mailbox

*Issue a warning at (GB):
1.9

*Prohibit send at (GB):
2

*Prohibit send and receive at (GB):
2.3

◉ Use the default retention settings from the

Save   Cancel

FIGURE 7-13 Use the quota settings to specify storage limits and deleted item retention on a per-user basis when necessary.

3. To set mailbox storage limits, select **Customize The Quota Settings For This Mailbox**. Then set one or more of the following storage limits:

- **Issue Warning At (GB)**   This limit specifies the size, in gigabytes, that a mailbox can reach before a warning is issued to the user. The warning tells the user to clean out the mailbox.

- **Prohibit Send At (GB)**   This limit specifies the size, in gigabytes, that a mailbox can reach before the user is prohibited from sending any new mail. The restriction ends when the user clears out the mailbox and the mailbox size is under the limit.
- **Prohibit Send And Receive At (GB)**   This limit specifies the size, in gigabytes, that a mailbox can reach before the user is prohibited from sending and receiving mail. The restriction ends when the user clears out the mailbox and the mailbox size is under the limit.

> **CAUTION**   Prohibiting send and receive might cause the user to think they've lost email. When someone sends a message to a user who is prohibited from receiving messages, an NDR is generated and delivered to the sender. The original recipient never sees the email. Because of this, you should rarely prohibit send and receive.

4. Click **Save**.

Users who have an archive mailbox have the mailbox type User (Archive). You set individual storage restrictions for archive mailboxes by completing the following steps:

1. Select the user name in Exchange Admin Center.

2. In the Details pane, scroll down until you see the In-Place Archive heading and the related options. Click **View Details**.

3. Enter the desired maximum size for the archive in the Archive Quota text box.

4. Enter the storage limit for issuing a storage warning in the Issue Warning At text box.

5. Click **OK**.

Setting Deleted Item Retention Time on Individual Mailboxes

Normally, when a user deletes a message in Outlook, the message is placed in the Deleted Items folder. The message remains in the Deleted Items folder until the user deletes it manually or allows Outlook to clear out the Deleted Items folder. With personal folders, the message is then permanently deleted and you can't restore it. With server-based mailboxes, the message isn't actually deleted from the Exchange database. Instead, the message is marked as hidden and kept for a specified period of time called the *deleted item retention period*.

> **NOTE** The standard processes can be modified in several different ways. A user could press Shift+Delete to bypass Deleted Items. As an administrator, you can create and apply policies that prevent users from deleting items

(even if they try to use Shift+Delete). You can also configure policy to retain items indefinitely.

Default retention settings are configured for each mailbox database in the organization. With Exchange Online, the retention settings are as follows:

- Deleted items are retained for a maximum of 30 days.
- Items removed from the Deleted Items folder are retained for a maximum of 14 days.
- Items in the Junk Folder are retained for a maximum of 30 days before they are removed.

To configure deleted item retention on a per database basis, you edit the properties of mailbox databases. In Exchange Admin Center, navigate to Servers > Databases. Open the Properties dialog box for the mailbox database by double-clicking the database name. On the Limits page, use the options provided to configure the deleted item retention settings.

You can override the database settings on a per-user basis by completing these steps:

1. Open the Properties dialog box for the mailbox-enabled user account by double-clicking the user name in Exchange Admin Center.

2. On the Mailbox Usage page, click **More Options** and then select Customize The Retention Settings For This Mailbox.

Joe Montgomery

general	
▸ mailbox usage	○ Use the default retention settings from the mailbox database
contact information	◉ Customize the retention settings for this mailbox
organization	
email address	*Keep deleted items for (days):
	30
mailbox features	
member of	☑ Don't permanently delete items until the database is backed up
MailTip	
mailbox delegation	

Save   Cancel

3. In the Keep Deleted Items For (Days) text box, enter the number of days to retain deleted items. An average retention period is 14 days. If you set the retention period to 0 and aren't using policies that prevent deletion,

messages aren't retained and can't be recovered. If you set the retention period to 0 but are using policies that prevent deletion, the messages are retained according to the established policies.

4. You can also specify that deleted messages should not be permanently removed until the mailbox database has been backed up. This option ensures that the deleted items are archived into at least one backup set. Click **Save**.

REAL WORLD   Deleted item retention is convenient because it allows the administrator the chance to salvage accidentally deleted email without restoring a user's mailbox from backup. I strongly recommend that you enable this setting, either in the mailbox database or for individual mailboxes, and configure the retention period accordingly.

Chapter 8. Managing Groups

Learning the ins and outs of distribution groups and address lists will greatly facilitate the efficiency and effectiveness of Microsoft Exchange Server and Exchange Online administration. Careful planning of your organization's groups and address lists can save you time and help your organization run more efficiently. Study the concepts discussed in this chapter and the next then use the step-by-step procedures to implement the groups and lists for your organization.

Using Security and Distribution Groups

You use groups to grant permissions to similar types of users, to simplify account administration, and to make it easier to contact multiple users. For example, you can send a message addressed to a group, and the message will go to all the users in that group. Thus, instead of having to enter 20 different email addresses in the message header, you enter one email address for all of the group members.

Group Types, Scope, And Identifiers

Windows defines several different types of groups, and each of these groups can have a unique scope. In Active Directory domains, you use three group types:

* **Security**   You use security groups to control access to network resources. You can also use user-defined security groups to distribute email.
* **Standard distribution**   Standard distribution groups have fixed membership, and you use them only as email distribution lists. You can't use these groups to control access to network resources.
* **Dynamic distribution**   Membership for dynamic distribution groups is determined based on a Lightweight Directory Access Protocol (LDAP) query; you use these groups only as email distribution lists. The LDAP query is used to build the list of members whenever messages are sent to the group.

Security groups can have different scopes—*domain local, global,* and *universal*—so that they are valid in different areas of your Active Directory forest. Exchange Server only supports groups with universal scope. You can mail-enable security groups with universal scope, and you can create new distribution groups with universal scope.

In Exchange Admin Center, you select Recipients in the Features pane and then select Groups to work with groups (see Figure 8-1). Only mail-enabled groups with universal scope are displayed. Groups with universal scope can do the following:

- Contain users and groups from any domain in the Active Directory forest
- Be added to other groups and assigned permissions in any domain in the Active Directory forest

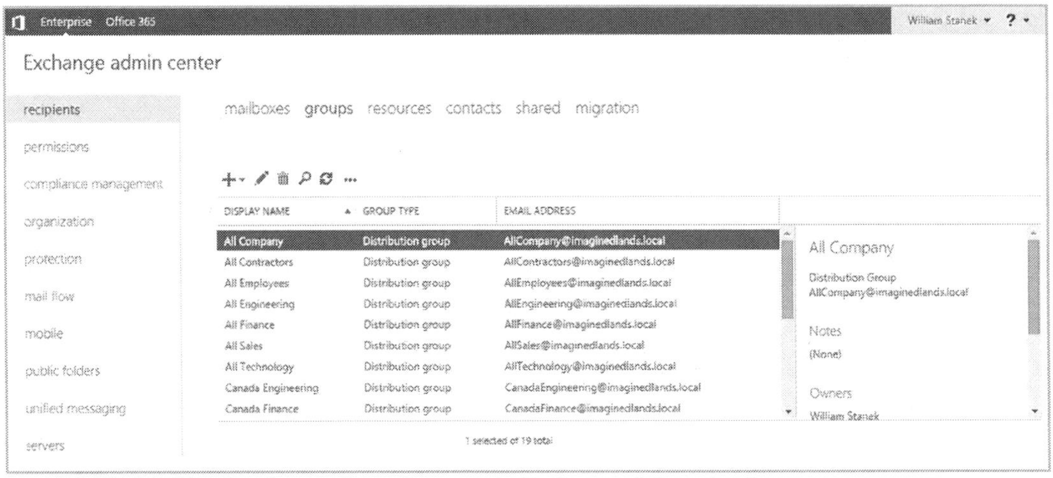

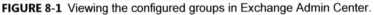

FIGURE 8-1 Viewing the configured groups in Exchange Admin Center.

When you work with dynamic distribution groups, keep in mind that the membership can include only members of the local domain, or it can include users and groups from other domains, domain trees, or forests. Scope is determined by the default apply-filter container you associate with the group when you create it. More specifically, the default apply-filter container defines the root of the search hierarchy and the LDAP query filters to recipients in and below the specified container. For example, if the apply-filter container you associate with the group is imaginedlands.com, the query filter is applied to all recipients in this domain. If the apply-filter container you associate with the organizational unit is Engineering, the query filter is applied to all recipients in or below this container.

As with user accounts, Windows uses unique security identifiers (SIDs) to track groups. This means that you can't delete a group, re-create it with the same name, and then expect all the permissions and privileges to remain the same. The new group will have a new SID, and all the permissions and privileges of the old group will be lost.

When to Use Security and Standard Distribution Groups

Rather than duplicating your existing security group structure with distribution groups that have the same purpose, you might want to selectively mail-enable your universal security groups, which converts them to distribution groups. For example, if you have a universal security group called Marketing, you don't need to create a MarketingDistList distribution group. Instead, you could enable Exchange mail on the original universal security group, which would then become a distribution group.

You might also want to mail-enable universal security groups that you previously defined. Then, if existing distribution groups serve the same purpose, you can delete the distribution groups.

To reduce the time administrators spend managing groups, Exchange defines several additional control settings, including

- **Group ownership**   Mail-enabled security groups, standard distribution groups, and dynamic distribution groups can have one or more owners. A group's owners are the users assigned as its managers, and they can control membership in the group. A group's managers are listed when users view the properties of the group in Microsoft Office Outlook. Additionally, managers can receive delivery reports for groups if you select the Send Delivery Reports To Group Manager option when configuring group settings.
- **Membership approval**   Mail-enabled security groups and standard distribution groups can have open or closed membership. There are separate settings for joining and leaving a group. For joining, the group can be open to allow users to join without requiring permission, be closed to allow only group owners and administrators to add members, or require owner approval to allow users to request membership in a group. Membership requests must be approved by a group owner. For leaving, a group can either be open to allow users to leave a group without requiring owner approval or closed to allow only group owners and administrators to remove members.

Your management tool of choice will determine your options for configuring group ownership and membership approval. When you create groups in Exchange Admin Center, you can specify ownership, membership, and approval settings when you create the group and can edit these settings at any time by editing the group's properties. When you create groups in Exchange Management Shell, you can configure additional advanced options that you'd otherwise have to manage after creating the group in Exchange Admin Center.

When to Use Dynamic Distribution Groups

It's a fact of life that over time users will move to different departments, leave the company, or accept different responsibilities. With standard distribution groups, you'll spend a lot of time managing group membership when these types of changes occur—and that's where dynamic distribution groups come into the picture. With dynamic distribution groups, there isn't a fixed group membership and you don't have to add or remove users from groups. Instead, group membership is determined by the results of an LDAP query sent to your organization's Global Catalog.

Dynamic distribution groups can be used with or without a dedicated expansion server. You'll get the most benefit from dynamic distribution without a dedicated expansion server when the member list returned in the results is relatively small (fewer than 25 members). In the case of potentially hundreds or thousands of members, however, dynamic distribution is inefficient and could require a great deal of processing to complete. Exchange 2016 shifts the processing requirements from the Global Catalog server to a dedicated expansion server (a server whose only task is to expand the LDAP queries). By default, Exchange 2016 uses the closest Mailbox server as the dedicated expansion server. For more information on expansion servers, see "Designating an expansion server" later in this chapter.

One other thing to note about dynamic distribution is that you can associate only one specific query with each distribution group. For example, you could create separate groups for each department in the organization. You could have groups called QD-Accounting, QD-BizDev, QD-Engineering, QD-Marketing, QD-Operations, QD-Sales, and QD-Support. You could, in turn, create a standard distribution group or a dynamic distribution group called AllEmployees that contains these groups as members—thereby establishing a distribution group hierarchy.

When using multiple parameters with dynamic distribution, keep in mind that multiple parameters typically work as logical AND operations. For example, if you create a query with a parameter that matches all employees in the state of Washington with all employees in the Marketing department, the query results do not contain a list of all employees in Washington or all Marketing employees. Rather, the results contain a list of recipients who are in Washington and are members of the Marketing group. In this case, you get the expected results by creating a dynamic distribution group for all Washington State employees, another dynamic distribution group for all Marketing employees, and a final group that has as members the other two distribution groups.

Working with Security and Standard Distribution Groups

As you set out to work with groups, you'll find that some tasks are specific to each type of group and some tasks can be performed with any type of group. Because of this, I've divided the group management discussion into three sections. In this section, you'll learn about the typical tasks you perform with security and standard distribution groups. The next section discusses tasks you'll perform only with dynamic distribution groups. The third section discusses general management tasks.

You can use Exchange Admin Center or Exchange Management Shell to work with groups.

Group Naming Policy

Whether you work at a small company with 50 employees or a large enterprise with 5,000 employees, you should consider establishing a group naming policy that ensures a consistent naming strategy is used for group names. For administrators, your naming policy should be implemented through written policies within your IT department and could be applied to both security groups and distribution groups.

Exchange 2016 and Exchange Online also allow you to establish official naming policy for standard distribution groups. Group naming policy is:

* Applied to non-administrators whenever they create or rename distribution groups.
* Applied to administrators only when they create or rename distribution groups using the shell (and omit the -IgnoreNamingPolicy parameter).

> **IMPORTANT**   Group naming policy doesn't apply to security groups or dynamic distribution groups. Each Exchange organization can have one and only one naming policy. Any naming policy you define is applied throughout the Exchange organization.

Understanding Group Naming Policy

You use group naming policy to format group names according to a defined standard. The rules for naming policy allow for one or more prefixes, a group name, and one or more suffixes, giving an expanded syntax of:

`<Prefix1><Prefix2>…<PrefixN><GroupName><Suffix1><Suffix2>…<SuffixN)`

You can use any Exchange attribute as the prefix or suffix. You also can use a text string as a prefix or suffix. The prefix, group name and suffix are combined without spacing. To improve readability, you can separate the prefix, name and suffix with a placeholder character, such as a space ( ), a period (.) or a dash (-).

Group naming policy works like this:

- A user creates a standard distribution group and specifies a display name for the group. After creating the group, Exchange applies the group naming policy by adding any prefixes or suffixes defined in the group naming policy to the display name.
- The display name is displayed in the distribution groups list in Exchange Admin Center, the shared address book, and the To:, Cc:, and From: fields in email messages.

You can create a naming policy with only a prefix and group name or with only a suffix and a group name. Common attributes that you might want to use as prefixes or suffixes include city, country code, department, office, and state. For example, you might want all distribution groups to have the following syntax:

`State_ GroupName`

To do this, you would create a naming policy with two prefixes. As shown in Figure 8-2, the first prefix would have the <State> attribute. The second prefix would have the _ text value. Thus, if a user in the state of New York (NY) creates a standard distribution group called Sales, Exchange adds the defined prefixes and the display name becomes NY_Sales.

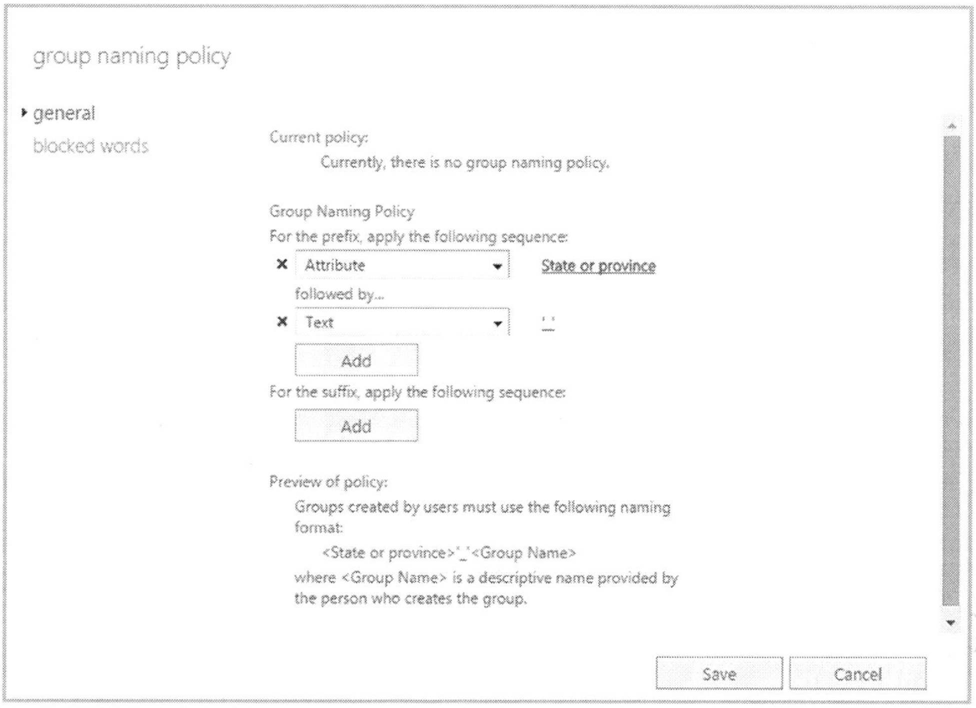

FIGURE 8-2 Creating a naming policy with two prefixes.

Group naming policy also allows you to specify blocked words. Users who try to use a word that you've blocked see an error message when they try to create the new group and are asked to remove the blocked word and create the group again.

Defining Group Naming Policy for Your Organization

Group naming policy formats display names so that they follow a defined standard. When setting the naming format, keep in mind that users enter the desired display name when they create the group and Exchange transforms the format according to the defined policy. Because the display name is limited to 64 characters, you must consider this limit when defining the prefixes and suffixes in your naming policy.

You can create the group naming policy for the Exchange organization by completing the following steps:

1. In Exchange Admin Center, select **Recipients** in the Features pane and then select **Groups**.

2. Click the **More** button (•••) and then select **Configure Group Naming Policy**. This displays the Group Naming Policy dialog box.

3. If you want the naming policy to have a prefix, do one of the following and then optionally click **Add** to add additional prefixes using the same technique:

- Use the selection list to choose Attribute as the prefix. In the Select The Attribute dialog box, select the attribute to use and then click OK.
- Use the selection list to choose Text as the prefix. In the Enter Text dialog box, select the text string to use and then click OK.

```
group naming policy

▸ general
  blocked words        Current policy:
                          Currently, there is no group naming policy.

                       Group Naming Policy
                       For the prefix, apply the following sequence:
                         ✗  [ Select one          ▾ ]
                              [     Add      ]
                       For the suffix, apply the following sequence:
                         ✗  [ Select one          ▾ ]
                              [     Add      ]

                       Preview of policy:
                          Currently, there is no group naming policy.

                                              [   Save   ]   [  Cancel  ]
```

4. If you want the naming policy to have a suffix do one of the following and then optionally click **Add** to add additional suffixes using the same technique:

- Use the selection list to choose Attribute as the suffix. In the Select The Attribute dialog box, select the attribute to use and then click OK.
- Use the selection list to choose Text as the suffix. In the Enter Text dialog box, select the text string to use and then click OK.

5. As you define the naming policy, the Preview Of Policy area shows the naming format. When you are satisfied with the naming format, click **Save**.

Defining Blocked Words in Group Naming Policy

Blocked words allow you to specify words that users can't use in the names of standard distribution groups they create. You can define or manage the blocked words list by completing the following steps:

1. In Exchange Admin Center, select **Recipients** in the Features pane and then select **Groups**.

2. Click the More button (•••) and then select Configure Group Naming Policy. This displays the Group Naming Policy dialog box.

3. On the Blocked Words page, any currently blocked words are displayed. Use the following techniques to manage the blocked word list:

- To add a blocked word, type the word in the text box provided and then click

   Add (✚). Alternatively, type the word to block in the text box provided and then press Enter.
- To modify a blocked word, select the word in the blocked word list and then click

   Edit (✏). Modify the word and then click outside the text box provided for editing. Alternatively, press Enter to apply the edits.
- To remove a blocked word, click the word to remove and then click Remove.

4. Click **Save**.

group naming policy

general
▸ blocked words

You can create a list of words that users can't use in the names of groups they create.

✏ —

enter a word to block ✚

Save   Cancel

Creating Security and Standard Distribution Groups

Security groups and distribution groups are available whether you are working with online or on-premises Exchange organizations. You use groups to manage permissions and to distribute email. As you set out to create groups, remember that you create groups for similar types of users. Consequently, you might want to create the following types of groups:

- **Groups for departments within the organization**   Generally, users who work in the same department need access to similar resources and should be a part of the same email distribution lists.
- **Groups for roles within the organization**   You can also organize groups according to the users' roles within the organization. For example, you could use a group called Executives to send email to all the members of the executive team and a group called Managers to send email to all managers and executives in the organization.
- **Groups for users of specific projects**   Often, users working on a major project need a way to send email to all the members of the team. To address this need, you can create a group specifically for the project.

You can create groups several ways. You can create a new distribution group, you can create a mail-enabled universal security group, or you can mail-enable an existing universal security group.

Creating a New Group

You can create a new distribution group or a new mail-enabled security group by completing the following steps:

1. In Exchange Admin Center, select **Recipients** in the Features pane and then select **Groups**.

2. Click **New** (   ) and then do one of the following:

- Select Distribution Group to create a new Distribution Group. This opens the New Distribution Group dialog box, shown in Figure 8-3.
- Select Security Group to create a new mail-enabled Security Group. This opens the New Security Group dialog box, and the options are the same as those for new distribution groups.

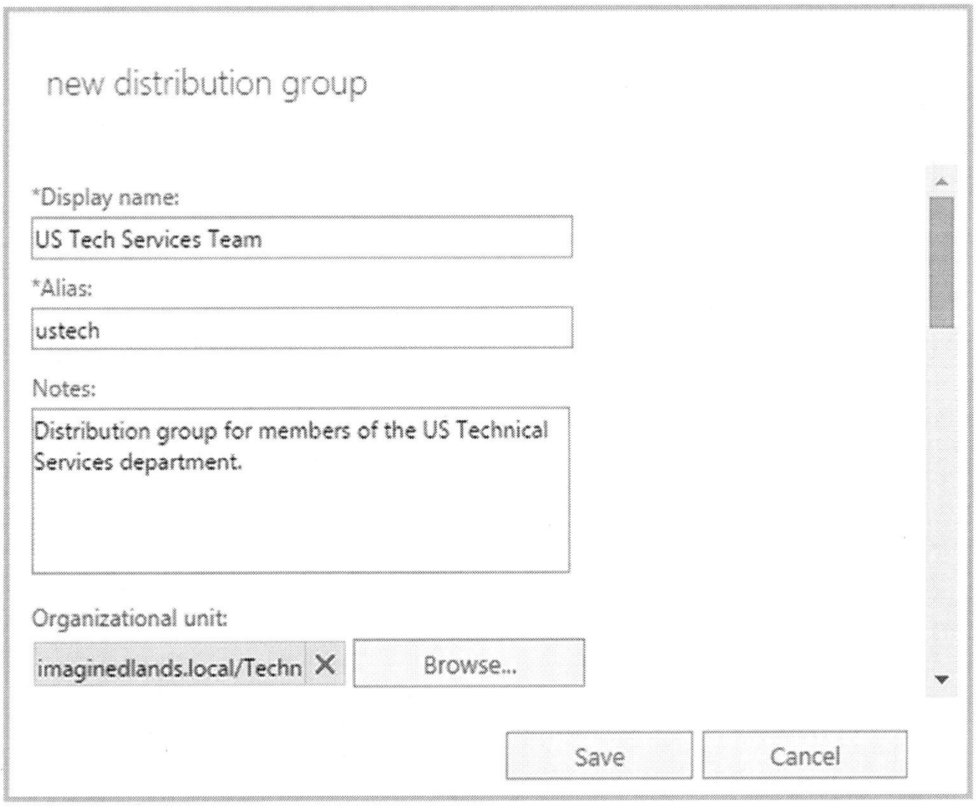

FIGURE 8-3 Configuring the group's settings.

3. In the Display Name text box, type a display name for the group. Group names aren't case-sensitive and can be up to 64 characters long. Keep in mind that group naming policy doesn't apply to administrators creating distribution groups in Exchange Admin Center (or to mail-enabled security groups in any way).

4. Like users, groups have Exchange aliases. Enter an alias. The Exchange alias is used to set the group's SMTP email address. Exchange Server uses the SMTP address for receiving messages.

5. For Exchange Online, the name and domain components of the default email address are displayed in the Email Address text boxes. As appropriate, change the default name and use the drop-down list to select the domain with which you want to associate the group. This sets the fully qualified email address, such as us-tech@imaginedlands.onmicrosoft.com.

6. With on-premises Exchange, the group account is created in the default user container, which typically is the Users container. To create the group in a specific organizational unit instead, click **Browse** to the right of the

Organizational Unit text box. In the Select Organizational Unit dialog box, choose the location where you want to store the account and then click **OK**.

7. Group owners are responsible for managing a group. To add owners, under Owners, click Add (➕). In the Select Owner dialog box, select users, groups, or both that should have management responsibility for the group. Select multiple users and groups using the Shift or Ctrl keys.

---

new distribution group

*Owners:

➕ ➖

> William Stanek

Members:

☑ Add group owners as members

➕ ➖

> US Technology

Save   Cancel

IMPORTANT While dynamic distribution groups don't have to have owners, every mail-enabled security group and standard distribution group must have at least one owner. By default, the account you are using is set as the group owner.

8. Members of a group receive messages sent to the group. By default, the group owners are set as members of the group. If you don't want the currently listed owners to be members of the group, clear the **Add Group Owners As Members** checkbox.

9. To add members, under Members, click Add (**+**). In the Select Members dialog box, select users, groups, or both that should be members of the group. Select multiple users and groups using the Shift or Ctrl keys.

10. Choose settings for joining the group. The options are:

* **Open**   Anyone can join this group without being approved by the group owners.
* **Closed**   Members can be added only by the group owners. All requests to join will be rejected automatically.
* **Owner Approval**   All requests are approved or rejected by the group owners.

11. Choose settings for leaving the group. The options are:

* **Open**   Anyone can leave this group without being approved by the group owners.
* **Closed**   Members can be removed only by the group owners. All requests to leave will be rejected automatically.

12. Click **Save** to create the group. If an error occurs during group creation, the related group will not be created. You need to correct the problem before you can complete this procedure. After creating a group, you might want to do the following:

* Set message size restrictions for messages mailed to the group.
* Limit users who can send to the group.
* Change or remove default email addresses.
* Add more email addresses.

> **NOTE**   By default, the new distribution group is open for joining and open for leaving.

new distribution group

Choose whether owner approval is required to join the group.

- ◉ Open: Anyone can join this group without being approved by the group owners.
- ○ Closed: Members can be added only by the group owners. All requests to join will be rejected automatically.
- ○ Owner approval: All requests are approved or rejected by the group owners.

Choose whether the group is open to leave.

- ◉ Open: Anyone can leave this group without being approved by the group owners.
- ○ Closed: Members can be removed only by the group owners. All requests to leave will be rejected automatically.

[Save] [Cancel]

In Exchange Management Shell, you can create a new distribution group using the New-DistributionGroup cmdlet. Sample 8-1 provides the syntax and usage. You can set the -Type parameter to Distribution for a distribution group or to Security for a mail-enabled security group.

SAMPLE 8-1 New-DistributionGroup cmdlet syntax and usage

Syntax

```
New-DistributionGroup -Name ExchangeName [-Alias ExchangeAlias]
[-DisplayName DisplayName] [-OrganizationalUnit OUName]
[-PrimarySmtpAddress SmtpAddress] [-SamAccountName PreWin2000Name]
[-Type <Distribution | Security>] {AddtlParams}

{AddtlParams}
[-ArbitrationMailbox ModeratorMailbox] [-BypassNestedModerationEnabled
<$true | $false>] [-CopyOwnerToMember {$true | $false}] [-DomainController
```

```
FullyQualifiedName] [-IgnoreNamingPolicy {$true | $false}] [-ManagedBy
RecipientIdentities] [-MemberDepartRestriction <Closed | Open |
ApprovalRequired>] [-MemberJoinRestriction <Closed | Open |
ApprovalRequired>] [-Members RecipientIdentities] [-ModeratedBy
Moderators] [-ModerationEnabled <$true | $false>] [-Notes String]
[-Organization OrgName] [-RoomList {$true | $false}]
[-SendModerationNotifications <Never | Internal | Always>]
```

Usage

```
New-DistributionGroup -Name 'CorporateSales' -Type 'Distribution'
 -OrganizationalUnit 'imaginedlands.com/Sales'
 -SamAccountName 'CorporateSales'
 -DisplayName 'Corporate Sales'
 -Alias 'CorporateSales'
```

Mail-Enabling Universal Security Groups

You can't use Exchange Admin Center to mail-enable a security group. In Exchange
Management Shell, you can mail-enable a universal security group using the Enable-
DistributionGroup cmdlet. Sample 8-2 provides the syntax and usage.

SAMPLE 8-2 Enable-DistributionGroup cmdlet syntax and usage

Syntax

```
Enable-DistributionGroup -Identity GroupIdentity [-Alias ExchangeAlias]
[-DisplayName DisplayName] [-DomainController FullyQualifiedName]
[-OverrideRecipientQuotas {$true | $false}]
[-PrimarySmtpAddress SmtpAddress]
```

Usage

```
Enable -DistributionGroup -Identity 'AllSales'
-DisplayName 'All Sales' -Alias 'AllSales'
```

> **NOTE** Group naming policy applies only to distribution groups.

You can manage mail-enabled security groups in several ways. You can add or
remove group members as discussed in the "Assigning and Removing Membership
for Individual Users, Groups, and Contacts" section of this chapter. If a group should

no longer be mail-enabled, you can use Disable-DistributionGroup to remove the Exchange settings from the group. If you no longer need a mail-enabled security group and it is not a built-in group, you can permanently remove it from Active Directory by selecting it in Exchange Admin Center and clicking Delete. Alternatively, you can delete a group using Delete-DistributionGroup.

Using Exchange Management Shell, you can disable a group's Exchange features using the Disable-DistributionGroup cmdlet, as shown in Sample 8-3.

SAMPLE 8-3 Disable-DistributionGroup cmdlet syntax and usage

Syntax

```
Disable-DistributionGroup -Identity GroupIdentity
[-DomainController FullyQualifiedName]
[-IgnoreDefaultScope {$true | $false}]
```

Usage

```
Disable-DistributionGroup -Identity 'AllSales'
```

Assigning and Removing Membership for Individual Users, Groups, and Contacts

All users, groups, and contacts can be members of other groups. To configure a group's membership, follow these steps:

1. In Exchange Admin Center, double-click the group entry. This opens the group's Properties dialog box.

2. On the Membership page, you'll see a list of current members. Click Add (

    ➕

) to add recipients to the group. In the Select Members dialog box, select users, groups, or both that should be members of the group. Select multiple users and groups using the Shift or Ctrl keys.

3. You can remove members on the Membership page as well. To remove a member from a group, select a recipient, and then click Remove (▬). When you're finished, click **Save**.

All Technology

general
ownership
▸ membership
membership approval
delivery management
message approval
email options
MailTip
group delegation

Members:

➕ ➖

Canada Technology
US Tech Services Team
US Technology
William Stanek

[Save] [Cancel]

In Exchange Management Shell, you can view group members using the Get-DistributionGroupMember cmdlet. Sample 8-4 provides the syntax and usage.

SAMPLE 8-4 Get-DistributionGroupMember cmdlet syntax and usage

Syntax

```
Get-DistributionGroupMember -Identity GroupIdentity [-Credential
Credential] [-DomainController FullyQualifiedName]
[-IgnoreDefaultScope {$true | $false}] [-ReadFromDomainController {$true
| $false}] [-ResultSize Size]
```

Usage

```
Get-DistributionGroupMember -Identity 'CorpSales'
```

You add members to a group using the Add-DistributionGroupMember cmdlet. Sample 8-5 provides the syntax and usage.

SAMPLE 8-5 Add-DistributionGroupMember cmdlet syntax and usage

Syntax

```
Add-DistributionGroupMember -Identity GroupIdentity [-Member
RecipientIdentity] [-BypassSecurityGroupManagerCheck {$true | $false}]
[-DomainController FullyQualifiedName]
```

```
Add-DistributionGroupMember -Identity 'CorpSales'
 -Member 'imaginedlands.com/Sales/April Stewart'
```

You remove members from a group using the Remove-DistributionGroupMember cmdlet. Sample 8-6 provides the syntax and usage.

SAMPLE 8-6 Remove-DistributionGroupMember cmdlet syntax and usage

Syntax

```
Remove-DistributionGroupMember -Identity GroupIdentity [-Member
RecipientIdentity] [-BypassSecurityGroupManagerCheck {$true | $false}]
[-DomainController FullyQualifiedName]
```

Usage

```
Remove-DistributionGroupMember -Identity 'CorpSales'
 -Member 'imaginedlands.com/Sales/April Stewart'
```

Adding and Removing Managers

Group owners are responsible for managing a group. Every group must have at least one owner. To configure a group's managers, follow these steps:

1. In Exchange Admin Center, double-click the group entry. This opens the group's Properties dialog box.

2. On the Ownership page, lists current owners. Click Add (**+**) to add recipients to the group. In the Select Owners dialog box, select users, groups, or both that should be owners of the group. Select multiple users and groups using the Shift or Ctrl keys.

3. You can remove owners on the Ownership page as well. To remove an owner from a group, select a recipient, then click Remove (**▬**). When you're finished, click **Save**.

In Exchange Management Shell, you can add or remove group managers using the -ManagedBy parameter of the Set-DistributionGroup cmdlet. To set this parameter, you must specify the full list of managers for the group by doing the following:

- Add managers by including existing managers and specifying the additional managers when you set the parameter.
- Remove managers by specifying only those who should be managers and excluding those who should not be managers.

If you don't know the current managers of a group, you can list the managers using Get-DistributionGroup. You'll need to format the output and examine the value of the -ManagedBy property.

Sample 8-7 provides syntax and usage examples for adding and removing group managers.

SAMPLE 8-7 Adding and removing group managers

Syntax

```
Get-DistributionGroup -Identity GroupIdentity | format-table
-property ManagedBy


Set-DistributionGroup -Identity GroupIdentity -ManagedBy GroupManagers
```

```
Get-DistributionGroup -Identity 'CorpSales' |
format-table -property ManagedBy
```

```
Set-DistributionGroup -Identity 'CorpSales'
-ManagedBy 'imaginedlands.com/Sales/Oliver Lee',
'imaginedlands.com/Users/Jamie Stark'
```

```
$g = Get-DistributionGroup -Identity 'CorpSales'
$h = $g.managedby + 'imaginedlands.com/Users/William Stanek'
```

```
Set-DistributionGroup -Identity 'CorpSales'
-ManagedBy $h
```

Configuring Member Restrictions and Moderation

Membership in distribution groups can be restricted in several ways. Groups can be open or closed for joining or require group owner approval for joining. Groups can be open or closed for leaving. Groups also can be moderated. With moderated groups, messages are sent to designated moderators for approval before being distributed to members of the group. The only exception is for a message sent by a designated moderator. A message from a moderator is delivered immediately because a moderator has the authority to determine what is and isn't an appropriate message.

To configure member restrictions and moderation, follow these steps:

1. In Exchange Admin Center, double-click the group entry. This opens the group's Properties dialog box.

2. On the Membership Approval page, choose settings for joining the group. The options are:

* **Open**   Anyone can join this group without being approved by the group owners.
* **Closed**   Members can be added only by the group owners. All requests to join will be rejected automatically.
* **Owner Approval**   All requests are approved or rejected by the group owner.

3. Choose settings for leaving the group. The options are:

- **Open**   Anyone can leave this group without being approved by the group owners.
- **Closed**   Members can be removed only by the group owners. All requests to leave will be rejected automatically.

4. The Message Approval page displays the moderation options. To disable moderation, clear the **Messages Sent To This Group Have To Be Approved By A Moderator** check box. To enable moderation, select the **Messages Sent To This Group Have To Be Approved By A Moderator** check box, and then use the options provided to specify group moderators, specify senders who don't require message approval, and configure moderation notifications.

5. Click **Save** to apply your changes.

In Exchange Management Shell, you manage distribution group settings using Set-DistributionGroup. You configure member restrictions for joining a group using the -MemberJoinRestriction parameter and configure member restrictions for leaving a group using the -MemberDepartRestriction parameter. If you want to check the current restrictions, you can do this using Get-DistributionGroup. You'll need to format the output and examine the values of the -MemberJoinRestriction property, the -MemberDepartRestriction property, or both.

Sample 8-8 provides syntax and usage examples for configuring member restrictions.

Syntax

```
Get-DistributionGroup -Identity GroupIdentity | format-table –property
Name, MemberJoinRestriction, MemberDepartRestriction

Set-DistributionGroup -Identity GroupIdentity
[-MemberJoinRestriction <Closed | Open | ApprovalRequired>]
[-MemberDepartRestriction <Closed | Open | ApprovalRequired>]
```

Usage

```
Get-DistributionGroup -Identity 'AllMarketing' |
format-table –property Name, MemberJoinRestriction,
MemberDepartRestriction

Set-DistributionGroup -Identity 'AllMarketing'
-MemberJoinRestriction 'Closed' -MemberDepartRestriction 'Closed'
```

Set-DistributionGroup parameters for configuring moderation include -ModerationEnabled, -ModeratedBy, -BypassModerationFromSendersOrMembers, and -SendModerationNotifications. You enable or disable moderation by using -ModerationEnabled. If moderation is enabled, you can do the following:

* Designate moderators using -ModeratedBy.
* Specify senders who don't require message approval by using -BypassModerationFromSendersOrMembers.
* Configure moderation notifications using -SendModerationNotifications.

Sample 8-9 provides syntax and usage examples for configuring moderation.

SAMPLE 8-9 Configuring moderation for groups

Syntax

```
Get-DistributionGroup -Identity GroupIdentity | format-table –property
Name, ModeratedBy, BypassModerationFromSendersOrMembers,
SendModerationNotifications

Set-DistributionGroup -Identity GroupIdentity
```

```
[-ModeratedBy Moderators] [-ModerationEnabled <$true | $false>]
[-BypassModerationFromSendersOrMembers Recipients]
[-SendModerationNotifications <Never | Internal | Always>]
```

Usage

```
Get-DistributionGroup -Identity 'AllMarketing' |
format-table -property Name, ModeratedBy,
BypassModerationFromSendersOrMembers, SendModerationNotifications
```

```
Set-DistributionGroup -Identity 'AllMarketing'
-ModerationEnabled $true -Moderators 'AprilC'
-SendModerationNotifications 'Internal'
```

Working with Dynamic Distribution Groups

Just as there are tasks that apply only to security and standard distribution groups, there are also tasks that apply only to dynamic distribution groups. These tasks are discussed in this section.

Creating Dynamic Distribution Groups

With dynamic distribution groups, group membership is determined by the results of an LDAP query. You can create a dynamic distribution group and define the query parameters by completing the following steps:

1. In Exchange Admin Center, select **Recipients** in the Features pane and then select **Groups**.

2. Click **New** ( ) and then select **Dynamic Distribution Group**. This opens the New Dynamic Distribution Group dialog box, shown in Figure 8-4.

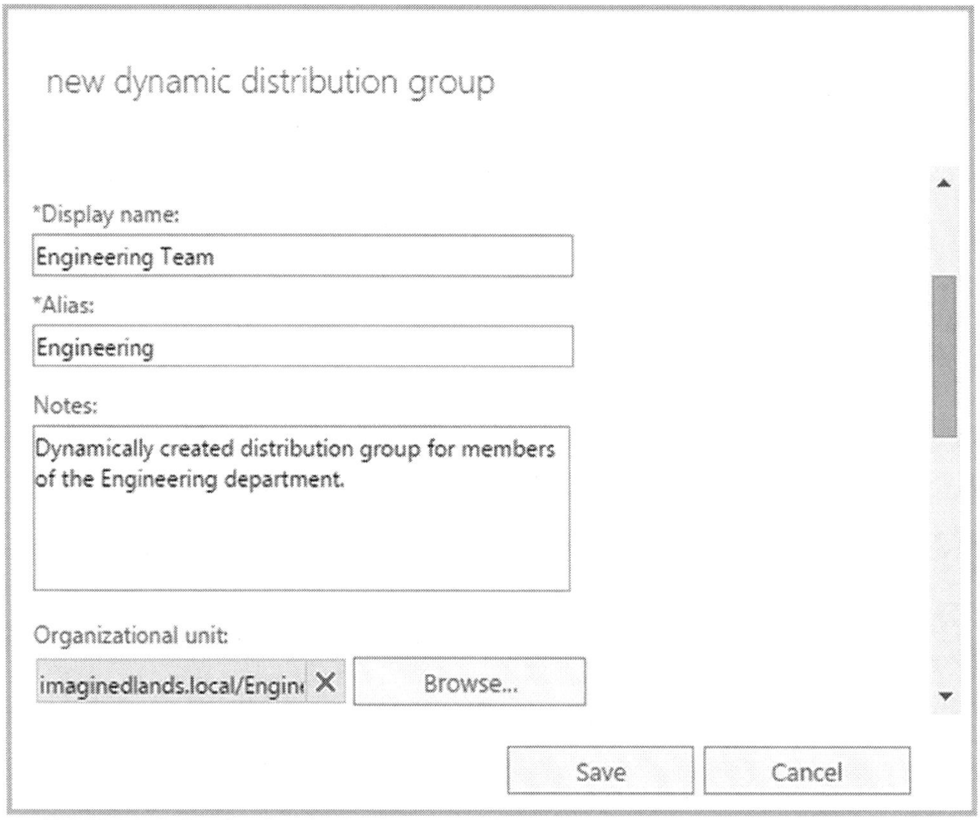

FIGURE 8-4 Configuring the basic settings for the dynamic distribution group.

3. In the Display Name text box, type a display name for the group. Group names aren't case-sensitive and can be up to 64 characters long. Keep in mind that group naming policy doesn't apply to administrators creating distribution groups in Exchange Admin Center.

4. Like users, groups have Exchange aliases. Enter an alias. The Exchange alias is used to set the group's SMTP e-mail address. Exchange Server uses the SMTP address for receiving messages.

5. With on-premises Exchange, the group account is created in the default user container, which typically is the Users container. To create the group in a specific organizational unit instead, click **Browse** to the right of the Organizational Unit text box. In the Select Organizational Unit dialog box, choose the location where you want to store the account and then click **OK**.

> **NOTE** With Exchange 2016, the organizational unit you specify is simply the storage container. Thus, unlike Exchange 2010, the selection is not used to scope or filter the LDAP query.

6. Group owners are responsible for managing groups. Unlike standard distribution groups, dynamic distribution groups don't need to be assigned an owner. If you want to specify an owner, under Owner, click Add (➕). In the Select Owner dialog box, select the user or group that should have management responsibility for the group.

7. Specify the recipients to include in the group. To allow any recipient type to be a member of the group, select **All Recipient Types**. Otherwise, choose **Only The Following Recipient Types** and then choose the types of recipients to include in the dynamic distribution group.

8. Membership in the group is determined by the rules you define. To define a rule, click **Add A Rule** and set the filter conditions. The following types of conditions as well as conditions for custom attributes are available:

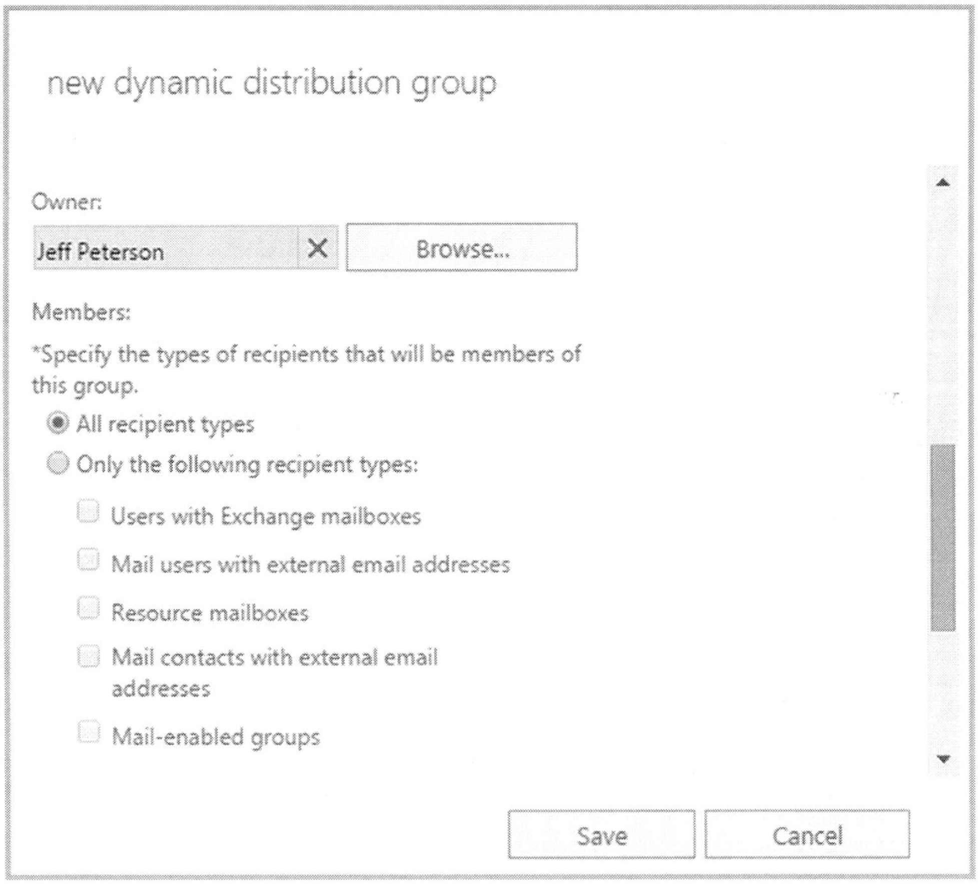

FIGURE 8-5 Configuring ownership and membership settings for the dynamic distribution group.

- **Recipient Container**   Filters recipients based on where the related account is stored in Active Directory. Selecting this option displays the Select An Organizational Unit dialog box. Click the container where the recipients are stored, such as Users or an organizational unit, and then click OK.
- **State Or Province**   Filters recipients based on the value of the State/Province text box on the Contact Information page in the related Properties dialog box. Selecting this option displays the Specify Words Or Phrases dialog box. Type a state or province identifier to use as a filter condition and then press Enter or click Add. Repeat as necessary, and then click OK.
- **Department**   Filters recipients based on the value of the Department text box on the Organization page in the related Properties dialog box. Selecting this option displays the Specify Words Or Phrases dialog box. Type a department name to use as a filter condition and then press Enter or click Add. Repeat as necessary, and then click OK.
- **Company**   Filters recipients based on the value of the Company text box on the Organization page in the related Properties dialog box. Selecting this option displays the Specify Words Or Phrases dialog box. Type a company name to use as a filter condition and then press Enter or click Add. Repeat as necessary, and then click OK.

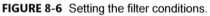

new dynamic distribution group

Membership in this group will be determined by the rules you set up below.

✕ State or province   ▼   'OR' or 'WA' ...

✕ Department   ▼   'Engineering'

✕ Company   ▼   'Imagined La...

add a rule

Save   Cancel

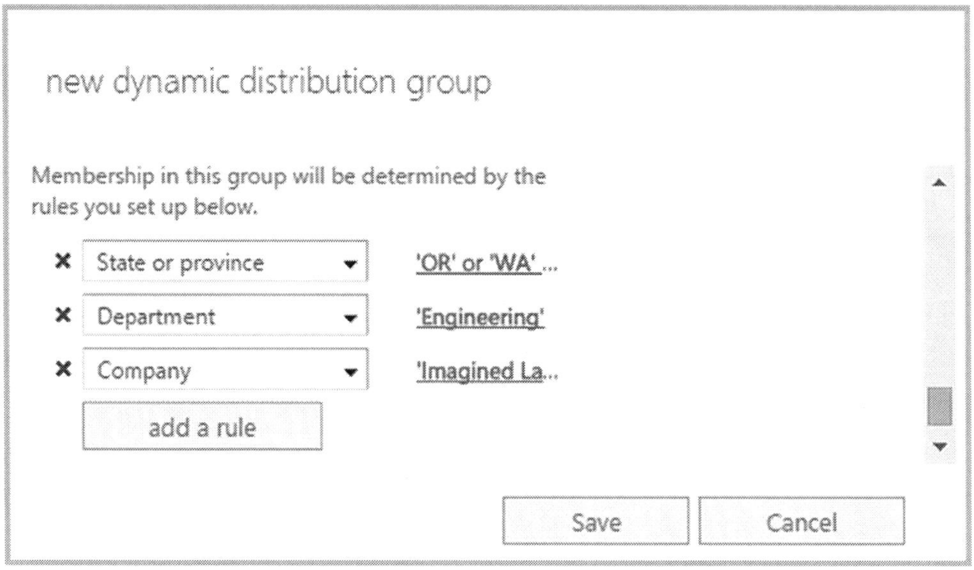

FIGURE 8-6 Setting the filter conditions.

> **IMPORTANT**   Although each rule acts as an OR condition for matches on specified values, the rules are aggregated as AND conditions. This means that a user that matches one of the values in a rule passes that filter but must be a match for all the rules to be included in the group. For example, if you were to define a state rule for Oregon, California, or Washington and a department rule for Technology, only users who are in Oregon, California, or

> Washington *and* in the Technology department match the filter and are included as members of the group.

9. Click **Save** to create the group. If an error occurs during group creation, the related group will not be created. You need to correct the problem before you can complete this procedure.

10. Creating the group isn't the final step. Afterward, you might want to do the following:

- Set message size restrictions for messages mailed to the group.
- Limit users who can send to the group.
- Change or remove default email addresses.
- Add more email addresses.

In Exchange Management Shell, you can create a dynamic distribution group using the New-DynamicDistributionGroup cmdlet. Sample 8-10 provides the syntax and usage.

SAMPLE 8-10 New-DynamicDistributionGroup cmdlet syntax and usage

Syntax

```
New-DynamicDistributionGroup -Name ExchangeName
-IncludedRecipients <None, MailboxUsers, MailContacts, MailGroups,
Resources, AllRecipients> [-Alias ExchangeAlias]
[-DisplayName DisplayName] [-OrganizationalUnit OUName]
[-ConditionalCompany CompanyNameFilter1, CompanyNameFilter2,...]
[-ConditionalCustomAttributeX Value1, Value2,...]
[-ConditionalDepartment DeptNameFilter1, DeptNameFilter2, ... ]
[-ConditionalStateOrProvince StateNameFilter1, StateNameFilter2, ...]
[-RecipientContainer ApplyFilterContainer] {AddtlParams}


New-DynamicDistributionGroup -Name ExchangeName -RecipientFilter Filter
[-Alias ExchangeAlias] [-DisplayName DisplayName] [-OrganizationalUnit
OUName] [-RecipientContainer ApplyFilterContainer] {AddtlParams}


{AddtlParams}
[-ArbitrationMailbox ModeratorMailbox] [-DomainController
FullyQualifiedName] [-ExternalDirectoryObjectId ObjectId]
[-ModeratedBy Moderators] [-ModerationEnabled <$true | $false>]
```

```
[-Organization OrgName] [-PrimarySmtpAddress SmtpAddress]
[-SendModerationNotifications <Never | Internal | Always>]
```

Usage

```
New-DynamicDistributionGroup -Name 'CrossSales'
 -OrganizationalUnit 'imaginedlands.com/Users' -DisplayName
'CrossSales' -Alias 'CrossSales'
 -IncludedRecipients 'MailboxUsers, MailContacts, MailGroups'
 -ConditionalCompany 'Imagined Lands'
 -ConditionalDepartment 'Sales','Marketing'
 -ConditionalStateOrProvince 'Washington','Oregon','California'
 -RecipientContainer 'imaginedlands.com'
```

Changing Query Filters and Filter Conditions

With dynamic distribution groups, the filter conditions determine the exact criteria that must be met for a recipient to be included in the dynamic distribution group. You can modify the filter conditions by completing the following steps:

1. In Exchange Admin Center, double-click the dynamic distribution group entry. This opens the group's Properties dialog box.

2. On the Membership page, use the Specify The Types Of Recipients options to specify the types of recipients to include in the query. Select either **All Recipient Types** or select **Only The Following Recipient Types**, and then select the types of recipients.

3. The Membership page lists the current conditions. The following types of conditions as well as conditions for custom attributes are available:

- **State Or Province**   Filters recipients based on the value of the State/Province text box on the Contact Information page in the related Properties dialog box. Click the related Enter Words link. In the Specify Words Or Phrases dialog box, type a state or province identifier to use as a filter condition and then press Enter or click Add. Repeat as necessary, and then click OK.
- **Department**   Filters recipients based on the value of the Department text box on the Organization page in the related Properties dialog box. Click the related Enter Words link. In the Specify Words Or Phrases dialog box, type a department name to use as a filter condition and then press Enter or click Add. Repeat as necessary, and then click OK.
- **Company**   Filters recipients based on the value of the Company text box on the Organization page in the related Properties dialog box. Click the related Enter

Words link. In the Specify Words Or Phrases dialog box, type a company name to use as a filter condition and then press Enter or click Add. Repeat as necessary, and then click OK.

4.   Click **Save** to apply the changes.

Designating an Expansion Server

When there are potentially hundreds or thousands of members, dynamic distribution groups are inefficient and can require a great deal of processing to complete. This is why Exchange 2016 shifts the processing requirements from Global Catalog servers to dedicated expansion servers. However, the routing destination is the ultimate destination for a message. A distribution group expansion server is the routing destination when a distribution group has a designated expansion server that's responsible for expanding the membership list of the group. A distribution group expansion server is always an Exchange 2016 Mailbox server, an Exchange 2013 Mailbox server or an Exchange 2010 Hub Transport server.

Each routing destination has a delivery group, which is a collection of one or more transport servers that are responsible for delivering messages to that routing destination. When the routing destination is a distribution group expansion server, the delivery group may contain Exchange 2016 Mailbox servers, Exchange 2013 Mailbox servers, and Exchange 2010 Hub Transport servers.

How the message is routed depends on the relationship between the source transport server and the destination delivery group. If the source transport server is in the destination delivery group, the routing destination itself is the next hop for the message. The message is delivered by the source transport server to the mailbox database or connector on a transport server in the delivery group.

On the other hand, if the source transport server is outside the destination delivery group, the message is relayed along the least-cost routing path to the destination delivery group. In a complex Exchange organization, a message may be relayed to other transport servers along the least-cost routing path or relayed directly to a transport server in the destination delivery group.

> **REAL WORLD**   Keep in mind that when a distribution group expansion server is the routing destination, the distribution group is already expanded when a message reaches the routing stage of categorization on the distribution group expansion server. Therefore, the routing destination from the distribution group expansion server is always a mailbox database or a connector.

By default, Exchange 2016 uses the closest Exchange server that has the Mailbox server role installed as the dedicated expansion server. Because routing destinations and delivery groups can also include Exchange 2013 Mailbox servers and Exchange 2010 Hub Transport servers in mixed environments, Exchange 2013 and Exchange 2010 servers could perform distribution group expansion in mixed Exchange organizations.

In some cases, you might want to explicitly specify the dedicated expansion server to handle expansion processing for some or all of your dynamic distribution groups. A key reason for this is to manage where the related processing occurs and in this way shift the processing overhead from other servers to this specified server. You can specify a dedicated expansion server using the -ExpansionServer parameter of the Set-DynamicDistributionGroup cmdlet.

Modifying Dynamic Distribution Groups Using Cmdlets

In Exchange Management Shell, you can use the Get-DynamicDistributionGroup cmdlet to get information about dynamic distribution groups and modify their associated filters and conditions using the Set-DynamicDistributionGroup cmdlet.

Sample 8-11 provides the syntax and usage for the Get-DynamicDistributionGroup cmdlet.

SAMPLE 8-11 Get-DynamicDistributionGroup cmdlet syntax and usage

Syntax

```
Get-DynamicDistributionGroup [-Identity GroupIdentify | -Anr Name
  | -ManagedBy Managers]
[-AccountPartition PartitionID] [-Credential Credential]
[-DomainController FullyQualifiedName] [-Filter FilterString]
[-IgnoreDefaultScope {$true | $false}] [-Organization OrgName]
[-OrganizationalUnit OUName] [-ReadFromDomainController {$true | $false}]
[-ResultSize Size] [-SortBy Value]
```

Usage

```
Get-DynamicDistributionGroup -Identity 'CrossSales'
```

Sample 8-12 provides the syntax and usage for the Set-DynamicDistributionGroup cmdlet.

SAMPLE 8-12 Set-DynamicDistributionGroup cmdlet syntax and usage

Syntax

```
Set-DynamicDistributionGroup -Identity GroupIdentity
[-Alias NewAlias] [-AcceptMessagesOnlyFrom Recipients]
[-AcceptMessagesOnlyFromDLMembers Recipients]
[-AcceptMessagesOnlyFromSendersOrMembers Recipients]
[-ArbitrationMailbox ModeratorMailbox]
[-BypassModerationFromSendersOrMembers Recipients]
[-ConditionalCompany Values] [-ConditionalDepartment Values]
[-ConditionalCustomAttributeX Values]
[-ConditionalStateOrProvince Values] [-CreateDTMFMap <$true | $false>]
```

[-DisplayName **Name**] [-DomainController **DCName**]

[-EmailAddresses **ProxyAddress**]

[-EmailAddressPolicyEnabled <$false|$true>]

[-ExpansionServer **Server**] [-ForceUpgrade <$false|$true>]

[-ExtensionCustomAttribute**X Value1, Value2,...**]

[-GrantSendOnBehalfTo **Mailbox**]

[-HiddenFromAddressListsEnabled <$false|$true>]

[-IgnoreDefaultScope {$true | $false}]

[-IncludedRecipients <None, MailboxUsers, MailContacts, MailGroups, Resources, AllRecipients>] [-MailTip **String**]

[-MailTipTranslations **Locale:TipString, Locale:TipString, ...**]

[-ManagedBy **Managers**] [-MaxReceiveSize **Size**] [-MaxSendSize **Size**]

[-ModeratedBy **Moderators**] [-ModerationEnabled <$true | $false>]

[-Name **Name**] [-Notes **Value**] [-PhoneticDisplayName **PhName**]

[-PrimarySmtpAddress **SmtpAddress**]

[-RecipientContainer **OUName**] [-RecipientFilter **String**]

[-RejectMessagesFrom **Recipients**]

[-RejectMessagesFromDLMembers **Recipients**]

[-RejectMessagesFromSendersOrMembers **Recipients**]

[-ReportToManagerEnabled <$false|$true>]

[-ReportToOriginatorEnabled <$false|$true>]

[-RequireSenderAuthenticationEnabled <$false|$true>]

[-SendModerationNotifications <Never | Internal | Always>]

[-SendOofMessageToOriginatorEnabled <$false|$true>]

[-SimpleDisplayName **Name**] [-UMDtmfMap **Values**]

[-WindowsEmailAddress **SmtpAddress**]

Usage

```
Set-DynamicDistributionGroup -Identity 'CrossSales'
 -IncludedRecipients 'AllRecipients'
 -ConditionalCompany 'Imagined Lands'
 -ConditionalDepartment 'Sales','Accounting'
 -ConditionalStateOrProvince 'Washington','Idaho','Oregon'
 -RecipientContainer 'imaginedlands.com'
```

```
Set-DynamicDistributionGroup -Identity 'CrossSales'
 -ForceUpgrade $true
```

Usage

```
Set-DynamicDistributionGroup -Identity 'CrossSales'
 -ExpansionServer 'CorpSvr127'
```

Previewing Dynamic Distribution Group Membership

You can preview a dynamic distribution group to confirm its membership and determine how long it takes to return the query results. The specific actions you take depend on the following factors:

* In some cases, membership isn't what you expected. If this happens, you need to change the query filters, as discussed earlier.
* In other cases, it takes too long to execute the query and return the results. If this happens, you might want to rethink the query parameters and create several query groups.

You can quickly determine how many recipients are in the group by checking how many recipients received the last message sent to the group. One way to do this is to follow these steps:

1. In Exchange Admin Center, select the dynamic distribution group entry.
2. In the details pane, look under Membership to see the number of recipients who received the last message sent to the group.

In Exchange Management Shell, you can determine the exact membership of a dynamic distribution group by getting the dynamic group and then using the associated recipient filter to list the members. Consider the following example:

```
$Members = Get-DynamicDistributionGroup "TechTeam"
Get-Recipient -RecipientPreviewFilter $Members.RecipientFilter
```

In this example, Get-DynamicDistributionGroup stores the object for the TechTeam group in the $Members variable. Then Get-Recipient lists the recipients that match the recipient filter on this object. Note that the Exchange identifier can be the display name or alias for the group.

Other Essential Tasks for Managing Groups

Previous sections covered tasks that were specific to a type of group. As an Exchange administrator, you'll need to perform many additional group management tasks. These essential tasks are discussed in this section.

Changing a Group's Name Information

Each mail-enabled group has a display name, an Exchange alias, and one or more email addresses associated with it. The display name is the name that appears in address lists. The Exchange alias is used to set the email addresses associated with the group.

Whenever you change a group's naming information, new email addresses can be generated and set as the default addresses for SMTP. These email addresses are used as alternatives to email addresses previously assigned to the group. To learn how to change or delete these additional email addresses, see the "Changing, adding, or deleting a group's email addresses" section later in this chapter.

To change the group's Exchange name details, complete the following steps:

1. In Exchange Admin Center, double-click the group entry. This opens the group's Properties dialog box.
2. On the General page, the first text box shows the display name of the group. If necessary, type a new display name.
3. The Alias text box shows the Exchange alias. If necessary, type a new alias. Click **Save**.

> **NOTE** When you change a group's display name, you give the group a new label. Changing the display name doesn't affect the SID, which is used to identify, track, and handle permissions independently from group names.

US Support

▸ general
ownership
membership
membership approval
delivery management
message approval
email options
MailTip
group delegation

*Display name:

US Support

*Alias:

USSupport

Notes:

☐ Hide this group from address lists

Organizational unit:

imaginedlands.local/Users

[Save] [Cancel]

Changing, Adding, or Deleting a Group's Email Addresses

When you create a mail-enabled group, default email addresses are created for SMTP. Any time you update the group's Exchange alias, new default email addresses can be created. The old addresses aren't deleted, however; they remain as alternative email addresses for the group.

To change, add, or delete a group's email addresses, follow these steps:

1. In Exchange Admin Center, double-click the group entry. This opens the group's Properties dialog box.

2. On the Email Options page, use the following techniques to manage the group's email addresses:

- **Create a new SMTP address** Click Add (✚). In the New Email Address dialog box, SMTP is selected as the address type by default. Enter the email address, and then click OK.

- **Create a custom address** Click Add (✚). In the New Email Address dialog box, select Custom Address Type. Enter a prefix that identifies the type of email address, and then enter the associated address. Click OK.

> **TIP** Use SMTP as the address type for standard Internet email addresses. For custom address types, such as X.400, you must manually enter the address in the proper format.

- **Set a new Reply To Address** Double-click the address that you want to use as the primary SMTP address. Select Make This The Reply Address, and then click OK. (Exchange Online Only)
- **Edit an existing address** Double-click the address entry. Modify the settings in the Address dialog box, and then click OK.
- **Delete an existing address** Select the address, and then click Remove.

Sample 8-13 provides syntax and usage examples for configuring a group's primary SMTP email address. If email address policy is enabled, you won't be able to update the email address unless you set -EmailAddressPolicyEnabled to $false.

SAMPLE 8-13 Configuring a group's primary SMTP email address

Syntax

```
Get-DistributionGroup -Identity GroupIdentity | format-list –property
Name, EmailAddresses, PrimarySmtpAddress

Set-DistributionGroup -Identity GroupIdentity
-PrimarySmtpAddress SmtpAddress -EmailAddressPolicyEnabled $false
```

```
Get-DistributionGroup -Identity 'AllSales' | format-list -property
Name, EmailAddresses, PrimarySmtpAddress
```

```
Set-DistributionGroup -Identity 'AllSales'
-PrimarySmtpAddress allsales@imaginedlands.com
-EmailAddressPolicyEnabled $false
```

Hiding Groups from Exchange Address Lists

By default, any mail-enabled security group or other distribution group that you create is shown in Exchange address lists, such as the global address list. If you want to hide a group from the address lists, follow these steps:

1. In Exchange Admin Center, double-click the group entry. This opens the group's Properties dialog box.

2. On the General page, select the **Hide This Group From Address Lists** check box. Click **OK**.

US Support

- general
- ownership
- membership
- membership approval
- delivery management
- message approval
- email options
- MailTip
- group delegation

*Display name:
US Support

*Alias:
USSupport

Notes:

☐ Hide this group from address lists

Save   Cancel

NOTE When you hide a group, it isn't listed in Exchange address lists. However, if a user knows the name of a group, he or she can still use it in the mail client. To prevent users from sending to a group, you must set message restrictions, as discussed in the next section, "Setting Usage Restrictions on Groups."

In Exchange Management Shell, you can return a list of groups hidden from address lists using either of the following commands:

```
Get-DistributionGroup -filter {HiddenFromAddressListsEnabled -eq $true}
```

```
Get-DistributionGroup | where {$_.HiddenFromAddressListsEnabled -eq $true}
```

Setting Usage Restrictions on Groups

Groups are great resources for users in an organization. They let users send mail quickly and easily to other users in their department, business unit, or office. However, if you aren't careful, people outside the organization could use groups as well. Would your boss like it if spammers sent unsolicited email messages to company employees through your distribution lists? Probably not—and you'd probably be sitting in the hot seat, which would be uncomfortable, to say the least.

To prevent unauthorized use of mail-enabled groups, groups are configured by default to accept mail only from authenticated users so that only senders inside an organization can send messages to groups. An authenticated user is any user accessing the system through a logon process. It does not include anonymous users or guests. If you use the default configuration, any message from a sender outside the organization is rejected. Off-site users will need to log on to Exchange before they can send mail to groups, which might present a problem for users who are at home or travelling.

send mail to the group; this is an approach that doesn't require any special groups with permissions to be created or maintained.

Alternatively, you can allow senders inside and outside the organization to send email to a group. This setting allows unrestricted access to the group, so anyone can send messages to the group. However, this exposes the group to spam from external mail accounts.

Another way to prevent unauthorized use of mail-enabled groups is to specify that only certain users or members of a particular group can send messages to the group. For example, if you create a group called AllEmployees, of which all company employees are members, you can specify that only the members of AllEmployees can send messages to the group. You do this by specifying that only messages from members of AllEmployees are acceptable.

To prevent mass spamming of other groups, you can set the same restriction. For example, if you have a group called Technology, you could specify that only members of AllEmployees can send messages to that group.

You can set or remove usage restrictions by completing the following steps:

1. In Exchange Admin Center, double-click the group entry. In the Properties dialog box for the group, select the **Delivery Management** page.
2. To ensure that messages are accepted only from authenticated users, select **Only Senders Inside My Organization**.
3. To accept messages from all email addresses, select **Senders Inside And Outside Of My Organization**.
4. To restrict senders, specify that messages only from the listed users, contacts, or groups be accepted. To do this, click Add (   ) to display the Select Allowed Senders dialog box. Select a recipient, and then click **OK**. Repeat as necessary.

> **TIP** You can select multiple recipients at the same time. To select multiple recipients individually, hold down the Ctrl key and then click each recipient that you want to select. To select a continuous sequence of recipients, select the first recipient, hold down the Shift key, and then click the last recipient.

5. Click **Save**.

US Engineering

general
ownership
membership
membership approval
▸ delivery management
message approval
email options
MailTip
group delegation

By default, only senders inside your organization can send messages to this group. You can also allow people outside the organization to send to this group. Choose one of the options below.

◉ Only senders inside my organization
◯ Senders inside and outside of my organization

If you want to restrict who can send messages to the group, add users or groups to the list below. Only the specified senders will be able to send to the group and mail sent by anyone else will be rejected.

+ −

All senders can send messages to this group.

Save   Cancel

Creating Moderated Groups

By default, senders don't require approval for their messages to be sent to all members of a group. Sometimes though you'll want to appoint moderators who must approve messages before they are sent to all members of the group. If you enable moderation but don't specify a moderator or moderators, the group owner is responsible for reviewing and approving messages. When moderation is enabled, you also can specify users who don't require approval for their messages to be sent to all members of the group.

To see how moderation could be used, consider the following example. A project team is set up to work on a restricted project. The team leader wants a moderated group for the project team so that she must review and approve all messages sent to the group before they are sent to members of the team. As the moderator, the team leader's messages don't require approval and are sent directly to all members of the group.

To configure moderation for a group, complete the following steps:

1. In Exchange Admin Center, double-click the group name to open the Properties dialog box for the group.

2. On the Message Approval page, do one of the following:

- To enable moderation, select Messages Sent To This Group Have To Be Approved By A Moderator. Next, use the options provided to specify moderators and senders who don't required message approval.
- To disable moderation, clear Messages Sent To This Group Have To Be Approved By A Moderator. Click Save and then skip the rest of the steps.

US Engineering

general
ownership
membership
membership approval
delivery management
▸ message approval
email options
MailTip
group delegation

☑ Messages sent to this group have to be
approved by a moderator

Group moderators:

+ −

If you don't select a moderator, the group owner
will review and approve messages.

Senders who don't require message approval:

+ −

You can select senders who can send messages
to the group without message approval.

[Save]   [Cancel]

3. Use the Group Moderators options to add moderators. If there are any senders who don't require message approval, add these as well using the options provided.

4. If a message addressed to the group isn't approved, the message isn't distributed to members of the group, and all users receive a nondelivery report (NDR) by default whether they are inside or outside the organization. Alternatively, you can notify only senders in your organization when their messages aren't approved or you can disable notification completely.

5. Click **Save**.

US Engineering

general
ownership
membership
membership approval
delivery management
▸ message approval
email options
MailTip
group delegation

Select moderation notifications:

◉ Notify all senders when their messages aren't approved.

◯ Notify senders in your organization when their messages aren't approved.

◯ Don't notify anyone when a message isn't approved.

| Save | Cancel |

Deleting Groups

If you are an owner of a group, you can delete it. Deleting a group removes it permanently. After you delete a security group, you can't create a security group with the same name and automatically restore the permissions that the original group was assigned because the SID for the new group won't match the SID for the old group. You can reuse group names, but remember that you'll have to re-create all permissions settings.

warning

Are you sure you want to delete the group "US Finance"?

| Yes | No |

You cannot delete built-in groups in Windows. In Exchange Admin Center, you can remove other types of groups by selecting them and clicking Delete. When prompted, click Yes to delete the group. If you click No, Exchange Admin Center will not delete the group.

In Exchange Management Shell, only a group's manager or other authorized user can remove a group. Use the Remove-DistributionGroup cmdlet to remove distribution groups, as shown in Sample 8-14.

SAMPLE 8-14 Remove-DistributionGroup cmdlet syntax and usage

Syntax

```
Remove-DistributionGroup -Identity GroupIdentity
[-BypassSecurityGroupManagerCheck {$true | $false}]
[-DomainController FullyQualifiedName]
[-IgnoreDefaultScope {$true | $false}]
```

Usage

```
Remove-DistributionGroup -Identity 'imaginedlands.com/Users/AllSales'
```

To remove dynamic distribution groups, you can use the Remove-DynamicDistributionGroup cmdlet. Sample 8-15 shows the syntax and usage.

SAMPLE 8-15 Remove-DynamicDistributionGroup cmdlet syntax and usage

Syntax

```
Remove-DynamicDistributionGroup -Identity GroupIdentity
[-DomainController FullyQualifiedName]
[-IgnoreDefaultScope {$true | $false}]
```

Usage

```
Remove-DynamicDistributionGroup -Identity 'CrossSales'
```

Chapter 9. Managing Addresses Online and Offline

Email addresses and other contact information stored in the Exchange organization are available via online address lists and offline address books. Address lists are collections of recipients in an Exchange organization that are selectable in the address book of client applications. Exchange can be configured to distribute copies of address books to authorized users so that address lists are accessible when working offline.

Managing Online Address Lists

You use address lists to organize recipients by department, business unit, location, type, and other criteria. The default address lists that Exchange Server creates, as well as any new address lists that you create, are available to the user community based on their view of the global address list. Users can navigate these address lists to find recipients to whom they want to send messages.

Using Default Address Lists

During setup, Exchange Server creates a number of default address lists that are selectable in the address book of client applications, including the following:

- **Default Global Address List**   Lists all mail-enabled users, contacts, and groups in the organization.
- **Default Offline Address Book**   Provides an address list for viewing offline that contains information on all mail-enabled users, contacts, and groups in the organization.
- **All Contacts**   Lists all mail-enabled contacts in the organization.
- **All Groups**   Lists all mail-enabled groups in the organization.
- **All Rooms**   Lists all resource mailboxes for rooms.
- **Public Folders**   Lists all public folders in the organization.
- **All Users**   Lists all mail-enabled users in the organization.

> **IMPORTANT**   Generally, whenever you specify address list paths in Exchange Management Shell, you must reference their position relative to the root container. The root container is identified as \. If the address list name contains spaces, you also must enclose the address list path in quotes. Thus, you reference the Default Address List as '\Default Address List' and All Rooms as '\All Rooms'.

The most commonly used address lists are the global address list and the offline address book. In Exchange Admin Center for your on-premises organization, you access online address lists and offline address books by selecting Organization in the Features pane and then selecting Address Lists. As Figure 9-1 shows, the main pane shows each address list by name and up-to-date status. If an address list isn't up-to-date, you can click the Update option to update it.

> **IMPORTANT**   Any address list created using the shell should be managed only with the shell. Address lists created with the GUI can be managed with either the GUI or the shell. That said, Microsoft recommends that you manage address lists from the shell whenever the list contains several thousand or more recipients. The reason for this is that Exchange Admin Center will be locked until the task is completed.

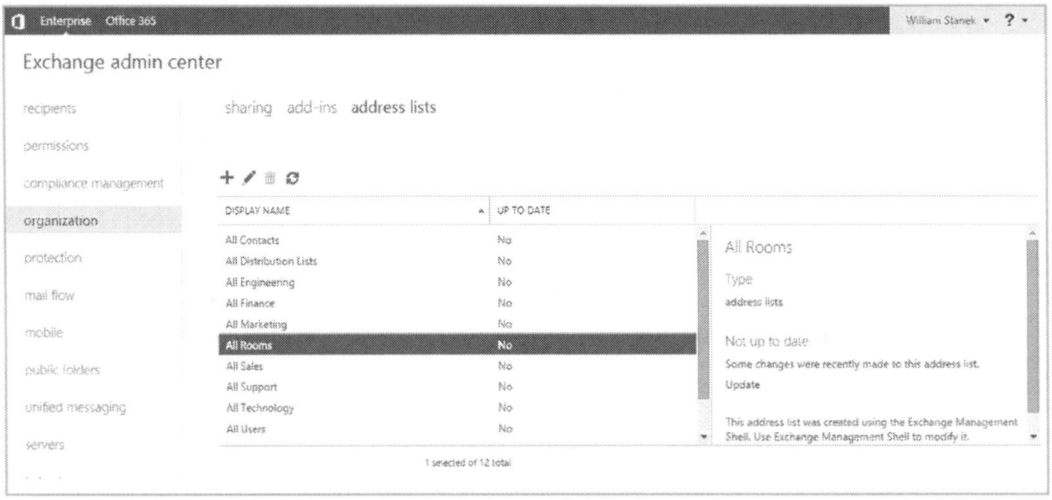

FIGURE 9-1 Accessing address lists in Exchange Admin Center.

Using Address Book Policies

Most Exchange organizations don't need address book policies. However, when multiple companies share one Exchange organization, you may want to segment the global address list to provide customized (scoped) views of recipient data to users in each separate company. You segment the global address list using address book policies. Each address book policy contains a global address list, an offline address book, a room list, and one or more address lists.

You use address book policies when you need to complete separation of the recipient data. Consider the following example:

TV Press merges with Reagent Press, resulting in a merged company called RP Media. While publicly a single company, internally the television and publishing operations are distinct and separate. The only overlap between the operations is in the top-level executive team.

The company has a single Exchange organization and wants those that work in one part of the operation to have access only to recipients and resources in that operation. Employees get scoped views of All Users, All Groups, and All Rooms as well as the default global address list and the default offline address list. These scoped views include only those that work as part of the television or publishing operations and not both.

The top-level executives and their direct support staff have access to the original, unscoped address lists. This ensures they can access recipients and resources in both operations areas.

Keep in mind that the need for custom views of recipients doesn't mean that your organization needs address book policies. You can create new address lists at any time and those address lists can be scoped however you'd like them to be scoped. For example, you could create an address list called All Marketing that includes only employees in the marketing department.

You can assign address book policy to recipients in both on-premises and online Exchange organizations. Before you can use address book policy, you must do the following:

1. Install and enable the Address Book Policy Routing Agent using these commands:

```
Install-TransportAgent -Name "ABP Routing Agent"
-TransportAgentFactory "Microsoft.Exchange.Transport.Agent
.AddressBookPolicyRoutingAgent
.AddressBookPolicyRoutingAgentFactory"
-AssemblyPath "C:\Program Files\Microsoft\Exchange Server\V15\
TransportRoles\Agents\AddressBookPolicyRoutingAgent\
Microsoft.Exchange.Transport.Agent
.AddressBookPolicyRoutingAgent.dll"


Enable-TransportAgent "ABP Routing Agent"
```

> **NOTE** Here, C:\Program Files\Microsoft\Exchange Server\V15\ is the Exchange install path. If you installed Exchange in a different location, revise the path as appropriate.

2. Next, you should restart the Microsoft Exchange Transport service and enable Address Book Policy routing in the organization using these commands:

```
Restart-Service MSExchangeTransport
Set-TransportConfig -AddressBookPolicyRoutingEnabled $true
```

3. Set an attribute on all recipients that can be used to segment the Exchange organization. For example, you could use a custom attribute to do this.

4. Create a one or more address lists that provide the segmented views of the organization-wide global address list. Typically, you'll want a list for mailbox users, contacts, distributions lists, and rooms. Use New-AddressList with recipient filters that look for the special attribute to create these lists. Here are examples:

```
New-AddressList -Name "B - All Users" -RecipientFilter
{(RecipientType -eq 'UserMailbox') -and
 (CustomAttribute8 -eq "CompanyB")}


New-AddressList -Name "B - All Contacts" -RecipientFilter
{((RecipientType -eq "MailUser") -or (RecipientType
-eq "MailContact")) -and (CustomAttribute8 -eq "CompanyB")}


New-AddressList -Name "B - All Groups" -RecipientFilter
{((RecipientType -eq "MailUniversalDistributionGroup")
-or (RecipientType -eq "DynamicDistributionGroup")
-or (RecipientType -eq "MailUniversalSecurityGroup"))
-and (CustomAttribute1 -eq "CompanyB")}


New-AddressList -Name "B - All Rooms" -RecipientFilter {(Alias
-ne $null) -and (CustomAttribute8 -eq "CompanyB")-and
(RecipientDisplayType -eq 'ConferenceRoomMailbox') -or
(RecipientDisplayType -eq 'SyncedConferenceRoomMailbox')}
```

> **NOTE** Address book policy requires a room list. If you don't use rooms, create an empty list.

5. Create a segmented global address list and then use this address list to create the segmented offline address book. Here are examples:

```
New-GlobalAddressList -Name "B - GAL" -RecipientFilter
{(CustomAttribute8 -eq "CompanyB")}
```

```
New-OfflineAddressBook -Name "B - OAB" -AddressLists "\B - GAL"
```

6. Create an address book policy for the first company within the organization and then assign this policy to the appropriate mailboxes. Here are examples:

```
New-AddressBookPolicy -Name "CompanyB ABP" -AddressLists
"\B - All Users", "\B - All Contacts", "\B - All Contacts"
-OfflineAddressBook "\B - OAB" -GlobalAddressList "\B - GAL"
-RoomList "\B - All Rooms"
```

```
Get-Mailbox -resultsize unlimited | where {$_.CustomAttribute8 -eq
"CompanyB"} | Set-Mailbox -AddressBookPolicy "CompanyB ABP"
```

7. As necessary, repeat Steps 4 through 6 to configure address lists and policies for each company within the Exchange organization.

Creating and Applying New Address Lists

You can create new address lists to create customized views of recipient data. For example, if your organization has offices in Seattle, Portland, and San Francisco, you might want to create separate address lists for each office.

To create an address list that users can select in their Outlook clients, follow these steps:

1. In Exchange Admin Center, select **Organization** in the Features pane and then select **Address Lists**.

2. Click **New** ( ). This opens the New Address List dialog box.

3. Type an internal Exchange name and a display name for the address list, as shown in Figure 9-2. The display name should describe the types of recipients that are viewed through the list. For example, if you're creating a list for recipients in the Boston office, you can call the list Boston Office.

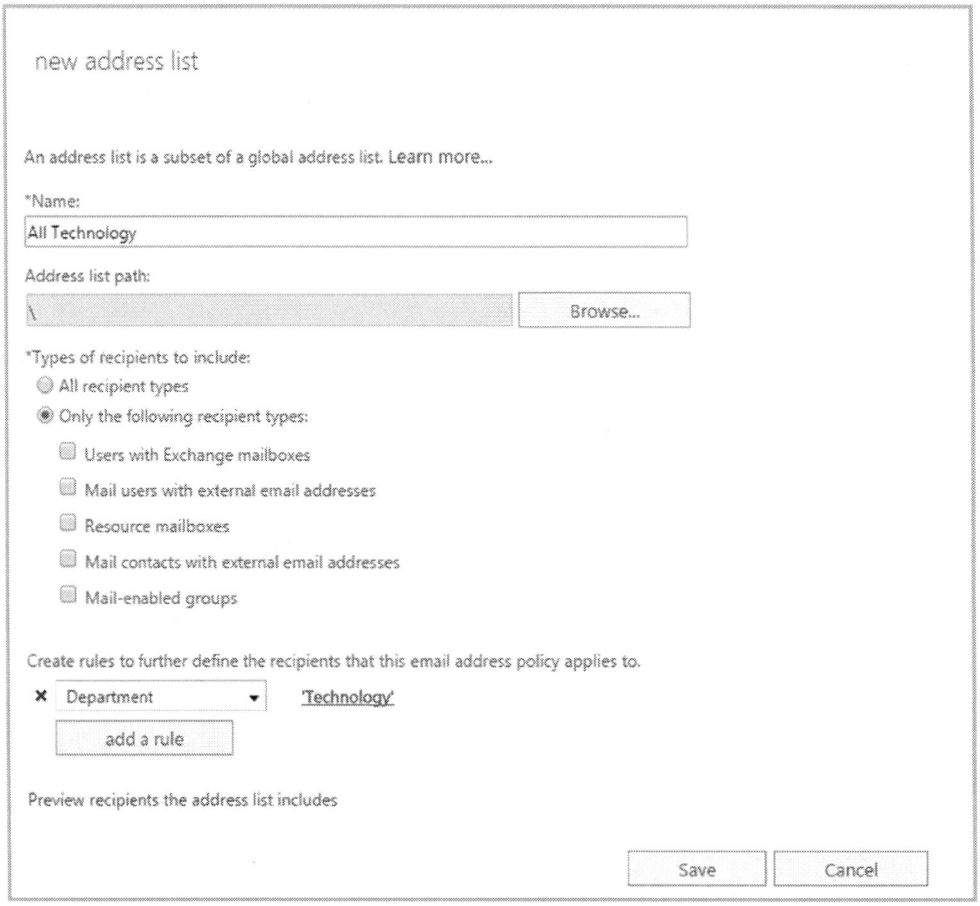

FIGURE 9-2 Specifying a name and configuring the address list.

4. The container on which you base the address list sets the scope of the list. The list will include recipients in address lists in and below the specified container. The default (root) container, \, specifies that all address lists are included by default. To specify a different container for limiting the list scope, click **Browse**, and then use the Address List Picker dialog box to select a container. In most cases, you'll want to select the default (root) container. The list path is fixed when you create a list, so you won't be able to specify a different list path later.

5. Use the Types Of Recipient To Include options to specify the types of recipients to include in the address list. Select All Recipient Types or select Only The Following Recipient Types and then select the types of recipients. You can include mailbox users, mail-enabled contacts, mail-enabled groups, mail-enabled users, and resource mailboxes.

6. Next, you can create rules that further filter the address list. Each rule acts as a condition that must be met. If you set more than one rule, each condition

must be met for there to be a match. To define a rule, click **Add A Rule** and then set the filter conditions. The following types of conditions are available as well as conditions for custom attributes:

- **Recipient Container**   Filters recipients based on where in Active Directory the related account is stored. Selecting this option displays the Select An Organizational Unit dialog box. Click the container where the recipients are stored, such as Users or an organizational unit, and then click OK.
- **State Or Province**   Filters recipients based on the value of the State/Province text box on the Contact Information page in the related Properties dialog box. Selecting this option displays the Specify Words Or Phrases dialog box. Type a state or province identifier to use as a filter condition and then press Enter or click Add. Repeat as necessary, and then click OK.
- **Department**   Filters recipients based on the value of the Department text box on the Organization page in the related Properties dialog box. Selecting this option displays the Specify Words Or Phrases dialog box. Type a department name to use as a filter condition and then press Enter or click Add. Repeat as necessary, and then click OK.
- **Company**   Filters recipients based on the value of the Company text box on the Organization page in the related Properties dialog box. Selecting this option displays the Specify Words Or Phrases dialog box. Type a company name to use as a filter condition and then press Enter or click Add. Repeat as necessary, and then click OK.

7. Click **Save** to create the address list. After the address list is created, users will be able to use the new address list the next time they start Outlook. In the Details pane, the new list will have a status of Not Up To Date.

Creating and fully populating address lists can be resource intensive, so new address lists aren't populated. You can populate the address list for the first time by updating it. To do this, click the address list and then click Update.

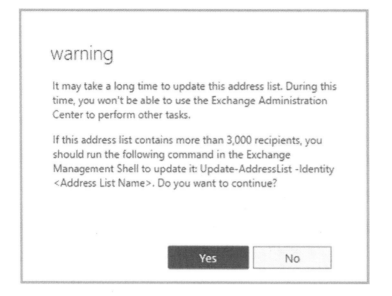

As shown, you'll see a warning prompt explaining that it could take a long time to update the address list. When you click Yes, Exchange Admin Center begins updating the address list and displays the update progress in a bar graph. If you find the update is taking too long, you can click Stop to halt the update. You can then restart the update process later.

In Exchange Management Shell, creating and applying address lists are two separate tasks. You can create address lists using the New-AddressList cmdlet. You apply address lists using the Update-AddressList cmdlet. Sample 9-1 provides the syntax and usage for the New-AddressList cmdlet. Sample 9-2 provides the syntax and usage for the Update-AddressList cmdlet. For -IncludedRecipients, you can include mailbox users, mail-enabled contacts, mail-enabled groups, mail-enabled users, and resource mailboxes.

> **TIP** Exchange Server 2016 does not support Recipient Update Service (RUS). To replace the functionality of RUS, you can schedule the Update-AddressList and Update-EmailAddressPolicy cmdlets to run periodically using Task Scheduler. Alternatively, you can run the cmdlets manually when you modify addresses.

SAMPLE 9-1 New-AddressList cmdlet syntax and usage

Syntax

```
New-AddressList -Name ListName [-Container BaseAddressList]
[-DisplayName DisplayName] [-IncludedRecipients <None, MailboxUsers,
MailContacts, MailGroups, MailUsers, Resources, AllRecipients>]
[-ConditionalCompany CompanyNameFilter1, CompanyNameFilter2,...]
[-ConditionalCustomAttributeX Value1, Value2, ...]
[-ConditionalDepartment DeptNameFilter1, DeptNameFilter2, ... ]
[-ConditionalStateOrProvince StateFilter1, StateFilter2, ...]
[-DomainController FullyQualifiedName] [-Organization OrgName]
[-RecipientContainer ApplyFilterContainer]


New-AddressList -Name ListName [-Container BaseAddressList]
[-DisplayName DisplayName] [-DomainController FullyQualifiedName]
[-Organization OrgName] [-RecipientContainer ApplyFilterContainer]
[-RecipientFilter Filter]
```

Usage

```
New-AddressList -Name 'West Coast Sales' -Container '\'
-DisplayName 'West Coast Sales' -IncludedRecipients 'MailboxUsers,
MailContacts, MailGroups, Resources'
-ConditionalCompany 'Imagined Lands'
-ConditionalDepartment 'Sales','Marketing'
-ConditionalStateOrProvince 'Washington','Idaho','Oregon'
```

SAMPLE 9-2 Update-AddressList cmdlet syntax and usage

Syntax

```
Update-AddressList -identity ListIdentity
[-DomainController FullyQualifiedName]
```

```
Update-AddressList -Identity '\West Coast Sales'
```

Updating Address List Configuration and Membership Throughout the Domain

Exchange Server doesn't immediately replicate changes to address lists throughout the domain. Instead, changes are replicated during the normal replication cycle, which means that some servers might temporarily have outdated address list information. Rather than waiting for replication, you can manually update address list configuration, availability, and membership throughout the domain. To do this, follow these steps:

1. In Exchange Admin Center, select **Organization** in the Features pane and then select **Address Lists**.
2. Click the address list you want to work with and then click **Update**.
3. You'll see a warning prompt explaining that it could take a long time to update the address list. Click **Yes**. Exchange Admin Center begins updating the address list and displays the update progress in a bar graph.
4. If you find the update is taking too long, you can click **Stop** to halt the update. You can then restart the update process later.

Alternatively, you can use the Update-AddressList cmdlet to update lists. See Sample 9-2 for syntax and usage.

Previewing and Editing Address Lists

Although you can't change the properties of default address lists, you can change the properties of address lists that you create using either Exchange Admin Center or Exchange Management Shell. You can edit a list's settings or preview the recipients in the list by completing the following steps:

1. In Exchange Admin Center, select **Organization** in the Features pane and then select **Address Lists**.
2. Click the address list you want to work with. If there's a note in the Details pane stating the list was created in Exchange Management Shell, you won't be able to modify its settings. You can, however, view the list's settings in the Address List dialog box.

3. Click **Edit** (✎). In the Address List dialog box, you'll see the name, path, and recipient filter associated with the list.

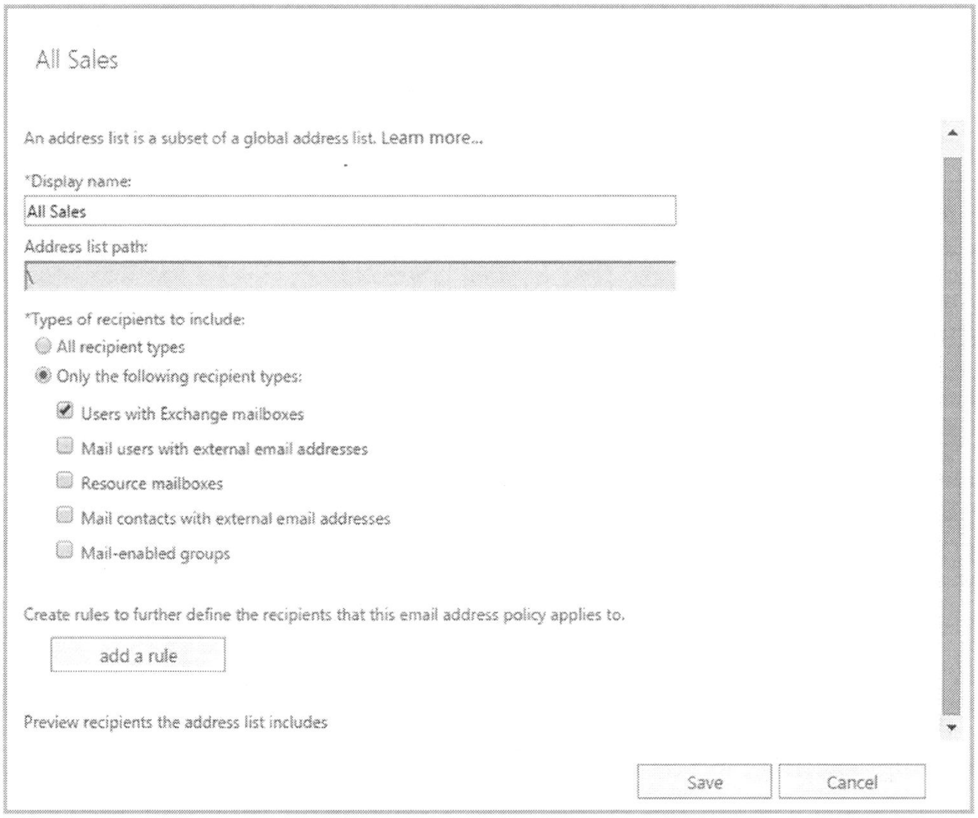

All Sales

An address list is a subset of a global address list. Learn more...

*Display name:

All Sales

Address list path:

\

*Types of recipients to include:

◯ All recipient types

◉ Only the following recipient types:

☑ Users with Exchange mailboxes

☐ Mail users with external email addresses

☐ Resource mailboxes

☐ Mail contacts with external email addresses

☐ Mail-enabled groups

Create rules to further define the recipients that this email address policy applies to.

    add a rule

Preview recipients the address list includes

    Save   Cancel

FIGURE 9-3 Modifying an address list.

4. To preview the recipients included in the list, click the link provided.

5. Modify the name as necessary. Use the Types Of Recipients To Include options to specify the types of recipients to include. Select **All Recipient Types** or select **Only The Following Recipient Types** and then select the types of recipients.

6. Create new rules or modify existing rules to further filter the recipients.

7. Click **Save**. A warning prompt is displayed stating the address list might not be up to date if you made changes. Click **OK**.

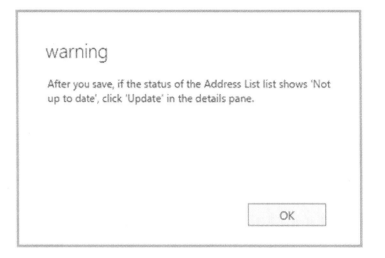

warning

After you save, if the status of the Address List list shows 'Not up to date', click 'Update' in the details pane.

OK

In Exchange Management Shell, you can modify an address list using the Set-AddressList cmdlet. Sample 9-3 provides the syntax and usage. When you modify an address list, you can make the changes visible by using the Update-AddressList cmdlet, as shown previously in Sample 9-2.

SAMPLE 9-3 Set-AddressList cmdlet syntax and usage

Syntax

```
Set-AddressList -Identity ListName
[-DisplayName DisplayName] [-IncludedRecipients <None, MailboxUsers,
MailContacts, MailGroups, Resources, AllRecipients>]
[-ConditionalCompany CompanyNameFilter1, CompanyNameFilter2,...]
[-ConditionalDepartment DeptNameFilter1, DeptNameFilter2, ...]
[-ConditionalStateOrProvince StateFilter1, StateFilter2, ...]
[-DomainController FullyQualifiedName] [-ForceUpgrade <$false|$true>]
[-RecipientContainer ApplyFilterContainer] [-RecipientFilter Filter]
```

Usage

```
Set-AddressList -Identity '\West Coast Sales' -Name 'Sales Team-West'
-IncludedRecipients 'MailboxUsers, MailContacts, MailGroups'
 -Company 'Imagined Lands'
 -Department 'Sales','Marketing'
 -StateOrProvince 'Washington','Idaho','Oregon'
```

```
Set-AddressList -Identity '\West Coast Sales' -Name 'Sales Team-West'
 -IncludedRecipients 'MailboxUsers, MailContacts, MailGroups'
 -ForceUpgrade $true
```

Configuring Clients to Use Address Lists

Address books are available to clients that are configured for corporate or workgroup use. To set the address lists used by the client, complete these steps:

1. In Office Outlook 2013 or Outlook 2016, on the Home panel, select **Address Book**. Alternatively, press **Ctrl+Shift+B**.

2. In the Address Book dialog box, from the Tools menu, select **Options**, and then set the following options to configure how address lists are used:

- **When Sending E-Mail, Check Address Lists In This Order**   Sets the order in which Outlook searches address books when you send a message or click Check Names. You can start with either the global address list or the contact folders. Or you can choose the Custom option and then use the up and down arrows to change the list order.
- **When Opening The Address Book, Show This Address List First**   Sets the address book that the user sees first whenever he or she works with the address book.

3. Click **OK**.

> **TIP**   When checking names, you'll usually want the global address list (GAL) to be listed before the user's own contacts or other types of address lists. This is important because users often put internal mailboxes in their personal address lists. The danger of doing this without first resolving names against the GAL is that although the display name might be identical, the properties of a mailbox might change. When changes occur, the entry in the user's address book is no longer valid, and any mail sent bounces back to the sender with a nondelivery report (NDR). To correct this, the user should either remove that mailbox from his or her personal address list and add it based on the current entry in the GAL, or change the check names resolution order to use the GAL before any personal lists.

Renaming and Deleting Address Lists

You can only rename or delete user-defined address lists.

- **Renaming address lists** To rename an address list, in Exchange Admin Center, select its entry and then select **Edit** (   ). Type a new name in the Display Name text box. In the Details pane, the modified list will have a status of Not Up To Date. To update the membership of the address list, click **Update**.
- **Deleting address lists** To delete an address list, in Exchange Admin Center, select its entry and then select **Remove** (   ). When prompted to confirm the action, click **Yes**.

In Exchange Management Shell, you can remove address lists using the Remove-AddressList cmdlet. Sample 9-4 provides the syntax and usage. If you also want to remove address lists that reference the address list you are removing and match a portion of it (child address lists), set the -Recursive parameter to $true. By default, the cmdlet does not remove child address lists of the specified list.

SAMPLE 9-4 Remove-AddressList cmdlet syntax and usage

Syntax

```
Remove-AddressList -Identity ListIdentity
[-DomainController FullyQualifiedName] [-Recursive {$true | $false}]
```

Usage

```
Remove-AddressList -Identity '\West Coast Sales'
```

Managing Offline Address Books

You configure offline address books differently than online address lists. To use an offline address book, the client must be configured to have a local copy of the server mailbox, or you can use personal folders. Clients using Outlook 2010 or later retrieve the offline address book from the designated offline address book (OAB) distribution point.

> **NOTE** Although future updates may change this, Exchange Admin Center doesn't have options for managing offline address books at the time of this writing. This means that you need to use Exchange Management Shell to manage offline address books.

> **IMPORTANT** An OAB distribution point is a virtual directory to which Outlook 2010 or later clients can connect to download the offline address book. OAB distribution points are hosted by Mailbox servers running Internet Information Services (IIS) as virtual directories. Each distribution point can have two URLs associated with it: one URL for internal (on-site) access and another for external (off-site) access.

Creating Offline Address Books

By default, the default offline address book includes all the addresses in the global address list. It does this by including the default global address list. All other offline address books are created by including the default global address list or a specific online address list as well.

> **NOTE** You can create other custom offline address books using Exchange Management Shell. You cannot use Exchange Admin Center to create other offline address books.

In Exchange Management Shell, you can create offline address books using the New-OfflineAddressBook cmdlet. You apply offline address books using the Update-OfflineAddressBook cmdlet. Sample 9-5 provides the syntax and usage for the New-OfflineAddressBook cmdlet. Sample 9-6 provides the syntax and usage for the Update-OfflineAddressBook cmdlet.

> **NOTE** Public folder distribution is no longer associated with offline address books. Public folders are now stored in special mailboxes, as discussed in Chapter 6, "Adding Special-Purpose Mailboxes."

SAMPLE 9-5 New-OfflineAddressBook cmdlet syntax and usage

Syntax

```
New-OfflineAddressBook -Name ListName -Server GenerationServer
 -AddressLists AddressList1, AddressList2, ...
[-VirtualDirectories  VirtualDir1, VirtualDir2, ...] {AddtlParams}


{AddtlParams}
[-DiffRetentionPeriod RetentionPeriod]
```

```
[-DomainController FullyQualifiedName]
[-GlobalWebDistributionEnabled <$true | $false>]
[-IsDefault <$true | $false>] [-Organization OrgName]
```

Usage

```
New-OfflineAddressBook -Name 'Offline – West Coast Sales'
 -Server 'CorpSvr127'
 -AddressLists '\West Coast Sales'
 -VirtualDirectories 'CORPSVR127\OAB (Default Web Site)'
```

SAMPLE 9-6 Update-OfflineAddressBook cmdlet syntax and usage

Syntax

```
Update-OfflineAddressBook -Identity OABName
[-DomainController FullyQualifiedName]
```

Usage

```
Update-OfflineAddressBook -Identity '\Offline – West Coast Sales'
```

When you create an offline address book, you must use the -AddressLists parameter to specify the address lists that are included. If you want the offline address book to include all recipients in the organization, specify that the Default Global Address List is the address list to include as shown in this example:

```
New-OfflineAddressBook -Name 'Offline – Entire Organization'
 -Server 'CorpSvr127'
 -AddressLists '\Default Global Address List'
 -VirtualDirectories 'CORPSVR127\OAB (Default Web Site)'
```

You can include multiple address lists using a comma-separated list, as shown in this example:

```
New-OfflineAddressBook -Name 'Offline – Sales & Marketing'
 -Server 'CorpSvr127'
 -AddressLists '\All Marketing', '\All Sales', '\Sales Teams'
 -VirtualDirectories 'CORPSVR127\OAB (Default Web Site)'
```

If you want the new offline address book to be the default, use the -IsDefault parameter.

Configuring Clients to Use an Offline Address Book

Offline address lists are available only when users are working offline. You can configure how clients use offline address books by completing the following steps:

1. Do one of the following:

*   In Outlook 2010, click the Office button. On the Info pane, select Download Address Book. The Offline Address Book dialog box appears.
*   In Outlook 2013 and Outlook 2016, on the File pane, click Info. On the Info page, click Account Settings and then select Download Address Book. The Offline Address Book dialog box appears.

2. Select the Download Changes Since Last Send/Receive check box to download only items that have changed since the last time you synchronized the address list. Clear this check box to download the entire contents of your address book.

3. Specify the information to download as either of the following two options:

*   **Full Details**   Select this option to download the address book with all address information details. Full details are necessary if the user needs to encrypt messages when using remote mail.
*   **No Details**   Select this option to download the address book without address information details. This reduces the download time for the address book.

4. If multiple address books are available, use the **Choose Address Book** drop-down list to specify which address book to download. Click **OK**.

Setting the Default Offline Address Book

Although you can create many offline address books, clients download only one. This address list is called the default offline address book. To specify the default offline address book, use Set-OfflineAddressBook with this basic syntax:

```
Set-OfflineAddressBook -Identity OABName -IsDefault
[-DomainController FullyQualifiedName]
```

In the following example, Offline – All Company is set as the default offline address book:

```
Set-OfflineAddressBook -Identity '\Offline - All Company' -IsDefault
```

Changing Offline Address Book Properties

The offline address book is based on other address lists that you've created in the organization. In Exchange Management Shell, you can modify offline address books using the Set-OfflineAddressBook cmdlet. Sample 9-7 provides the syntax and usage.

SAMPLE 9-7 Set-OfflineAddressBook cmdlet syntax and usage

Syntax

```
Set-OfflineAddressBook -Identity OABName
[-AddressLists AddressList1, AddressList2, ... ]
[-ApplyMandatoryProperties {$true | $false}]
[-ConfiguredAttributes Attributes]
[-DiffRetentionPeriod RetentionPeriod]
[-DomainController FullyQualifiedName]
[-GlobalWebDistributionEnabled <$true | $false>]
[-IsDefault <$true | $false>] [-MaxBinaryPropertySize Size]
[-MaxMultivaluedBinaryPropertySize Size]
[-MaxMultivaluedStringPropertySize Size] [-MaxStringPropertySize Size]
[-Name Name] [-PublicFolderDistributionEnabled <$false|$true> ]
[-Schedule Schedule] [-UseDefaultAttributes {$true | $false}]
[-Versions Versions] [-VirtualDirectories  VirtualDir1, VirtualDir2, ...]
```

Usage

```
Set-OfflineAddressBook -Identity '\Offline - West Coast Sales'
 -Name 'West Coast Sales - Offline'
 -AddressLists '\West Coast Sales'
 -PublicFolderDistributionEnabled $true
 -VirtualDirectories 'CORPSVR127\OAB (Default Web Site)'
```

One way to modify an offline address book is to modify the list of included address lists. You can make additional address lists a part of the offline address book. If you no longer want an address list to be a part of the offline address book, you can remove it. To perform either task, use the -AddressLists parameter. This parameter specifies the exact list of address lists to include, and you must always explicitly specify each address list that should be included. Consider the following example:

```
Get-OfflineAddressBook
```

```
Name                          Versions    AddressLists
----                          --------    ------------
Default Offline Address Book  {Version4}  {\Default Global Address List}
Temp Employees Address Book   {Version4}  {\All Support, \All Temps}
```

In this example, the organization has two offline address books. One for full-time employees and one for temporary employees who provide onsite support. For temporary employees, the offline address book includes recipient data only for members of the support team and other temps on the support team. If the offline address book for temporary employees should also include recipient data for All Help Desk, you could add this address list as shown in this example:

```
Set-OfflineAddressBook -Identity '\Temp Employees Address Book'
-AddressLists '\All Support', '\All Temps', 'All Help Desk'
```

If you later decided to remove All Help Desk from this offline address book, you could do so by entering the following command:

```
Set-OfflineAddressBook -Identity '\Temp Employees Address Book'
-AddressLists '\All Support', '\All Temps'
```

Designating OAB Generation Servers and Schedules

In Exchange 2016, the organization has a dedicated OAB generation server. This server is responsible for generating the offline address books for the entire organization. Although the first Mailbox server you install with Exchange 2016 may be designated as the OAB generation server, this isn't always the case.

To identify the OAB generation server, you need to locate the arbitration mailbox that handles the offline address book generation. In Exchange 2016, an arbitration mailbox with the persisted capability "OrganizationCapabilityOABGen" handles offline address book generation. You can locate this mailbox and identify the server and database it resides on using the following command:

```
Get-Mailbox -Arbitration | where {$_.PersistedCapabilities -like "*oab*"} |
ft name, servername, database
```

If your Mailbox servers are configured in an availability group, ensure you've identified the active copy of the database using the following command:

```
Get-MailboxDatabaseCopyStatus DatabaseName
```

where DatabaseName is the database to check. The active copy has the status Mounted.

By default, the OAB generation server rebuilds offline address books on a daily schedule and does so once each day. You can confirm the current settings using the following command:

```
Get-MailboxServer -Identity OABGenerationServer | fl OABGeneratorWorkCycle,
OABGeneratorWorkCycleCheckpoint
```

where OABGenerationServer is the Mailbox server hosting the OAB generation mailbox. The output of this command is as shown here:

```
OABGeneratorWorkCycle           : 1.00:00:00
OABGeneratorWorkCycleCheckpoint : 1.00:00:00
```

> **NOTE**   In Exchange 2010, offline address book generation occurs according to a fixed schedule set with the -Schedule parameter of Set-OfflineAddressBook. In Exchange 2016, this schedule is not used.

The Mailbox server uses the default daily schedule and will rebuild the offline address books once each day. The schedule uses the following format:

```
D.HH:MM:SS
```

where D is the number of days, HH sets the hours, MM sets the minutes, and SS sets the seconds.

You can configure a different schedule using Set-MailboxServer. Use -OABGeneratorWorkCycle to set the master schedule and -OABGeneratorWorkCycleCheckpoint to set the rebuild interval within this schedule.

For example, if you want address books to be rebuild daily and update every six hours, use the following command:

```
Set-MailboxServer -OABGeneratorWorkCycle 1.00:00:00
-OABGeneratorWorkCycleCheckpoint  06:00:00
```

The OAB generation server manages and propagates the offline address books. If the OAB generation server is being overutilized and you want to move the offline address book generation responsibility to a server with more resources, you can do this using several different techniques. When the database and server are part of an availability group, you can move the OAB generation mailbox from one server in the group to another server in the group. However, to do this, you must activate the corresponding mailbox database on the other server (and thereby inactivate the mailbox database on its current server). Consider the following example:

```
Move-ActiveMailboxDatabase Database42 -ActivateOnServer MailServer22
```

In this example, MailServer22 hosts an inactive copy of the mailbox database that contains the OAB generation mailbox and this database is activated. When Database42 is activated, MailServer22 becomes the OAB generation server.

When the database and server are not part of an availability group, you can use a standard move request to move the OAB generation mailbox from a database on one server to a database on another server. Consider the following example:

```
Get-Mailbox -Arbitration -database Database42| where
{$_.PersistedCapabilities -like "*oab*"} | New-MoveRequest
-TargetDatabase Database14
```

When the move request is completed and final, the new server becomes the OAB generation server. As may be required for load balancing, fault tolerance, or geographically disbursed Exchange organizations, you can create an additional OAB generation mailbox. To do this, use the following commands:

```
New-Mailbox -Arbitration -Name "OAB 2" -Database Database42
-UserPrincipalName oab2@imaginedlands.com -DisplayName "OAB Mailbox 2"
```

```
Set-Mailbox -Arbitration oab2 -OABGen $true
```

Rebuilding the OAB

Although the offline address book is generated automatically according to the generator work cycle, you can force the OAB generator to rebuild offline address books manually. To do this, use the Update-OfflineAddressBook cmdlet as shown in this example:

```
Update-OfflineAddressBook -Identity '\Default Offline Address Book'
```

This example initiates an update of the default offline address book. This command initiates an RPC request to each mailbox server hosting an active OAB generation mailbox.

You also can force Exchange to rebuild the offline address book if you restart the Mailbox Assistance service on the server hosting an active OAB generation mailbox.

Deleting Offline Address Books

If an offline address book is no longer needed, you can delete it as long as it isn't the default offline address book. Before you can delete the default offline address book, you must set another address book as the default.

In Exchange Management Shell, you can delete an offline address book using the Remove-OfflineAddressBook cmdlet. Sample 9-8 provides the syntax and usage. Set the -Force parameter to $true to force the immediate removal of an offline address book.

SAMPLE 9-8 Remove-OfflineAddressBook cmdlet syntax and usage

Syntax

```
Remove-OfflineAddressBook -Identity 'OfflineAddressBookIdentity'
[-Force <$false|$true>] [-DomainController FullyQualifiedName]
```

Usage

```
Remove-OfflineAddressBook -Identity '\Offline - West Coast Sales'
```

Chapter 10. Configuring Exchange Clients

Knowing how to configure and maintain Exchange clients is essential for Microsoft Exchange administrators. With Microsoft Exchange Server 2016 and Exchange Online, you can use any mail client that supports standard mail protocols. For ease of administration, however, you'll want to choose specific clients for users. I recommend focusing on Microsoft Office Outlook 2010 and later and Outlook Web App as your clients of choice. Each client supports a slightly different set of features and messaging protocols, and each client has its advantages and disadvantages, including the following:

* With Outlook 2010 or later, you get a full-featured client that on-site, off-site, and mobile users can use. Outlook 2010 or later is part of the Microsoft Office system of applications. They are the only mail clients that support the latest messaging features in Exchange Server. Corporate and workgroup users often need their rich support for calendars, scheduling, voice mail, and email management.
* With Outlook Web App, you get a mail client that you can access securely through a standard web browser whether you are using Windows desktop, Windows Server, iOS or Android. With Microsoft Edge, Internet Explorer 11.0 or later, and current versions of Firefox, Chrome and Safari, Outlook Web App supports many of the features found in Outlook 2010 and later, including calendars, scheduling, and voice mail. With other browsers, the client functionality remains the same, but some features might not be supported. You don't need to configure Outlook Web App on the client, and it's ideal for users who want to access email while away from the office.

Outlook 2010 and later versions are the most common Exchange clients for corporate and workgroup environments. With the MAPI over HTTP feature of Exchange, which eliminates the need for a virtual private network (VPN) to securely access Exchange Server over the Internet by using the Messaging Application Programming Interface (MAPI) over Secure Hypertext Transfer Protocol (HTTPS) connections, Outlook 2010 and later versions might also be your clients of choice for off-site and mobile users.

> **NOTE** With Exchange 2016 and Exchange Online, MAPI over HTTP is enabled by default in a standard configuration. However, if you upgraded to Exchange 2016 from Exchange 2013, you'll need to enable MAPI over HTTP, as the feature was disabled by default in Exchange 2013. Note also that only Outlook 2016 supports MAPI over HTTP without any updates. Outlook 2010 requires Service Pack 2 and updates KB2956191 and KB2965295 to support MAPI over HTTP. Outlook 2013 requires Service Pack 1.

This chapter shows you how to manage Outlook 2010 and later. For ease of reference, I will refer to Outlook 2010 and later simply as Outlook, unless I need to differentiate between them.

Mastering Outlook Web App essentials

Outlook Web App is a standard Microsoft Exchange Server 2016 technology that allows users to access their mailboxes using a web browser. If public folders are hosted by Exchange 2016, users will be able to access public folder data as well. The technology works with standard Internet protocols, including HTTP and Secure HTTP (HTTPS).

When users access mailboxes and public folder data over the web, Client Access and Mailbox servers are working behind the scenes to grant access and transfer files to the browser. Because you don't need to configure Outlook Web App on the client, it's ideally suited for users who want to access email while away from the office and may also be a good choice for users on the internal network who don't need the full version of Microsoft Outlook. Outlook Web App is automatically configured for use when you install the Client Access and Mailbox server roles for Exchange Server 2016. This makes Outlook Web App easy to manage. That said, there are some essential concepts you should know to manage Outlook Web App more effectively, and the following section explains these concepts.

Getting started with Outlook Web App

Outlook Web App is installed automatically when you install the Mailbox server role for Exchange Server 2016. If users will be accessing Outlook Web App over the Internet, the server must be able to accept connections from external clients on an external URL.

In most cases, you need to open only TCP port 443 on your organization's firewall to allow users to access mailboxes and public folder data over the web. After that, you simply tell users the URL path that they need to type into their browser's Address text box in order to access Outlook Web App when they're off-site.

Outlook Web App for Exchange 2016 has a streamlined interface that is optimized for PCs, tablets, and mobile devices. The browser used to access Outlook Web App determines the experience and supported features. The following two versions are available:

- **Standard** Provides a rich experience with performance that closely approximates Microsoft Office Outlook, including a folder hierarchy that you can expand or collapse, drag-and-drop functionality, move and copy functionality, and shortcut menus that you can access by right-clicking. In addition, you can use all of the following features: appearance color schemes, calendar views, file share integration, notifications, personal distribution lists, public folder access, recover deleted items, reminders, search, server-side rules, voice mail options, and WebReady Document Viewing.
- **Light** Provides a basic experience with a simplified user interface when the user's browser cannot support the standard version. This version can also be useful when working over low-bandwidth connections or when there are accessibility needs. No Standard-only features are available. In addition, calendar options are limited and messages can be composed only as plain text. Outlook Web App shortcut menus are not displayed when you right-click. The Outlook Web App toolbar has slightly different options, and the Options page itself is simplified as well.

> **IMPORTANT** By default, all users see the standard version when their browser supports it. Additionally, Outlook Web App for Exchange 2016 doesn't include a spellchecker as this functionality is now being built into web browsers. Microsoft Internet Explorer 10 and later as well as some other web browsers have built-in spell checkers.

Outlook Web App uses HTML 4.0 and JavaScript [European Computer Manufacturers Association (ECMA)] script. The standard version of Outlook Web App is available for PCs, servers, tablets and smart phones running current versions of Windows, Android and iOS

Outlook Web App for Exchange Server 2016 has many features, including:

- **Apps** Users and administrators can add apps to the interface to add functionality. Several apps are installed and made available to users by default, including the following apps created by Microsoft: Action Items, Bing Maps, Suggested Meetings and Unsubscribe. Other apps can be added from the Office Store, from a URL, or from a file.
- **Inbox Rules** Users can create Inbox rules to automatically sort incoming email into folders. Users create rules on the Inbox Rules tab or by right-clicking a message on which they want to base a rule, and then selecting Create Rule.
- **Text Messaging Notifications** Users can set up text messaging notifications to be sent to their mobile devices. Notifications are triggered by calendar events, such as meetings and Inbox rules.

- **Message attachments**   Users can attach files, meeting requests, and other messages to messages by clicking the attach file icon on the toolbar.
- **Delivery Reports**   Users can generate delivery reports to search for delivery information about message they've sent or received during the previous two weeks.
- **Personal Groups**   Users can create personal groups that will appear in their address book.
- **Public groups**   Users can create distribution groups that will appear in the global address book for everyone to use.

Using message options, you can specify message sensitivity as Normal, Personal, Private or Confidential. You also can request delivery receipt, read receipt or both.

Connecting to Mailboxes and Public Folder Data Over the Web

With Outlook Web App, you can easily access mailboxes and public folder data over the web and a corporate intranet. To access a user's mailbox, type the Exchange Outlook Web App URL into your browser's Address text box, and then enter the user name and password for the mailbox you want to access. The complete step-by-step procedure is as follows:

1. In a web browser, enter the secure URL for Outlook Web App. If you are outside the corporate network, enter the external URL, such as https://*servername.yourdomain.com*/owa, where *servername* is a placeholder for the web server hosted by Exchange Server and *yourdomain.com* is a placeholder for the external domain. For example, if your Mailbox server is configured to use mail as the external DNS name and your external domain is imaginedlands.com, you type **https://mail.imaginedlands.com/owa**.

The version of Outlook Web App displayed depends on the version of Exchange running on the Mailbox server hosting your personal mailbox. Exchange 2010 runs version 14 and you can specify this version explicitly by appending **?ExchClientVer=14** to the internal or external URL.

Exchange 2016 runs version 15 and you can specify this version explicitly by appending **?ExchClientVer=15** to the internal or external URL. For example, if your external URL is https://mail.imaginedlands.com, you could enter **https://mail.imaginedlands.com/owa?ExchClientVer=15** as the URL.

> **NOTE**   By default, you must use HTTPS to connect. If you don't, you'll see an error stating "Access is denied." Using HTTPS ensures data transmitted between the client browser and the server is encrypted and in this way secured.

2. By default, Mailbox servers are configured to use Secure HTTP (HTTPS) for Outlook Web App. When you install Exchange Server 2016, a self-signed security certificate is issued for the Mailbox server automatically. Because this default certificate is not issued by a trusted certificate authority, you might see a warning that there is a problem with the website's security certificate. If your browser displays a security alert stating there's a problem with the site's security certificate or that the connection is untrusted, proceed anyway.

- With Internet Explorer, the error states "There's a problem with this website's security certificate". You proceed by selecting the Continue To This Web Site (Not Recommended) link.
- With Google Chrome, the error states "The site's security certificate is not trusted". You continue by selecting the Proceed Anyway button.

- With Mozilla Firefox, the error states "This connection is untrusted." You proceed by selecting I Understand The Risks and then selecting Add Exception. Finally, in the Add Security Exception dialog box, you select Confirm Security Exception.

    3. You'll see the logon page for Outlook Web App. Enter your user name and password, and then click **Sign In**.

    Be sure to specify your user name in DOMAIN\username format. The domain can either be the DNS domain, such as imaginedlands.com, or the NetBIOS domain name, such as pocket-consulta. For example, the user MikeL could specify his logon name as imaginedlands.com\mikel or imaginedlands\mikel.

    4. If you are logging in for the first time, select your preferred display language and time zone, and then click **Save**.

After a user has accessed his mailbox in Outlook Web App, he can access public folders data that is available as well as long as the public folders are hosted on Exchange 2016. To access public folders, follow these steps:

1. In the left pane of the Outlook Web App window, right-click Favorites.

2. Select Add Public Folder To Favorites. In the Add Public Folder dialog box, you'll see a list of the available top levels to which you have access

3. Select a public folder and then click Add To Favorites.

4. Repeat Steps 1 through 3 to add other public folders.

The public folders you've added are listed under the Favorites heading in the left pane. To access a folder and display its contents in the main pane, simply select it in the left pane.

Working with Outlook Web App

After you enter the Outlook Web App URL into a browser's Address text box and log in, you'll see the view of Outlook Web App compatible with your browser. Figure 10-1 shows the full-featured view of Outlook Web App. Most users see this view of Outlook Web App automatically. If their browsers don't support a necessary technology for the full-featured view, some features or options won't be available, or they might see the Light view instead. If they can right-click and see a shortcut menu, they have the full-featured view.

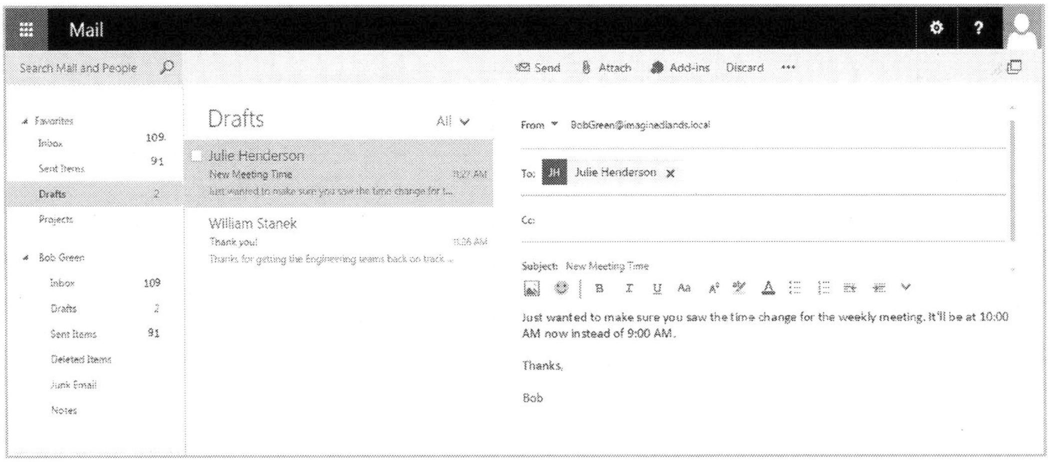

FIGURE 10-1 Outlook Web App has nearly all of the features of Microsoft Office Outlook.

As shown in Figure 10-1, the latest version of Outlook Web App has a toolbar that provides quick access to the following key features:

 Apps – Displays a list of the available apps you can switch to, including Mail, Calendar, People and Tasks.

 Help – Use this option to access online help for Outlook Web App. You can search for topics, print help text and more.

 Settings – Provides quick access to settings for managing automatic replies, display settings, Outlook apps, offline settings, themes, and the user's password. Also allows the user to access the Options page to configure Outlook Web App properties or view current configuration details.

 Account – Displays the user's name. Provides options for opening another mailbox and signing out. Also allows you to set the mailbox picture.

 Open Window– Opens the message or other item you are working with in a separate window.

Outlook Web App can be configured to allow users to connect their account other email accounts. This allows users to keep send, receive, and read email from other email services. Users also can forward email from their Outlook Web App to another account. If users want to add their contacts from Facebook and LinkedIn to Outlook Web App contacts, Outlook Web App can be configured to do this, too.

Outlook Web App can be configured to allow users to work offline. Users can continue to work when they are disconnected from the Internet when Outlook Web App is configured to cache mail items and other information on the users' computers. When Offline mode is allowed in the Outlook Web App configuration, users can enable offline settings by completing the following steps:

1. In Outlook Web App, select Settings (), Offline Settings, choose Turn On Offline Access. This starts the Offline Settings Wizard.

2. As the cached mail and other information stored on a user's computer could be accessed by other users of a computer, the wizard prompts to ensure the current user is the only person who uses the computer. Click **Yes** to confirm.

3. As a user's browser caches the mail data, the size of the browser cache and other related settings might need to be changed. If prompted to grant more storage to the browser, click **Yes**.

4. Click **Next** to continue. When prompted, press Ctrl+D to create a bookmark for quickly accessing Outlook Web App.

5. Click **Next** and then click **OK**.

By default, the Inbox and Drafts folder, as well as recently used folders are synced for offline use. To designate folders that should always be synced:

1. In Outlook Web App, select Settings (   ), Offline Settings.
2. Up to five folders can be selected for syncing. Any currently selected folder is listed by name in one of the five designated slots.

✓ OK   ✗ Cancel

Offline settings

After you turn on offline access, you can use this computer when it's not connected to a network.

☑ Turn on offline access

The Inbox and Drafts folders are always synced so you can view them offline. Five other folders you recently used are also synced. You can choose other folders to sync instead.

Select folder	✛
Select folder	✛

You can now add or remove synced folders:

- To add a folder, click **Select Folder**. In the Select Folder dialog box, click the folder to sync, such as Sent Items, and then click **OK**.

- To remove a folder, click the Remove button (   ) to the right of the folder name.

The primary offline data for Outlook Web App and the user's mailbox is cached under %LocalAppData%\Microsoft\Windows\WebCache on the computer. After offline access is enabled, the browser reads data from this cache, allowing users to continue to work with Outlook Web App and access mail, contacts, and other mail data when their computers aren't connected to the Internet.

If offline mode has been enabled, you can turn this feature off by:

1. In Outlook Web App, select Settings ( ), Offline Settings.
2. Clear the Turn On Offline Access checkbox and then click **OK**.

Disabling offline access doesn't remove the cached data, nor does clearing the browser cache. Because the cached mail data is persistent across browser sessions and independent of the browser's local cache, you must manually remove this data if you want to be certain the data can no longer be accessed.

Enabling and Disabling Web Access for Users

Exchange Server 2016 enables Outlook Web App for each user by default and applies the Default Outlook Web App Mailbox policy to each user. Outlook Web App Mailbox policy controls the features that are enabled for each user and allows users to:

* Use Instant Messaging, text messaging, unified messaging, and Exchange Active Sync
* Create and manage personal contacts, and access all internal address lists
* Use Journaling, notes, Inbox rules, and recover deleted items
* Change their password and configure junk email filters
* Use themes, the premium client, and email signatures
* Manage calendars, tasks, reminders, and notifications

If necessary, you can enable or disable Outlook Web App or set a new default policy for specific users by completing the following steps:

1. In Exchange Admin Center, select Recipients in the Feature pane, and then select Mailboxes. You should now see a list of users with Exchange mailboxes in the organization.
2. Select the user you want to work with in the main pane.
3. In the details pane, the current status of Outlook Web App is listed under the Email Connectivity heading, as shown in Figure 10-2.

Exchange admin center

recipients

permissions

compliance management

organization

protection

mail flow

mobile

public folders

unified messaging

servers

mailboxes   groups   resources   contacts   shared   migration

+ ▾   ✎   🗑   🔎   🔄   ···

DISPLAY NAME	▲	MAILBOX TYPE	EMAIL ADDRESS
Bob Green		User	BobGreen@imaginedlands.local
Cindy Richards		User	cindyr@imaginedlands.local
Debbie Tanner		User	debbiet@imaginedlands.local
Jeff Peterson		User (Archive)	jeffp@imaginedlands.local
Joe Montgomery		User (Archive)	joem@imaginedlands.local
Kyle Brunner		User (Archive)	kyleb@imaginedlands.local
Mark Vance		User	markv@imaginedlands.local
Nancy Thomas		User	NancyThomas@imaginedlands.local
Sarah Johnson		User	SarahJohnson@imaginedlands.local
William Stanek		User	williams@imaginedlands.local

In-Place Hold
User isn't under hold

Email Connectivity
Outlook on the web: Enabled
Disable | View details

Move Mailbox
To another database

1 selected of 10 total

FIGURE 10-2 Use the options under Email Connectivity to manage a user's web access settings.

- To disable Outlook Web App for the user you selected, click Disable. When prompted to confirm, click Yes.

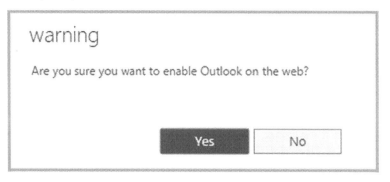

warning

Are you sure you want to disable Outlook on the web?

Yes   No

- To enable Outlook Web App for the user you selected, click Enable. When prompted to confirm, click Yes.

warning

Are you sure you want to enable Outlook on the web?

Yes   No

While you are working with Outlook Web App, you may want to determine the mailbox policy currently being applied. To view or change a user's Outlook Web App mailbox policy, do the following:

- Click **View Details**. In the Outlook Web App Mailbox Policy dialog box, the currently assigned policy is listed or the policy entry is blank, which means the default policy is currently applied.
- To assign a different policy, click **Browse**. Select a policy to view its enabled features. When you've selected the policy you want to use, click **OK**, and then click **Save**.

Outlook Web App mailbox policy

| | Browse... |

| Save | Cancel |

Configuring Mail Support for Outlook

You can install Outlook as a client on a user's computer. This section looks at the following topics:

- Understanding address lists, offline address books, and autodiscover
- Configuring Outlook for the first time
- Adding Internet mail accounts to Outlook
- Reconfiguring Outlook mail support

Unless specified otherwise, the procedures in this section work with desktop computers running current versions of Windows and Windows Server. Additionally, unless noted otherwise, the procedures work with Outlook 2010, Outlook 2013 and Outlook 2016.

Understanding Address Lists, Offline Address Books, and Autodiscover

Address lists are collections of recipients in an Exchange organization. Offline address books (OABs) are copies of address lists that are downloaded and cached on a computer so an Outlook user can access the address book while disconnected from the Exchange organization.

Every Exchange organization has a global address list and a default OAB. In the Exchange organization, address lists reside in Active Directory. If mobile users are disconnected from the Internet, they are unable to access the address lists stored on Exchange Online. If mobile users are disconnected from the corporate network, they are unable to access the address lists stored on Exchange 2016. To allow users to continue working when disconnected from the network, Exchange 2016 and Exchange Online generate offline address books and make them accessible to Outlook clients so that they can be downloaded and cached for use while working offline.

Although Exchange 2016 and Exchange Online continue to support public folders, public folders are not required for access to the global address list or the OAB. Exchange 2016 and Exchange Online provide these features through a web-based distribution point. Outlook clients use the web-based distribution point to obtain the global address list and the OAB automatically.

Exchange Online largely manages the default address lists and OABs automatically. On-premises Exchange, however, includes many configuration options, as discussed in the remainder of this section. For more information on global address lists and OABs, see "Managing Online Address Lists" and "Managing Offline Address Books" in Chapter 9 "Managing Addresses Online and Offline."

A designated Mailbox server, referred to as the *generation server,* is responsible for creating and updating the OABs. OAB data is produced by the Microsoft Exchange OABGen Service and stored in a special arbitration mailbox with the persisted capability "OrganizationCapabilityOABGen." When a client initiates an OAB distribution request, the request is directed through a Mailbox server that routes the request to the Mailbox server hosting the OAB data. The OAB data is then distributed directly from the Mailbox server to the client.

Outlook 2010 and later as well as some mobile devices use the Autodiscover service to automatically configure themselves for access to Exchange. Outlook relies on DNS lookups to locate a host service (SRV) resource record for the Autodiscover service, then uses the user's credentials to authenticate to Active Directory and search for the

Autodiscover connection points. After retrieving the connection points, the client connects to the first Mailbox server in the list and obtains the profile information. The connection point uses the globally unique identifier (GUID) for the user's mailbox plus the at symbol (@) and the domain portion of the user's primary SMTP address. The profile information includes the user's display name, the location of the user's mailbox server, connection settings for internal and external connectivity, MAPI over HTTP settings, and the URLs for Outlook features including those for free-busy data, the OAB, and Unified Messaging.

When you install a Mailbox server, an Autodiscover virtual directory is created on the default website in Internet Information Services (IIS), and an internal URL is set up for automatic discovery and other features, such as the OAB (which can be automatically discovered as well). Typically, the Autodiscover URL is either https://*domain*/autodiscover/autodiscover.xml or https://autodiscover.*domain*/autodiscover/autodiscover.xml, where *domain* is your organization's primary SMTP domain address, such as https://autodiscover.imaginedlands.com/autodiscover/autodiscover.xml. When you deploy multiple Mailbox servers, a connection point is created for each. This connection point stores the server's fully qualified domain name (FQDN) in the form https://*servername*/autodiscover/autodiscover.xml, where *servername* is the FQDN of the Mailbox server, such as https://server18.imaginedlands.com/autodiscover/autodiscover.xml.

The OAB virtual directory is the web-based distribution point for the OAB. By default, when you install a Mailbox server, this directory is created on the default website in IIS and configured for internal access. You can specify an external URL as well. Typically, the internal URL is set as https://*servername*/OAB, where *servername* is the FQDN of the Mailbox server, such as https://server18.imaginedlands.com/OAB.

For MAPI over HTTP to be automatically configured by using the Autodiscover service, external users running Outlook 2010 or later clients must have a valid Secure Sockets Layer (SSL) certificate on the Mailbox server that includes both the common name, such as mail.imaginedlands.com, and a Subject Alternative name for the Autodiscover service, such as autodiscover.imaginedlands.com. Also, the external URLs for the offline address book, Exchange Web Services, and MAPI over HTTP must be configured.

To configure the external URL for the OAB, you can use the -ExternalUrl parameter of the Set-OABVirtualDirectory cmdlet. In the following example, you set the OAB external URL and configure it for use with SSL:

```
Set-OABVirtualDirectory -identity "Mailserver01\OAB (Default Web Site)"
-externalurl https://mail.imaginedlands.com/OAB -RequireSSL $true
```

To configure the external URL for Exchange Web Services, you can use the -ExternalUrl parameter of the Set-WebServicesVirtualDirectory cmdlet. The following example sets the Exchange Web Services external URL and configures it for use with basic authentication:

```
Set-WebServicesVirtualDirectory -identity "Mailserver01\EWS (Default Web
Site)" -externalurl https://mail.imaginedlands.com/EWS/Exchange.asmx
-BasicAuthentication $True
```

To configure the external URL for MAPI over HTTP, you can use the -ExternalUrl parameter of the Set-MapiVirtualDirectory cmdlet. The following example sets the MAPI over HTTP external URL and configures it for use with NTLM and Negotiate authentication:

```
Set-MapiVirtualDirectory -identity "Mailserver01\mapi (Default Web
Site)" -externalurl https://mail.imaginedlands.com/mapi
-IISAuthenticationMethods NTLM,Negotiate
```

If you want older clients to be able to use Outlook Anywhere, you can use the -ExternalHostname parameter of Set-OutlookAnywhere. The following example sets the external host name and configures authentication:

```
Set-OutlookAnywhere -Server Mailserver01 -ExternalHostname
"mail.imaginedlands.com" -ExternalClientAuthenticationMethod Negotiate
-InternetClientAuthenticationMethod NTLM
-IISAuthenticationMethods Basic, NTLM, Negotiate
-SSLOffloading $False
```

Once you've configured these options, you can test the Availability service, Outlook Anywhere, and the Offline Address Book service by using Test-OutlookWebServices. Here are examples:

```
Test-OutlookWebServices -ClientAccessServer "Mailserver01"
```

```
Test-OutlookWebServices -Identity "willams@imaginedlands.com"
```

Use Test-MapiConnectivity to test MAPI over HTTP. Here are examples:

```
Test-MapiConnectivity -Server "Mailserver01"
```

```
Test-MapiConnectivity -Identity "willams@imaginedlands.com"
```

Configuring Outlook for the First Time

You can install Outlook as a standalone product or as part of Microsoft Office. Outlook can be used to connect to the following types of email servers:

*   **Microsoft Exchange** Connects directly to Exchange Server, Exchange Online, or both; best for users who are connected to the organization's network. Users will have full access to Exchange. If users plan to connect to Exchange using MAPI over HTTP or Outlook Anywhere (RPC over HTTP), this is the option to choose as well. With Exchange, users can check mail on an email server and access any private or public folders to which they have been granted permissions. If you define a personal folder and specify that new email messages should be delivered to it, messages can be delivered to a personal folder on a user's computer.
*   **POP3** Connects to Exchange 2016 or another POP3 email server through the Internet; best for users who are connecting from a remote location, such as a home or a remote office, using dial-up or broadband Internet access. With POP3, users can check mail on an email server and download it to their inboxes. Users can't, however, synchronize mailbox folders or access private or public folders on the server. By using advanced configuration settings, the user can elect to download the mail and leave it on the server for future use. By leaving the mail on the server, the user can check mail in Outlook Web App or on a home computer and then still download it to an office computer later.
*   **IMAP4** Connects to Exchange 2016 or another IMAP4 email server through the Internet; best for users who are connecting from a remote location, such as a home or a remote office, using dial-up or broadband Internet access. Also well suited for users who have a single computer, such as a laptop, that they use to check mail both at the office and away from it. With IMAP4, users can check mail on an email server and synchronize mailbox folders. Users can also download only message headers and then access each message individually to download it. Unlike POP3, IMAP4 has no option to leave mail on the server. IMAP4 also lets users access public and private folders on an Exchange server.
*   **ActiveSync** Connects to an Exchange ActiveSync compatible service, such as Outlook.com, through the Internet; best as an additional email configuration

option. Users can have an external email account with a web-based email service that they can check in addition to corporate email.

- **Additional server types**   Connects to a third-party mail server or other services, such as Outlook Mobile Text Messaging. If your organization has multiple types of mail servers, including Exchange Server, you'll probably want to configure a connection to Exchange Server first and then add more email account configurations later.

To begin, log on to the computer as the user whose email you are configuring or have the user log on. If the computer is part of a domain, log on using the user's domain account. If you are configuring email for use with a direct Exchange 2016 or Exchange Online connection rather than a POP3, IMAP4, or ActiveSync connection, ensure that the user's mailbox has been created. If the user's mailbox has not been created, auto-setup will fail, as will the rest of the account configuration.

The first time you start Outlook, the application runs the Welcome Wizard. You can use the Welcome Wizard to configure email for Exchange, POP3, IMAP4, and ActiveSync mail servers, as discussed in the sections that follow.

First-Time Configuration: Connecting to Exchange Server

With Outlook 2010 or later, you can use the Welcome Wizard to configure email for Exchange 2016 or Exchange Online in Outlook by completing the following steps:

1. Start Outlook and click **Next** on the Welcome page. The procedure is nearly identical whether you are working with Outlook 2010, Outlook 2013 or Outlook 2016.

2. When prompted to indicate whether you would like to configure an email account, verify that Yes is selected and then click **Next**.

Use Outlook to connect to email accounts, such as your organization's Microsoft Exchange Server or an Exchange Online account as part of Microsoft Office 365. Outlook also works with POP, IMAP, and Exchange ActiveSync accounts.

Do you want to set up Outlook to connect to an email account?

⦿ Yes
◯ No

---

3. The next page of the wizard varies depending on the computer's current configuration:

- For computers that are part of a domain and for users that have an existing Exchange Server mailbox, the wizard uses the Autodiscover feature to automatically discover the required account information.

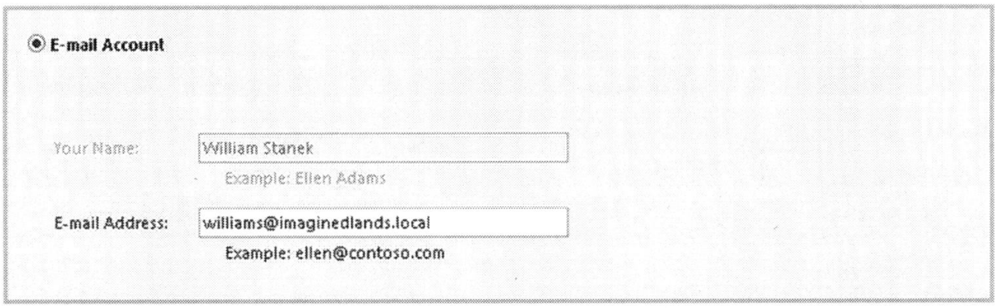

E-mail Account	
Your Name:	William Stanek
	Example: Ellen Adams
E-mail Address:	williams@imaginedlands.local
	Example: ellen@contoso.com

- For computers that are part of a domain and for users without an on-premises Exchange mailbox, leave the wizard open, create the user's Exchange mailbox, and then proceed with the wizard once the mailbox is automatically discovered.
- For all other configurations, including computers that are part of a workgroup, and computers on which you are logged on locally, Outlook assumes you want to configure an Internet email account for the user. Enter the user's account name and email address. Then type and confirm the user's password (see Figure 10-3).

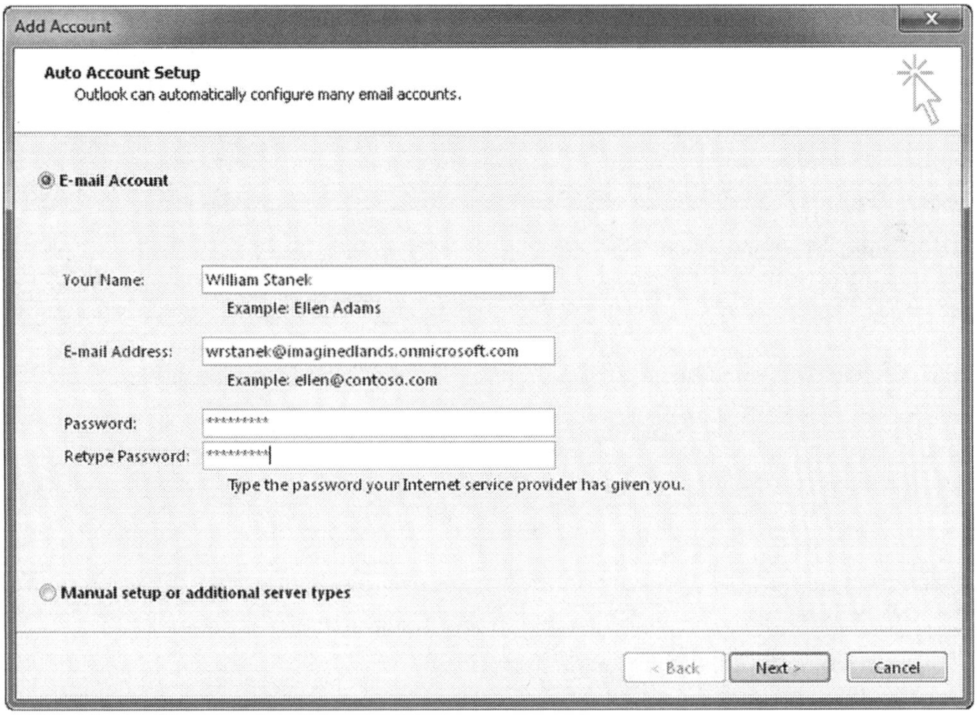

Add Account

Auto Account Setup
Outlook can automatically configure many email accounts.

◉ E-mail Account

Your Name:	William Stanek
	Example: Ellen Adams
E-mail Address:	wrstanek@imaginedlands.onmicrosoft.com
	Example: ellen@contoso.com
Password:	*********
Retype Password:	*********
	Type the password your Internet service provider has given you.

○ Manual setup or additional server types

< Back   Next >   Cancel

FIGURE 10-3 Although the Wizard can automatically fill in account information when you are logged on to a domain, the wizard does not do this for other configurations.

4. After you click Next, the wizard uses the new Auto Account Setup feature to automatically discover the rest of the information needed to configure the account and then uses the settings to log on to the server. If the auto-configuration and server logon are successful, click **Finish** and skip the remaining steps in this procedure. The wizard then sets up the user's Exchange mailbox on the computer as appropriate.

5. If auto-configuration is not successful, click **Next** so that the wizard can attempt to establish an unencrypted connection to the server. If the auto-configuration and server logon are successful this time, click **Finish** and then skip the remaining steps in this procedure.

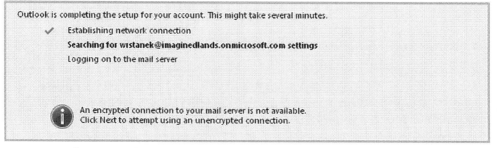

6. If auto-configuration fails twice, you'll see a prompt to confirm the user's email address. If the email address is incorrect, correct it, and then click **Retry**. If the auto-configuration and server logon are successful this time, click **Finish** and then skip the remaining steps in this procedure.

Outlook is completing the setup for your account. This might take several minutes.

   ✓   Establishing network connection

   ✗   **Searching for wrstanek@imaginedlands.onmicrosoft.com settings (unencrypted)**

       Log on to server (unencrypted)

We are having trouble connecting to your account. Verify the settings below and make changes if necessary.

E-mail Address: wrstanek@imaginedlands.onmicrosoft.com

              Example: ellen@contoso.com

☐ Change account settings

7. If all attempts at auto-configuration fail, you can try to configure settings manually (and might also want to confirm that the Autodiscover service is working properly). Click **Next**. On the Choose Service page, select a service. Click **Next**. On the next wizard page, complete the necessary information for the type of email service you selected. If necessary, click More Settings. Use the Properties dialog box to configure the additional required settings and

then click **OK**. Click **Next** and then click **Finish** to complete the mail configuration.

First-Time Configuration: Connecting to Internet Email Servers

When a user is logged on to a domain, Outlook automatically attempts to configure itself for use with the user's Exchange mailbox as part of its initial configuration. This configuration works for internal users but not for remote users who need or prefer to access Exchange using POP3 or IMAP4 (rather than MAPI over HTTP or Outlook Anywhere [which uses RPC over HTTP]). For these users, you can complete the first-time configuration of Outlook by following these steps:

1. In the Welcome Wizard, prompted to indicate whether you would like to configure an email account, verify that Yes is selected and then click **Next**.

2. Select the manual setup option. In Outlook 2010, this checkbox is labeled as Manually Configure Server Settings Or Additional Server Types. In Outlook 2013 and Outlook 2016, this checkbox is labeled as Manual Setup Or Additional Server Types. Click **Next**.

3. On the Choose Service page, choose the service to use. In Outlook 2010, choose Internet E-Mail as the service. In Outlook 2013 and Outlook 2016, choose POP Or IMAP as the service. Click **Next**.

Outlook.com or Exchange ActiveSync compatible service
Connect to a service such as Outlook.com to access email, calendars, contacts, and tasks

POP or IMAP
Connect to a POP or IMAP email account

Other
Connect to a server type that is listed below

Fax Mail Transport

4. In the Your Name text box, type the name to appear in the From field of outgoing messages for this user, such as **William Stanek**.

5. In the E-Mail Address text box, type the email address of the user. Be sure to type the email user name as well as the domain name, such as **williams@imaginedlands.com**.

6. From the Account Type list, select POP3 or IMAP4 as the type of protocol to use for the incoming mail server. The advantages and disadvantages of these protocols are as follows:

- POP3 is used to check mail on an email server and download it to the user's inbox. The user can't access private or public folders on the server. By using advanced configuration settings, the user can elect to download email and leave it on the server for future use. By leaving the email on the server, the user can check a message on a home computer and still download it to an office computer later.

- IMAP4 is used to check mail on an email server and download message headers. The user can then access each email individually and download it. Unlike POP3, IMAP4 has no option to leave mail on the server. IMAP4 also lets users access public and private folders on an Exchange server. It is best suited for users who have a single computer, such as a laptop, that they use to check mail both at the office and away from it.

User Information

Your Name: William Stanek

Email Address: williams@imaginedlands.co

Server Information

Account Type: POP3

Incoming mail server: pop3.imaginedlands.com

Outgoing mail server (SMTP): smtp.imaginedlands.com

Logon Information

User Name: williams@imaginedlands.co

Password: *********

☑ Remember password

☑ Require logon using Secure Password Authentication (SPA)

Test Account Settings

We recommend that you test your account to ensure that the entries are correct.

Test Account Settings ...

☑ Automatically test account settings when Next is clicked

Deliver new messages to:

◉ New Outlook Data File

○ Existing Outlook Data File

Browse

More Settings ...

7. Enter the FQDN for the incoming and outgoing mail servers. Although these entries are often the same, some organizations have different incoming and outgoing mail servers. If you are not certain of your mail servers' FQDN, contact your network administrator.

> **NOTE** If you're connecting to Exchange with POP3 or IMAP4, you should enter the FQDN for the Exchange server rather than just the host name. For example, you would use MailServer.imaginedlands.com instead of MailServer. This ensures Outlook will be able to find the Exchange server.

8. Under Logon Information, type the user's logon name and password. If the mail server requires secure logon, select the Require Logon Using Security Password Authentication check box.

9. To verify the settings, click **Test Account Settings**. Outlook verifies connectivity to the Internet and then logs on to the Mail server. Next, Outlook sends a test message to the specified mail server. If the test fails, note the errors and make corrections as necessary.

10. If necessary, click More Settings. Use the Properties dialog box to configure the additional required settings and then click **OK**. When you are ready to continue, click **Next**, and then click **Finish** to complete the configuration.

Configuring Outlook for Exchange

If you didn't configure Outlook to use Exchange the first time it was started and elected to use Outlook without an email account, don't worry: You can change the Outlook configuration to use Exchange. It does take a bit of extra work, however.

Follow these steps to configure Outlook to use Exchange:

1. In Outlook 2013 or Outlook 2016, click **File** and then select **Add Account**. If you are using Outlook 2010, you must select Tools, Account Settings, New and then select Microsoft Exchange as the e-mail service.

2. Outlook assumes you want to configure an Internet email account for the user. You will, however, provide the information needed for Exchange. Enter the user's account name and email address for Exchange. Then type and confirm the user's domain password.

◉ **E-mail Account**

Your Name:	William Stanek
	Example: Ellen Adams
E-mail Address:	williams@imaginedlands.local
	Example: ellen@contoso.com
Password:	*********
Retype Password:	*********
	Type the password your Internet service provider has given you.

---

3. Click **Next**. The wizard uses the new Auto Account Setup feature to automatically discover the rest of the information needed to configure the account and then uses the settings to log on to the server. If the auto-configuration and server logon are successful, click **Finish**.

Configuring

Outlook is completing the setup for your account. This might take several minutes.

✓ Establishing network connection
✓ **Searching for williams@imaginedlands.local settings**
✓ Logging on to the mail server

Congratulations! Your email account was successfully configured and is ready to use.

Adding Internet Mail Accounts to Outlook

Through email account configuration, each mail profile for Outlook supports only one Exchange Server account at a time. If you need access to multiple Exchange Server mailboxes in the same mail profile, you must configure access to these mailboxes as discussed in the section "Accessing Multiple Exchange Mailboxes" later in the chapter.

Although you can configure only one Exchange email account for each mail profile, Outlook allows you to retrieve mail from both Exchange Online and Exchange Server as well as from multiple Internet servers. For example, you can configure Outlook to check mail on the corporate Exchange server, a personal account with an ActiveSync compatible service, and Exchange Online.

You can add Internet mail accounts to Outlook. In Outlook, complete the following steps:

1. In Outlook 2013 or Outlook 2016, click **File** and then select **Add Account**. If you are using Outlook 2010, you must select Tools, Account Settings, New and then select POP3, IMAP, Or HTTP as the e-mail service.

2. Click **Next**. The wizard tries to use the new Auto Account Setup feature to automatically discover the rest of the information needed to configure the account and then uses the settings to log on to the server.

3. If the auto-configuration and server logon are successful, click **Finish**. Otherwise, follow steps 2–10 outlined previously in the "First-time configuration: Connecting to Internet email servers" section.

Repairing and Changing Outlook Mail Accounts

When you first configure Outlook on a computer, you can configure it to connect to an Exchange server, to Exchange Online, to Internet email, or to another email server. With Exchange Server, Outlook can use MAPI over HTTP or RPC over HTTP to connect to the appropriate Mailbox server and access the appropriate mailbox. If a user's mailbox is moved to a different server within the Exchange organization, the user is connected to this server automatically the next time he or she starts Outlook. If, for some reason, a user has a problem connecting to Exchange or needs to update configuration settings, you can use a repair operation. Repairing the user's account restarts the Auto Account Setup feature.

With non-Exchange servers, access to email very much depends on the account and server configuration remaining the same. If the account or server configuration changes, the account configuration in Outlook must be updated. The easiest way to do this is with a repair operation.

To start a repair, follow these steps:

1. Log on as the domain account of the user for whom you are repairing email.

2. In Outlook 2010, click the Office button, click **Account Settings**, and then select the **Account Settings** option. In Outlook 2013 or Outlook 2016, on the File pane, click **Account Settings**, and then select the **Account Settings** option.

3. In the Account Settings dialog box, the E-Mail tab lists all currently configured email accounts by name. Select the account to repair and then click **Repair**.

4. On the Auto Account Setup page, check the account settings. With Exchange accounts for domain users and with Exchange Online, you cannot change the displayed information. With other accounts, you can modify the user's email address and password, as necessary.

5. When you click **Next**, the Repair E-Mail Account Wizard contacts the mail server and tries to determine the correct account settings. If the auto-configuration and server logon are successful, click **Finish**. Skip the remaining steps in this procedure.

6. If auto-configuration is not successful, click **Next** so that the wizard can attempt to establish an unencrypted connection to the server. If the auto-configuration and server logon are successful this time, click **Finish** and then skip the remaining steps in this procedure. You must restart Outlook.

> **NOTE** You may be prompted to confirm the user's credentials. If so, type the user's password, select the Remember My Credentials checkbox, and then click OK.

7. If auto-configuration fails twice, you can try to configure settings manually. Select the manual setup option, and then click Next.

8. Use the fields provided to update the mail account configuration. If you need to configure additional settings beyond the user, server, and logon information, click the More button (•••), and then use the Properties dialog box to configure the additional required settings. When you are finished, click **OK** to close the Properties dialog box.

9. To check the new settings, click **Test Account Settings**.

10. Click **Next**, and then click **Finish**.

In some cases, if you've incorrectly configured Exchange, you might not be able to start Outlook and access the Account Settings dialog box. In this case, you can repair the settings using the following procedure:

1. Start the Mail utility. In Control Panel, click **Small Icons** on the View By list and then start the Mail app by clicking its icon or by double-clicking its icon.

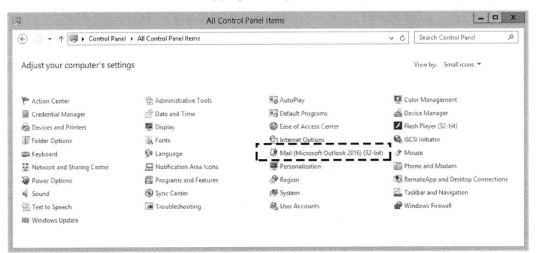

2. In the Mail Setup–Outlook dialog box, click **E-Mail Accounts**. The Accounts Settings dialog box appears.

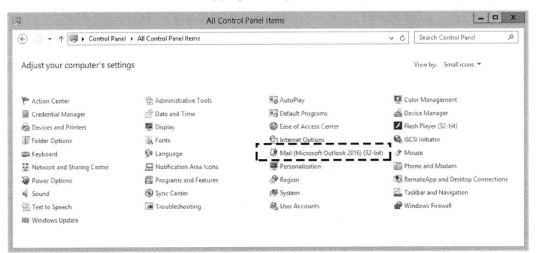

3. In the Account Settings dialog box, the E-Mail tab is selected by default. Click the incorrectly configured Exchange account and then do one of the following:

■ Click Change to modify the Exchange settings using the techniques discussed previously.

- Click Remove to remove the Exchange settings so that they are no longer used by Outlook.

4. When you are finished, close the Mail Setup–Outlook dialog box, and then start Outlook.

For POP3 or IMAP4, you can change a user's email configuration at any time by completing the following steps:

1. In Outlook 2010, click the Office button, click **Account Settings**, and then select the **Account Settings** option. In Outlook 2013 or Outlook 2016, on the File pane, click **Account Settings**, and then select the **Account Settings** option.

2. In the Account Settings dialog box, the E-Mail tab lists all currently configured email accounts by name. Select the account you want to work with, and then click **Change**.

3. Use the fields provided to update the mail account configuration. If you need to configure additional settings beyond the user, server, and logon information, click the More button (•••), and then use the Properties dialog box to configure the additional required settings. When you are finished, click **OK** to close the Properties dialog box.

4. To check the new settings click **Test Account Settings**.

5. Click **Next**, and then click **Finish**.

Leaving Mail on the Server with POP3

If the user connects to an Internet e-mail server, an advantage of POP3 is that it lets a user leave mail on the server. By doing this, the user can check mail on a home computer and still download it to an office computer later.

With Outlook, you can configure POP3 accounts to leave mail on the server by completing the following steps:

1. In Outlook 2010, click the Office button, click **Account Settings**, and then select the **Account Settings** option. In Outlook 2013 or Outlook 2016, on the File pane, click **Account Settings**, and then select the **Account Settings** option.

2. In the Account Settings dialog box, select the POP3 mail account you want to modify and then click **Change**.

3. Click the More button (●●●)to display the Internet E-Mail Settings dialog box.

4. In the Internet E-Mail Settings dialog box, click the **Advanced** tab, as shown in Figure 10-5.

5. Use the options below Delivery to configure how and when mail should be left on the server. To enable this option, select the **Leave A Copy Of Messages On The Server** check box. The additional options depend on the client configuration. Options you might see include the following:

▪ **Remove From Server After *N* Days**   Select this option if the user will be connecting to an Internet service provider (ISP) and you want to delete messages from the server after a specified number of days. By deleting ISP mail periodically, you ensure that the mailbox size doesn't exceed the limit.

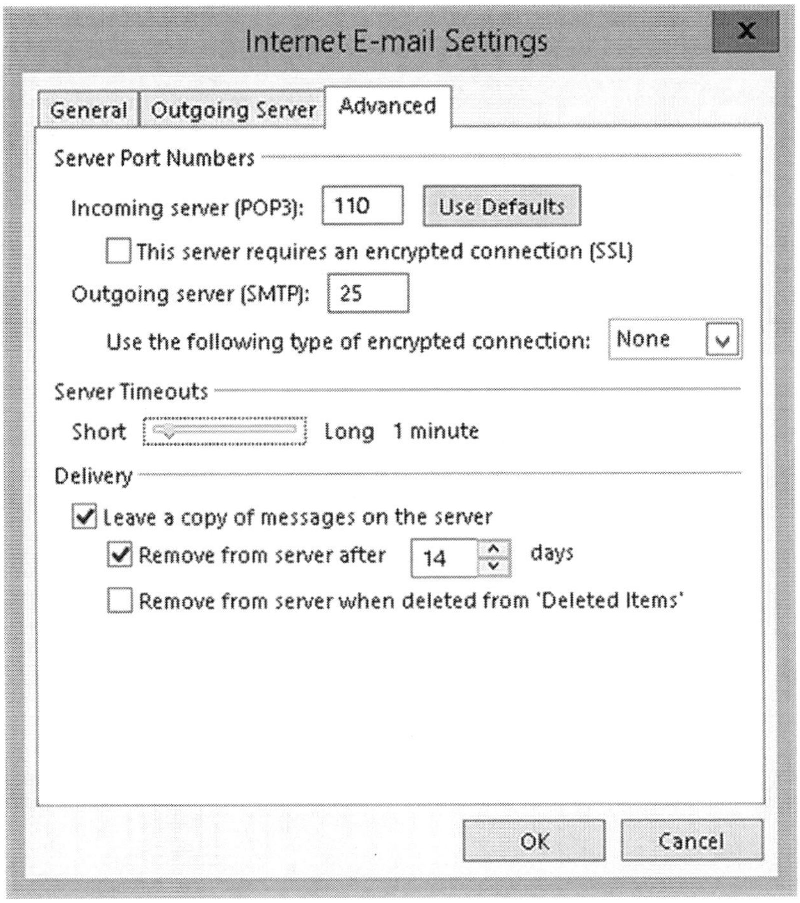

FIGURE 10-5 Using the Advanced tab to configure how and when mail should be left on the server.

- **Remove From Server When Deleted From "Deleted Items"** Select this option to delete messages from the server when the user deletes them from the Deleted Items folder. You'll see this option with Internet-only Outlook configurations.

6. Click **OK** when you've finished changing the account settings.

7. Click **Next**, and then click **Finish**. Click **Close** to close the Account Settings dialog box.

Checking Private and Public Folders with IMAP4 and UNIX Mail Servers

With IMAP4, you can check public and private folders on a mail server. This option is enabled by default, but the default settings might not work properly with UNIX mail servers.

With Outlook, you can check or change the folder settings used by IMAP4 by completing the following steps:

1. Start Outlook. In Outlook 2010, click the Office button, click **Account Settings**, and then select the **Account Settings** option. In Outlook 2013, on the File pane, click **Account Settings**, and then select the **Account Settings** option.

2. In the Account Settings dialog box, select the IMAP4 mail account you want to modify and then click **Change**.

3. Click the More button (•••) to display the Internet E-Mail Settings dialog box.

4. In the Internet E-Mail Settings dialog box, click the **Advanced** tab, as shown in Figure 10-6.

5. If the account connects to a UNIX mail server, enter the path to the mailbox folder on the server, such as **~williams/mail**—don't end the folder path with a forward slash (/)—and then click **OK**.

6. Click **Next**, and then click **Finish**.

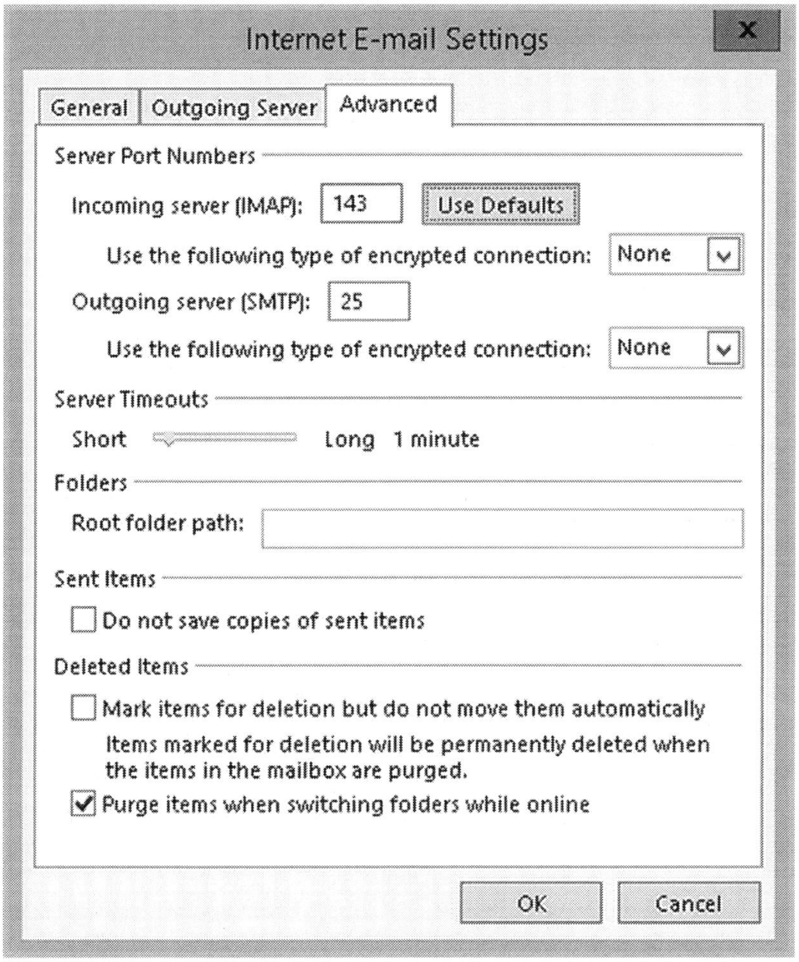

FIGURE 10-6 Using the Advanced tab to configure how folders are used with IMAP4 mail accounts.

Managing the Exchange Configuration in Outlook

Whenever you use Outlook to connect to Exchange, you have several options for optimizing the way mail is handled. These options include the following:

- Email delivery and processing
- Remote mail
- Scheduled connections
- Multiple mailboxes

Each of these options is examined in this section.

Managing Delivery and Processing Email Messages

When Outlook uses Exchange, you have strict control over how email is delivered and processed. Exchange mail can be delivered in one of two ways:

- To server mailboxes with local copies
- To personal folders

Exchange mail can be processed by any of the information services configured for use in Outlook. These information services include the following:

- Microsoft Exchange
- Internet email

Let's look at how you use each of these delivery and processing options.

Using Server Mailboxes

When you are using Outlook 2010 or later with Exchange 2016 or Exchange Online, server mailboxes with local copies are the default configuration option. With server mailboxes, new email is delivered to a mailbox on the Exchange server, and users can view or receive new mail only when they're connected to Exchange. When users are connected to Exchange, Outlook retrieves their mail and stores a local copy on their computer in addition to the email stored on Exchange.

The local copy of a user's mail is stored in an offline folder .ost file. With Windows 7 and later, the default location of a .ost file is *%LocalAppData%*\Microsoft\Outlook, where *%LocalAppData%* is a user-specific environment variable that points to a user's local application data. Using server mailboxes offers users protected storage and the ability to have a single point of recovery in case something happens to their computer.

Using Personal Folders

An alternative to using server mailboxes is to use personal folders. Personal folders are stored in a .pst file on the user's computer. With personal folders, you can specify that mail should be delivered to the user's inbox and stored on the server or that mail should be delivered only to the user's inbox. Users have personal folders when

Outlook is configured to use Internet email or other email servers. Users might also have personal folders if the auto-archive feature is used to archive messages.

> **REAL WORLD**   With Windows 7 and later, the default location of a .pst file is %LocalAppData%\Microsoft\Outlook, where %LocalAppData% is a user-specific environment variable that points to a user's local application data. Personal folders are best suited for mobile users who check mail through dial-up connections and who might not be able to use a dial-up connection to connect directly to Exchange.
>
> Users with personal folders lose the advantages that server-based folders offer—namely, protected storage and the ability to have a single point of recovery in case of failure. In addition, .pst files have many disadvantages. They get corrupted more frequently and, on these occasions, you must use the Inbox Repair Tool to restore the file. If the hard disk on a user's computer fails, you can recover the mail only if the .pst file has been backed up. Unfortunately, most workstations aren't backed up regularly (if at all), and the onus of backing up the .pst file falls on the user, who might or might not understand how to do this.

Determining the Presence of Personal Folders

You can determine the presence of personal folders by following these steps:

1. Start Outlook. In Outlook 2010, click the Office button, click **Account Settings**, and then select the **Account Settings** option. In Outlook 2013 or Outlook 2016, on the File pane, click **Account Settings**, and then select the **Account Settings** option.

2. In the Account Settings dialog box, click the **Data Files** tab.

3. The location of the data file associated with each email account is listed. If the file name ends in .pst, the account is using a personal folder.

Account Settings

Data Files
  Outlook Data Files

| E-mail | Data Files | RSS Feeds | SharePoint Lists | Internet Calendars | Published Calendars | Address Books |

🔳 Add... 🏛 Settings... ✅ Set as Default ✖ Remove 📂 Open File Location...

Name	Location
Outlook Data ...	C:\Users\williams\Documents\Outlook Files\Outlook.pst
williams@imag...	C:\Users\williams\AppData\Local\Microsoft\Outlook\williams@imaginedlands.local.ost

Select a data file in the list, then click Settings for more details or click Open File Location to display the folder that contains the data file. To move or copy these files, you must first shut down Outlook.

Tell Me More...

Close

Creating New or Opening Existing Personal Folders

If personal folders aren't available and you want to configure them, follow these steps:

1. Start Outlook. In Outlook 2010, click the Office button, click **Account Settings**, and then select the **Account Settings** option. In Outlook 2013 or Outlook 2016, on the File pane, click **Account Settings**, and then select the **Account Settings** option.

2. In the Account Settings dialog box, click the **Data Files** tab.

3. Click **Add**. If the New Outlook Data File dialog box appears, Office Outlook Personal Folders File (.pst) should be selected by default. Click **OK**.

4. Use the Create Or Open Outlook Data File dialog box, as shown in Figure 10-7, to create a new .pst file or open an existing .pst file:

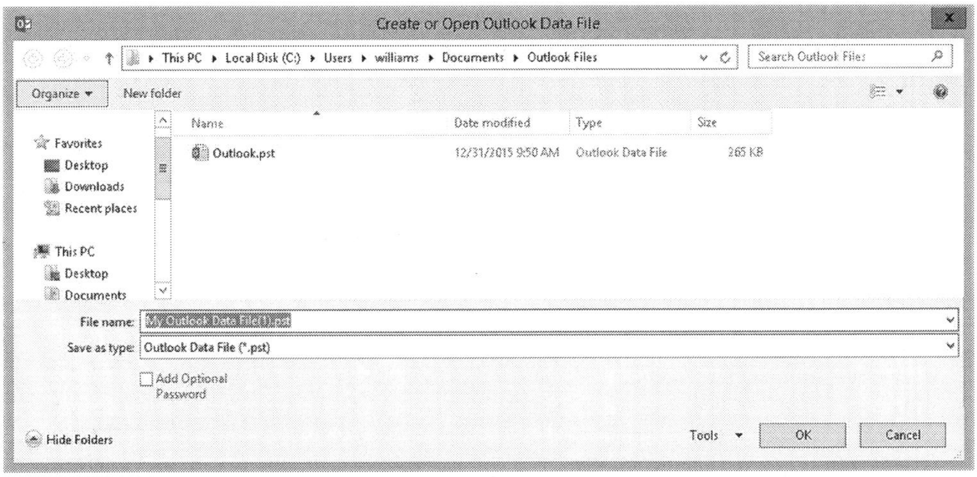

FIGURE 10-7 Using the Create Or Open Outlook Data File dialog box to search for an existing .pst file or to create a new one.

- To create a new .pst file in the default folder, type a name for the Outlook data file in the text box provided or accept the default value. To secure the file and ensure only a person with this password can access the file, select the Add Optional Password checkbox. In the Create Microsoft Personal Folders dialog box, specify a password, verify a password for the .pst file, and click OK.
- To create a new .pst file in a nondefault folder, click Browse Folders to show the folder view if it is hidden. Browse for the folder you want to use, type the file name in the text box provided or accept the default value, and then click OK. Optionally, select the Add Optional Password checkbox. In the Create Microsoft Personal Folders dialog box, specify a password, verify a password for the .pst file, and click OK.
- To open an existing .pst file, click Browse Folders to show the folder view if it is hidden. Browse to the folder containing the .pst file. Select the .pst file, and then click OK. In the Personal Folders dialog box, use the options provided to change the current password or compact the personal folder, and then click OK.

> **NOTE** It is important to be aware that Exchange Server does not ship with any password recovery utility for .pst files. If a user sets a password on a .pst file and forgets it, the Exchange administrator has no way to reset it. You might find third-party vendors who make password-cracking or recovery tools, but they are not guaranteed to work and they are not supported by Microsoft.

5. Click **Close**. The personal folder you've selected or created is displayed in the Outlook folder list. You should see related subfolders as well.

Delivering Mail to Personal Folders

When you configure mail to be delivered to a personal folder, Outlook saves email messages only locally on the computer. As a result, Outlook removes the messages from Exchange Server after delivery and you can access the messages only on the currently logged-on computer.

If you want mail to be delivered to a personal folder, complete the following steps:

1. Start Outlook. In Outlook 2010, click the Office button, click **Account Settings**, and then select the **Account Settings** option. In Outlook 2013 or Outlook 2016, on the File pane, click **Account Settings**, and then select the **Account Settings** option.
2. In the Account Settings dialog box, click the **Data Files** tab.
3. Select the .pst file to use in the list of data files provided, and then click **Set As Default**.
4. When prompted to confirm, click **Yes** and then click **Close**.
5. Exit and restart Outlook. Outlook will now use personal folders.

If you want mail to resume using server-stored mail, complete the following steps:

1. Start Outlook. In Outlook 2010, click the Office button, click **Account Settings**, and then select the **Account Settings** option. In Outlook 2013 or Outlook 2016, on the File pane, click **Account Settings**, and then select the **Account Settings** option.
2. In the Account Settings dialog box, click the **Data Files** tab.
3. Select the .ost file to use in the list of data files provided, and then click **Set As Default**.
4. When prompted to confirm, click **OK** and then click **Close**.
5. Exit and restart Outlook. Outlook will now use personal folders.

Repairing .pst data files

When Outlook uses personal folders, you can use the Inbox Repair tool (scanpst.exe) to analyze and repair corrupted data files.

- With Office 2010 and Office 2013, this tool is stored in the %SystemDrive%\Program Files\Microsoft Office\Office*Version* folder, where *Version* is the internal version of Office you are using, such as Office15 for Outlook 2013.
- With Office 2016, this tool is stored in the %SystemDrive%\Program Files\Microsoft Office\root\Office16 folder, such as c:\program files (x86)\Microsoft Office\root\Office16.

If a .pst file won't open or is damaged, you can use the Inbox Repair tool to repair it by completing the following these steps:

1. Exit Outlook. Open the Office folder in File Explorer and then double-click the Inbox Repair tool (scanpst.exe).

2. Click **Browse**. In the Select File To Scan dialog box, browse to the folder where .pst files are stored, select the .pst file you want to work with, and then click **Open**. Generally, .pst files are either stored in *%LocalAppData%*\Microsoft\Outlook, where *%LocalAppData%* is a user-specific environment variable that points to a user's local application data, or in the %UserProfile%\Documents\Outlook Files folder, where %UserProfile% is a user-specific environment variable that points to the user's local profile data.

3. Click **Start**, and the Inbox Repair tool will begin analyzing the file. The larger the file the longer the analysis will take.

4. If errors are found, click **Repair** to start the repair process. The Inbox Repair tool will create a copy of the .pst file before attempting the repair operation. During the repair, the Inbox Repair tool will rebuild the .pst file. This backup will be stored in the same folder as the original .pst file.

Microsoft Outlook Inbox Repair Tool

The following file has been scanned:
C:\Users\williams\Documents\Outlook Files\Outlook.pst

Errors were found in this file. To repair these errors, click Repair.

Folders found in this file: 24
Items found in this file: 0

☑ Make backup of scanned file before repairing
Enter name of backup file:

C:\Users\williams\Documents\Outlook Files\Ol   [Browse...]

[Details...]   [Repair]   [Cancel]

5. Start Outlook with the profile that contains the .pst file that you repaired. Press Ctrl+6 to display the Folder List view and look for a folder named Recovered Personal Folders. This folder contains the default Outlook folders as well as a Lost And Found folder, which contains any items recovered by the Inbox Repair tool.

> **NOTE** You can also display the Folders List view by clicking the More button (•••) in the Features pane and then selecting Folders.

6. Create a new .pst data file to store your mail items. Drag the items from the Lost And Found folder into the appropriate folder under the new Personal folders. When you've moved all the items, you can remove the Recovered Personal Folders .

7. The Inbox Repair tool creates a backup of the original .pst file and names it with the .bak file extension. By default this file is stored in the same location as the original .pst file. If you make a copy of this file and name it with a .pst extension, you may be able to recover additional items. To do this, add the .pst file to the mail profile and then move any additional mail items from this old .pst file to the new data file created in step 6.

Repairing .ost data files

When Outlook uses server mailboxes, .ost data files contain copies of information saved on the server. If an .ost file won't open or is damaged, you can re-create the file by completing the following these steps:

1. Exit Outlook. Start the Mail utility. Press the Windows key +I and then click **Control Panel**. In Control Panel, click **Small Icons** on the View By list and then start the Mail app by double-clicking its icon.

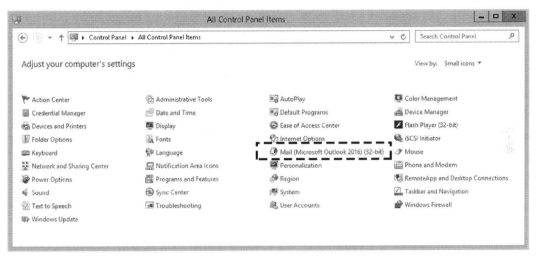

2. In the Mail Setup–Outlook dialog box, click **Data Files**. This opens the Account Settings dialog box with the Data Files tab selected.

3. Select the Exchange account and then click **Open File Location**. This opens File Explorer to the location of the data file. Note this location. By default, .ost files are stored in *%LocalAppData%*\Microsoft\Outlook, where *%LocalAppData%* is a user-specific environment variable that points to a user's local application data.

4. Close the Account Settings and Mail Setup dialog boxes. In File Explorer, right-click the .ost file and then click **Delete**. If you are unable to delete the file, make sure all mail and Office windows are closed.

5. Start Outlook. Download a copy of the mail items again to automatically re-create the .ost file.

Accessing Multiple Exchange Mailboxes

Earlier in the chapter, I discussed how users could check multiple Internet mail accounts in Outlook. You might have wondered whether users could check multiple Exchange mailboxes as well—and they can. Users often need to access multiple Exchange mailboxes for many reasons:

- Help desk administrators might need access to the help desk mailbox in addition to their own mailboxes.
- Managers might need temporary access to the mailboxes of subordinates who are on vacation.
- Project team members may need to access mailboxes set up for long-term projects.
- Resource mailboxes might need to be set up for accounts payable, human resources, corporate information, and so on.

Normally, a one-to-one relationship exists between user accounts and Exchange mailboxes. You create a user account and add a mailbox to it; only this user can access the mailbox directly through Exchange. To change this setup, you must change the permissions on the mailbox. One way to change mailbox access permissions is to do the following:

1. Log on to Exchange as the owner of the mailbox.

2. Delegate access to the mailbox to one or more additional users.

3. Have users with delegated access log on to Exchange and open the mailbox.

The sections that follow examine each of these steps in detail.

Logging on to Exchange as the Mailbox Owner

Logging on to Exchange as the mailbox owner allows you to delegate access to the mailbox. Before you can do this, however, you must complete the following steps:

1. Log on as the user or have the user log on for you.

2. Start Outlook. Make sure that mail support is configured to use server mailboxes. If necessary, configure this support, which creates the mail profile for the user.

3. After you configure Outlook to use Exchange, you should be able to log on to Exchange as the mailbox owner.

TIP With multiple mailbox users, you should configure the mailbox to deliver mail to the server rather than to a personal folder. In this way, the mail can be checked by one or more mailbox users.

Delegating Mailbox Access

After you've logged on as the mailbox owner, you can delegate access to the mailbox by completing these steps:

1. Start Outlook. Open the Delegates dialog box by doing one of the following:

- In Outlook 2010, click the Office button, click **Account Settings**, and then select the **Account Settings** option. On the Delegates tab or in the Delegates dialog box, click **Add**.
- In Outlook 2013 or Outlook 2016, on the File pane, click **Account Settings**, and then select the **Delegate Access** option. In the Delegates dialog box, click **Add**.

2. The Add Users dialog box appears. To add users, double-click the name of a user who needs access to the mailbox. Repeat this step as necessary for other users, and then click **OK** when you're finished.

Delegates

Delegates can send items on your behalf, including creating and responding to meeting requests. If you want to grant folder permissions without giving send-on-behalf-of permissions, close this dialog box, right-click the folder, click Change Sharing Permissions, and then change the options on the Permissions tab.

[Add...]
[Remove]
[Permissions...]
[Properties...]

Deliver meeting requests addressed to me and responses to meeting requests where I am the organizer to:

(•) My delegates only, but send a copy of meeting requests and responses to me (recommended)

( ) My delegates only

( ) My delegates and me

[OK]   [Cancel]

Add Users

Search: (•) Name only   ( ) More columns   **Address Book**

[   ] [Go]   Global Address List - williams@imaginedla ∨   Advanced Find

Name	Title	Business Phone	Location
Alert William Stanek			
All Company			
All Contractors			
All Employees			
All Engineering			
All Finance			
All Sales			
All Technology			
Bob Green			
Canada Engineering			
Canada Finance			
Canada Sales			
Canada Service			
Canada Support			
Canada Technology			

[Add ->]   Bob Green

[OK]   [Cancel]

3. In the Delegate Permissions dialog box, assign permissions to the delegates for the Calendar, Tasks, Inbox, Contacts, and Notes. The available permissions include

- **None**   No permissions
- **Reviewer**   Grants read permission only
- **Author**   Grants read and create permissions
- **Editor**   Grants read, create, and modify permissions

> **NOTE**   If the user needs total control over the mailbox, you should grant the user Editor permission for all items.

4. Click **OK** twice. These changes go into effect when the user restarts Outlook.

Delegated users can access the mailbox and send mail on behalf of the mailbox owner. To change this behavior, set folder permissions as described later in the "Granting permission to access folders without delegating access" section.

Opening Additional Exchange Mailboxes

The final step is to let Exchange Server know about the additional mailboxes the user can open. To do this, follow these steps:

1. Have the user who will be accessing additional mailboxes log on and start Outlook.

2. In Outlook 2010, click the Office button, click **Account Settings**, and then select the **Account Settings** option. In Outlook 2013 or Outlook 2016, on the File pane, click **Account Settings**, and then select the **Account Settings** option.

3. Select the Microsoft Exchange Server account, and then click **Change**.

E-mail Accounts
You can add or remove an account. You can select an account and change its settings.

| E-mail | Data Files | RSS Feeds | SharePoint Lists | Internet Calendars | Published Calendars | Address Books |

New... 🔧 Repair... 🖆 Change... ② Default ✕ Remove ⬆ ⬇

Name	Type
williams@imaginedlands.local	Microsoft Exchange (send from this account by def... ①

Microsoft Exchange ✕

| General | Advanced | Security |

Mailboxes

Open these additional mailboxes:

Add...

Remove

Cached Exchange Mode Settings

☑ Use Cached Exchange Mode
  ☑ Download shared folders
  ☐ Download Public Folder Favorites

Outlook Data File Settings...

Mailbox Mode

Outlook is running in Unicode mode against Microsoft Exchange.

OK   Cancel   Apply

4. In the Change Account dialog box, click **More Settings**.

5. In the Microsoft Exchange dialog box, on the Advanced tab, click **Add**.

6. Type the name of a mailbox to open. Generally, this is the same name as the mail alias for the user or account associated with the mailbox. Click **OK**. Repeat this step to add other mailboxes.

7. Click **Next**, and then click **Finish**.

8. Click **Close**. The additional mailboxes are displayed in the Outlook folder list.

Granting Permission to Access Folders Without Delegating Access

When a mailbox is stored on the server, you can grant access to individual folders in the mailbox. Granting access in this way allows users to add the mailbox to their mail profiles and work with the folder. Users can perform tasks only for which you've granted permission.

To grant access to folders individually, follow these steps:

1. Right-click the folder for which you want to grant access, and then select **Properties**. In the Properties dialog box, select the **Permissions** tab, as shown in Figure 10-8.

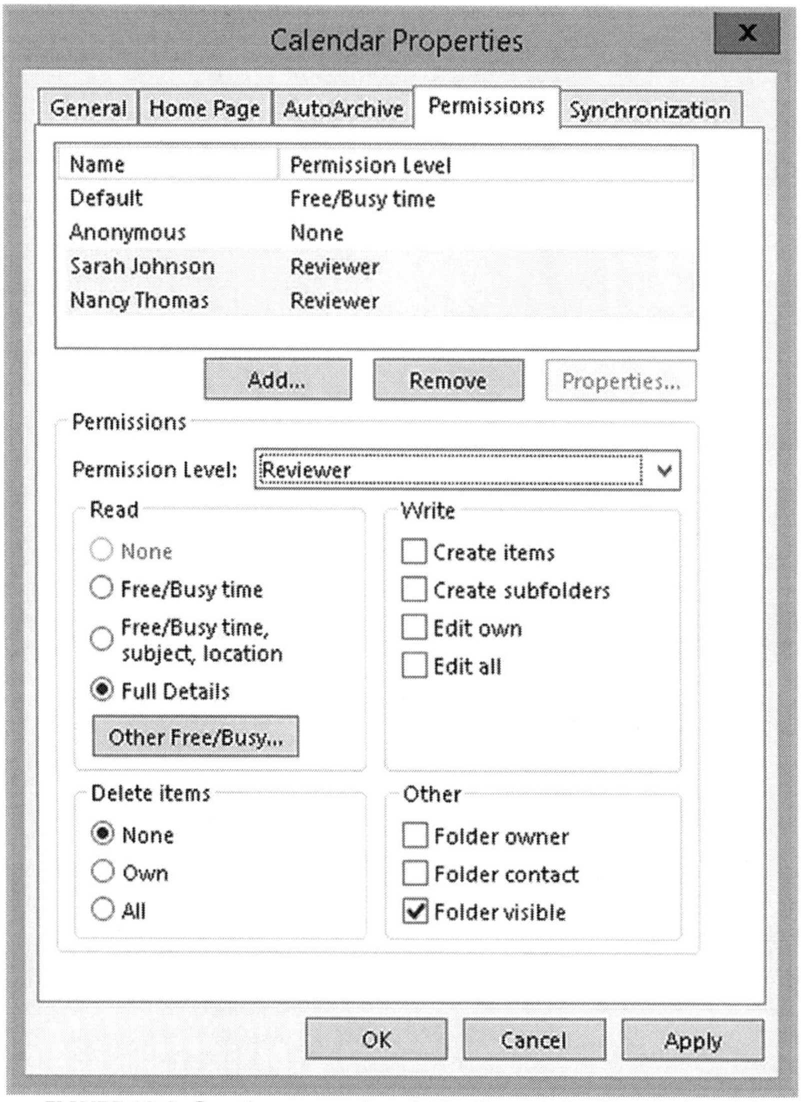

FIGURE 10-8 Granting access to a folder through the Permissions tab.

2. The Name and Permission Level lists display account names and their permissions on the folder. Two special names might be listed:

- **Default** Provides default permissions for all users.
- **Anonymous** Provides permissions for anonymous users, such as those who anonymously access a published public folder through the web.

3. To grant permission that differs from the default permission, click **Add**.

4. In the Add Users dialog box, double-click the name of a user who needs access to the mailbox. Repeat this step as necessary for other users, and click **OK** when finished.

5. In the Name and Role lists, select one or more users whose permissions you want to modify. Then use the Permission Level list to assign permissions or select individual permission items. The roles are defined as follows:

- **Owner** Grants all permissions in the folder. Users with this role can create, read, modify, and delete all items in the folder. They can create subfolders and change permissions on folders as well.
- **Publishing Editor** Grants permission to create, read, modify, and delete all items in the folder. Users with this role can create subfolders as well.
- **Editor** Grants permission to create, read, modify, and delete all items in the folder.
- **Publishing Author** Grants permission to create and read items in the folder, to modify and delete items the user created, and to create subfolders.
- **Author** Grants permission to create and read items in the folder and to modify and delete items the user created.
- **Nonediting Author** Grants permission to create and read items in the folder.
- **Reviewer** Grants read-only permission.
- **Contributor** Grants permission to create items but not to view the contents of the folder.
- **None** Grants no permission in the folder.

6. When you're finished granting permissions, click **OK**.

Using Mail Profiles to Customize the Mail Environment

The mail profile used with Outlook determines which information services are available and how they are configured. A default mail profile is created when you install and configure Outlook for the first time. This mail profile is usually called Outlook.

The active mail profile defines the mail setup for the user who is logged on to the computer. You can define additional profiles for the user as well. You can use these additional profiles to customize the user's mail environment for different situations. Here are two scenarios:

- A manager needs to check the Technical Support and Customer Support mailboxes only on Mondays when she writes summary reports. On other days, the manager doesn't want to see these mailboxes. To solve this problem, you create two mail profiles: Support and Standard. The Support profile displays the manager's mailbox as well as the Technical Support and Customer Support mailboxes. The Standard profile displays only the manager's mailbox. The manager can then switch between these mail profiles as necessary.
- A laptop user wants to check Exchange mail directly while connected to the LAN. When at home, the user wants to use remote mail with scheduled connections. On business trips, the user wants to use SMTP and POP3. To solve this problem, you create three mail profiles: On-Site, Off-Site, and Home. The On-Site profile uses the Exchange Server service with a standard configuration. The Off-Site profile configures Exchange Server for remote mail and scheduled connections. The Home profile uses the Internet mail service instead of the Exchange information service.

Common tasks you'll perform to manage mail profiles are examined in this section.

Creating, Copying, and Removing Mail Profiles

You manage mail profiles through the Mail utility. To access this utility and manage profiles, follow these steps:

1. Exit Outlook. Start the Mail utility. In Control Panel, click **Small Icons** on the View By list and then start the Mail app by clicking its icon or by double-clicking its icon.

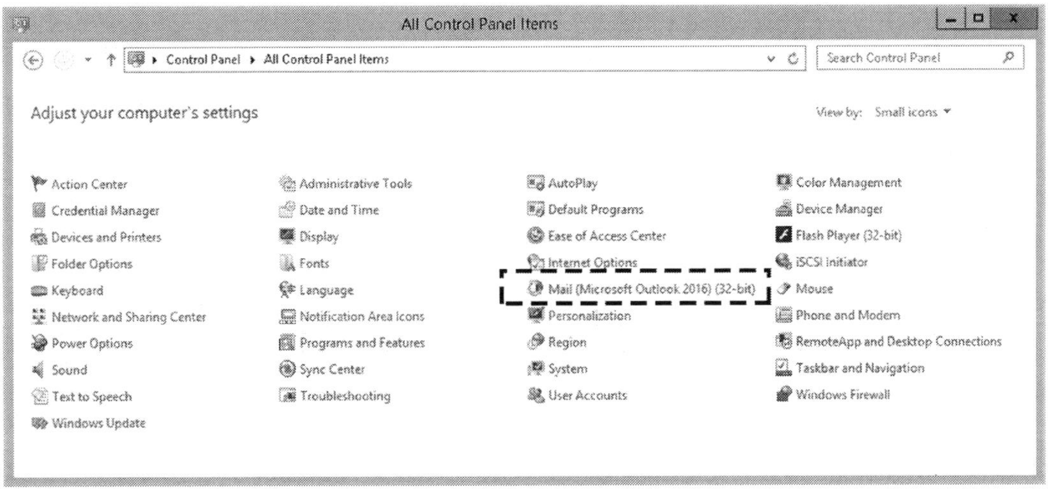

2. In the Mail Setup–Outlook dialog box, click **Show Profiles**.

3. As Figure 10-9 shows, you should see a list of mail profiles for the current user.

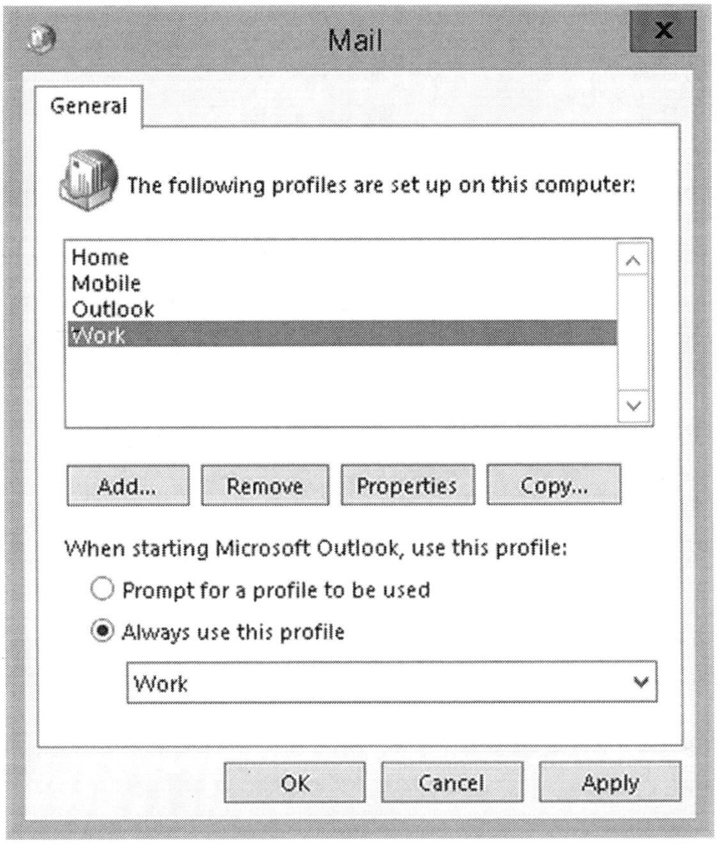

FIGURE 10-9 Using the Mail dialog box to add, remove, or edit mail profiles.

4. Mail profiles for other users aren't displayed. You can now perform the following actions:

- Click Add to create a new mail profile using the Account Settings Wizard.
- Delete a profile by selecting it and clicking Remove.
- Copy an existing profile by selecting it and clicking Copy.
- View a profile by selecting it and clicking Properties.

Selecting a Specific Profile to use on Startup

You can configure Outlook to use a specific profile on startup or to prompt for a profile to use.

To start with a specific profile, follow these steps:

1. Start the Mail utility. Press the Windows key +I and then click **Control Panel**. In Control Panel, click **Small Icons** on the View By list and then start the Mail app by clicking its icon or by double-clicking its icon.

2. In the Mail Setup–Outlook dialog box, click **Show Profiles**.

3. Select **Always Use This Profile**, and then use the drop-down list to choose the startup profile. Click **OK**.

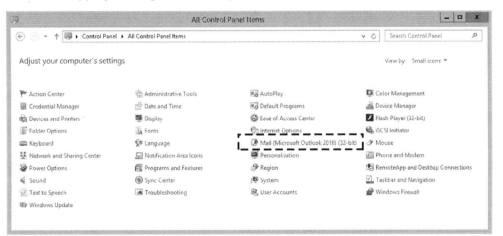

To prompt for a profile before starting Outlook, follow these steps:

1. Start the Mail utility. Press the Windows key +I and then click **Control Panel**. In Control Panel, click **Small Icons** on the View By list and then start the Mail app by clicking its icon or by double-clicking its icon.

2. In the Mail Setup–Outlook dialog box, click **Show Profiles**.

3. Select **Prompt For A Profile To Be Used**, and then click **OK**.

The following profiles are set up on this computer:

Home
Mobile
Outlook
Work

Add... | Remove | Properties | Copy...

When starting Microsoft Outlook, use this profile:

⊙ Prompt for a profile to be used
○ Always use this profile

Work

OK | Cancel | Apply

Chapter 11. Customizing & Troubleshooting the Exchange Shell

As discussed earlier in the text, the Exchange Management Shell is a command-line management interface built on Windows PowerShell. You use the Exchange Management Shell to manage any aspect of an Exchange Server 2016 configuration that you can manage in the Exchange Admin Center. This means that you can typically use either tool to configure Exchange Server 2016. However, only the Exchange Management Shell has the full complement of available commands, and this means that some tasks can be performed only at the shell prompt.

Running and using the Exchange Management Shell

After you've installed the Exchange management tools on a computer, you can start to use the Exchange Management Shell and the following techniques:

- With Windows 8.1, Windows 10 as well as Windows Server 2012 and Windows Server 2016, you can start Exchange Management Shell by using the Apps Search box. Type **shell** in the Apps Search box, and then select Exchange Management Shell. Or click Start and then choose Exchange Management Shell.
- With Windows 7 and Windows Server 2008 R2, you can start Exchange Management Shell by clicking Start, pointing to All Programs, clicking Microsoft Exchange Server 2016, and then clicking Exchange Management Shell.

The Exchange Management Shell is designed to be run only on domain-joined computers. Whether you are logged on locally to an Exchange server or working remotely, this opens a custom Windows PowerShell console. The console does the following:

1. Connects to the closest Exchange 2016 server using Windows Remote Management (WinRM).

2. Performs authentication checks that validate your access to the Exchange 2016 server and determine the Exchange role groups and roles your account is a member of. You must be a member of at least one management role.

3. Creates a remote session with the Exchange 2016 server. A remote session is a runspace that establishes a common working environment for executing commands on remote computers.

Selecting the shell in this way starts the Exchange Management Shell using your user credentials. This enables you to perform any administrative tasks allowed for your user account and in accordance with the Exchange role groups and management roles you're assigned. As a result, you don't need to run the Exchange Management Shell in elevated, administrator mode, but you can. To do so, right-click Exchange Management Shell, and then click Run As Administrator.

The actual command that runs when you start the shell is:

```
C:\Windows\System32\WindowsPowerShell\v1.0\powershell.exe -noexit -command
". 'C:\Program Files\Microsoft\Exchange Server\V15\bin\RemoteExchange.ps1';
Connect-ExchangeServer -auto -ClientApplication:ManagementShell "
```

As you can see, the command starts PowerShell, runs the RemoteExchange.ps1 profile file, and then uses the command Connect-ExchangeServer to establish the remote session. Note the parameters passed in for Connect-ExchangeServer. The –ClientApplication parameter specifies that client-side application is the Exchange Management Shell. The –Auto parameter tells the cmdlet to automatically discover and try to connect to an appropriate Exchange 2016 server. Discovery works like this:

1. When you run the command on an Exchange 2016 server, the local server is tried first.
2. Next, the command tries to connect to a Mailbox server in the current Active Directory site.
3. Finally, the command tries to connect to a Mailbox server in the current Active Directory site.
4. If no server is available, the command exits.

The RemoteExchange.ps1 profile file sets aliases, initializes Exchange global variables, and loads .NET assemblies for Exchange. It also modifies the standard PowerShell prompt so that it is scoped to the entire Active Directory forest and defines the following Exchange-specific functions:

*   **Functions**   Allows you to list all available functions by typing **functions**.
*   **Get-Exbanner**   Displays the Exchange Management Shell startup banner whenever you type **get-exbanner**.
*   **Get-Exblog**   Opens Internet Explorer and accesses the Exchange blog at Microsoft whenever you type **get-exblog**.

- **Get-Excommand**   Allows you to list all available Exchange commands by typing **get-excommand**.
- **Get-Pscommand**   Allows you to list all available PowerShell commands by typing **get-pscommand**.
- **Get-Tip**   Displays the tip of the day whenever you type **get-tip**.
- **Quickref**   Opens Internet Explorer and allows you to download the Exchange Management Shell quick start guide whenever you type **quickref**.

The RemoteExchange.ps1 profile loads the ConnectFunctions.ps1 script, which defines a number of functions that enable AutoDiscover and Connect features. The functions include the following:

- Connect-ExchangeServer
- CreateOrGetExchangeSession
- Discover-EcpVirtualDirectoryForEmc
- Discover-ExchangeServer
- _AutoDiscoverAndConnect
- _CheckServicesStarted
- _ConnectToAnyServer
- _GetCAFEServers
- _GetMailservers
- _GetCurrentVersionServers
- _GetExchangeServersInSite
- _GetHostFqdn
- _GetHubMailboxUMServers
- _GetLocalForest
- _GetServerFqdnFromNetworkAddress
- _GetSites
- _GetWebServiceServers
- _GetURL
- _NewExchangeRunSpace
- _OpenExchangeRunSpace
- _PrintUsageAndQuit
- _SelectVdir

These functions are available for you to use whenever you work with the Exchange Management Shell or have loaded the ConnectFunctions.ps1 script. However, only Connect-ExchangeServer, CreateOrGetExchangeSession, Discover-EcpVirtualDirectoryForEmc and Discover-ExchangeServer are meant to be called directly. The other functions are helper functions.

When you are working with the Exchange Management Shell or have run ConnectFunctions.ps1, you can view the source for a function by typing **functions** followed by the name of the function, such as **functions connect-exchangeserver**.

If you want to access Exchange features from a manual remote shell (as discussed later in this chapter under "Using a Manual Remote Shell to Work with Exchange") or within scripts, you need to load the RemoteExchange.ps1 profile file. You can find an example of the command required to do this by viewing the properties of the shortcut for the Exchange Management Shell. In the Properties dialog box, the Target text is selected by default. Press Ctrl+C to copy this text so that you can use it. For example, if you copy the Target text and paste it into an elevated command prompt (cmd.exe), you can access the Exchange Management Shell and work with Exchange Server. If you copy the Target text and paste it into a script, you can be sure that the manual remote session is established when you run the script.

You also can customize the way the Exchange Management Shell is initialized by editing the shortcut properties or by copying the shortcut that starts the Exchange Management shell and then editing the properties. With Windows 8.1, Windows 10 as well as Windows Server 2012 and Windows Server 2016, one way to create a new shortcut for Exchange Management Shell is to do the following:

1. If an Exchange Management Shell shortcut is not pinned to the desktop taskbar, open the Start screen. Next, right-click **Exchange Management Shell** and then select **Pin To Taskbar**.

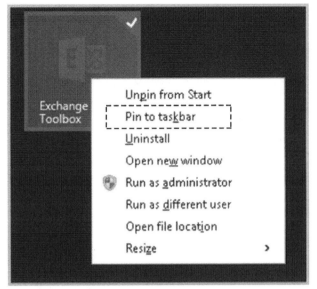

2. On the desktop, right-click the taskbar shortcut for Exchange Management Shell. This displays the Tasks dialog box.

3. In the Tasks dialog box, right-click **Exchange Management Shell** and then select **Properties**. This opens the Properties dialog box for the shortcut with the Shortcut tab selected.

4. Click in the Target box. The text should be selected automatically so you can copy it in the next step. If the text isn't selected, press **Ctrl+A** to select all of the related text.

Exchange Management Shell Properties X

Colors	Security	Details	Previous Versions
General	Shortcut	Options	Font	Layout

Exchange Management Shell

Target type: Application

Target location: v1.0

Target: Server -auto -ClientApplication:ManagementShell "

Start in:

Shortcut key: None

Run: Normal window

Comment: Manages the Exchange e-mail system with the co

[Open File Location]   [Change Icon...]   [Advanced...]

[OK]   [Cancel]   [Apply]

5. Press **Ctrl+C** to copy the selected text and then click **OK** to close the Properties dialog box.

6. Right-click an open area of the desktop, select **New**, and then select **Shortcut**. This opens the Create Shortcut dialog box.

7. In the Create Shortcut dialog box, click in the Type The Location Of The Item box and then press **Ctrl+V** to paste the previously selected text.

8. Click **Next**. Type a name for the shortcut, such as Custom EMC. Click **Finish** to create the shortcut.

9. Run the shortcut with your custom options by double-clicking it on the desktop.

An extra command must always be added to the Target text. This additional command is Connect-ExchangeServer, a command enabled when the ConnectFunctions.ps1 script runs. To customize the initialization of remote sessions, other parameters are available:

* **–ClearCache**   A troubleshooting option that allows you to clear registry entries and exported modules and then re-create the registry settings and import modules again. After you clear the cache, you can try to connect again using options you need.

```
connect-exchangeserver -clearcache
```

* **–Forest**   Allows you to specify a single part name or the fully qualified domain name (FQDN) of the Active Directory forest in which to perform discovery. You must be able to authenticate in the forest. User credentials you provide for the – Username parameter are not used for discovery. Use with –Auto.

```
connect-exchangeserver -auto -forest ForestName
```

* **–Prompt**   Prompts you for the FQDN of the Exchange server to connect to. If you use –Prompt with –Auto, you are prompted only if PowerShell cannot connect automatically. If you use –Prompt with –ServerFqdn, you are prompted only if PowerShell cannot connect to the specified server.

```
connect-exchangeserver -auto -prompt
```

* **–ServerFqdn**   Allows you to specify the FQDN of the Exchange server to connect to.

```
connect-exchangeserver -serverfqdn ExServerFQDN
```

* **–Username**   Allows you to specify the user name to use for authentication. You will be prompted for the user's password. You can also pass in a Credential object. Use with –ServerFqdn or –Auto.

```
connect-exchangeserver -serverfqdn ExServerFQDN
-username UserName
```

> **REAL WORLD**   When you are working with some cmdlets and objects in PowerShell, you might need to specify a credential for authentication. To do this, use Get-Credential to obtain a Credential object and save the result in a variable for later use. Consider the following example:

```
$cred = get-credential
```

PowerShell reads this command, prompts you for a user name and password, and then stores the credentials provided in the *$cred* variable. You also can specify that you want the credentials for a specific user in a specific domain. The following example requests the credentials for the ExAdmin account in the Imaginedlands.com domain:

```
$cred = get-credential –credential imaginedlands\exadmin
```

A Credential object has UserName and Password properties that you can work with. Although the user name is stored as a regular string, the password is stored as a secure, encrypted string. Simply pass in the credential instead of the user name as shown in this example:

```
$cred = get-credential –credential imaginedlands\exadmin
get-hotfix –credential $cred –computername MailServer22
```

IMPORTANT   When you prompt for credentials, integrated Windows authentication is used for authentication. However, if the credentials are not set when prompted, such as when the user selects Cancel, Kerberos authentication is used with the user's default credentials.

REAL WORLD   Where a domain name is required for credentials, you typically can use either the NET BIOS domain name or the DNS domain name. In the previous examples, I entered the NET BIOS domain name **pocket-consulta** rather than the DNS name **imaginedlands.com**.

When you call Connect-ExchangeServer, the function does one of two things: It opens a remote session by using implicit credentials (the credentials of the user who is running Exchange Management Shell) or by using specified credentials (credentials you've explicitly provided). One of the final things Connect-ExchangeServer does is call _OpenExchangeRunSpace, which in turn calls _NewExchangeRunspace to establish the remote session.

In the script, the core code for _OpenExchangeRunSpace is:

```
$global:remoteSession = _NewExchangeRunspace $fqdn $credential $UseWIA
$SuppressError $ClientApplication $AllowRedirection
```

And the core code for _NewExchangeRunspace is:

```
$so = New-PSSessionOption -OperationTimeout $sessionOptionsTimeout
-IdleTimeout $sessionOptionsTimeout -OpenTimeout $sessionOptionsTimeout;
```

```
New-PSSession -ConnectionURI "$connectionUri" -ConfigurationName
Microsoft.Exchange -SessionOption $so
```

The code sample creates a global variable named *$remoteSession* to hold the remote session. A global variable is used to ensure that the session remains active and available when the script exits. The session is established using New-PSSession with a connection URI for a particular Exchange server. For example, if the Exchange server's FQDN is MailServer15.Imaginedlands.local, the connection URI is https://mailserver15.imaginedlands.local/powershell. The –ConfigurationName parameter sets the configuration namespace as Microsoft.Exchange (in place of the default Microsoft.PowerShell). The –SessionOption parameter sets session options that were defined previously using the New-PSSessionOption cmdlet. The session options include the operation timeout value, the idle timeout value, and the open session timeout value. By default, all three are set to 180,000 milliseconds (180 seconds) via the *$sessionOptionsTimeout* variable defined in the first section of the ConnectFunctions.ps1 script.

You can use the *MsExchEmsTimeout* environment variable to set the default timeout values. If you set this environment variable to a value of 900,000 milliseconds or less (15 minutes or less), the timeouts are set accordingly. If you set this environment variable to a value greater than 900,000 milliseconds, the timeout values revert to the 3-minute default value.

> **REAL WORLD**   When you connect to Exchange Admin Center in a browser, the browser version determines your experience level, and the location of your mailbox determines whether you see the console for Exchange 2010, Exchange 2013, or Exchange 2016. This is not the case when you are working with the shell. With the shell, the experience level is always set to FULL. Further, the HKLM:\SOFTWARE\Microsoft\ExchangeServer\v15\Setup key in the registry is examined to determine the Exchange version and the build number, and then this information is used to set the client version compatibility level. Thus, a precise connection URI is set as http://$fqdn/powershell?serializationLevel=Full;ExchClientVer=$clientVersion.

Managing the PowerShell Application

Microsoft Internet Information Services (IIS) handles every incoming request to a website within the context of a web application. A web application is a software program that delivers web content to users over HTTP or HTTPS. Each website has a default web application and one or more additional web applications associated with it. The default web application handles incoming requests that aren't assigned to other web applications. Additional web applications handle incoming requests that specifically reference a particular application.

When you connect to a server using a URL, such as https://mailserver15.imaginedlands.local/powershell, you are performing remote operations via the PowerShell application running on the web server providing Exchange services. Like all web applications, the PowerShell application has a virtual directory associated with it. The virtual directory sets the application name and maps the application to the physical directory that contains the application's content.

You can manage the PowerShell application using IIS Manager GUI and the Exchange Management Shell. The related commands for the Exchange Management Shell are:

* **Get-PowerShellVirtualDirectory** Displays information about the PowerShell application running on the web server providing services for Exchange.

```
Get-PowerShellVirtualDirectory [-Identity 'AppName']
[-DomainController 'DomainControllerName']
```

```
Get-PowerShellVirtualDirectory -Server 'ExchangeServerName'
[-DomainController 'DomainControllerName']
```

* **New-PowerShellVirtualDirectory** Creates a new PowerShell application running on the web server providing services for Exchange.

```
New-PowerShellVirtualDirectory -Name 'AppName'
[-AppPoolId 'AppPoolName'] [-BasicAuthentication <$true | $false>]
[-CertificateAuthentication <$true | $false>] [-DomainController
'DomainControllerName'] [-ExternalUrl 'URL'] [-InternalUrl 'URL']
[-Path 'PhysicalDirectoryPath']
[-WindowsAuthentication <$true | $false>]
```

* **Remove-PowerShellVirtualDirectory** Removes a specified PowerShell application running on the web server providing services for Exchange.

```
Remove-PowerShellVirtualDirectory -Identity 'AppName'
[-DomainController 'DomainControllerName']
```

- **Set-PowerShellVirtualDirectory**   Modifies the configuration settings for a specified PowerShell application running on the web server providing services for Exchange.

```
Set-PowerShellVirtualDirectory -Identity 'AppName'
[-BasicAuthentication <$true | $false>] [-CertificateAuthentication
<$true | $false>] [-DomainController 'DomainControllerName']
[-ExternalUrl 'URL'] [-InternalUrl 'URL']
[-LiveIdBasicAuthentication <$true | $false>]
[-WindowsAuthentication <$true | $false>]
```

At the Exchange Management Shell prompt, you can confirm the location of the PowerShell application by typing **get-powershellvirtualdirectory**.

GetPowerShellVirtualDirectory lists the name of the application, the associated directory and website, and the server on which the application is running, as shown in the following example:

```
Name                           Server
-------                        -------
PowerShell (Default Web Site)  CorpServer45
```

In this example, a standard configuration is being used where the application named *PowerShell* is running on Default Web Site on CorpServer45. You can use Set-PowerShellVirtualDirectory to specify the internal and external URL to use as well as the permitted authentication types. Authentication types you can enable or disable include basic authentication, Windows authentication, certificate authentication, and Live ID basic authentication. You can use New-PowerShellVirtualDirectory to create a new PowerShell application on the web server providing services for Exchange and Remove-PowerShellVirtualDirectory to remove a PowerShell application.

> **REAL WORLD**   Any change you make to the PowerShell virtual directory configuration requires careful pre-planning. For every potential change, you'll need to determine whether you need to modify the WinRM configuration and the PowerShell path in ConnectFunctions.ps1 scripts on management computers and Exchange servers as well as the specific changes you'll need to make with regard to IIS on your Mailbox servers.
>
> Microsoft cautions against modifying the default configuration for the PowerShell virtual directory as any mistakes you make could prevent you from managing Exchange Server. Because Exchange configuration data is

stored in Active Directory and the affected IIS metabase, you would need to be able to restore Exchange data in Active Directory and the affected IIS metabase to a previous state to recover.

Customizing Exchange Management Shell

Now that you know how the Exchange Management Shell environment works, you can more easily customize the shell to work the way you want it to. One way to do this is to modify the menu shortcut that starts the Exchange Management Shell or create copies of this menu shortcut to change the way the Exchange Management Shell starts. For example, if you want to connect to a named Exchange server rather than any available Exchange server, you can do the following:

1. In the Properties dialog box for the shortcut that starts Exchange Management Shell, the Target text is selected by default. Press the right arrow key to move to the end of the command text.

2. Delete **–Auto** and type **–ServerFqdn** followed by the FQDN of the Exchange server, such as **–ServerFQDN MailServer12.Imaginedlands.local**. Click **OK**.

That said, this entire sequence of tasks is meant to simplify the task of establishing an interactive remote session with a single Exchange server. As implemented in the default configuration, you have a one-to-one, interactive approach for remote management, meaning you establish a session with a specific remote server and work with that specific server simply by executing commands.

When you are working with PowerShell outside of Exchange Management Shell, you might want to use the Enter-PSSession cmdlet to start an interactive session with an Exchange server or any other remote computer. The basic syntax is **Enter-PSSession ComputerName**, where *ComputerName* is the name of the remote computer, such as the following:

```
enter-pssession mailserver15
```

After you enter this command, the command prompt changes to show that you are connected to the remote computer, as shown in the following example:

```
[MailServer15]: PS C:\Users\wrstanek.cpand1\Documents>
```

Now, the commands that you type run on the remote computer just as if you had typed them directly on the remote computer. In most cases, you need to ensure you are running an elevated, administrator shell and that you pass credentials along in the session. When you connect to a server in this way, you use the standard PowerShell remoting configuration and do not go through the PowerShell application running on a web server. You can end the interactive session by using the command Exit-PSSession or typing **exit**.

To access an Exchange server in the same way as the ConnectFunctions.ps1 script, you need to use the –ConnectionURI parameter to specify the connection URI, the –ConfigurationName parameter to specify the configuration namespace, the –Authentication parameter to set the authentication type to use, and optionally, the –SessionOption parameter to set session options. Consider the following example:

```
 enter-pssession -connectionURI
http://mailserver12.imaginedlands.local/powershell
-ConfigurationName Microsoft.Exchange -Authentication Kerberos
```

Here, you set the connection URI as https://mailserver12.imaginedlands.local/powershell, set the configuration namespace as Microsoft.Exchange, and use Kerberos authentication with the implicit credentials of your user account. If you don't specify the authentication method, the default authentication method for WinRM is used. If you want to use alternate credentials, you can pass in credentials as shown in this example:

```
$cred = get-credential -credential imaginedlands\williams
```

```
enter-pssession -connectionURI
https://mailserver12.imaginedlands.local/powershell
-ConfigurationName Microsoft.Exchange -credential $cred
-Authentication Kerberos
```

Here, you set the connection URI as https://mailserver12.imaginedlands.local/powershell, set the configuration namespace as Microsoft.Exchange, and use alternate credentials. When PowerShell reads the Get-Credential command, you are prompted for the password for the specified account. Because the authentication type is not defined, the session uses the default authentication method for WinRM.

To put this all together, one way to create a script that runs on an Exchange server is to run the RemoteExchange.ps1 profile file and then run the ConnectFunctions.ps1 script to autoconnect to Exchange. The commands you insert into your script to do this are the following:

```
$s = $env:ExchangeInstallPath + "bin\RemoteExchange.ps1"
&$s
$t = $env:ExchangeInstallPath + "bin\ConnectFunctions.ps1"
&$t
```

Here, you define variables that point to the RemoteExchange.ps1 and ConnectFunctions scripts in the Exchange installation path, and then you use the & operator to invoke the scripts. The environment variable *ExchangeInstallPath* stores the location of the Exchange installation. If you enter the full path to a script, you don't need to assign the path to a variable and then invoke it. However, you then have a fixed path and might need to edit the path on a particular Exchange server. Be sure to run the script at an elevated, administrator PowerShell prompt.

To create a script that runs on your management computer and then executes commands remotely on an Exchange server, insert commands in your script to create a new session and then invoke commands in the session using the techniques discussed in the next section.

Performing One-to-Many Remote Management

PowerShell also lets you perform one-to-many remote management. To do so, you must work with an elevated, administrator shell and can either invoke remote commands on multiple computers or establish remote sessions with multiple computers. When you remotely invoke commands, PowerShell runs the commands on the remote computers, returns all output from the commands, and establishes connections to the remote computers only for as long as is required to return the output. When you establish remote sessions, you can create persistent connections to the remote computers and then execute commands within the session. Any command you enter while working in the session is executed on all computers to which you are connected, whether this is 1 computer, 10 computers, or 100 computers.

> **TIP** As discussed in Chapter 1, "Welcome to Exchange Server 2016," WinRM must be appropriately configured on any computer you want to remotely manage. While WinRM is configured on Exchange servers and most others computers running current versions of Windows and Windows Server, WinRM listeners generally are not created by default. You can create the required listeners by running winrm quickconfig.

The following command entered as a single line invokes the Get-Service and Get-Process commands on the named servers:

```
invoke-command -computername MailServer12, Mailserver19, MailServer32
-scriptblock {get-service; get-process}
```

The following command establishes a remote session with the named computers:

```
$s = new-PSSession -computername MailServer12, Mailserver19, MailServer32
-Credential Cpandl\WilliamS
```

When you connect to a server in this way, you use the standard PowerShell remoting configuration and are not going through the PowerShell application running on a web server. After you establish the session, you can then use the $s session with Invoke-Command to return commands on all remote computers you are connected to. This example looks for stopped Exchange services on each computer:

```
invoke-command –session $s
-scriptblock {get-service mse* | where { $_.status -eq "stopped"}}
```

In this example, you pipe the output of Get-Service to the Where-Object cmdlet and filter based on the Status property. Because the $_ automatic variable operates on the current object in the pipeline, PowerShell examines the status of each service in turn and lists only those that are stopped in the output.

In addition to working with remote commands and remote sessions, some cmdlets have a ComputerName parameter that lets you work with a remote computer without using Windows PowerShell remoting. PowerShell supports remote background jobs as well. A background job is a command that you run asynchronously in an interactive or noninteractive session. When you start a background job, the command prompt returns immediately, and you can continue working while the job runs. For a complete discussion of these remoting features, see *Windows PowerShell: The Personal Trainer* (Stanek & Associates, 2014).

Using a Manual Remote Shell to Work with Exchange

Although the easiest way to work remotely with Exchange 2016 is to install the management tools on your computer, you can connect to and manage Exchange 2016 if you don't have the management tools installed. To do this, you can use a manual remote shell to connect to an Exchange 2016 server. However, you lose the benefits of the preconfigured tools which set up the environment and manage the Exchange connection for you. You also can use a manual remote shell to connect to and work with Exchange Online.

Preparing to Use the Remote Shell

As you might expect, there are several prerequisites for creating a manual remote shell. The computer you use to connect an Exchange server must be running a current version of Windows or Windows Server.

The computer must have Windows Management Framework, which includes Windows PowerShell and WinRM, and Microsoft .NET Framework. Although current versions of Windows and Windows Server include these components, Windows 7 and Windows Server 2008 R2 do not.

> **REAL WORLD** When you install the Mailbox server role for Exchange 2016, the server is configured automatically with a Windows PowerShell gateway that is configured as a proxy service. This proxy service allows you to run remote commands in web browsers and in remote sessions. Whenever you work with Exchange Admin Center or Exchange Management Shell, the commands are executed via this proxy—even if you logged on locally.

Before you can work remotely, WinRM must be running and the authentication mechanisms you want to use must be enabled. As Exchange Online uses Basic authentication, you may need to enable this. At an elevated, administrator PowerShell prompt, enter the following commands to check the status of WinRM:

```
get-service "winrm"
```

If WinRM isn't running, start the service by entering:

```
start-service "winrm"
```

Next, ensure that the authentication mechanisms you want to use are enabled for use with WinRM. To do this, enter the following command:

```
winrm get winrm/config/client/auth
```

Although you are working in the PowerShell window, this command is passed through to the command prompt and the output states the status of available authentication mechanisms:

```
Auth
    Basic = false
    Digest = true
    Kerberos = true
    Negotiate = true
    Certificate = true
    CredSSP = false
```

If Basic authentication isn't enabled and you want to work with Exchange Online, you must enable it. Unfortunately, there's no easy way to pass a complex command through to the command prompt. Because of this, you'll need to open an elevated command prompt and then enter the following command:

```
winrm set winrm/config/client/auth '@{Basic="true"}'
```

> **IMPORTANT** Exchange Management Shell and Exchange Admin Center require integrated Windows authentication. Exchange Online uses Basic authentication.

Once you've ensured WinRM is running and configured appropriately, you can check the status of script execution by entering the following command at the PowerShell prompt:

```
Get-ExecutionPolicy
```

Windows PowerShell script execution must be enabled on your computer. Typically, you'll want to use the RemoteSigned execution policy. If so, enter the following command at an elevated, administrator PowerShell prompt:

```
Set-ExecutionPolicy RemoteSigned
```

When you connect to a remote Exchange server, you can use your current network credentials or you can specify another set of credentials. Either way, the user account that you want to use for remote management must be a member of a management role group or be enabled for remote shell.

By default, when you create a new mailbox user for Exchange 2016 or Exchange Online, the mailbox user has remote PowerShell enabled. You can view the access status for all users in the Exchange organization by entering the following command:

```
Get-User -ResultSize unlimited |
Format-Table Name,DisplayName,RemotePowerShellEnabled
```

If you want to display a list of only users who don't have access, you could filter the results for this value by running the following command instead:

```
Get-User -ResultSize unlimited -Filter {RemotePowerShellEnabled -eq $false}
```

Set the filtered value to $true if you want to see a list of only users who have access. You can check the access status of a specific user as well by specifying the SAM account name, display name, or login name of the user, as shown in these examples:

```
Get-User "williams" | Format-List RemotePowerShellEnabled
```

```
Get-User "William Stanek" | Format-List RemotePowerShellEnabled
```

```
Get-User "williams@imaginedlands.com" | Format-List
RemotePowerShellEnabled
```

Connecting Manually to Exchange 2016 Servers

In an elevated, administrator Windows PowerShell window, you can establish a connection to the remote Exchange server using a PowerShell session. When your management computer is joined to the domain, you can use either HTTP or HTTPS with Kerberos authentication to establish the session. However, HTTPS is normally disabled by default in the client configuration. The basic syntax is:

```
$Session = New-PSSession -ConfigurationName Microsoft.Exchange
-ConnectionUri http://Exchange2016MSName/PowerShell/
-Authentication Kerberos
```

where *Exchange2016MSName* is the host name or FQDN of the Exchange 2016 Mailbox server to which you want to connect and *PowerShell* is the name of the PowerShell virtual directory on the server, such as:

```
$Session = New-PSSession -ConfigurationName Microsoft.Exchange
-ConnectionUri http://mailserver35.imaginedlands.com/PowerShell/
-Authentication Kerberos
```

With Kerberos authentication, your current credentials are used to establish the session. Keep in mind that with Kerberos authentication you must use the server name or the FQDN and cannot use an IP address.

If you want to use an authentication mechanism other than Kerberos or your computer isn't connected to a domain, you must use HTTPS as the transport (or the destination server must be added to the TrustedHosts configuration settings for

WinRM, and HTTP must be enabled in the client configuration). You also must explicitly pass in a credential using the –Credential parameter.

You also can specify the authentication mechanism, such as Basic, Digest or Negotiate. All communications are encrypted with HTTPS. The modified syntax is then:

```
$Session = New-PSSession -ConfigurationName Microsoft.Exchange
-ConnectionUri https://Exchange2016MSNameOrIP/PowerShell/
-Authentication Negotiate -Credential Credential
```

where *Exchange2016MSNameOrIP* is the FQDN or IP address of the Exchange 2016 Mailbox server to which you want to connect, *PowerShell* is the name of the PowerShell virtual directory on the server, and *Credential* sets the user name under which the session is established. Consider the following example:

```
$Session = New-PSSession -ConfigurationName Microsoft.Exchange
-ConnectionUri https://mailserver35.imaginedlands.com/PowerShell/
-Authentication Negotiate -Credential imaginedlands\williams
```

Here, you establish a session with MailServer35 using integrated Windows authentication and store this session in the $Session object. As you are passing in a credential for Williams, you are prompted for and must enter the account password. You also can store the credential in a Credential object and then use Get-Credential to request the credentials. The syntax then becomes:

```
$Cred = Get-Credential
$Session = New-PSSession -ConfigurationName Microsoft.Exchange
-ConnectionUri https://mailserver35.imaginedlands.com/PowerShell/
-Authentication Negotiate -Credential $Cred
```

> **IMPORTANT**   Regardless of whether you use Kerberos or another authentication mechanism, the Exchange server's SSL certificate must contain a common name (CN) that matches the identifier you are using. Otherwise, you won't be able to connect.

Connecting Manually to Exchange Online

Connecting manually to Exchange Online is similar to connecting manually to on-premises servers running Exchange 2016. In an elevated, administrator Windows PowerShell window, you can establish a connection to Exchange Online using a PowerShell session. You can use a stand-alone computer or a domain-joined computer that meets the requirements discussed earlier under "Preparing to use the remote shell."

The basic syntax for connecting manually to Exchange Online is:

```
$Cred = Get-Credential
$Session = New-PSSession -ConfigurationName Microsoft.Exchange
-ConnectionUri https://ps.outlook.com/powershell/
-Authentication Basic -Credential $Cred -AllowRedirection
```

Here, you use HTTPS with Basic authentication for the session and establish a connection to the Exchange Online URL provided by Microsoft, which typically is https://ps.outlook.com. To establish the connection, you must pass in your Exchange Online user name and password. This example stores credentials in a Credential object and then uses Get-Credential to prompt for the required credentials. You also could specify the credentials explicitly, as shown here:

```
$Session = New-PSSession -ConfigurationName Microsoft.Exchange
-ConnectionUri https://ps.outlook.com/powershell/
-Authentication Basic -Credential wrs@imaginedlands.onmicrosoft.com
-AllowRedirection
```

Here, you are prompted for the password for the account.

> **NOTE** When you work with Exchange Online, keep in mind that not all of the cmdlets are available as compared to an on-premises installation. This is because the operating environments are different. Exchange Online runs on Windows Azure rather than Windows Server. You can connect to and work directly with the Microsoft Online service and Windows Azure as discussed in Chapter 2, "Working with Exchange Online."

Managing Remote Sessions

After you establish a session with an Exchange 2016 server or Exchange Online, you must import the server-side PowerShell session into your client-side session by running the following command:

```
Import-PSSession $Session
```

You can then work with the remote server.

When you are finished, you should disconnect the remote shell from Exchange server. It's important to note that, beginning with Windows PowerShell 3.0, sessions are persistent by default. When you disconnect from a session, any command or scripts that are running in the session continue running, and you can later reconnect to the session to pick up where you left off. You also can reconnect to a session if you were disconnected unintentionally, such as by a temporary network outage.

> **IMPORTANT** With Exchange Online, each account can have only three connections to sever-side sessions at a time. If you close the PowerShell window without disconnecting from the session, the connection remains open for 15 minutes and then disconnects.

To disconnect a session without stopping commands or releasing resources, run the following command:

```
Disconnect-PSSession $Session
```

The $Session object was instantiated when you created the session. As long as you don't exit the PowerShell window in which this object was created, you can use this object to reconnect to the session by entering:

```
Connect-PSSession $Session
```

When you are completely finished with the session, you should remove it. Removing a session stops any commands or scripts that are running, ends the session, and releases the resources the session was using. Remove a session by running the following command:

```
Remove-PSSession $Session
```

Troubleshooting Exchange Management Shell

Note that the ConnectionFunctions.ps1 script relies on your organization having a standard Exchange Server configuration. By default, Exchange is configured for management using HTTP with the URL *http://ServerName/powershell*. If you've modified the Web Server configuration on your Exchange servers to use a different path, such as might be required to enhance security, you need to update the connection URIs used in the ConnectionFunctions.ps1 script.

When you invoke the PowerShell application, the web server to which you connect runs the PowerShell plug-in (Pwrshplugin.dll) and the Exchange Authorization plug-in (Microsoft.Exchange.AuthorizationPlugin.dll). The PowerShell plug-in runs as a Microsoft.Exchange shell and has the following initialization parameters:

- PSVersion, which sets the PowerShell version as appropriate
- ApplicationBase, which sets the base path for the Exchange server as %ExchangeInstallPath%Bin
- AssemblyName, which sets the name of the .NET assembly to load as Microsoft.Exchange.Configuration.ObjectModel.dll

The Authorization plug-in handles Exchange authorization and authentication. Together, these plug-ins create an authorized shell environment for the remote session.

The physical directory for the PowerShell application is %ExchangeInstallPath%\ClientAccess\PowerShell. This application runs in the context of an application pool named MSExchangePowerShellAppPool. In a large organization, you might want to optimize settings for this and other application pools, as discussed in the *IIS Web Applications, Security & Maintenance: The Personal Trainer* (Stanek & Associates, 2015).

In the %ExchangeInstallPath%\ClientAccess\PowerShell directory on your server, you'll find a web.config file that defines the settings for the PowerShell application. This file contains a role-based access control (RBAC) configuration section that loads the assemblies and web controls for the application.

> **TIP** Microsoft recommends against changing the PowerShell application configuration. However, there's nothing magical or mystical about the PowerShell application or MSExchangePowerShellAppPool. You can re-

create these features to enable remote management in alternate configurations, such as on nondefault websites or websites with alternate names. However, be sure to copy the PowerShell application's web.config file to the physical directory for your base application. Before you make any changes to a live production environment, you should plan and test your changes in a nonproduction test environment.

The web server to which you connect processes your remote actions via the Exchange Control Panel (ECP) application running on the default website. With Exchange 2016, you see the ECP as the Exchange Admin Center. The physical directory for this application is %ExchangeInstallPath%\ClientAccess\Ecp. This application runs in the context of an application pool named MSExchangeECPAppPool.

In the %ExchangeInstallPath%\ClientAccess\ECP directory on your server, you'll find a web.config file that defines the settings for the ECP application. This file contains an RBAC configuration section that loads the assemblies and web controls for the application.

Because of the interdependencies created by accessing Exchange via web applications, you'll want to examine related features as part of troubleshooting any issues you experience with remote sessions. Generally, your troubleshooting should follow these steps:

1. Examine the status and configuration of the WinRM on your local computer and the target Exchange server. The service must be started and responding.

2. Check the settings of any firewall running on your local computer, the target Exchange server, or any device between the two, such as a router with a firewall.

3. Check the status of the World Wide Web Publishing Service on the Exchange server. The service must be started and responding.

4. Check the configuration settings of the PowerShell and ECP applications on the web server. By default, the applications don't have access restrictions, but another administrator could have set restrictions.

5. Check the status of MSExchangePowerShellAppPool and MSExchangeECPAppPool. You might want to recycle the application pools to stop and then start them.

6. Check the configuration settings of MSExchangePowerShellAppPool and MSExchangeECPAppPool. By default, the application pools are configured to use only one worker process to service requests.

7. Check to ensure the PowerShell application's web.config file is present in the physical directory for the application, and also that the file has the appropriate settings.

8. Check to ensure the ECP application's web.config file is present in the physical directory for the application and also that the file has the appropriate settings.

Chapter 12. Customizing & Configuring Exchange Security

You manage Exchange security using either the Active Directory tools or the Exchange management tools. In Active Directory, you manage security using permissions. Users, contacts, and security groups all have permissions assigned to them. These permissions control the resources that users, contacts, and groups can access and the actions they can perform. You use auditing to track the use of these permissions, as well as log ons and log offs. In addition to the standard permissions, Exchange also supports *role-based access control* (RBAC), which are unique to Exchange.

Configuring Standard Exchange Permissions

Active Directory is the central repository for information in domains. Because Active Directory also stores most Exchange information, you can use the features of Active Directory to manage standard permissions for Exchange across the organization.

Assigning Permissions: Exchange Server and Online

Users, contacts, and security groups are represented in Active Directory as objects. These objects have many attributes that determine how they are used. The most important attributes are the permissions assigned to the objects. Permissions grant or deny access to objects and resources. For example, you can grant a user the right to create public folders but deny that same user the right to create mail-enabled contacts.

Permissions assigned to an object can be applied directly to the object, or they can be inherited from another object. Generally, objects inherit permissions from *parent objects*. A parent object is an object that is above another object in the object hierarchy. However, you can override inheritance. One way to do this is to assign permissions directly to an object. Another way is to specify that an object shouldn't inherit permissions.

In Exchange Server 2016, permissions are inherited through the organizational hierarchy. The root of the hierarchy is the *domain*. All other containers in the tree inherit the permissions of the domain container. Sometimes, however, you want to create structures that represent parts of the organization or you want to limit administrative access for part of the organization. To do this, you use organizational units. *Organizational units* (OUs) are containers for objects that you not only want to group together but that you also want to manage together.

For the management of Exchange information and servers, Exchange Server 2016 uses several predefined groups. These predefined security groups have permissions to manage the Exchange organization, Exchange servers, and Exchange recipient data in Active Directory. In Active Directory Users And Computers, you can view and work with the Exchange-related groups using the Microsoft Exchange Security Groups organizational unit (see Figure 12-1).

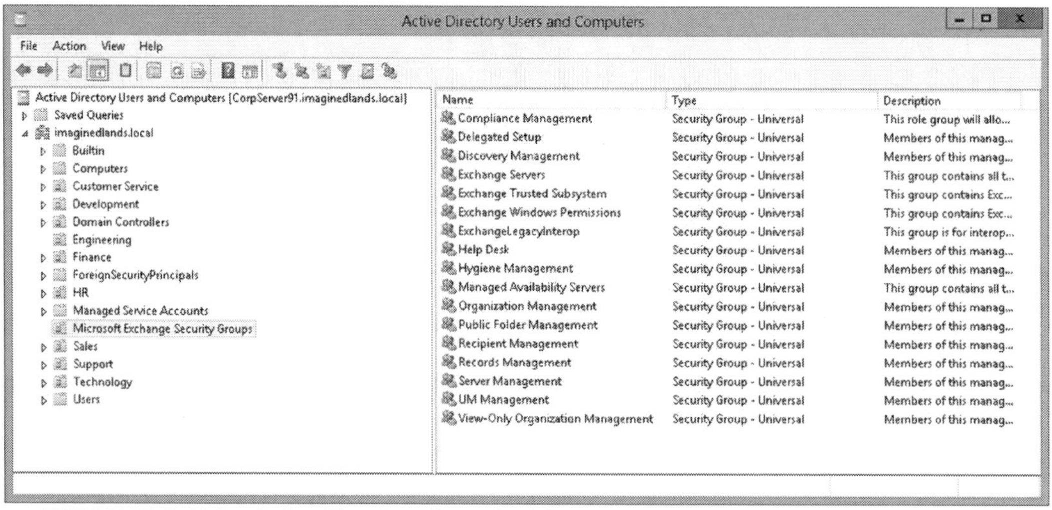

FIGURE 12-1 Using Active Directory Users And Computers to work with Exchange management groups.

In Active Directory Users And Computers, there's a hidden container of Exchange objects called Microsoft Exchange System Objects. You can display this container by selecting Advanced Features on the View menu.

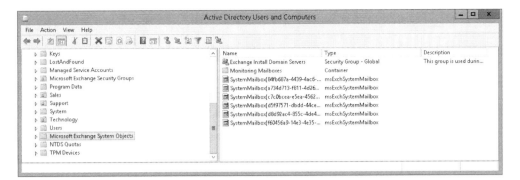

FIGURE 12-2 Viewing the Exchange system objects.

> **NOTE** Throughout this chapter, I will often refer to Active Directory security groups simply as *security groups* or *groups*. Exchange also has distribution groups. Although distribution groups are created as objects in Active Directory, they aren't used to control access to resources.

When you are working with Exchange Online, you can view the Exchange Management groups as well. To do this, connect to Windows Azure and Microsoft Online Services in Windows PowerShell and then enter the Get-Group command. For more information on using Windows PowerShell to work with the online service, see Chapter 2 "Working with Exchange Online."

Understanding Exchange Management Groups

Table 12-1 lists predefined groups created in Active Directory for Exchange Server 2016. As the table shows, each group has a slightly different usage and purpose. Several of the groups are used by Exchange servers. These groups are Exchange Servers, Exchange Trusted Subsystem, Exchange Windows Permissions, and ExchangeLegacyInterop. You use the other groups for role-based access control and assigning management permissions. Role groups marked with an asterisk (*) are also available with Exchange Online.

TABLE 12-1 Security groups created for Exchange 2016

GROUP	DESCRIPTION
Compliance Management*	A role group. Members of this universal security group have permission to manage compliance settings.
Delegated Setup	A role group. Members of this universal security group have permission to install and uninstall Exchange on provisioned servers.
Discovery Management*	A role group. Members of this universal security group can perform mailbox searches for data that meets specific criteria.
Exchange Install Domain Servers	Members of this global security group include domain controllers on which Exchange Server is installed. You can see this group only when you select View and then click Advanced Features in Active Directory Users And Computers.
Exchange Servers	Members of this universal security group are Exchange servers in the organization. This group allows Exchange servers to work together. By default, all computers running Exchange Server 2016 are members of this group; you should not change this setup.
Exchange Trusted Subsystem	Members of this universal security group are Exchange servers that run Exchange cmdlets using Windows Remote Management (WinRM). Members of this group have permission to read and modify all Exchange configuration settings as well as user accounts and groups.

GROUP	DESCRIPTION
Exchange Windows Permissions	Members of this universal security group are Exchange servers that run Exchange cmdlets using WinRM. Members of this group have permission to read and modify user accounts and groups.
ExchangeLegacyInterop	This group is universal security used for interoperability with Exchange Server 2003 bridgehead servers. (Shouldn't be deleted even though it is not used with Exchange 2016.)
Help Desk*	A role group. Members of this universal security group can view any property or object within the Exchange organization and have limited management permissions.
Hygiene Management*	A role group. Members of this universal security group can manage the anti-spam and antivirus features of Exchange.
Managed Availability Servers	All Mailbox servers are members of this universal security group.
Organization Management*	A role group. Members of this universal security group have full access to all Exchange properties and objects in the Exchange organization with some exceptions, such as Discovery Management.
Public Folder Management	A role group. Members of this universal security group can manage public folders and perform most public folder management operations.
Recipient Management*	A role group. Members of this universal

GROUP	DESCRIPTION
	security group have permission to modify Exchange user attributes in Active Directory and perform most mailbox operations.
Records Management*	A role group. Members of this universal security group can manage compliance features, including retention policies, message classifications, and transport rules.
Server Management	A role group. Members of this universal security group can manage all Exchange servers in the organization but do not have permission to perform global operations.
UM Management*	A role group. Members of this universal security group can manage all aspects of unified messaging (UM), including the Unified Messaging service configuration and UM recipient configuration.
View-Only Organization Management*	A role group. Members of this universal security group have read-only access to the entire Exchange organization tree in the Active Directory configuration container and read-only access to all the Windows domain containers that have Exchange recipients.

Also available with Exchange Online

Table 12-2 lists predefined groups and administrative roles used with Exchange Online and Office 365. These groups and roles are used for role-based access controls and assigning management permissions. However, HelpDeskAdmins and TenantAdmins aren't managed in Exchange Online. Instead, you add users to the related Office 365 role to get the desired permissions.

TABLE 12-2 Security groups and administrative roles for the Exchange Online and Office 365

GROUP/ROLE	DESCRIPTION
Billing Administrator	Used with Office 365. Members of this role are responsible for managing subscriptions and making purchases. They also can manage support tickets and monitor service health.
Exchange Administrator	Used with Office 365. Members of this role have full access to Exchange Online.
Global Administrator	Used with Office 365. Members of this role have full access to all Office 365 features and are the only ones who can assign other admin roles. Except for password admins, they also are the only ones who can reset passwords for other admins.
HelpDeskAdmins	Used with Exchange Online. Members of this group have the Password Administrator role in the Office 365 organization.
Password Administrator	Used with Office 365. Members of this role are responsible for managing passwords for standard users and other password admins. They also can manage service requests and monitor service health.
Service Administrator	Used with Office 365. Members of this role are responsible for managing service requests and monitoring service health.
SharePoint Administrator	Used with Office 365. Members of this role have full access to SharePoint.
Skype for Business Administrator	Used with Office 365. Members of this role can manage Skype for Business.
TenantAdmins	Used with Exchange Online. Members of this group have the Global Administrator role in the Office 365 organization.

GROUP/ROLE	DESCRIPTION
User Management Administrator	Used with Office 365. Members of this role are responsible for managing standard users and groups. They can reset passwords for standard users, manage service requests, and monitor service health.

When working with Exchange-related groups, keep in mind that Organization Management grants the widest set of Exchange management permissions possible. Members of this group can perform any Exchange management task, including organization, server, and recipient management. Members of the Recipient Management group, on the other hand, can manage only recipient information, and Public Folder Management can manage only public folder information. View-Only Organization Management can view Exchange organization, server, and recipient information, but this group cannot manage any aspects of Exchange.

Table 12-3 provides an overview of the default group membership for the Exchange groups in an on-premises organization. Membership in a particular group grants the member the permissions of the group. Exchange groups that aren't listed don't have any default members or membership.

TABLE 12-3 Default membership for Exchange security groups

GROUP	MEMBERS	MEMBER OF
Exchange Install Domain Servers	Individual Exchange servers	Exchange Servers
Exchange Servers	Exchange Install Domain Servers, individual Exchange servers	Windows Authorization Access Group, Managed Availability Group
Exchange Trusted Subsystem	Individual Exchange servers	Exchange Windows Permissions
Exchange Windows Permissions	Exchange Trusted Subsystem	n/a
Managed Availability Servers	Exchange Servers, Mailbox servers	n/a

With Exchange Online, the TenantAdmins group is a member of the Organization Management role group and inherits its permissions from this role group. Rather than add members directly to TenantAdmins, you add members to this role by granting the Global Administrator role to users in Office 365 Admin Center.

Similarly, the HelpDeskAdmins group is a member of the View-Only Organization Management role group and inherits its permissions from this role group. Rather than add members directly to HelpDeskAdmins, you add members to this role by granting the Global Administrator role to users in Office 365 Admin Center.

Assigning Management Permissions

To grant Exchange management permissions to a user or group of users, all you need to do is make the user or group a member of the appropriate Exchange management group. For on-premises Exchange, one of the tools you can use to manage users and groups is Active Directory Users And Computers. You can make users, contacts, computers, or other group members part of an Exchange management group by completing the following steps:

1. Open Server Manager, click Tools, and then select Active Directory Users And Computers.

2. In Active Directory Users And Computers, double-click the Exchange management group you want to work with. This opens the group's Properties dialog box.

3. Click the Members tab, as shown in Figure 12-3.

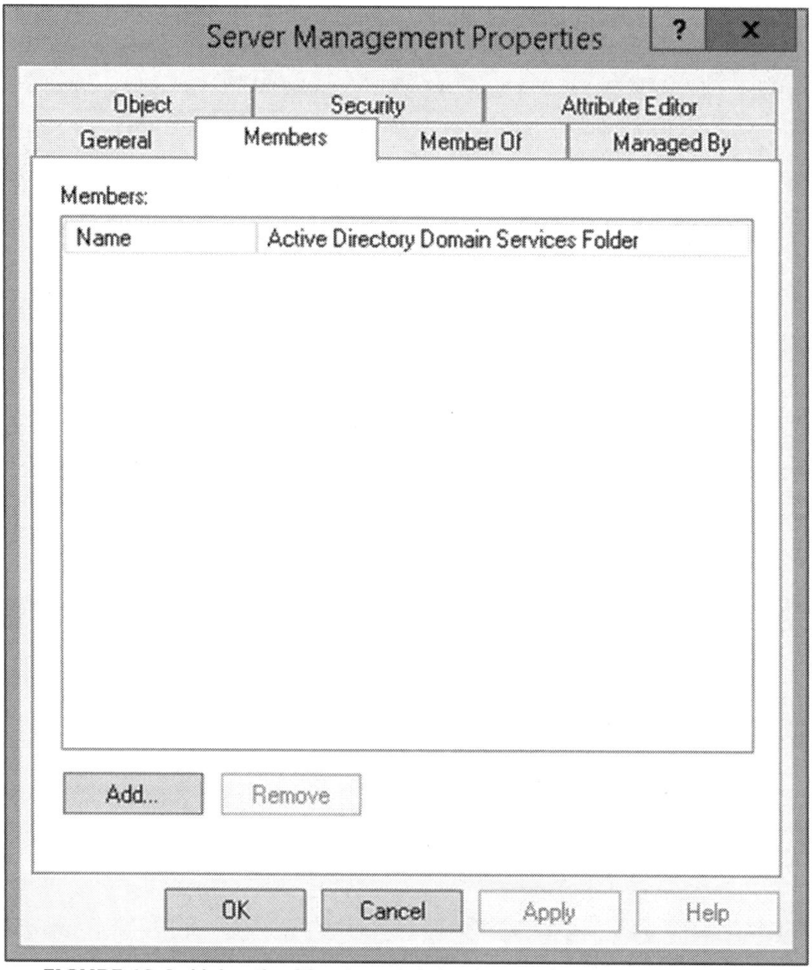

FIGURE 12-3 Using the Members tab to view and manage membership in a group.

4. To make a user or group a member of the selected group, click Add. The Select Users, Contacts, Computers, Service Accounts, Or Groups dialog box appears, as shown in Figure 12-4.

FIGURE 12-4 Specifying the name of the user, contact, computer, service account, or group to add.

5. Type the name of the account to which you want to grant permissions, and then click **Check Names**. If matches are found, select the account you want to use and then click **OK**. If no matches are found, update the name you entered, and try searching again. Repeat this step as necessary. Click **OK**.

You can remove a user, contact, computer, service account, or other group from an Exchange management group by completing the following steps:

1. In Active Directory Users And Computers, double-click the Exchange management group with you want to work with. This opens the group's Properties dialog box.

2. On the Members tab, click the user or group you want to remove and then click **Remove**. When prompted to confirm, click **Yes**, and then click **OK**.

For both on-premises Exchange and Exchange Online, you use Exchange Admin Center to manage membership in Exchange role groups. When you are managing the organization, select Permissions in the Features pane and then select Admin Roles to work with Exchange role groups. When you select a role, the right-most pane provides a description of the role, lists the assigned roles, and also shows the current members (see Figure 12-5). While working with this view, you can double-click a group entry to view and manage its membership.

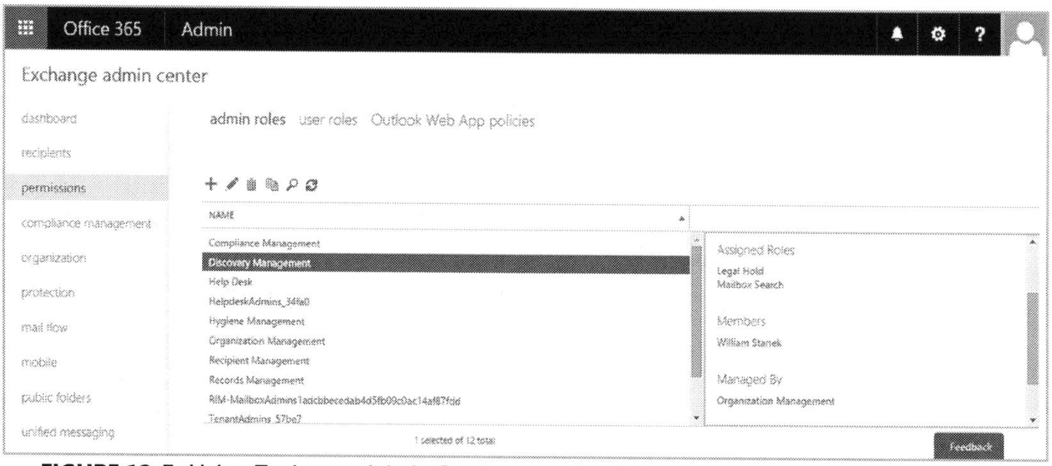

FIGURE 12-5 Using Exchange Admin Center to work with Exchange role groups.

You use Office Admin Center to manage membership in Office 365 role groups. When you are managing the Office 365 service, select **Users & Groups** in the Features pane and then select **Active Users** to view a list of all active users in the organization.

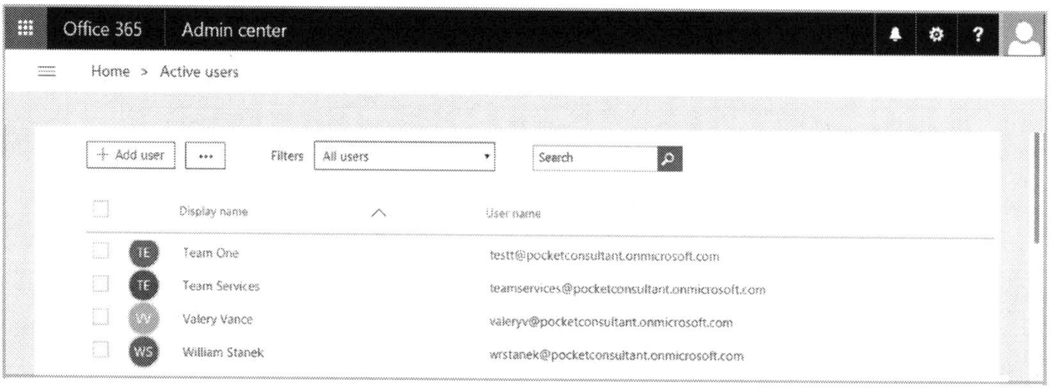

When you select a user, the properties page for the user is displayed. Next, select **Edit** in the Roles pan.

Sign-in status	🖉 Edit
Current users sign in status is **Blocked**	
Roles	🖉 Edit
Products	🖉 Edit

If you want the user to have administrator privileges, complete the following steps:

1. Choose the role to assign. For example, choose Global Administrator to make the user a member of TenantAdmins or Password Administrator to make the user a member of HelpDeskAdmins in the Exchange Online organization.

2. As necessary, enter an alternative email address for the user. Every Office 365 admin must have an alternate email address.

3. Click **Save** to apply the changes.

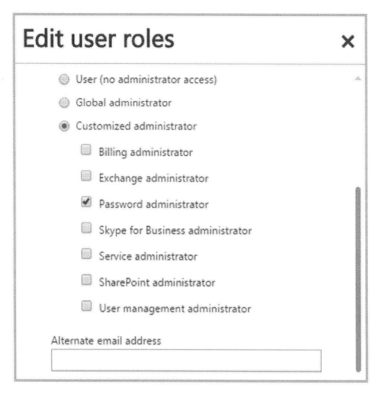

Understanding Advanced Exchange Server Permissions

Active Directory objects are assigned a set of permissions. These permissions are standard Microsoft Windows permissions, object-specific permissions, and extended permissions.

Table 12-4 summarizes the most common object permissions. Keep in mind that some permissions are generalized. For example, with Read Value(s) and Write Value(s), Value(s) is a placeholder for the actual type of value or values.

TABLE 12-4 Common permissions for Active Directory objects

PERMISSION	DESCRIPTION
Full Control	Permits reading, writing, modifying, and deleting
List Contents	Permits viewing object contents

Read All Properties	Permits reading all properties of an object
Write All Properties	Permits writing to all properties of an object
Read Value(s)	Permits reading the specified value(s) of an object, such as general information or group membership
Write Value(s)	Permits writing the specified value(s) of an object, such as general information or group membership
Read Permissions	Permits reading object permissions
Modify Permissions	Permits modifying object permissions
Delete	Permits deleting an object
Delete Subtree	Permits deleting the object and its child objects
Modify Owner	Permits changing the ownership of the object
All Validated Writes	Permits all types of validated writes
All Extended Writes	Permits all extended writes
Create All Child Objects	Permits creating all child objects
Delete All Child Objects	Permits deleting all child objects
Add/Remove Self As Member	Permits adding and removing the object as a member
Send To	Permits sending to the object

Send As	Permits sending as the object
Change Password	Permits changing the password for the object
Receive As	Permits receiving as the object

Table 12-5 summarizes Exchange-specific permissions for objects. If you want to learn more about other types of permissions, I recommend that you read *Windows Server 2016: Essentials for Administration* (Stanek & Associates, 2016).

TABLE 12-5 Extended permissions for Exchange Server

PERMISSION	DESCRIPTION
Read Exchange Information	Permits reading general Exchange properties of the object
Write Exchange Information	Permits writing general Exchange properties of the object
Read Exchange Personal Information	Permits reading personal identification and contact information for an object
Write Exchange Personal Information	Permits writing personal identification and contact information for an object
Read Phone and Mail Options	Permits reading phone and mail options of an object
Write Phone and Mail Options	Permits writing phone and mail options of an object

Although you can use standard Windows permissions, object-specific permissions, and extended permissions to control Exchange management and use, Microsoft recommends that you use role-based access controls instead. My recommendation is to use the role-based access controls whenever possible in place of specific permissions.

Assigning Advanced Exchange Server Permissions

In Active Directory, different types of objects can have different sets of permissions. Different objects can also have general permissions that are specific to the container in which they're defined. For troubleshooting or fine-tuning your environment, you might occasionally need to modify advanced permissions. You can set advanced permissions for Active Directory objects by following these steps:

1. Open Active Directory Users And Computers. If advanced features aren't currently being displayed, select **Advanced Features** on the View menu.

2. Right-click the user, group, service account, or computer account with which you want to work.

> **CAUTION**   Only administrators with a solid understanding of Active Directory and Active Directory permissions should manipulate advanced object permissions. Incorrectly setting advanced object permissions can cause problems that are difficult to track down and may also cause irreparable harm to the Exchange organization.

3. Select **Properties** from the shortcut menu, and then click the Security tab in the Properties dialog box, as shown in Figure 12-6.

4. Users or groups with access permissions are listed in the Group Or User Names list box. You can change permissions for these users and groups by doing the following:

- Select the user or group you want to change.
- Use the Permissions list box to grant or deny access permissions.
- When inherited permissions are dimmed, override inherited permissions by selecting the opposite permissions.

5. To set access permissions for additional users, computers, or groups, click **Add**. Then use the Select Users, Computers, Security Accounts, Or Groups dialog box to add users, computers, security accounts, or groups.

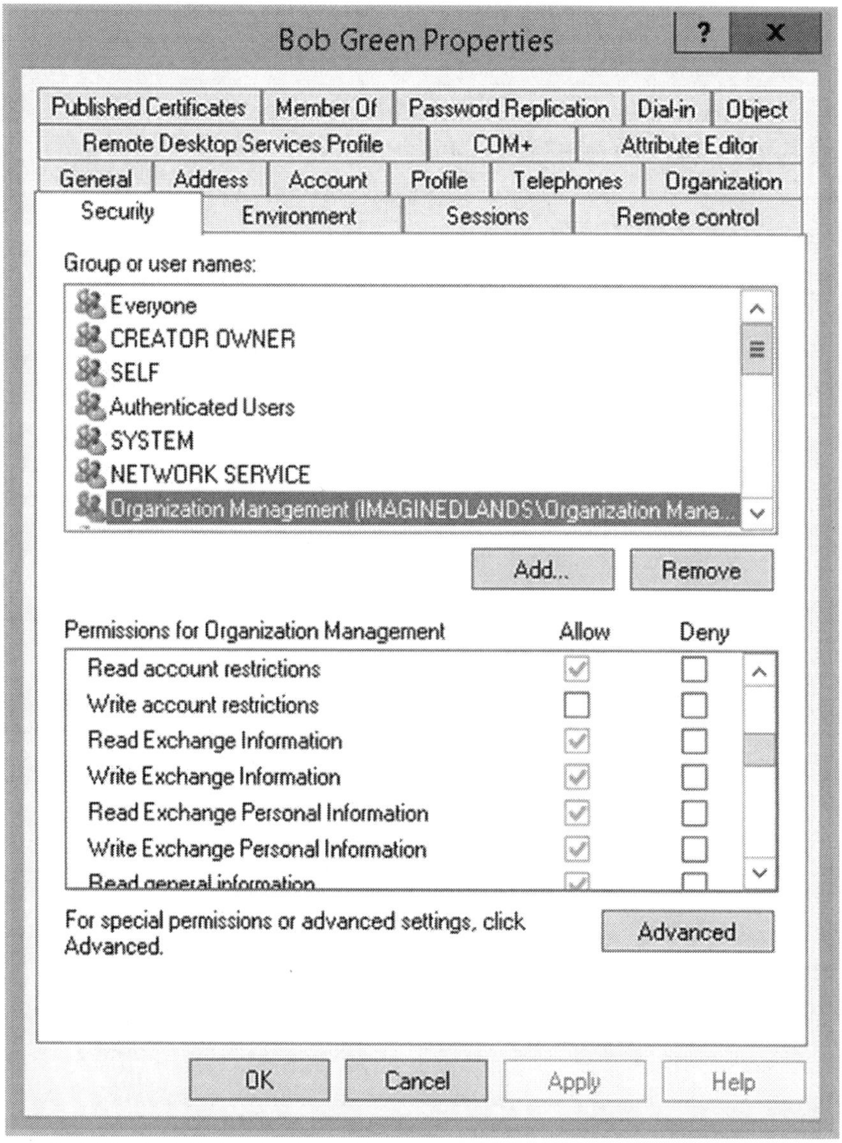

FIGURE 12-6 Using the Security tab to manage advanced permissions.

6. Select the user, computer, service account, or group you want to configure in the Group Or User Names list box, click **Add**, and then click **OK**. Then use the fields in the Permissions area to allow or deny permissions. Repeat this step for other users, computers, service accounts, or groups. Click **OK** when you're finished.

Configuring Role-Based Permissions for Exchange

Exchange 2016 and Exchange Online implement role-based access controls that allow you to easily customize permissions for users in the organization. You use role-based access controls to do the following:

* Assign permissions to groups of users
* Define policies that assign permissions
* Assign permissions directly to users

Before I discuss each of these tasks, I'll discuss essential concepts related to role-based permissions. Because the permissions model is fairly complex, I recommend reading this entire section to understand your implementation options before starting to assign permissions.

Understanding Role-Based Permissions

Role-based access control is a permissions model that uses role assignment to define the management tasks a user or group of users can perform in the Exchange organization. Exchange defines many built-in management roles that you can use to manage your Exchange organization. Each built-in role acts as a logical grouping of permissions that specify the management actions that those assigned the role can perform. You also can create custom roles.

You can assign roles to role groups or directly to users. You also can assign roles through role policies that are then applied to role groups, users, or both. By assigning roles, you grant permission to perform management tasks.

At the top of the permissions model is the role group, which is a special type of security group that has been assigned one or more roles. Keep the following in mind when working with role-based permissions:

* You can assign role-based permissions to any mailbox-enabled user account. Assigning a role to a user grants the user the ability to perform a specific management action.
* You can assign role-based permissions to any universal security group. Assigning a role to a group grants members of the group the ability to perform a specific management action.
* You cannot assign role-based permissions to security groups with the domain local or global scope.

- You cannot assign role-based permissions to distribution groups regardless of scope.

As Table 12-1 showed previously, Exchange 2016 and Exchange Online include a number of predefined role groups. These role groups are assigned fixed management roles by default. As a result, you do not need to explicitly add roles to these groups to enable management, nor can you add or remove roles associated with the built-in groups. You can, however, manage the members of the predefined role groups using the procedures discussed previously. You can also create your own role groups and manage the membership of those groups.

When you assign a role to a group, the management scope determines where in the Active Directory hierarchy that objects can be managed by users assigned a management role. The scope is either implicitly or explicitly assigned. Implicit scopes are the default scopes that apply based on a particular type of management role.

Table 12-6 lists key management roles with an organization scope. A role with an organization scope applies across the whole Exchange organization. Table 12-7 lists key management roles with an organization scope that apply to individual servers. Table 12-8 lists key management roles with a user scope. A role with a user scope applies to an individual user. When you create a role group, you also can set an explicit scope, such as for objects in the Customer Service organizational unit or objects in the Technology organizational unit.

TABLE 12-6 Management roles with an organization scope

MANAGEMENT ROLE	ENABLES MANAGERS TO...
Active Directory Permissions	Configure Active Directory permissions in an organization. Keep in mind that permissions set directly on Active Directory objects cannot be enforced through RBAC.
Address Lists	Manage address lists, the global address list, and offline address lists in an organization.
Audit Logs	Manage audit logs in an organization.
Cmdlet Extension Agents	Manage cmdlet extension agents in an organization.
Data Loss Prevention	Configure data loss prevention settings in an organization.
Database Availability Groups	Manage database availability groups in an organization.
Disaster Recovery	Restore mailboxes and database availability groups in an organization.
Distribution Groups	Create and manage distribution groups and distribution group members in an organization.
Edge Subscriptions	Manage edge synchronization and subscription configuration between Edge Transport servers and Mailbox servers in an organization.
E-Mail Address Policies	Manage email address policies in an organization.
Exchange Connectors	Manage routing group connectors, delivery agent connectors, and other connectors used for transport. This role doesn't enable administrators to manage Send and Receive connectors.

MANAGEMENT ROLE	ENABLES MANAGERS TO...
Federated Sharing	Manage cross-forest and cross-organization sharing in an organization.
Information Rights Management	Manage the Information Rights Management (IRM) features of Exchange in an organization.
Journaling	Manage journaling configuration in an organization.
Legal Hold	Configure whether data within a mailbox should be retained for litigation purposes in an organization.
Mail Enabled Public Folders	Configure whether individual public folders are mail enabled or mail disabled in an organization.
Mail Recipient Creation	Create mailboxes, mail users, mail contacts, distribution groups, and dynamic distribution groups in an organization.
Mail Recipients	Manage existing mailboxes, mail users, mail contacts, distribution groups, and dynamic distribution groups in an organization. This does not enable administrators to create these recipients.
Mail Tips	Manage mail tips in an organization.
Message Tracking	Track messages in an organization.
Monitoring	Monitor the Microsoft Exchange services and component availability in an organization.
Move Mailboxes	Move mailboxes between servers in an organization and between servers in the local organization and another organization.
Organization Configuration	Manage basic organization-wide settings. This role type doesn't include the permissions included in the

MANAGEMENT ROLE	ENABLES MANAGERS TO...
	Organization Client Access or Organization Transport Settings role types.
Organization Transport Settings	Manage organization-wide transport settings, including system messages, site configuration, and so forth. This role doesn't enable administrators to create or manage transport Receive or Send connectors, queues, hygiene, agents, remote and accepted domains, or rules.
Public Folders	Manage public folders in an organization. This role type doesn't enable administrators to manage whether public folders are mail enabled or to manage public folder replication.
Send Connectors	Manage transport send connectors in an organization.
Recipient Policies	Manage recipient policies, such as provisioning policies, in an organization.
Remote and Accepted Domains	Manage remote and accepted domains in an organization.
Reset Password	Reset users' password in an organization.
Retention Management	Manage retention policies in an organization.
Role Management	Manage management role groups, role assignment policies, management roles, role entries, assignments, and scopes in an organization. Users assigned roles associated with this role type can override the Managed By property for role groups, configure any role group, and add or remove members to or from any role group.
Security Group Creation and Membership	Create and manage security groups and their memberships in an organization.

MANAGEMENT ROLE	ENABLES MANAGERS TO...
Team Mailboxes	Define site mailbox provisioning policies and manage site mailboxes.
Transport Agents	Manage transport agents in an organization.
Transport Hygiene	Manage antivirus and anti-spam features in an organization.
Transport Rules	Manage transport rules.
UM Mailboxes	Manage the unified messaging (UM) configuration of mailboxes and other recipients.
UM Prompts	Create and manage custom UM voice prompts.
Unified Messaging	Manage Unified Messaging settings. This role doesn't enable administrators to manage UM-specific mailbox configuration or UM prompts.
User Options	View the Microsoft Outlook Web Access options for users.
View-Only Configuration	View all of the nonrecipient Exchange configuration settings.
View-Only Recipients	View the configuration of recipients, including mailboxes, mail users, mail contacts, distribution groups, and dynamic distribution groups.
View-Only Audit Logs	Search the administrator audit logs and view results.

TABLE 12-7 Management roles for individual servers

MANAGEMENT ROLE	ENABLES MANAGERS TO...
Database Copies	Manage mailbox database copies on individual servers.
Databases	Create, manage, mount, and dismount mailbox and public folder databases on individual servers.
Exchange Server Certificates	Create, import, export, and manage Exchange server certificates on individual servers.
Exchange Servers	Manage Exchange server configuration on individual servers.
Exchange Virtual Directories	Manage Autodiscover, Outlook Web App, Exchange ActiveSync, offline address book (OAB), Windows PowerShell, and Web administration interface virtual directories on individual servers.
Migration	Migrate mailboxes and mailbox content into or out of a server.
POP3 and IMAP4 Protocols	Manage Post Office Protocol version 3 (POP3) and Internet Message Access Protocol version 4 (IMAP4) configuration, such as authentication and connection settings, on individual servers.
Receive Connectors	Manage transport Receive connector configuration, such as size limits on an individual server.
Transport Queues	Manage transport queues on an individual server.

TABLE 12-8 Management roles for user scope

MANAGEMENT ROLE	ENABLES INDIVIDUAL USERS TO...
MyBaseOptions	View and modify the basic configuration of their own mailboxes and associated settings.
MyContactInformation	Modify their contact information. This information includes their addresses and phone numbers.
MyDiagnostics	Perform basic diagnostics on their mailboxes.
MyDistributionGroupMembership	View and modify their membership in distribution groups in an organization, provided that those distribution groups allow manipulation of group membership.
MyDistributionGroups	Create, modify, and view distribution groups and modify, view, remove, and add members to distribution groups they own.
MyProfileInformation	Modify their names.
MyRetentionPolicies	View their retention tags and view and modify their retention tag settings and defaults.
MyTeamMailboxes	Create and connect site mailboxes.
MyTextMessaging	View and modify their text messaging settings.
MyVoiceMail	View and modify their voice mail settings.

Role assignment policies grant users permissions to configure their Outlook Web App options and perform limited management tasks. When you install Exchange 2016, the setup process creates the Default Role Assignment Policy and sets this as the default for all new mailboxes. This policy grants users the MyBaseOptions, MyContactInformation, MyDistributionGroupMembership, and MyVoiceMail roles, but it does not grant users the MyDistributionGroups and MyProfileInformation roles.

Exchange Online has a Default Role Assignment policy as well. This default policy, assigned to all Exchange Online users, grants all of the management roles. You can create other role assignment policies as well.

Working with Role Groups

By default, members of the Organization Management group can manage any role group in the Exchange organization. Anyone designated as a manager of a role group can manage the role group. You assign a user as a manager of a role group using the -ManagedBy parameter, which can be set when you create or modify a role group.

To view the currently available role groups and the roles they've been assigned, select **Permissions** in the Features pane and then select **Admin Roles**. As shown in Figure 12-7, when you select a role group, the details pane lists the assigned roles and members.

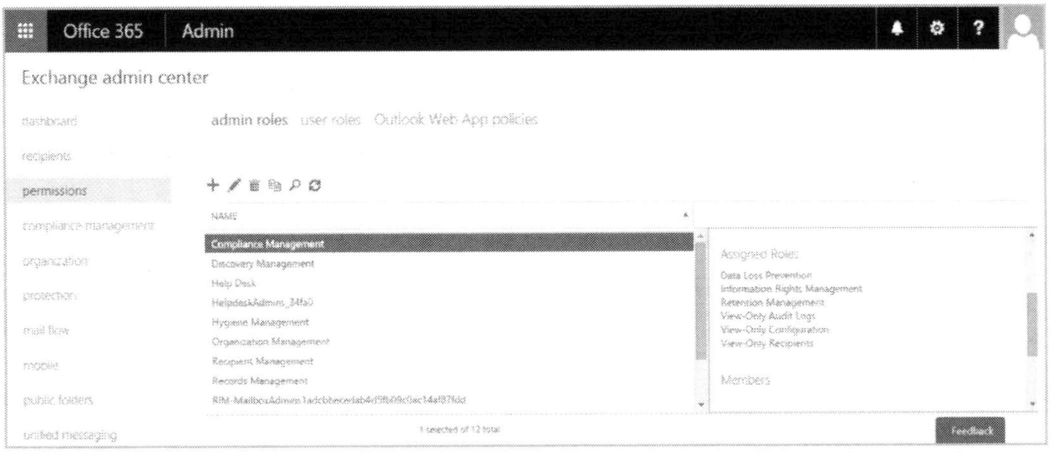

FIGURE 12-7 Viewing the role groups and the assigned roles and members of a selected group.

To create a role group, complete the following steps:

1. In Exchange Admin Center, select **Permissions** in the Features pane and then select **Admin Roles**.

2. Click **New** (✚). In the New Role Group dialog box, shown in Figure 12-8, type a descriptive name for the role group. By default, the role group will use the implicit write scope.

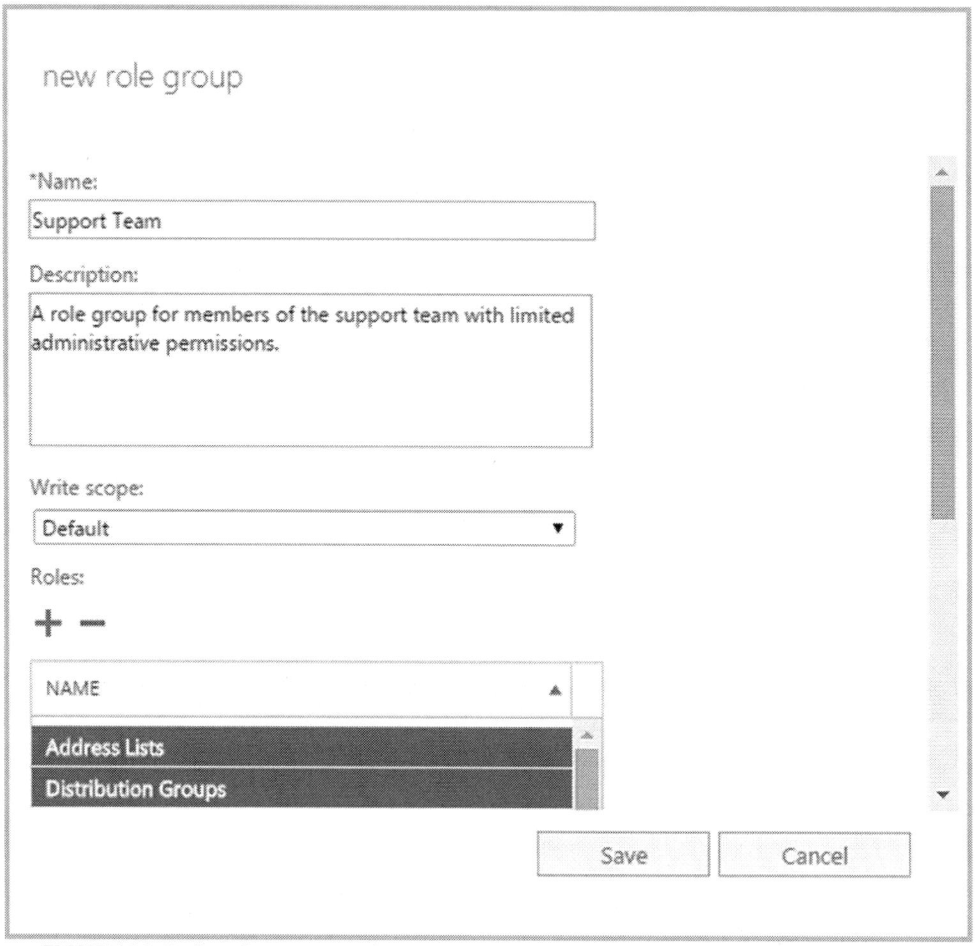

new role group

*Name:

Support Team

Description:

A role group for members of the support team with limited administrative permissions.

Write scope:

Default ▼

Roles:

✚ ━

NAME ▲

Address Lists

Distribution Groups

Save   Cancel

FIGURE 12-8 Creating a new role group.

3. Under Roles, click Add (✚). In the Select A Role dialog box select roles to assign to the role group and then click **Add**. You can select multiple roles using the Shift or Ctrl key, or you can simply select and add each role individually. When you are finished adding roles, click OK.

DISPLAY NAME ▲

DISPLAY NAME	
Org Marketplace Apps	
Organization Client Access	Reset Password
Organization Configuration	
Organization Transport Settings	This role enables users to reset their own passwords and administrators to reset users' passwords in an organization.
Public Folders	
Recipient Policies	
Remote and Accepted Domains	Default recipient scope
Reset Password	Organization
Retention Management	
Role Management	Default configuration scope
Security Group Creation and Membership	OrganizationConfig

1 selected of 48 total

add -> Address Lists[remove]; Distribution Groups[remove]; Mail Enabled Public Folders[remove]; Public Folders[remove]; Reset Password[remove];

OK   Cancel

4. Under Members, click Add (   ). In the Select Members dialog box select members to add to the role group and then click **Add**. You can select multiple members using the Shift or Ctrl key, or you can simply select and add each member individually. When you are finished, click OK.

5. Click **Save** to create the role group.

NAME ▲	DISPLAY NAME
Records Management	
RIM-MailboxAdmins1adcbbecedab4d5fb09c0ac14af87fdd	
Team One	Team One
Team Services	**Team Services**
TenantAdmins_57be7	Company Administrator
UM Management	

1 selected of 19 total

add -> George Tall[remove]; Team Services[remove];

OK   Cancel

In the shell, commands you use to work with role groups include the following:

* **Get-RoleGroup** Displays a complete or filtered list of role groups. When specifying filters, use parentheses to define the filter, such as **–Filter { RolegroupType –Eq** "Linked" **}**.

```
Get-RoleGroup [-Identity RoleGroupName] {AddtlParams}
```

```
{AddtlParams}
[-AccountPartition PartitionID] [-DomainController FullyQualifiedName]
[-Filter {LinkedGroup | ManagedBy | Members | Name | RoleGroupType |
DisplayName}] [-Organization OrganizationID] [-ReadFromDomainController
{$True|$False}] [-ResultSize Size] [-SortBy {LinkedGroup |
ManagedBy | Members | Name | RoleGroupType | DisplayName}]
[-ShowPartnerLinked {$True|$False}] [-UsnForReconciliationSearch Num]
```

* **New-RoleGroup** Creates a new role group. When specifying roles, you must use the full role name, including spaces. Enclose the role names in quotation marks and separate each role with a comma, such as **"Mail Recipient Creation"**, **"Mail Recipients"**, **"Recipient Policies"**.

```
New-RoleGroup –Name RoleGroupName [-Roles Roles]
[-ManagedBy ManagerIds] [-Members MemberIds] {AddtlParams}
```

```
{AddtlParams}
[-CustomConfigWriteScope Scope] [-CustomRecipientWriteScope Scope]
[-Description Description] [-DisplayName DisplayName]
[-DomainController FQDN] [-ExternalDirectoryObjectId ObjId]
[-Organization OrganizationID] [-PartnerManaged {$True|$False}]
[-RecipientOrganizationalUnitScope Scope]
[-SamAccountName PreWin2000Name] [-ValidationOrganization OrgId]
[-WellKnownObjectGUID GUID]
```

```
[-LinkedCredential Credential] [-LinkedDomainController LinkedDC]
[-LinkedForeignGroup LinkedGroup]
```

* **Remove-RoleGroup** Removes a role group. If a role group has designated managers, you must be listed as a manager to remove the role group or use the -BypassSecurityGroupManagerCheck parameter and be an organization manager.

```
Remove-RoleGroup -Identity RoleGroupName {AddtlParams}
```

```
{AddtlParams}
[-BypassSecurityGroupManagerCheck {$True|$False}]
[-DomainController FullyQualifiedName] [-ForReconciliation
{$True|$False}] [-RemoveWellKnownObjectGUID {$True|$False}]
```

- **Set-RoleGroup** Configures role group properties. If you specify managers, you must provide the complete list of managers because the list you provide overwrites the existing list of managers. To manage role assignment, see the "Assigning roles directly or via policy" section later in the chapter.

```
Set-RoleGroup -Identity RoleGroupName [-ManagedBy ManagerIds]
[-Name NewName] {AddtlParams}
```

```
{AddtlParams}
[-BypassSecurityGroupManagerCheck {$True|$False}]
[-Description Description] [-DisplayName DisplayName]
[-DomainController FullyQualifiedName]
[-ExternalDirectoryObjectId ObjId]
```

```
[-LinkedCredential Credential] [-LinkedDomainController LinkedDC]
[-LinkedForeignGroup LinkedGroup]
```

You use New-RoleGroup to create role groups. When you create a role group, you must specify the group name and the roles assigned to the group. You should also specify the managers and members of the group. The managers and members can be individual users or groups identified by their display name, alias, or distinguished name. If you want to specify more than one manager or member, separate each entry with a comma. The following example creates the Special Recipient Management role group to allow members of the group to manage (but not create) recipients:

```
New-RoleGroup -Name "Special Recipient Management"
-Roles "mail recipients", "recipient policies"
-ManagedBy "juliec", "tylerk", "ulij"
-Member "mikeg", "lylep", "rubyc", "yus"
```

By default, the scope of the role group is the organization. You can also set a specific scope for an organizational unit. The following example creates a role group named LA Recipient Management and sets the scope to the LA Office organizational unit to allow members of the group to manage recipients in the LA Office organizational unit:

```
New-RoleGroup -Name "LA Recipient Management"
-Roles "mail recipient creation", "mail recipients", "recipient policies"
-ManagedBy "LA Managers" -Member "LA Help Desk"
-RecipientOrganizationalUnitScope "LA Office"
```

A linked role group links the role group to a universal security group in another forest. Creating a linked role group is useful if your Exchange servers reside in a resource forest and your users and managers reside in a separate user forest. If you create a linked role group, you can't add members directly to it. You must add the members to the universal security group in the foreign forest.

When you create linked role groups, you use the -LinkedDomainController parameter to specify the fully qualified domain name or IP address of a domain controller in the foreign forest. This domain controller is used to get security information for the foreign universal security group, which is specified by the -LinkedForeignGroup parameter. If you use the -LinkedDomainController parameter, you must specify a foreign universal security group with the -LinkedForeignGroup parameter, and you can't use the -Members parameter. Optionally, you can use the -LinkedCredential parameter to specify credentials to use to access the foreign forest. To pass in the credentials, use a Credential object.

The following example creates a linked role group that enables the members of the Chicago Managers universal security group to manage recipients located in the Chicago office:

```
$cred = Get-Credentials

New-RoleGroup -Name "Chicago Recipient Managers"
-LinkedDomainController corpserver26.cpusers.imaginedlands.com
-LinkedCredential $cred -LinkedForeignGroup "Chicago Managers"
-CustomRecipientWriteScope "Chicago Recipients" -Roles "mail recipients"
```

In this example, Chicago Managers is a group created in the user forest and the administrator is logged on to the resource forest. When PowerShell reads the Get-Credentials command, a prompt for the user name and password for the user forest appears.

Role groups are created as universal security groups in the Active Directory database. In Active Directory Users And Computers, you'll find role groups in the Microsoft Exchange Security Groups container. After you create a role group, you can manage it using Active Directory Users And Computers or Exchange Management Shell. The management tasks you can perform depend on which tool you are using. In Active Directory Users And Computers, you can manage group membership, rename the group, or delete the group. Additional tasks you can perform when you use Exchange Management Shell include setting managers and modifying role assignments.

> **NOTE**   Although you can edit a group's managers or other attributes in Active Directory Users And Computers, you shouldn't do this because some values are linked and set differently than you'd expect. For example, you set the ManagedBy property to the distinguished name of the first manager and define additional managers using the msExchCoManagedByLink property.

You can list available role groups using Get-RoleGroup. If you type Get-RoleGroup at the Exchange Management Shell prompt, you see a list of all role groups defined in the Exchange organization to which you are connected. You can filter the output in a variety of ways using standard PowerShell filtering techniques. Get-RoleGroup also has a -Filter parameter that you can use to filter the output according to specific criteria you set. The following example looks for a role group named CS Recipient Management and lists all its properties:

```
Get-RoleGroup -filter {Name -eq "CS Recipient Management"} |
format-list
```

You can use Set-RoleGroup to change the name of a role group or to define a new list of managers. To delete a role group, use Remove-RoleGroup.

Managing Role Group Members

By default, members of the Organization Management group can manage the membership of any role group in the Exchange organization. Anyone designated as a manager of a role group can manage the membership of that role group as well.

In the shell, commands you use to configure role group membership include the following:

* **Add-RoleGroupMember** Adds a user or universal security group as a member of a role group. If a role group has designated managers, you must be listed as a manager to add role group members or use the -BypassSecurityGroupManagerCheck parameter and be an organization manager.

```
Add-RoleGroupMember -Identity RoleGroupName -Member MemberIds
[-BypassSecurityGroupManagerCheck {$True|$False}]
[-DomainController FullyQualifiedName]
```

* **Get-RoleGroupMember** Lists the members of a role group.

```
Get-RoleGroupMember -Identity RoleGroupName
[-DomainController FullyQualifiedName]
[-ReadFromDomainController {$True|$False}]
[-ResultSize Size]
```

* **Remove-RoleGroupMember** Removes a user or universal security group from a role group. If a role group has designated managers, you must be listed as a manager to remove role group members or use the -BypassSecurityGroupManagerCheck parameter and be an organization manager.

```
Remove-RoleGroupMember -Identity RoleGroupName -Member MemberIds
[-BypassSecurityGroupManagerCheck {$True|$False}]
[-DomainController FullyQualifiedName]
```

* **Update-RoleGroupMember** Replaces the current group membership with the list of members you provide.

```
Update-RoleGroupMember -Identity RoleGroupName -Members NewMemberIds
[-BypassSecurityGroupManagerCheck {$True|$False}]
[-DomainController FullyQualifiedName]
```

You add members to a role group using Add-RoleGroupMember. When you add a member to a role group, the member is given the effective permissions provided by the management roles assigned to the role group. If the role group has designated managers, you must be a role group manager or use the -BypassSecurityGroupManagerCheck parameter to override the security group management check. The following example adds a user to the LA Recipient Management role group:

```
Add-RoleGroupMember –Identity "LA Recipient Management"
-Member "joym"
```

Whether you are working with Exchange Online or on-premises Exchange at the shell prompt, don't forget that all the features of PowerShell are at your disposal. The following example lists all users with mailboxes in the Technology department and adds them to the Technology Management role group:

```
Get-User –Filter { Department –Eq "Technology" –And –RecipientType
-Eq "UserMailbox" } | Get-Mailbox | Add-RoleGroupMember
"Technology Management"
```

You can list members of a particular role group using Get-RoleGroupMember. Members are listed by name and recipient type as shown in the following example and sample output:

```
Get-RoleGroupMember –Identity "CS Recipient Management"
```

Name	RecipientType
Riis Anders	UserMailbox
Darren Waite	UserMailbox

You can delete role group members using Remove-RoleGroupMember. When you remove a member from a role group, the user or group of users can no longer perform the management tasks made available by that role group. However, keep in mind that the user or group of users might be a member of another role group that grants management permissions. If so, the user or group of users will still be able to perform management tasks.

> **NOTE** For linked role groups, you can't use Remove-RoleGroupMember to remove members from the role group. Instead, you need to remove members from the foreign universal security group (USG) that's linked to the linked role group. Use Get-RoleGroup to identify the foreign group.

Assigning Roles Directly or Via Policy

You can assign built-in or custom roles to users, role groups, and universal security groups in one of two ways:

- Directly using role assignment
- Via assignment policy

Directly assigning roles is accomplished using role assignment commands. By adding, removing, or modifying role assignments, you can control the management tasks that users can perform. Although you can assign roles directly to users or universal security groups, this approach increases the complexity of the permissions model in your Exchange organization. A more flexible solution is to assign roles via assignment policy. Assigning roles via assignment policy requires you to do the following:

1. Create assignment policies.
2. Assign roles to these policies.
3. Assign policies to users or groups as appropriate.

Management roles define the specific tasks that can be performed by the members of a role group assigned the role. A role assignment links a management role and a role group. Assigning a management role to a role group grants members of the role group the ability to perform the management tasks defined in the management role. Role assignments can use management scopes to control where the assignment can be used.

In the shell, commands you use to work with role assignment include the following:

- **Get-ManagementRoleAssignment** Displays a complete or filtered list of role assignments for a role group. You can examine role assignments by name, assignment type, or scope type as well as whether the assignment is enabled or disabled.

```
Get-ManagementRoleAssignment [-Identity RoleAssignmentToRetrieve]
{AddtlParams}


Get-ManagementRoleAssignment [-Role RoleID] [-RoleAssignee IdentityToCheck]
[-AssignmentMethod {Direct | SecurityGroup |
RoleAssignmentPolicy}] {AddtlParams}


{AddtlParams}
[-ConfigWriteScope <None | NotApplicable | OrganizationConfig |
CustomConfigScope | PartnerDelegatedTenantScope |
 ExclusiveConfigScope>] [-CustomConfigWriteScope ManagementScopeId]
[-CustomRecipientWriteScope ManagementScopeId] [-Delegating <$true
| $false>] [-DomainController FullyQualifiedName] [-Enabled <$true
| $false>] [-Exclusive <$true | $false>]
[-ExclusiveConfigWriteScope ManagementScopeId]
[-ExclusiveRecipientWriteScope ManagementScopeId]
[-GetEffectiveUsers <$true | $false>]
[-GetEffectiveUsers <$true | $false>]
[-Organization OrganizationId] [-RecipientOrganizationalUnitScope
OrganizationalUnitId] [-RecipientWriteScope <None | NotApplicable
| Organization | MyGAL | Self | MyDirectReports | OU |
CustomRecipientScope | MyDistributionGroups | MyExecutive |
ExclusiveRecipientScope>] [-RoleAssigneeType <User |
SecurityGroup | RoleAssignmentPolicy | MailboxPlan |
ForeignSecurityPrincipal | RoleGroup | LinkedRoleGroup>]
[-WritableDatabase DatabaseId] [-WritableRecipient GeneralRecipientId]
[-WritableServer ServerId]
```

- **New-ManagementRoleAssignment** Creates a new role assignment, and
  assigns it directly to a user or group or assigns it via an assignment policy.

```
New-ManagementRoleAssignment –Name RoleAssignmentName
-SecurityGroup Group -Role Roles {AddtlParams}


New-ManagementRoleAssignment –Name RoleAssignmentName
-Policy Policy -Role Roles {AddtlParams}
```

```
New-ManagementRoleAssignment -Name RoleAssignmentName
-User User -Role Roles {AddtlParams}

New-ManagementRoleAssignment -Name RoleAssignmentName
-Computer Computer -Role Roles {AddtlParams}

{AddtlParams}
[-CustomConfigWriteScope Scope][-CustomRecipientWriteScope Scope]
[-Delegating {$True|$False}] [-DomainController FullyQualifiedName]
[-ExclusiveConfigWriteScope Scope] [-ExclusiveRecipientWriteScope
Scope] [-Organization OrganizationId]
[-RecipientOrganizationalUnitScope Scope]
[-RecipientRelativeWriteScope <None | NotApplicable | Organization
| MyGAL | Self | MyDirectReports | OU |CustomRecipientScope |
MyDistributionGroups | MyExecutive | ExclusiveRecipientScope>]
[-UnscopedTopLevel {$True|$False}]
```

* **Remove-ManagementRoleAssignment** Removes a role assignment.

```
Remove-ManagementRoleAssignment -Identity RoleAssignmentName
[-DomainController FullyQualifiedName]
```

* **Set-ManagementRoleAssignment** Configures role assignment properties.

```
Set-ManagementRoleAssignment -Identity RoleAssignmentName
[-DomainController FullyQualifiedName] [-Enabled {$True|$False}]
{AddtlParams1 | AddtlParams2 | AddtlParams3 | AddtlParams4}

{AddtlParams1}
[-CustomConfigWriteScope Scope] [-RecipientOrganizationalUnitScope
OUId] [-RecipientRelativeWriteScope <None | NotApplicable |
Organization | MyGAL | Self | MyDirectReports | OU |
CustomRecipientScope | MyDistributionGroups | MyExecutive |
ExclusiveRecipientScope>]

{AddtlParams2}
[-CustomConfigWriteScope Scope]
[-CustomRecipientWriteScope Scope]
```

```
{AddtlParams3}
  [-CustomConfigWriteScope Scope]
[-DomainController FullyQualifiedName]

{AddtlParams4}
[-ExclusiveConfigWriteScope Scope]
[-ExclusiveRecipientWriteScope Scope]
```

You can list role assignments using Get-ManagementRoleAssignment. You use New-ManagementRoleAssignment to assign roles. The following example assigns the Retention Management role to the Central Help Desk group:

```
New-ManagementRoleAssignment –Name "Central Help Desk_Retention"
–Role "Retention Management" –SecurityGroup "Central Help Desk"
```

The following example assigns the Mail Recipients role to members of the Marketing Help Desk group and restricts the write scope to the Marketing organizational unit:

```
New-ManagementRoleAssignment –Name "Marketing_Options"
–Role "Mail Recipients" –SecurityGroup "Marketing Help Desk"
–RecipientOrganizationalUnitScope "imaginedlands.com/Marketing"
```

This allows users who are members of the Marketing Help Desk group to manage existing mailboxes, mail users, mail contacts, distribution groups, and dynamic distribution groups in the Marketing organizational unit. This does not enable these users to create recipients in this organizational unit. To create recipients, the users need to be assigned the Mail Recipient Creation role.

You can modify role assignment using Set-ManagementRoleAssignment. The following example disables the Central Help Desk_Retention role assignment:

```
Set-ManagementRoleAssignment –Identity "Central Help Desk_Retention"
–Enabled $False
```

When you disable a role assignment, the users assigned the role can no longer perform the management tasks granted by the role. However, keep in mind that a user might have been granted the permission in another way. By disabling a role assignment rather than removing it, you can easily enable the role assignment again as shown in the following example:

```
Set-ManagementRoleAssignment -Identity "Central Help Desk_Retention"
-Enabled $True
```

However, if you are sure you no longer want to use a particular role assignment, you can remove it using Remove-ManagementRoleAssignment as shown in the following example:

```
Remove-ManagementRoleAssignment -Identity "Central Help Desk_Retention"
```

When you create a new assignment policy, you can assign it to users using the New-Mailbox, Set-Mailbox, or Enable-Mailbox cmdlet. If you make the new assignment policy the default assignment policy, it's assigned to all new mailboxes that don't have an explicitly designated assignment policy. After you create an assignment policy, you must assign it at least one management role for permissions to apply to a mailbox. Without any roles assigned to it, users assigned the policy won't be able to manage any of their mailbox configurations. To assign a management role, use New-ManagementRoleAssignment.

In the shell, commands you use to work with role assignment policy include the following:

- **Get-RoleAssignmentPolicy**   Lists all policies or a specified role assignment policy.

```
Get-RoleAssignmentPolicy [-Identity AssignmentPolicyName]
[-DomainController FullyQualifiedName] [-Organization
OrganizationId]
```

- **New-RoleAssignmentPolicy**   Creates a new role assignment policy.

```
New-RoleAssignmentPolicy -Name AssignmentPolicyName
[-Description Description] [-DomainController FullyQualifiedName]
[-IsDefault {$True|$False}] [-Organization OrganizationId]
```

- **Remove-RoleAssignmentPolicy**   Removes a role assignment policy.

```
Remove-RoleAssignmentPolicy -Identity AssignmentPolicyName
[-DomainController FullyQualifiedName]
```

- **Set-RoleAssignmentPolicy** Changes the name of a role assignment policy, or sets a role assignment policy as the default.

```
Set-RoleAssignmentPolicy -Identity AssignmentPolicyName
[-Description Description] [-DomainController FullyQualifiedName]
[-IsDefault {$True|$False}] [-Name NewName]
```

You can list role assignment policies using Get-RoleAssignmentPolicy. Rather than view all available assignment policies, you can easily filter the output to look for default assignment policies. Here is an example:

```
Get-RoleAssignmentPolicy | Where { $_.IsDefault -eq $True }
```

You use New-RoleAssignmentPolicy to create role assignment policies. The following example creates the Standard User Policy and assigns it as the default:

```
New-RoleAssignmentPolicy -Name "Standard User Policy"
```

When you create a new assignment policy, you can assign it to users using New-Mailbox, Set-Mailbox, or Enable-Mailbox as shown in the following example:

```
Set-Mailbox -Identity "tommyj" -RoleAssignmentPolicy "Standard User
Policy"
```

If you make the new assignment policy the default assignment policy, it's assigned to all new mailboxes that don't have an explicitly designated assignment policy. You can specify that a policy is the default when you create it using -IsDefault. You can also designate a policy as the default using Set-RoleAssignmentPolicy as shown in this example:

```
Set-RoleAssignmentPolicy -Identity "Standard User Policy" -IsDefault
```

After you create an assignment policy, you must assign at least one management role to it for it to apply permissions to a mailbox. Without any roles assigned to it, users assigned the policy won't be able to manage any of their mailbox configuration. To assign a management role, use New-ManagementRoleAssignment.

You can remove policies using Remove-RoleAssignmentPolicy. The assignment policy you want to remove can't be assigned to any mailboxes or management roles.

Also, if you want to remove the default assignment policy, it must be the last assignment policy. Because of this, you need to use Set-Mailbox to change the assignment policy for any mailbox that's assigned the assignment policy before you can remove it. If the assignment policy is the default assignment policy, use Set-RoleAssignmentPolicy to select a new default assignment policy before you remove the old default policy. You don't need to do this if you're removing the last assignment policy. Additionally, keep in mind that you can use Remove-ManagementRoleAssignment to remove any management role assignments assigned to a policy.

With this in mind, the following series of examples show how you can modify and remove assignment policy. The first example removes the assignment policy called "Standard User Policy" by finding all of the mailboxes assigned the policy and then assigning a different policy:

```
Get-Mailbox | Where {$_.RoleAssignmentPolicy -Eq "Standard User Policy"}
 | Set-Mailbox -RoleAssignmentPolicy "New User Policy"
```

Next, you can remove all the role assignments assigned to an assignment policy:

```
Get-ManagementRoleAssignment -RoleAssignee "Standard User Policy" |
Remove-ManagementRoleAssignment
```

Afterward, you can remove the assignment policy by entering the following:

```
Remove-RoleAssignmentPolicy "Standard User Policy"
```

Configuring Account Management Permissions

Exchange 2016 and Exchange Online user roles control the settings that users can configure on their own mailboxes and on distribution groups they own. These settings determine whether users can:

- Change the display name, contact information, text messaging settings, voice mail settings, and more.
- View and modify apps, mail subscriptions, and retention policies.
- Modify the basic configuration of the mailbox.
- Create and connect site mailboxes.
- Manage text messaging and voice mail settings
- Create, modify, and view distribution groups

- Manage membership of distribution groups they own.
- Manage their membership in distribution groups.

The Exchange organization has a default role assignment policy that grants users permission to configure all user-manageable settings. You can create one or more additional role assignment policies and assign them to users at any time using Exchange Admin Center. To view the currently available policies, select **Permissions** in the Features pane and then select **User Roles** as shown in Figure 12-9.

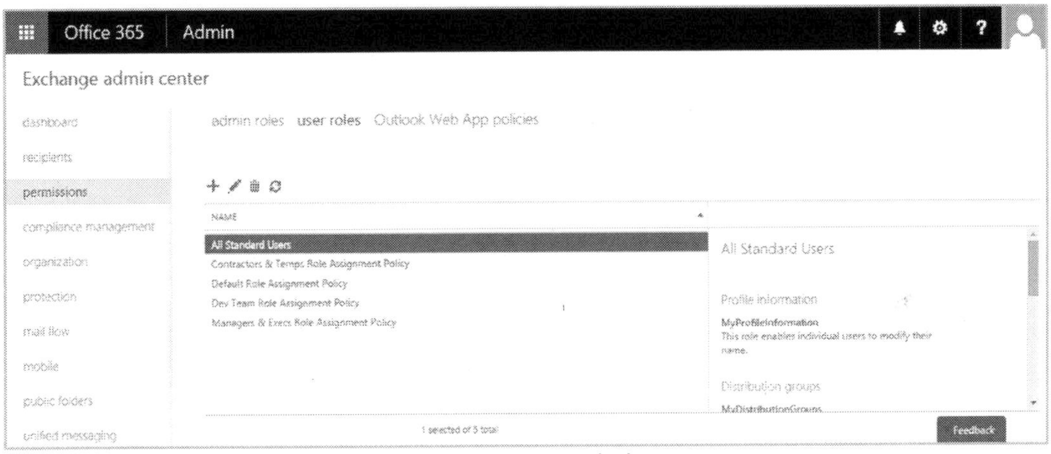

FIGURE 12-9 Configuring user roles to manage permissions.

To create a policy, click **New** (). In the Role Assignment Policy dialog box, type a descriptive name for the policy, such as All Standard Users. To grant a role to users, select the related check box. To not grant a role to users, clear the related check box. At a minimum, be sure to grant MyBaseOptions to the policy so that those assigned the policy can access their mailbox and basic settings.

Finally, click **Save** to create the policy and update the organization settings. It may take several minutes to update the organization settings. If an error occurs, try to create the policy again before you begin any troubleshooting. Sometimes, a complex process won't be completed fully the first time and retrying will resolve the problem.

role assignment policy

*Name:

Contractors & Temps Role Assignment Policy

Description:

Contact information:
☐ MyContactInformation
This role enables individual users to modify their contact information, including address and phone numbers.

    ☐ MyAddressInformation

    ☐ MyMobileInformation

    ☐ MyPersonalInformation

Save   Cancel

To assign a policy to a user, follow these steps:

1. In Exchange Admin Center, select **Recipients** in the Features pane and then select **Mailboxes**. Double-click the entry for the user.

2. On the Mailbox Features page, use the Role Assignment Policy selection list to choose the policy that you want to apply.

3. Click **Save**.

Jeff Peterson

general
mailbox usage
contact information
organization
email address
▸ mailbox features
member of
MailTip
mailbox delegation

Select the mailbox settings, phone and voice features, and email connectivity options for this mailbox. Learn more

Sharing policy:
[Default Sharing Policy ▾]

Role assignment policy:
[Contractors & Temps Role Assignment Policy ▾]

Retention policy:
[Default MRM Policy ▾]

Address book policy:
[[No Policy] ▾]

[Save] [Cancel]

Managing Advanced Permissions

Advanced permissions areas you can work with are related to custom management roles, management scopes, and role entries. Management roles define the management tasks users can perform. Management scopes identify the objects that are allowed to be managed. Role entries are the individual permission entries on a management role that allow users to perform management tasks.

Adding Custom Roles

The built-in roles were listed previously in Tables 12-6 to 12-8. The built-in roles are fixed, and you cannot create role entries to define additional management tasks for built-in roles. You can, however, create your own custom roles based on built-in roles and then extend the custom roles as necessary to meet the needs of your organization. In this way, custom management roles allow you to do things you can't do with the built-in roles.

Commands you use to create custom roles and to view any existing roles include the following:

- **Get-ManagementRole** Displays a complete or filtered list of management roles defined in the organization. Role types are the same as those listed previously without spaces in their names.

```
Get-ManagementRole [-Identity RoleName] [-DomainController
FullyQualifiedName] [-Organization OrganizationId] [-RoleType RoleType]
{AddtlParams}
```

```
{AddtlParams}
{ [-Cmdlet Cmdlet] [-CmdletParameters Parameters] |
[-GetChildren {$True|$False}] |
[-Script Script] [-ScriptParameters Parameters] |
[-Recurse {$True|$False}] }
```

- **New-ManagementRole** Creates a new management role.

```
New-ManagementRole -Name RoleName
[-Parent ParentRoleToCopy | -UnScopedTopLevel {$True|$False}]
[-Description Description] [-DomainController FullyQualifiedName]
[-Organization OrganizationId]
```

- **Remove-ManagementRole** Removes a management role.

```
Remove-ManagementRole [-Identity RoleName]
[-DomainController FullyQualifiedName] [-Recurse {$True|$False}]
[-UnScopedTopLevel {$True|$False}]
```

To view management roles, you use Get-ManagementRole. Entering Get-ManagementRole by itself without parameters lists all the roles in your organization. Additional options include using

- **-Identity** to view information about a specific role
- **-Cmdlet** to list all roles that include a specified cmdlet
- **-CmdletParameters** to list all roles that include the specified cmdlet parameter or parameters
- **-GetChildren** to list only the child roles of a specified parent role
- **-Recurse** to list the role specified in the -Identity parameter, its child roles, and all subsequent children until all the roles that were created based on the parent role have been fully identified.
- **-RoleType** to list all roles of a particular type
- **-Script** to list all roles that include a specified script

- **-ScriptParameters** to list all roles that include the specified script parameter or parameters

The following example lists all the roles associated with the Mail Recipient Creation role:

```
Get-ManagementRole "Mail Recipient Creation" -Recurse
```

You can create your own custom roles using New-ManagementRole. New roles can either be empty top-level roles or based on an existing parent role. For example, the following command creates an empty role:

```
New-ManagementRole -Name "Change Management"
-UnscopedTopLevel
```

In the following example, a new role is created based on the Organization Client Access role:

```
New-ManagementRole -Name "Organization Client Access View-Only"
-Parent "Organization Client Access"
```

After you create a role based on another role, you might need to remove role entries that are not required. For example, the following command ensures the Organization Client Access View-Only role grants view-only permission for Client Access information by removing any entries for commands that don't begin with Get:

```
Get-ManagementRoleEntry "Organization Client Access View-Only\*" |
Where { $_.Name -NotLike "Get*" } | Remove-ManagementRoleEntry
```

To remove a custom role, you use Remove-ManagementRole. You can remove a role by name as shown in the following example:

```
Remove-ManagementRole "Organization Client Access View-Only"
```

Using the -Recurse parameter, you can remove all child roles of a role. Using the -UnscopedTopLevel parameter, you can remove an unscoped top-level role. You also can use Get-ManagementRole to obtain a list of roles to remove as shown in this example:

```
Get-ManagementRole *MyTestRole* | Remove-ManagementRole
```

> **TIP** To avoid accidentally removing a number of important roles, you should run Get-ManagementRole by itself first or add the -WhatIf parameter to Remove-ManagementRole. Either technique will ensure you know exactly which roles you are working with.

Adding Custom Role Scopes

Every management role has a management scope that determines where in Active Directory objects can be viewed or modified by users assigned the management role. Management scopes can be defined as either regular or exclusive. Regular scopes can be either implicitly or explicitly created. They are simply the standard type of scope, and they define the set of recipients that can be managed. Exclusive scopes, on the other hand, must always be explicitly created, and they allow you to deny users access to objects contained within the exclusive scope if those users aren't assigned a role associated with the exclusive scope.

Scopes can be:

* Inherited from the management role
* Specified as a predefined relative scope on a management role assignment
* Created using custom filters and added to a management role assignment

Scopes inherited from management roles are called *implicit scopes,* while predefined and custom scopes are called *explicit scopes*. Implicit scopes include:

* **Recipient read scope**   Determines which recipient objects the user assigned the management role is allowed to read from Active Directory.
* **Recipient write scope**   Determines which recipient objects the user assigned the management role is allowed to modify in Active Directory.
* **Configuration read scope**   Determines which configuration objects the user assigned the management role is allowed to read from Active Directory.
* **Configuration write scope**   Determines which organizational and server objects the user assigned the management role is allowed to modify in Active Directory.

Commands you use to work with scopes include the following:

* **Get-ManagementScope**   Displays a complete or filtered list of management scopes defined in the organization.

```
Get-ManagementScope [-Identity ScopeName]
[-Exclusive {$True|$False}] [-DomainController FullyQualifiedName]
[-Organization OrganizationId] [-Orphan {$True|$False}]
```

- **New-ManagementScope**   Creates a new management scope.

```
New-ManagementScope -Name ScopeName -RecipientRestrictionFilter
Filter [-RecipientRoot Root] {AddtlParams}
```

```
New-ManagementScope -Name ScopeName
-ServerList Servers | -ServerRestrictionFilter Filter {AddtlParams}
```

```
New-ManagementScope -Name ScopeName
-DatabaseList Servers | -DatabaseRestrictionFilter Filter {AddtlParams}
```

```
{AddtlParams}
[-DomainController FullyQualifiedName] [-Organization OrganizationId]
[-Exclusive {$True|$False}] [-Force {$True|$False}]
```

- **Remove-ManagementScope**   Removes a management scope.

```
Remove-ManagementScope [-Identity Scope]
[-DomainController FullyQualifiedName]
```

- **Set-ManagementScope**   Modifies the settings of a management scope.

```
Set-ManagementScope -Identity ScopeName -ServerRestrictionFilter
Filter [-DomainController FullyQualifiedName] [-Name Name]
```

```
Set-ManagementScope -Identity ScopeName -RecipientRestrictionFilter
Filter [-RecipientRoot Root] [-DomainController FullyQualifiedName]
[-Name Name]
```

```
Set-ManagementScope -Identity ScopeName -DatabaseRestrictionFilter
Filter [-DomainController FullyQualifiedName] [-Name Name]
```

You use Get-ManagementScope to retrieve a list of existing management scopes. If you want to list only exclusive scopes, use the -Exclusive parameter. If you want to list only management scopes that aren't associated with role assignments, use the -Orphan parameter, as shown here:

```
Get-ManagementScope -Orphan
```

You can create custom management scopes using New-ManagementScope. After you create a regular or exclusive scope, you need to associate the scope with a management role assignment. One way to do this is to use New-ManagementRoleAssignment.

You define scopes using recipient restriction filters, explicit server lists, or server restriction filters. For example, the following command creates the Sales Team scope that applies only to mailboxes located in the Sales organizational unit:

```
New-ManagementScope -Name "Sales Team Scope" -RecipientRoot
"imaginedlands.com/Sales" -RecipientRestrictionFilter {RecipientType -eq
"UserMailbox"}
```

The following example creates a scope that applies only to MailServer14 and MailServer22:

```
New-ManagementScope -Name "Main Server Scope" -ServerList
"MailServer14", "MailServer22"
```

The following example creates a scope that applies only to servers in the Active Directory site called Seattle-First-Site:

```
New-ManagementScope -Name "Seattle Site Scope" -ServerRestrictionFilter
{ServerSite -eq "Seattle-First-Site"}
```

Exclusive scopes work a bit differently. When an exclusive scope is created, all users are immediately blocked from modifying the recipients that match the exclusive scope until the scope is associated with a management role assignment. If other role assignments are associated with other exclusive scopes that match the same recipients, those assignments can still modify the recipients. For example, the following command creates a Protected Managers exclusive scope for users that contain the string "Manager" in their job titles:

```
New-ManagementScope -Name "Protected Managers"
-RecipientRestrictionFilter { Title -Like "*Manager*" } -Exclusive
```

After creating an exclusive scope, you then need to associate it with a management role assignment that assigns the appropriate management roles to the appropriate role group or groups. In the following example, members of the Level 5 Administrators security group are granted permission to work with Protected Manager mailboxes:

```
New-ManagementRoleAssignment -Name "Level 5 Administrators_Mail
Recipients" -SecurityGroup "Level 5 Administrators" -Role "Mail
Recipients" -CustomRecipientWriteScope "Protected Managers"
```

You use Set-ManagementScope to modify the settings of a management scope. If you change a scope that has been associated with management role assignments, the updated scope applies to all of the associated role assignments. To remove a management scope, you can use Remove-ManagementScope. However, you can't remove a management scope if it's associated with a role assignment.

Adding Custom Role Entries

Role entries determine the management actions that members of a role group can perform. You create a role entry by specifying the permitted management command and any permitted command parameters.

Assigning a management role to a role group is essentially similar to creating the related role entries that allow a user or group to perform related management tasks. Another way to grant permission to perform a management action is to create a management role entry and add it to a management role. However, keep in mind that you can't add role entries to built-in roles.

Commands you use to work with role entries include:

* **Add-ManagementRoleEntry** Adds role entries to a custom management role. You can't add role entries to built-in roles. The -UnScopedTopLevel parameter allows you to specify that you're adding a custom script or non-Exchange cmdlet to an unscoped top-level management role.

```
Add-ManagementRoleEntry -Identity RoleEntryToAdd
[-DomainController FullyQualifiedName] [-Parameters CmdletParametersToUse]
[-PSSnapinName SnapinThatContainsCmdlet] [-Type <Cmdlet | Script |
ApplicationPermission | All>] [-Overwrite {$True|$False}]
```

```
[-UnScopedTopLevel {$True|$False}]
```

```
Add-ManagementRoleEntry -ParentRoleEntry ParentRoleEntry
-Role Role [-DomainController FullyQualifiedName]
[-Overwrite {$True|$False}]
```

* **Get-ManagementRoleEntry** Lists the role entries configured on a particular role. You can list role entries that match specific criteria such as role name, cmdlet name, parameter name, role entry type, or associated PowerShell snap-in.

```
Get-ManagementRoleEntry -Identity RoleEntry
[-DomainController FullyQualifiedName]
[-Parameters CmdletParameters] [-PSSnapinName Snapin]
[-Type <Cmdlet | Script | ApplicationPermission | All>]
```

* **Remove-ManagementRoleEntry** Removes a management role entry.

```
Remove-ManagementRoleEntry -Identity RoleEntry
[-DomainController FullyQualifiedName]
```

* **Set-ManagementRoleEntry** Modifies a management role entry.

```
Set-ManagementRoleEntry -Identity RoleEntry
[-AddParameter {$True|$False} | -RemoveParameter {$True|$False}]
[-Parameters ParametersToAddOrRemove]
```

```
[-DomainController FullyQualifiedName]
[-UnScopedTopLevel {$True|$False}]
```

Every management role must have at least one management role entry. A role entry consists of a single cmdlet and its parameters, a script, or a special permission that you want to make available. If a cmdlet or script doesn't appear as an entry on a management role, that cmdlet or script isn't accessible via that role. Similarly, if a parameter isn't specified in a role entry, the parameter on that cmdlet or script isn't accessible via that role.

The way you create and work with role entries depends on whether they are based on the built-in roles or unscoped roles. Roles based on built-in roles can contain only role entries that are Exchange cmdlets. To use custom scripts or non-Exchange cmdlets, you need to add them as unscoped role entries to an unscoped top-level role.

You can't add management role entries to child roles if the entries don't appear in parent roles. For example, if the parent role doesn't have an entry for New-Mailbox, the child role can't be assigned that cmdlet. Additionally, if Set-Mailbox is on the parent role but the -Database parameter has been removed from the entry, the -Database parameter on the Set-Mailbox cmdlet can't be added to the entry on the child role. With this in mind, you need to carefully choose the parent role to copy when you want to create a new customized role.

Role entry names are a combination of the management role that they're associated with and the name of the cmdlet or script that you want to make available. The role name and the cmdlet or script are separated by a backslash character (\). For example, the role entry name for the New-Mailbox cmdlet on the Mail Recipient Creation role is Mail Recipient Creation\New-Mailbox.

You can use the wildcard character (*) in the role entry name to return all of the role entries that match the input you provide. The wildcard character can be used with role names as well as with cmdlet or script names. For example, you can use ** to return a list of all role entries for all roles, *\New-Mailbox to return a list of all role entries that contain the New-Mailbox cmdlet, or Mail Recipient Creation* to return a list of all role entries on the Mail Recipient Creation role.

When you create a role entry, you need to specify all of the parameters that can be used. Exchange will try to verify the parameters that you provide when you add the role entry. Only the parameters that you include are available to the users assigned to the role. You need to update role entries manually if parameters available for cmdlets or scripts change.

To avoid errors, keep the following in mind:

* Scripts that you add to an unscoped role entry must reside in the Exchange 2016 scripts directory on every server where administrators and users connect using Exchange Management Shell. The default scripts directory is C:\Program Files\Microsoft\Exchange Server\V15\Scripts.
* Non-Exchange cmdlets that you add to an unscoped role entry must be installed on every Exchange 2016 server where administrators and users connect using the Exchange Management Shell. When you add a non-Exchange cmdlet, you must

specify the Windows PowerShell snap-in name that contains the non-Exchange cmdlet.

You use Get-ManagementRoleEntry to list role entries that have been configured on roles. For example, the following command lists all the role entries that exist on the Mail Recipient Creation role:

```
Get-ManagementRoleEntry "Mail Recipient Creation\*"
```

You also can list all the role entries that contain a particular command, as shown here:

```
Get-ManagementRoleEntry *\Get-Recipient
```

You can list role entries that match specific criteria such as role name or cmdlet name. Using Add-ManagementRoleEntry, you can specify role entries to add to a role. You specify the role entry to add using the -Identity parameter and the basic syntax for the identity as RoleName\CmdletName. Role entries are either based on a parent role entry or are unscoped (the default), specified using the -ParentRoleEntry or -UnScopedTopLevel parameter, respectively. The -Role parameter specifies the role to which the new role entry is added.

For example, the following command adds a role entry for the Get-Mailbox cmdlet to the LA Recipient Managers role:

```
Add-ManagementRoleEntry -Identity "LA Recipient Managers\Get-Mailbox"
```

This entry assigns permission for the Get-Mailbox cmdlet to members of the LA Recipient Managers role. You can specify the exact parameters that are permitted as shown in the following example:

```
Add-ManagementRoleEntry -Identity "LA Recipient Managers\Get-Mailbox"
-Parameters Archive, Identity, Filter, OrganizationalUnit, SortBy
```

You can also assign permission for multiple commands. Consider the following example:

```
Get-ManagementRoleEntry "Mail Recipients\Get-Mailbox*" |
Add-ManagementRoleEntry -Role "Central Help Desk"
```

Here, Get-ManagementRoleEntry is used to retrieve a list of all the role entries for the Mail Recipients role that begin with the string "Get-Mailbox" in the cmdlet name, and then add them to the Central Help Desk role using the Add-ManagementRoleEntry cmdlet. The role entries are added to the child role exactly as they're configured on the parent role, Mail Recipients.

You use Set-ManagementRoleEntry to change the available parameters on an existing management role entry. With the -AddParameter parameter, the parameters you specify are added to the role entry. With the -RemoveParameter parameter, the parameters you specify are removed from the role entry. Otherwise, only the parameters you specify are included in the role entry. For example, with Get-Mailbox you might want users to be able to specify a server and limit the result set size, and you can do this by adding the -Server and -ResultSize parameters as shown in this example:

```
Set-ManagementRoleEntry –Identity "LA Recipient Managers\Get-Mailbox"
–AddParameter Server, ResultSize
```

To remove all parameters, set -Parameters to $Null and don't use either -AddParameter or -RemoveParameter as shown in this example:

```
Set-ManagementRoleEntry –Identity "LA Recipient Managers\Get-Mailbox"
–Parameters $Null
```

You use Remove-ManagementRoleEntry to remove role entries. However, you can't remove role entries from built-in management roles.

Working with Shared and Split Permissions

When you deploy Exchange 2016, you can use a shared permissions model or one of two split permissions models. Which permissions model your organization uses depends squarely on who should have the right to create and manage security principals in Active Directory.

Using Shared Permissions

The shared permissions model is the default. With the shared permissions model, management of Exchange and Active Directory are not separated within the

Exchange management tools. Administrators can use the Exchange management tools to create security principals in Active Directory. In this model, the Mail Recipient Creation role allows administrators to create security principals, such as Active Directory users, and the Security Group Creation And Membership role allows administrators to create security groups and manage security group membership.

Two Exchange role groups have these roles by default:

* The Organization Management role group has the Mail Recipient Creation role and the Security Group Creation And Membership role. This means members of this role group can create users, security groups, and other security principals in Active Directory. They also can manage security group membership.
* The Recipient Management role group has the Mail Recipient Creation role. This means members of this role group can create security principals in Active Directory, but cannot create security groups or manage the membership of security groups.

If you want other users to be able to create security principals and manage the membership of security groups, you have several choices. You can assign the Mail Recipient Creation role, the Security Group Creation And Membership role, or both roles to other role groups, users, and security groups. You also can make the appropriate users, security groups, or both members of the appropriate role group.

> **IMPORTANT** Permissions for working with security groups are separated from permissions for working with other security principals because Exchange administrators typically don't need to be able to create or manage security groups. In fact, in the base model, anyone who needs to be able to create or manage security groups is assumed to be an advanced administrator or manager who requires organization-wide management permissions.

An option for extending the shared permissions model is to grant the Security Group Creation And Membership role to the Recipient Management role group. This approach:

* Allows members of the Recipient Management role group to create and manage security groups in Active Directory.
* Doesn't require granting the role to individual users and security groups as may be needed for management of the Exchange organization.

I recommend this configuration only when Exchange administrators need to create security groups as part of their regular routine. With this option, you can continue to grant the Mail Recipient Creation role, the Security Group Creation And Membership role, or both roles to other role groups, users, and security groups as well.

Using Split Permissions

Some organizations require strict management of who can create security principals, and this is where split permissions are useful. With split permissions, you remove the default settings that allow members of Recipient Management and Organization Management to create security principals in Active Directory. Thereafter the process of creating security principals and the process of configuring Exchange attributes for security principals are completely separate. As a result, Active Directory administrators are responsible for creating security principals and Exchange administrators are responsible for configuring the Exchange attributes associated with security principals.

With split permissions, you have two configuration options. You can use:

* **RBAC split permissions**   With RBAC split permissions, only those who are members of the appropriate role groups can create Active Directory security principals and manage group membership.
* **Active Directory split permissions**   With Active Directory split permissions, permissions to create and manage security principals and group membership are not available in the Exchange management tools. You must use Active Directory management tools to create and manage security principals.

> **TIP**   For organizations that require split permissions, Microsoft recommends using RBAC split permissions and so do I. With RBAC split permissions, you can continue to use the Exchange management tools to create and manage security principals in Active Directory, and this gives you more flexibility in how you can use and work with Exchange.

Each Exchange organization has one and only one permissions model. Your Exchange organization is either configured to use a shared model that allows for RBAC split permissions or it's is configured to use Active Directory split permissions. During installation of Exchange 2016, you can specify whether you want to use Active Directory split permissions. If you select this option, the shared permissions and RBAC split permissions models are not available.

To move between the shared model that allows for RBAC split permissions and the Active Directory split permissions model or vice versa, you must run the following command from the Exchange 2016 installation media:

```
setup.exe /PrepareAD /ActiveDirectorySplitPermissions: {$true|$false}
```

where $true sets the organization to use Active Directory split permissions and $false sets the organization to use the shared model that allows for RBAC split permissions. You have to prepare Active Directory in each instance because many changes to groups and group membership will be made in the background. Next, you must either wait for Active Directory to replicate an access token to all servers running Exchange 2010 or Exchange 2016, or you must restart all servers running Exchange 2010 or Exchange 2016. Finally, you must implement your permissions model. A step-by-step procedure with examples follows:

1. Create a role group for Active Directory administrators and assign the Mail Recipient Creation role and the Security Group Creation And Membership role to this role group. If you want members of this role group to be able to create role assignments, include the Role Management role. Complete this step by adding members to the new role group.

```
New-RoleGroup "AD Admins" -Roles "Mail Recipient Creation",
"Security Group Creation and Membership", "Role Management"
Add-RoleGroupMember "AD Admins" -Member williams, timb, anneh, mikel
```

2. If you want members of the new role group to be able to delegate any of the roles they've been assigned, you can create delegating assignments.

```
New-ManagementRoleAssignment -Role "Mail Recipient Creation"
-SecurityGroup "AD Admins" -Delegating
```

```
New-ManagementRoleAssignment -Role "Security Group Creation and
Membership" -SecurityGroup "AD Admins" -Delegating
```

3. If you only want members of the new role group to be able to manage the group membership, replace the delegate list on the role group.

```
Set-RoleGroup "Active Directory Administrators" -ManagedBy
"AD Admins"
```

4. If you are implementing RBAC split permissions, remove the Mail Recipient Creation role and the Security Group Creation And Membership role assignments from the Recipient Management and Organization Management role groups.

```
Get-ManagementRoleAssignment -Role "Mail Recipient Creation" | Where
{ $_.RoleAssigneeName -eq "Recipient Management" or
$_.RoleAssigneeName -eq "Organization Management"} |
Remove-ManagementRoleAssignment -Whatif


Get-ManagementRoleAssignment -Role " Security Group Creation and
Membership " | Where { $_.RoleAssigneeName -eq "Recipient Management"
or $_.RoleAssigneeName -eq "Organization Management"} |
Remove-ManagementRoleAssignment -Whatif
```

> **CAUTION**   I recommend running the commands in the step with the -Whatif parameter first. This will ensure the command does exactly what you think it will. Before you remove these roles, confirm that the new role group has been assigned these roles and that the new role group has the appropriate members. Your account should be a member of the new role group.

5. Determine what groups have been assigned the Mail Recipient Creation role and the Security Group Creation And Membership role. Optionally, remove the Mail Recipient Creation role and the Security Group Creation And Membership role assignments from all other users and groups.

```
Get-ManagementRoleAssignment -Role *Creation* | Format-List Name, Role,
RoleAssigneeName


Get-ManagementRoleAssignment -Role "Mail Recipient Creation" | Where
{ $_.RoleAssigneeName -NE "AD Admins" } |
Remove-ManagementRoleAssignment -Whatif


Get-ManagementRoleAssignment -Role "Security Group Creation and
 Membership" | Where { $_.RoleAssigneeName -NE "AD Admins" } |
Remove-ManagementRoleAssignment -Whatif
```

When you use split permissions, only members of the group created in the previous procedure will be able to use the Exchange management tools to:

- Create mailbox users, mail-enabled users, mail-enabled contacts, remote mailbox users, and security groups.
- Remove mailbox users, mail-enabled users, mail-enabled contacts, remote mailbox users, and security groups.

This means Exchange administrators and others won't be able to use New-Mailbox, New-MailContact, New-MailUser, New-RemoteMailbox, Remove-Mailbox, Remove-MailContact, Remove-MailUser, or Remove-RemoteMailbox. Additionally, with Active Directory split permissions, only members of the group will be able to create distribution groups and manage their membership. Thus, only members of the group will be able to use the following cmdlets:

- Add-DistributionGroupMember, New-DistributionGroup
- Remove-DistributionGroup, Remove-DistributionGroupMember
- Update-DistributionGroupMember

Exchange administrators will still be able to configure Exchange attributes on existing Active Directory security principals. They will also be able to create and manage Exchange-specific objects.

Index

About the Author

William R. Stanek (*http://www.williamrstanek.com*) has more than 20 years of hands-on experience with advanced programming and development. He is a leading technology expert, an award-winning author, and a pretty-darn-good instructional trainer. Over the years, his practical advice has helped millions of programmers, developers, and network engineers all over the world. In 2013, William celebrated the publication of his 150th book.

William has been involved in the commercial Internet community since 1991. His core business and technology experience comes from more than 11 years of military service. He has substantial experience in developing server technology, encryption, and Internet solutions. He has written many technical white papers and training courses on a wide variety of topics. He frequently serves as a subject matter expert and consultant.

William has an MS with distinction in information systems and a BS in computer science, magna cum laude. He is proud to have served in the Persian Gulf War as a combat crewmember on an electronic warfare aircraft. He flew on numerous combat missions into Iraq and was awarded nine medals for his wartime service, including one of the United States of America's highest-flying honors, the Air Force Distinguished Flying Cross. Currently, he resides in the Pacific Northwest with his wife and children.

William recently rediscovered his love of the great outdoors. When he's not writing, he can be found hiking, biking, backpacking, traveling, or trekking in search of adventure with his family! In his spare time, William writes books for children, including *The Bugville Critters Explore the Solar System* and *The Bugville Critters Go on Vacation*.

Find William on Twitter at http://www.twitter.com/WilliamStanek and on Facebook at http://www.facebook.com/William.Stanek.Author.

Windows Server 2016
Essentials for Administration

William R. Stanek
Author & Series Editor

William R. Stanek, Jr.
Contributor

IT Pro
Solutions

Exchange Server 2016
Server Infrastructure

William R. Stanek
Author & Series Editor

William R. Stanek, Jr.
Contributor

IT Pro
Solutions

Made in the USA
Lexington, KY
11 July 2018